THE MURDER

THE MURDER GUIDE

TO GREAT BRITAIN

---

100 Extraordinary, Bizarre and Gruesome Murders

Brian Lane

Robinson
London

Robinson Publishing Ltd
7 Kensington Church Court
London W8 4SP

First published in this collected paperback edition, 1993
Copyright © Brian Lane 1988, 1989 and 1991
Previously published in part as The Murder Club Guides

ISBN 1 85487 236 2
D.L.TO: 1548–1992

A copy of the British Library Cataloguing in Publication
Data is available from the British Library

Typeset by Hewer Text Composition Services, Edinburgh
Printed in E.C.

CONTENTS

CONTENTS

CONTENTS

SOUTH-WEST ENGLAND

CONTENTS

ACKNOWLEDGEMENTS

No author can assemble a collection of material such as that contained in The Murder Guide without incurring many debts of gratitude, both to individuals and to institutions.

As always, my thanks go to those members of The Murder Club on whose contributions to our Archive much of this work is based. In particular credit must be given to Steve Wheatley, whose efforts on the overall concept of The Murder Club was of immense value, as are his contributions to the section on London crimes. Thanks also to Susan Dunkley for her imaginative treatment of the Armstrong, Crippen and Smith cases; and to Wilf Gregg for allowing such ready access to his time and library. I would like to express my gratitude to the many people who have allowed me to browse among their collections and given permission to use their material in the Guide; and to any whose copyright I have failed to trace may I apologise in advance.

For the kindness and generosity that I have been shown in scores of libraries and museums, large and small, all over Britain, and for all those people who knew about things and were willing to share, I hope this book may represent my thanks.

INTRODUCTION

On Apologias

> *Madame Life's a piece in bloom*
> *Death goes dogging everywhere;*
> *She's the tenant of the room,*
> *He's the ruffian on the stair.*
> (W.E. Henley, 1849–1903)

A disturbing by-product of the new fashionable 'human-ism' and its inseparable partner 'attitude-baring' is that the individual is under constant pressure to apologise for his passions. And nothing needs an apologia quite as much as a fascination with the darker sides of humankind.

There can be few notions more difficult to promote than that an interest in, say, the ritual of Magic does not of itself lead to nocturnal harvesting of the parish graveyard; or that a diet of gangster movies does not result in St Valentine's Day madness. An interest in crime is viewed as decidedly sinister; but a fascination with the crime of Murder – be it as academic or aficionado – renders a person particularly vulnerable, particularly in need of an apologia.

And so, for all those former members, and closet members of The Murder Club, here are some excellent precedents for our common need to justify.

One of the earliest examples can be found in the first issue of what was to become a popular illustrated weekly paper for a number of years around the turn of the century. Though its title was *Famous Crimes Past and Present*, as in so many similar magazines of the period 'crime' meant 'murder'. Editor Harold Furniss wrote, 'Down the vista of crime which stretches from the first transgression of our Father Adam to the last little boy punished for stealing a pennyworth of sweets, there stand at intervals landmarks – milestones, as it were – on the road of iniquity. These are the doings of great criminals, of men whose cunning, wickedness or brutality have thrown out their lives into relief against the sordid background of everyday transgressors. It is of these that we propose to write, and we do so with a two-fold purpose; firstly that those who are interested in criminology, and desirous of furthering the science by which the moral welfare of the country is preserved may have before them a reliable record of typical criminals; and secondly, that as the natural bent of man tends towards crime, we may provide him with reading matter, interesting and dramatic, which will afford him food for thought.'[1]

That there was a lighter side to the 'interest in criminology' even earlier is evidenced by David Jardine's *Criminal Trials* being published, in 1835, by The Society for the Diffusion of Useful Knowledge as part of its series 'The Library of Entertaining Knowledge'. Just why such material should be considered 'Entertaining' is spelt out by another chronicler of the Courts, Horace Wyndham: 'Of course, the real truth is (as De Quincey, who was something of a connoisseur on such matters, has asserted) crime in itself is intrinsically interesting. We may protest to the contrary, but there is no getting over the fact that the traffic of the dock does make an appeal. An extended one, too. Still, there is abundant reason for this. After all, "crime books" are concerned with human happenings, with real life, with the stir and fret and thrill of everyday occurrences. Again, crime is essentially dramatic, and touches the whole emotional gamut. Thus, there is tragedy; there is comedy; there is melodrama; and there is occasionally sheer farce. Even romance, too, at times. Anyway, plot and passion and swift moving incident from the rise to the fall of the curtain. Hence, not nearly so astonishing that such volumes are popular as that they are not still more popular.'[2]

Other writers have sought to give equal stress to the 'Useful' and to the 'Entertaining' sides of the crime story. Few people have done more consistently to popularize the twilight world of the criminal than the much respected writer, broadcaster, and former barrister, Edgar Lustgarten: 'The main aim of one approach is to probe psychology

– and thereby to illuminate and instruct. The main aim of the other is to tell a story – and thereby to divert and entertain.'[3] But, whichever of these two caps Mr Lustgarten chooses to wear, he is clear on the moral foundation of his apologia, 'Certainly the arrangement adopted in the construction of the book does not signify any departure by the author from the received opinion that murder is the wickedest and gravest of all crimes.'[4]

A different approach is taken by Colin Wilson, whose prolific path has taken him through such dangerous territory as Black Magic, Extra-Terrestrialism, ESP, Assassination, and Murder. One of his contentions is that the study of murder is a necessity – indeed, an obligation – if one is to understand the counter-balance, which is man's great creative potential. We have to be very grateful to Wilson for much of our contemporary understanding of 'criminality', though it is an approach which has led to accusations of pomposity – not much dispelled by his published feelings about some fellow-authors: 'It will be observed that my references to certain other writers on murder – particularly Edmund Pearson, William Roughead and William Bolitho – are hardly complimentary. I dislike the "murder for pleasure" approach. I consider this book, like the *Encyclopaedia of Murder*, as a tentative contribution to a subject that does not yet exist as a definite entity, a science that has not yet taken shape.'[5] Wilson's co-author on the *Encyclopaedia of Murder* was Patricia Pitman, who took a rather less pedantic view of the task in hand, concluding that the fascination with murderers is that they are so utterly different from us, and that that fascination is perfectly natural. Further, she brings a refreshing down-to-earthness to it all by adding that, aside from psychological justifications, the *Encyclopaedia* can provide '. . . plots for novels, questions for quizes, and innocent entertainment for eerie winter evenings.'[6]

But what of the 'murder for pleasure' approach so despised by Wilson?

The late Edmund Pearson, tireless recorder of the classic American murders and controversial authority on the Lizzie Borden case does, it is true, seem to take a wholesome relish in the retelling of a great murder story; England's own 'Brides in the Bath' killer, George Joseph Smith, he laments as a man 'who only went to ruin because, like so many great artists, he could not resist one more farewell performance' [see page 184].[7] In the essay 'What Makes a Good Murder?', Pearson treats 'collectors' of murders with the respect that he feels due to a discerning cognoscenti, noting that '. . . failure to recognise the elementary principle of an attractive murder is characteristic of many who should be better informed'.[8]

Back on this side of the Atlantic, Pearson would recognize a soul-mate in Nigel Morland, who steers a course happily between detective fiction and criminology; he too is adamant about quality in a murder – 'the critical eyes of aficionados recognise two distinct divisions of murder in the United States. There are the common-or-garden majority, whose ultimate destiny is the pages of popular magazines with lurid covers. The second, numerically minute, division is concerned with murders acceptable to the discerning taste, and here time has made certain classics'.[9]

Edward Spencer Shew was one of the pioneers, with Wilson and Pitman, of the encyclopaedic approach to the recording of murder, and in the frank introduction to his indispensable *Second Companion to Murder*, Shew comes dangerously close to appearing to enjoy his subject: 'Here the emphasis falls upon naked violence, raw and uncompromising, like the mallet strokes which destroyed Francis Mawson Rattenbury, or the blows of the iron-stone brick with which Irene Munro was battered to death upon the sands of the Crumbles. Here murder wears its most savage face'[10] a face that Ivan Butler recognises: 'it is in the strange vagaries of human behaviour that the persisting interest lies . . . the bizarre, the mysterious, the tragic, the gruesome, the just plain vicious'.[11]

Two novel and distinguished vindications are advanced by Gordon Honeycombe in his introductory pages to *The Murders of the Black Museum* – 'But the Black Museum made me realise what a policemen must endure in the course of his duty; what sights he sees, what dangers he faces, what depraved and evil people he has to deal with so that others may live secure'.[12] And later, 'Murder is a very rare event in England. Its exceptional nature is in fact part of its fascination.'

A counterpoint to this approach is provided by journalistic investigators, such as Paul Foot and Ludovic Kennedy. Their immediate motivation is the righting of a particular injustice, but they also have a wider purpose. As Kennedy writes in his introduction to 'Wicked Beyond Belief': '. . . once we start selecting those whom we think worthy or unworthy of Justice, we shall all in the end be diminished; for even if Justice is sometimes rough in practice, it is not for Cooper and McMahon alone that this book has been assembled: but for all those who, if Justice is allowed to go by default, may come to suffer in their time.'[13] Kennedy's intention is to expose those attitudes and processes of the police, the courts, lawyers and judges which create an institutional tendency towards injustice.

A more academic, but no less absorbing, motive for the study of Murder derives from the fact that murder cases have tended to be so much better documented than the less notorious fields of human endeavour. The wealth of detailed information which can be gleaned from Court testimony and newspaper reports provides an eloquent picture of the everyday behaviour, social conditions, and moral attitudes of times past. We would, undoubtedly, be far more ignorant of conditions in London's East End in the 1880s if it were not for Jack the Ripper; the description of repressive middle-class life presented by the cases of Dr Crippen and Major Armstrong [see pages 7 and 303] is, surely, as vivid as any novelist could invent; an examination of the predicament of Florence Maybrick or Edith Thompson provides a telling case study of the moral taboos of their time.

To be generous to the field, an example should be given of the 'There but for the Grace of God . . .' argument. Take Tony Wilmot's introduction to *Murder and Mayhem*,: 'Why do we like reading crime stories, especially murder? For murder, that most heinous of crimes, both horrifies and fascinates at one and the same time . . . Could it be that deep down, we suspect that we are capable of committing murder, or other serious crimes, if we knew we could get away with it? That, perhaps, the only thing that holds us back is the fear of being caught and paying the price?'[14]

Probably not. But the one certainty is that there are as many reasons for a fascination with the 'ruffian on the stair' as there are people to be fascinated by him.

[1] *Famous Crimes Past and Present*, Ed. Harold Furniss. Vol.1. No.1, 1903.

[2] *Famous Trials Retold*, Horace Wyndham. Hutchinson, London, 1925.

[3] *Illustrated Story of Crime*, Edgar Lustgarten. Weidenfeld and Nicolson, London, 1976.

[4] *Ibid.*

[5] *A Casebook of Murder*, Colin Wilson. Leslie Frewin, London, 1969.

[6] *Encyclopaedia of Murder*, Colin Wilson and Patricia Pitman. Arthur Barker, London, 1961.

[7] *Masterpieces of Murder*, Edmund Pearson. Hutchinson, London, 1969.

[8] *Ibid.*

[9] *Background to Murder*, Nigel Morland. Werner Laurie, London, 1955.

[10] *Second Companion to Murder*, E. Spencer Shew. Cassell, London, 1961.

[11] *Murderers' London*, Ivan Butler. Hale, London, 1973.

[12] *Murders of the Black Museum 1870–1970*, Gordon Honeycombe. Hutchinson, London, 1982.

[13] *The Luton Murder Case*, Ed. Ludovic Kennedy. Granada Publishing, London, 1980.

[14] *Murder and Mayhem*, Ed. Tony Wilmot. Harmsworth Publications, London, 1983.

LONDON

'REJECT ALL THE VALUES OF SOCIETY...'

**The Murder of Joe Orton
by Kenneth Halliwell
On Wednesday, 9th August 1967 at 25 Noel
Road, London N1**

It was in 1951 that the unlikely affair began between two drama students which set a ball rolling that would lead, within a decade and a half, to brutal murder and suicide.

The affair was unlikely only because of the dissimilarity of the partners. At the age of seventeen, Joe Orton was a virtual rural innocent, the product of very basic formal teaching, and having never travelled outside his native Leicester. By comparison, Kenneth Halliwell was the urbane sophisticate; 25 years old, and with the benefit of a classical education. In addition to this he had the two great social assets, his own flat and a car – certainly the symbols of a young man with prospects. The couple met at the Royal Academy of Dramatic Arts, where they studied acting, and each must have recognised the comfort and support of a fellow homosexual in a world less tolerant than today.

Within a very short time they had set up home together. Home was the one small room in which they were to live . . . and to die.

It was in this curious hermetic world that the brilliance of young Joe Orton was given its early foundation; Kenneth adapted to the role of teacher and guide as well as of lover, steering Joe through a rapid literary education. They read together, they wrote together; and with the flowering of confidence Joe Orton began rapidly to overtake his companion. He began to develop a purposeful determination, and with it that brand of flamboyant sexuality which has caused him so often to be compared with another young giant of a former age – with Oscar Fingall O'Flahertie Wills Wilde. Like Wilde, too, he had achieved a remarkable and individual style of play-writing, and a firm position in the ephemeral artistic society of 1960s 'swinging' London.

1963 was Joe Orton's year – the year the BBC broadcast his *Ruffian on the Stair*, that *Entertaining Mr Sloane* was to open on the West End stage, with *Loot* soon to follow. Joe was being wooed by the media; he was in demand at social gatherings. He was leaving poor Kenneth behind. He had – to use the phrase of his biographer John Lahr – 'edited Halliwell out'.

Kenneth would never recover from the real or the imagined rejections, and his inability to adopt a 'supporting role' to Joe's by now extravagant life-style and promiscuous sexuality signalled disaster for them both.

Kenneth Halliwell's collage design for the poster for Orton's *Loot*

Drawing of Orton by Patrick Proctor, 1967

On 9th August, 1967, Kenneth Halliwell smashed in his lover's head with a hammer. The life and times of Joe Orton had come to an untimely end, followed quickly by that of the tragic Ken – victim of a self-administered overdose of Nembutals. After his suicide, Halliwell's enigmatic 'last words' were found by police in a hastily scribbled note: 'if you read his diary all will be explained.' Orton's diary covering the period from December 1966 until his death, was published in 1987,* and even if Kenneth Halliwell's sad clue is not so dramatically apparent, the journal does reveal points at which Orton – wittingly or not – appeared to be deliberately goading his partner with the blatant sexual promiscuity that so hurt and frightened Halliwell; exploits that were written in colourful and wildly explicit prose into the pages of the 'diary' and then deliberately left where his companion could hardly fail to see them:

'We went into the lavatory. Only one man was there. I stood next to him . . . He was a Greek-Cypriot. He wasn't very young. About thirty-five. Very stupid looking. 'Come to the park,' he said, in an ice-cream seller's accent, 'I'll shag you.' I thought it was a stupid idea. And when we got to the park it seemed

* *The Orton Diaries*, edited by John Lahr. Published Methuen, London, 1987.

as though I had met a maniac. 'See over there,' he said. 'Two men. They shag. And over there,' he said, pointing to a clump of trees that were perhaps three feet away from a well-lighted pavement. 'Please let me shag you,' he said, 'I'll be quick.' 'But we're in the light!' I said. 'We can be seen.' 'Naw,' he said, 'nobody notice.' Up against a tree, I dropped my trousers and he fucked me. He was quick. Afterwards he tossed me off. As we were walking away he said, 'I shag a boy last week. I pay him £2. You don't want money, do you?' 'No,' I said, 'I've plenty of money.'

(13th July 1967)

There is acknowledgement, too, of the rapid degeneration of Ken Halliwell's reason: the black moods of hatred and self-doubt:

'Suddenly I realised Kenneth was looking tight-lipped and white-faced. We were in the middle of talks of suicide and 'you'll have to face up to the world one day'. And 'I'm disgusted by all this immorality' . . . and after a particularly sharp outburst, alarmed me by saying 'Homosexuals disgust me!' I didn't attempt to fathom this one out. He said he wasn't going to come away to Morocco. He was going to kill himself. 'I've led a dreadful, unhappy life. I'm pathetic. I can't go on suffering like this'. After talking until about eight he suddenly shouted out and hammered on the wall. 'They treated me like shit! I won't be treated like this.'

(1st May 1967)

What is perhaps remarkable is that, despite such painstaking observation and meticulous record-keeping, Orton was quite unable to read the imminent danger; a naivety that kept him in blissful unconcern until he felt the first frenzied blow of the hammer . . .

THE HEN-PECKED KILLER

**The Murder of Mrs Cora Crippen (called
Belle Elmore) by Dr Hawley Harvey Crippen**
On or about Monday, 31st January 1910 at
39 Hilldrop Crescent, London N7

The kitchen at 39 Hilldrop Crescent, Holloway, was an
unappetizing sight. Piles of unwashed dishes made a
squalid litter with bits of discarded female clothing, a box
of spilled face powder and several empty gin bottles. At
one end of the room a small and obviously depressed
figure was furiously polishing several pairs of muddy
boots. He was a dapper little man with a drooping
moustache and gold-rimmed spectacles protecting protu-
berant blue eyes which from time to time glanced
anxiously at the kettle on the stove. When it eventually
boiled he made morning tea with the precise gestures of a
man of science, belying the role of the kitchen drudge.

Hawley Harvey Crippen – a trained doctor in America
but not qualified to practise in his adopted London – was
doing the morning chores before his wife would let him go
to work. Each morning the lodgers' boots must be cleaned
and their breakfasts cooked while his wife, Cora – or Belle
Elmore as she preferred to be known to her theatrical
friends and audiences – still lay dreaming of dresses and
diamonds, champagne and compliments; and the time
when her name would blaze in lights to dazzle the whole
of England. In the meantime she vented her many frus-
trations on the meek little man to whom she had accorded,
to her mind, the inestimable honour of marriage.

Crippen first met Cora Turner (whose real name was
Kunigunde Mackamotzki) in New York and was dazzled

by the vivacity of the attractive Polish-German girl. Cora, at 19, had already been the mistress of a wealthy stove manufacturer and she now looked to Crippen to keep her in the manner to which she felt entitled as a potential star of the operatic stage.

In 1900 Crippen's employers – Munyon's Remedies, a patent medicine company – sent him to England, and Cora prepared to take the London theatre by storm. Sadly, her ambition was wildly out of proportion to her talent and she never achieved more than occasional music hall or smoking concert engagements. But she did become something of a personality in off-stage theatrical circles and even attained the position of treasurer of the Music Hall Ladies' Guild, so enlarging her large circle of friends and admirers. When Crippen was called to Philadelphia for six months on business, she made good use of the time to enjoy a tempestuous affair with an American performer and ex-prizefighter called Bruce Miller.

Crippen desperately tried to keep pace with his wife's imperious demands for all the trappings of luxury. He moved from venture to venture, all in vaguely medical fields, and even practised illegally for a time as a dentist and women's consultant; but their bank balance still would not stand the strain of Cora's extravagance and to make ends meet they were forced to take in lodgers in the large gloomy house they rented at Hilldrop Crescent. While Crippen was dispensing quack medicines to keep Cora in ermine, fox and jewels, she ruled him with a rod of iron, choosing all his clothes for him – right down to his underwear – humiliating him in front of the lodgers and her friends and treating him as a domestic skivvy.

She was unable to have children due to the ovariectomy that she had undergone shortly after her marriage, and so was free to use her time as she pleased. She divided her energies between two personas – the charming and delightful Belle Elmore, beloved by her many friends, and the coarse and bullying Cora Crippen, cruel tormentor of her husband.

Then Cora discovered that her husband was having an affair with his secretary – Ethel Le Neve. The love that had grown up between the 48-year-old Crippen and the younger Ethel was the only ray of happiness and pride in his otherwise miserable existence. Cora mocked and taunted him about the affair, cheapening it into something sordid and absurd and she used the situation to indulge her own extramarital adventures more openly. That is, until she found out that Ethel was pregnant. This was too much for the childless Cora, who set out to spread slanderous stories about Ethel among all her friends and acquaintances. Finally, she threatened to desert Crippen and to take everything in their joint bank account with her, leaving him penniless.

When Ethel suffered a miscarriage, Cora decided to stay put, but by this time a resolve had formed itself in the mind of the otherwise mild and inoffensive Crippen – a resolve so desperate that it did not stop short at murder – and he quietly laid the groundwork for the plan that would rid him of the intolerable incubus of his wife. His first step was to visit a chemist in New Oxford Street where he bought five grains of hyoscine hydrobromide – an obscure but effective poison . . .

On the evening of 31st January 1910, Mr and Mrs Martinetti, retired mime artists and friends of the Crippens, dined at Hilldrop Crescent – Crippen insisted that they should keep the engagement despite Mr Martinetti's ill-health and the fact that Cora was not in her finest fettle either with a slight cold. When the Martinettis left at around 1.30am, she waved them goodbye from an upstairs window so as not to risk the chill of the cold night air. It was the last time that anyone, other than her husband, was ever to see Cora Crippen alive.

The day after the dinner party, Crippen called on the Martinettis to see if they had enjoyed the evening, and he promised to pass on Mrs Martinetti's love to Cora. The following day he was pawning some of Cora's jewellery, and Ethel Le Neve spent the night at Hilldrop Crescent. Two days later, the Music Hall Ladies' Guild received two letters signed 'Belle Elmore' – but not in Cora's handwriting – resigning her membership of the Guild. The reason given was an urgent visit to America due to a family illness. Crippen made another sally to the pawnshop and, on 20th February, three weeks after Cora's supposed departure for the US, he coolly took Ethel, wearing one of Cora's brooches, to the Music Hall Ladies' annual ball. Neither the brooch nor the relationship escaped the scandalized eyes of the Ladies and their escorts and when on 12th March, Ethel openly moved into Hilldrop Crescent, the clicking of tongues became a clamour. Crippen started spreading the story that Cora had developed pneumonia in America and was dangerously ill. Finally, on 24th March, on his way to Dieppe for an Easter 'honeymoon' with Ethel, he sent a cable from Victoria Station to the Martinettis saying baldly – 'Belle died yesterday at six o'clock'.

The clamour of gossip became a tumult, and on his return to England Crippen was bombarded with questions from Cora's friends demanding details of the death and funeral arrangements. Crippen calmly told them that Belle had died with relatives in Los Angeles – even going into details of who was by her bedside at the end; he assured them that it was too late to send flowers to America – Cora's ashes were already on their way.

Crippen continued his normal quiet routine, returning each evening to Hilldrop Crescent and Ethel, who was now openly wearing Cora's furs and jewels. Then in May an old friend of Cora's returned from a business trip to California; a hurried visit to Los Angeles had revealed no trace of Cora Crippen or Belle Elmore, either alive or dead. His suspicions aroused, he took them straight to Scotland Yard.

Chief Inspector Walter Dew had been instructed to launch an enquiry into the disappearance and on 8th July he began by visiting 39 Hilldrop Crescent; he was received by Ethel Le Neve and a French maid. Later Crippen courteously showed the Inspector over the house, pointing out the trunks of clothing, furs and jewellery belonging to his wife. Then, with a shamefaced and dejected look, Crippen 'confessed' to the Inspector how he had fabricated the story of Cora's death to cover up the scandal of the 'real story' – that she had run away with her lover (the American Bruce Miller) and the couple had disappeared together, he knew not where. Inspector Dew felt sorry for the pathetic little man and after making him promise to write a description of Cora for the US newspapers, he left Crippen with a warm handshake. His reaction was rather cooler when he returned to the house a few days later to find nothing but the signs of hurried flight.

Pictures and descriptions of the couple were circulated, and on July 13th the police began a systematic search of the house. It was not until the third day that Dew, armed with a poker, prised up some loose bricks in the cellar floor and discovered something wrapped up in a pyjama jacket and buried in quicklime. In the parcel was part of a human body – a headless, armless and legless torso which, unbelievably, had been filleted.

Piece by piece the grisly remains were taken to the mortuary for analysis; side by side with the stoppered jars containing the body's organs were others displaying variously a pair of bloodstained combinations coated with lime, brown human hair in a curler, a tattered handkerchief, a cotton camisole and portions of a flannelette pyjama jacket which matched trousers found in Crippen's bedroom. A final jar contained a piece of skin from the abdomen which exhibited an old operation scar – the sort of scar that Cora Crippen bore as a reminder of the operation she had undergone when she was younger. Analysis of the organs revealed traces of hyoscine – the first time that this obscure poison had been used for the purpose of murder.

A warrant was issued for the arrest of both Crippen and Le Neve and the story exploded into the headlines of every newspaper in the country.

Captain Henry Kendall of the *S.S. Montrose*, bound for Canada, fancied himself as an amateur detective, using his powers of observation to protect passengers and crew against the sprinkling of conmen and troublemakers that such voyages inevitably attract. On this particular voyage he was keeping a weather eye on a curious couple who had boarded the ship at Antwerp; Mr and Master Robinson, who shared a double cabin, were not, Captain Kendall decided, quite what they appeared to be. He watched them more closely and before long came to the positive conclusion that Master Robinson was a woman in disguise; and Mr Robinson he noted, was in the habit of carrying a revolver under his jacket.

A police notice about Crippen and Le Neve reached Captain Kendall and he studied the photographs minutely; despite the lack of spectacles and moustache, he felt a shock of excitement as he realized that in the Robinsons he had found the fugitives Crippen and Le Neve. He took the dramatic step of sending a radio-telegraph to Scotland Yard – the first time that the new wireless device had been used in the battle against crime. As soon as the news reached Inspector Dew, he boarded a fast ship and caught up with the *S.S. Montrose* before she docked at Montreal.

The international press were running a high fever about the story by this time, and a boatload of journalists, disguised as shipwrecked sailors, had to be bribed from upstaging Dew, himself disguised as a harbour pilot, in getting aboard the *Montrose.*

Eventually the Chief Inspector was welcomed on board by Captain Kendall and had little trouble recognizing Mr Robinson as his quarry. Crippen, however, was at a disadvantage without his spectacles and did not at first recognise Dew in his pilot's uniform. The Inspector greeted him: 'Good morning Dr Crippen', and was rewarded with a fleeting look of surprise, followed by fear, and finally resignation as the cornered Crippen struggled to regain his composure.

Ethel Le Neve, awaiting Crippen in their cabin, collapsed in a dead faint as Dew burst into the compartment. The couple were arrested, handcuffed and searched on board the *Montrose.* In Crippen's pocket Dew found two cards – both printed 'John Robinson' and inscribed with pencilled messages. The first read: 'I cannot stand the horror I go through every night any longer and as I see nothing ahead and money has come to an end, I have made up my mind to jump overboard tonight. I know I have spoiled your life but I'll hope some day you can learn to forgive me. Last words of love. Yours H.' The other card read: 'Shall we wait till tonight about 10 or 11? If not, what time?' . . . Were these genuine suicide messages, or were they part of a plan to mislead the police when they searched the ship at Montreal? Crippen maintained at his trial that he had bribed someone to smuggle him ashore before the ship docked and that Ethel would have handed the two cards to the police saying that he had jumped overboard during the night. Such a plan might well have succeeded but for Dew's speed in reaching the *Montrose* when he did.

Crippen's trial at the Old Bailey became such a star attraction that over 4,000 applications were received for seats, and half-day-only tickets were specially issued. The trial opened on 18th October and lasted for five days – the prisoner behaving throughout with courageous dignity – even when the jury pronounced the inevitable 'guilty' verdict and sentence was passed. Only when the Appeal Court upheld the verdict did Crippen give way to a moment's black despair; he penned his last love letter to Ethel: '. . . Death has no terror for me . . .' he wrote, 'but Oh! wifie my love, my own, the bitterness of the thought that I must leave you alone without me in the world . . .'

On 23rd November 1910, at Pentonville Prison, Hawley Harvey Crippen calmly met his death by the hangman's rope and was buried in an unmarked grave in the prison yard. In compliance with his last modest request, Ethel's photograph and letters were buried with him.

Ethel Le Neve was acquitted of any complicity in the murder and to escape further publicity she emigrated to Canada soon after the trial. There she later married and had children and returned after many years to Britain where she died in old age and obscurity in 1965.

By all accounts, Hawley Harvey Crippen was a courteous, pleasant and unselfish man – in fact one witness at his trial described him as one of the nicest men she had ever met. Perhaps it is Cora Crippen who should have gone down in history as the villain of the piece – in driving her husband beyond the bounds of what human dignity could stand and into a ghastly crime for which they both paid with their lives.

'THIS ALL COUNTS FOR NOTHING'

The Murder of Ken Ockenden, Malcolm Barlow, Billy Sutherland, Martyn Duffey, John Howlett, and Stephen Sinclair by Dennis Andrew Nilsen
On various dates between December 1979 and January 1983 at 23 Cranley Gardens, London N10, and 195 Melrose Avenue, London NW2

Stumbling on a Mass Murderer

Twenty-Three Cranley Gardens is a large, Edwardian, semi-detached house in the North London suburb of Muswell Hill. Most of the houses in the street are occupied by middle-class families, but in the early 1980s Number 23 had been converted into six bedsit flats.

On Thursday, 3rd February 1983, a number of the tenants were irritated to discover that their lavatories wouldn't flush properly. The local plumber was called, but when he arrived on the Saturday he realized that it was too serious a job for him to handle. Jim Alcock, the boyfriend of one of the tenants, Fiona Bridges, decided to telephone 'Dyno-Rod', the large plumbing company, while his girlfriend attempted to get in touch with the landlord.

It was not until 6.15pm on the Tuesday evening that Mike Cattran, a 'Dyno-Rod' engineer, arrived to investigate the problem. He managed to trace the blockage to a manhole at the side of the house without any difficulty, but when he removed the cover he was assailed by the most revolting stench. As he shone his torch into the murky depths he could just make out, twelve feet below him, a layer of white sludge, which was flecked with what looked appallingly like blood. Holding his breath and suppressing the desire to retch, he climbed down the rungs into the manhole. In the sludge he came upon what he was now certain were pieces of rotting white meat, some with hair still on the skin. After climbing back up he discussed his unpleasant discovery with the tenants. Had anybody been trying to flush pieces of chicken or pork down the toilet? They hadn't, but the man in the top flat did have a dog. Perhaps he knew something about it? Mike Cattran turned to 'Des' Nilsen, a quiet man in his thirties who usually kept himself very much to himself. Had he been flushing meat down the lavatory? No, he replied, he was just as puzzled about the plumbing problem as everyone else. Mike Cattran was still suspicious. He hardly dared think it, but the meat just might be human remains. It didn't look like any meat he had ever seen before, and for some time he considered telephoning the police. Instead, he informed his supervisor of what he'd found and arranged to return to Cranley Gardens to take a further look in daylight.

Next morning Mike Cattran, accompanied by his supervisor, Gary Wheeler, prised open the manhole cover again, with considerable trepidation. To his surprise there was no nasty smell and when he looked down, the layer of white sludge had also disappeared. Had he been imagining things? He decided to climb down the manhole to have another good look. Feeling with his hand along the pipe which led into the manhole, he pulled out a chunk of flesh and four pieces of bone. The bones were horrifyingly reminiscent of human fingers. At that moment Fiona Bridges came out of the house. She and Jim had heard somebody scrabbling about outside during the night. Jim had gone out to investigate and nearly bumped into Des Nilsen coming back in. Nilsen had explained that he had just popped out for a pee, but both Jim and Fiona had been quite upset and had had some difficulty in getting back to sleep afterwards. Cattran and Wheeler decided it was time to call the police.

Detective Chief Inspector Peter Jay arrived at Cranley Gardens at eleven o'clock. A full search of the manhole was immediately begun and further pieces of flesh and bone were recovered from the drain. These were then taken in a plastic bag to Hornsey mortuary for identification, and from there to Charing Cross Hospital for detailed analysis by David Bowen, the Professor of Forensic Medicine at University College, London. Professor Bowen examined the remains at 3.30 in the afternoon and pronounced them human, the flesh coming from the neck region and the various bones from a male human hand.

By 4.30 DCI Jay was back at Cranley Gardens, accompanied by DI Stephen McCusker and DC Jeffrey Butler. They had to wait until 5.40pm for Dennis Nilsen to return from his work as a clerical officer in a Job Centre in Central London. Meeting Nilsen at the door, DCI Jay explained that he was a police officer and he had come about the drains. Nilsen expressed surprise that the police should be interested in something as mundane as drains, and the four men climbed the stairs. As they reached his flat and walked into the bedroom, Nilsen was informed that human remains had been found in the outside drain. 'Good grief! How awful!' he replied. DCI Jay then said 'Don't mess about, where's the rest of the body?' To his great surprise Nilsen replied, quite calmly, 'In two plastic bags in the wardrobe next door, I'll show you,' and led the detectives into the front room, offering DCI Jay the key to the wardrobe. The smell alone was enough to confirm Nilsen's statement without further investigation. Nilsen continued, unprompted, 'It's a long story. It goes back a long time. I'll tell you everything. I want to get it all off my chest, not here but at the police station.' Nilsen was cautioned and then arrested on a charge of murder.

While Nilsen was being taken by car to Hornsey Police Station, Detective Inspector McCusker turned and asked him, 'Are we talking about one body or two?' Nilsen replied: 'Fifteen or sixteen, since 1978. I'll tell you everything. It's a relief to be able to get it all off my mind.'

In the charge room the questioning began: 'Let's get this straight. Are you telling us that since 1978 you have killed sixteen people?' 'Yes, three at Cranley Gardens and about thirteen at my previous address, 195 Melrose Avenue, Cricklewood.'

The police were at first flabbergasted by Nilsen's apparent frankness, his cold, matter-of-fact approach to the situation, and by the sheer scale of his claims. They also found themselves in the unlikely position of having found their murderer almost before the investigation had begun. Their task was to – literally – piece together who he had killed, when and where the crimes had occured and how such an orgy of killing could have gone so completely unnoticed for so long.

With Nilsen secure in a cell in Hornsey Police Station, Chief Inspector Jay returned to Cranley Gardens at nine o'clock that evening, accompanied by Professor Bowen and Detective Chief Superintendent Peter Chambers, the head of 'Y' Division, who had now been placed in charge of the inquiry. They took two large plastic bags from Nilsen's wardrobe and returned to Hornsey mortuary to inspect the contents. Both of the bags contained a number of smaller, sealed carrier bags of the kind provided by supermarkets and department stores. The inventory of the first large bag listed the following: the left side of a man's chest; the right side of a man's chest with an arm attached; a torso minus legs, arms and head; a mess of internal organs, consisting of a heart, two lungs, a spleen, a liver, a gall bladder, kidneys and intestines. The second large plastic bag contained a torso with the arms attached, but the hands cut off; a skull with the flesh boiled away; a head with most of the flesh and hair attached, but the face removed.

On the morning of the following day, 11th February, at a quarter to eleven, the intensive questioning of Dennis Nilsen began, a process which was to take up a total of thirty hours over the next week. Throughout this ordeal Nilsen was always co-operative, straining his memory to recall the details of his murderous career. On the first morning he helpfully suggested that the police would find further remains under a drawer in the bathroom and in a tea chest in the front room at Cranley Gardens. In the tea chest, which was liberally garnished with mothballs and air freshener, they found another bundle of plastic bags under an old velvet curtain and some screwed up pages of The *Guardian*. Inside was another torso, a skull, and an assortment of bones. In a plastic bag in the bathroom they discovered the complete lower half of a body.

The police next turned their attention to the other address that Nilsen had mentioned, 195 Melrose Avenue, Willesden. The house (which had been renovated since Nilsen's tenancy) was literally pulled apart. Nilsen had also confessed to burning as many as thirteen bodies in the garden. A team of policemen in green boiler suits and thirty police cadets working in shifts systematically sifted every inch of ground over a period of thirteen days and nights. The trawl of Melrose Avenue brought in a heap of over a thousand charred bone fragments, including a piece of rib, part of a hipbone, a jaw with the teeth intact and a six-inch length of thigh-bone. In addition, a cheque book, a silver medallion, a pen and several fragments of clothing were recovered, all the possessions of Nilsen's hapless victims.

Gradually, through the long hours of interrogation, the police had begun to put together a picture of Dennis Nilsen's secret life of crime. His victims had all been unattached young men, many of them homosexual and most of them destitute. Few of them were missed when they disappeared, and this had undoubtedly been to

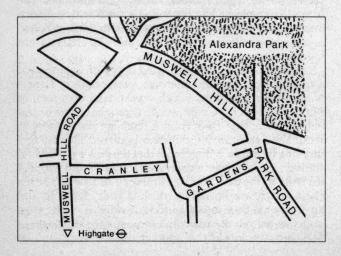

Nilsen's advantage. Nevertheless, the extraordinary catalogue of crimes that Nilsen admitted to the police makes chilling reading.

The Case History of a Mass Murderer
23rd November 1945
Dennis Nilsen was born, second of the three children of Betty Whyte and Olav Nilsen, a Norwegian soldier. The couple had been married three years earlier, but from the beginning the marriage was unhappy, with Olav frequently absent from home and usually drunk. The situation resolved itself in divorce in 1949; Mrs Nilsen and her children living at 47 Academy Road, Fraserburgh, Aberdeenshire, the home of Mrs Nilsen's parents, Andrew and Lily Whyte. The grandparents were the driving influence in the strict Presbyterian upbringing of the children.

31st October 1951
Nilsen's grandfather, Andrew Whyte, whom he idolized, died suddenly at sea at the age of 61. Nilsen was much affected by seeing the dead body of his grandfather laid out in the parlour.

1954
Betty Nilsen married Adam Scott, a builder, and the family moved to 73 Mid Street in nearby Strichen. Nilsen developed into a solitary child and disliked his stepfather.

August 1961
Nilsen enlisted in the Army Catering Corps at the age of 15 to escape from home. He was trained at Aldershot for the next three years.

1964
Nilsen was posted to Osnabruck in Germany as a cook. It was at this time that he began to drink heavily and to discover his homosexuality. Over the next eight years he was relatively happy in the Army, being posted at various times to Berlin, Cyprus and Sharjah in the Persian Gulf.

October 1972
Nilsen decided to resign from the Army, partly because he was appalled by the way it was being used in Northern Ireland.

November 1972
Joined the Metropolitan Police, and was trained at Hendon before being posted to Willesden Police Station.

December 1973
He resigned from the Police force, being unhappy both with the discipline and the restriction it put on his homosexual social life. He took a room at 9 Manstone Road, NW8, and began work as a security guard protecting various government buildings in Central London.

May 1974
After resigning his job as a security guard, Nilsen was accepted by the Manpower Services Commission as a clerical officer at the Denmark Street Job Centre, in Soho. He continued in this employment until his arrest in February 1983. A large part of his work was to interview the unemployed, the down-and-out, and the young rootless who hung about in Central London. At this time he was also regularly frequenting those public houses which attracted a homosexual clientele.

1974
Nilsen was evicted from his room in Manstone Road for entertaining male visitors late at night. He found new accommodation at 80 Teignmouth Road, Willesden.

1975
A young man named David Painter claimed that he had been attacked after rejecting Nilsen's sexual advances. Nilsen had met him at the Job Centre and invited him back to the flat. It was Nilsen who actually called the police after Painter had cut his arm in the struggle. Nilsen was interrogated for some time before being allowed to leave the police station.

November 1975
Nilsen met an unemployed man named David Gallichan at the Champion public house in Bayswater Road. After being invited back by Nilsen to his home, the pair decided to share a flat and moved to 195 Melrose Avenue.

May 1977
David Gallichan left Nilsen, who felt humiliated and rejected by the sudden departure.

30th December 1978
Nilsen meets a young Irishman at The Cricklewood Arms.
After inviting him back to his flat to continue drinking,
Nilsen strangled his guest with a tie during the night. The
body was carefully undressed and washed, before being
stored under the floorboards, a procedure that became the
pattern in Nilsen's subsequent crimes.

11th August 1979
Nilsen burnt the body of the Irishman in the garden. It
had, until then, been stored in pieces in two plastic bags.

October 1979
Nilsen picked up a Chinese student, Andrew Ho, in The
Salisbury public house in St Martin's Lane and took him
back to his flat. Ho offered sex and agreed to be tied up.
Nilsen attempted to strangle Andrew, but he broke free and
ran off to inform the police. Nilsen claimed that Ho had
been trying to 'rip him off' and the matter was dropped.

3rd December 1979
Nilsen met a 23-year-old Canadian student, Ken Ockenden, at the Princess Louise in High Holborn; Ockenden
was in London on holiday after graduating. This victim
was also strangled in Nilsen's flat and placed under the
floorboards. Nilsen tore up Ockenden's money 'because it
would be stealing'. Uniquely, Ockenden was missed, and
his parents came to London creating considerable publicity over his disappearance, but to no effect.

May 1980
Nilsen's next victim was a 16-year-old butcher called
Martyn Duffey; he took his place beside Ken Ockenden
under the floorboards.

July–September 1980
26-year-old Billy Sutherland, a Scot, went on a pub crawl
with Nilsen and ended up with Duffey and Ockenden.

12th November 1980
Nilsen met Scottish barman Douglas Stewart at The Red
Lion in Dean Street and took him back to Melrose Avenue.
There he tried to strangle him, then threatened him with a
carving knife, before deciding to let him go.

1980–81

A succession of victims followed. A Filipino or Mexican was picked up at The Salisbury, followed by another Irishman, a building worker. There followed a half-starved down-and-out that Nilsen had picked up in a doorway on the corner of Oxford Street and Charing Cross Road. He was burnt whole in the garden almost immediately because Nilsen was so horrified by his emaciated condition. Of the next victim Nilsen could remember nothing, except that he had cut the body into three pieces and burnt it about a year later. The ninth victim was a young Scotsman picked up in The Golden Lion in Dean Street, followed by another 'Billy Sutherland' type. The next to fall prey was a 'skinhead' who was heavily tattooed, including a dotted line round his neck, inscribed 'Cut here'. Nilsen obliged when dissecting him.

May 1981

Nilsen had a major body-burning session in the garden at 195 Melrose Avenue.

17th September 1981

Malcolm Barlow was sitting against a garden wall in Melrose Avenue, complaining that he couldn't use his legs when Nilsen found him; he phoned for an ambulance and accompanied Barlow to hospital. The next day, Barlow went back to Nilsen's flat to thank him. Nilsen cooked them both a meal, and strangled his guest when he fell asleep. Malcolm Barlow was the last of the Melrose Avenue victims.

October 1981

As a sitting tenant, Nilsen was offered £1000 to leave the flat in Melrose Avenue, so that it could be renovated. After a bonfire to remove the last vestiges of his murderous activities, Dennis Nilsen moved into the top flat at 23 Cranley Gardens, Muswell Hill.

25th November 1981

Nilsen met a homosexual student, Paul Nobbs, in The Golden Lion in Soho. Nobbs woke up next morning at Cranley Gardens with a worse than usual hangover; he went to University College Hospital for a check up and was told that someone had tried to strangle him. Nobbs did not pursue the matter.

March 1982

Nilsen met John Howlett, a young criminal known as 'John the Guardsman' in The Salisbury, and discovered that they had drunk there before, back in December 1981. Nilsen invited Howlett back to Cranley Gardens and tried to strangle him, but John put up a struggle and Nilsen had to bang his head against the bedrest before drowning him in the bath. This victim was quickly dismembered and portions of the body boiled in a pot because an old friend was expected to stay with Nilsen over the weekend.

May 1982

Picked up Carl Stotter, a homosexual revue artist known as 'Khara Le Fox' at The Black Cap in Camden High Street. Nilsen tried to strangle Stotter and then drown him in the bath, but seems to have relented half-way through. Next morning Carl Stotter went for a walk in the woods with Nilsen, who hit him violently over the head, picked him up again and continued walking. The two agreed to meet again, but Stotter wisely avoided Nilsen from then on.

Late 1982

The next victim was Graham Allen, who was picked up in Shaftesbury Avenue. He was invited to the Cranley Gardens flat, and fell asleep while eating an omelette. Allen was dissected, some parts being put in a tea chest, some in a plastic bag, and others flushed down the lavatory.

26th January 1983

Stephen Sinclair, a 20-year-old 'punk' and drug addict, was picked up in Leicester Square and taken to Nilsen's home. Stephen's body was left, covered by a blanket, for several days and Nilsen was in the process of dismembering it at the time of his arrest.

9th February 1983

Nilsen arrested.

12th February 1983

Remanded in custody for seven days by the Highgate

Magistrates Court. This became a regular weekly routine while police were investigating the case.

26th May 1983
Nilsen committed for trial at the Old Bailey on six counts of murder (Ken Ockenden, Malcolm Barlow, Billy Sutherland, Martyn Duffey, John Howlett, Stephen Sinclair) and two counts of attempted murder (Douglas Stewart, Paul Nobbs). The remains of Graham Allen were identified from dental records too late to be included in the first indictment. Likewise, Karl Stotter was traced too late for inclusion in the second, though his harrowing experience was used as evidence at the trial.

24th October 1983
The trial of Dennis Nilsen opened in Court No.1 at the Old Bailey, Mr Justice Croom Johnson presiding, with Mr Allan Green representing the Crown and Ivan Lawrence QC, MP, defending. That Nilsen had committed the crimes was never disputed. The main thrust of the defence was a plea for manslaughter on the grounds of diminished responsibility.

4th November 1983
After a day and a half's retirement the jury found Nilsen guilty by a majority of ten to two on all six counts of murder and two of attempted murder. He was sentenced to life imprisonment and removed from the court to Wormwood Scrubs Prison, and thence to Parkhurst on the Isle of Wight after he had been slashed across the cheek with a razor by a fellow prisoner.

Nilsen is at present serving his sentence at Wakefield Prison and, still the somewhat obstreperous union campaigner that was at work on the outside, is now keenly observant of prisoners' rights and the 'failings' of prison staff. Nilsen was sentenced, to a period of not less than twenty-five years, though it remains a matter of great doubt whether society will ever feel it safe to release him.

The Reflections of a Mass Murderer
Dennis Nilsen is an intelligent, articulate and self-analytical man. On the surface he was caring, compassionate

and particularly socially aware, with strong left-wing political sympathies and a highly developed sense of morality which motivated his work in the Denmark Street Job Centre, and as a trade-union official. His personal life, however, became increasingly sad and unsatisfactory, leading him to seek solace in excessive quantities of alcohol and a succession of casual homosexual encounters, the unfortunate ingredients which brought about an appalling murderous obsession. Nilsen himself was fascinated by this apparent paradox in his personality and

I like to see people in happiness.
I like to do good.
I love democracy.
I detest any criminal acts.
I like kids.
I like all animals.
I love public and community service.
I hate to see hunger, unemployment, oppression, war, aggression, ignorance, illiteracy, etc.
I was a trades union officer.
I was a good soldier and N.C.O.
I was a fair policeman.
I was an effective civil servant.
STOP. THIS ALL COUNTS FOR NOTHING when I can kill fifteen men (without any reason) and attempt to kill about nine others – in my home and under friendly circumstances.
Am I mad? I don't feel mad. Maybe I am mad.

(Poem written by Dennis Nilsen)

Never a man so sore afraid
To let his feelings shine;
Never a man so helpless
To stop and notice mine.

(Poem written by Dennis Nilsen in prison For David Martin, the bi-sexual police killer, for whom Nilsen developed a strong attachment during his period on remand)

constantly explored his confused feelings through the written word.

RED MONSTER LURES YOUNG MEN TO THEIR DEATHS IN HOMOSEXUAL HOUSE OF HORROR

Dennis Andrew Nilsen, 37, once believed to have close links with the Militant Tendency and the Socialist Workers Party (and personal supporter of Red Ken [Livingstone]) appeared at the Old Bailey today to face 15 charges of murder and nine charges of attempted murder.

Nilsen, who has been to East Berlin, sat in court in sombre suit and tie. He appeared unmoved and emotionless as the prosecution evidence was read out. It was revealed that Nilsen, a misfit and extremist trade union agitator, had butchered his helpless victims on his kitchen floor and burnt the pieces in front of neighbourhood children.

It is believed that during the Garners Steak House dispute he had 'bullied' staff at the Job Centre into blacking of legal job vacancies. 'He always intimidated us', said a spokesman for the staff at the Job Centre. While maintaining a respectable front in the Civil Service he prowled the streets of London.

(Spoof newspaper article written by Nilsen a week after his arrest)

IN AND OUT *THE EAGLE*

The Murder of Phyllis Dimmock
On Wednesday, 11th September 1907 at 29 St
Paul's Road (now Agar Grove), London NW1
and the Trial and Acquittal of Robert Wood for
the crime

The body in the case, that of 23-year-old Phyllis Dimmock, was found by Bertram Shaw, the man with
whom she had shared the previous nine months of her life.
Shaw was employed as a cook on the Midland Railways'
dining cars which plied the late night and early morning
runs between London St Pancras and Sheffield; a job that
had the double advantage of leaving Phyllis both the time
and the space to pursue her own, more historic calling. In
short, she made use of Shaw's nights away to hire out her
natural, God-given, attributes to such men as could afford
her company.

On the morning of Thursday, 12th September, 1907,
Bert Shaw arrived home off the 11 o'clock from Sheffield.
Getting no reply to his enthusiastic knocks on the door of
their first-floor flat, he obtained access via the duplicate
key held against such emergencies by the landlady downstairs. The sight that confronted him in the parlour behind
that front door was a shambles; cupboards and drawers
had been ransacked and their contents scattered about the
floor; there were the stale remains of a meal set for two,
and some empty beer bottles on the table. The door to the
bedroom was locked, obliging Shaw to put his shoulder to
it. The tableau that greeted his horrified eyes was worse by
far than anything he might have imagined. The body lay
naked on the bed; blood had seeped everywhere from a
throat cut so far through that it was only the vertebrae that

had prevented decapitation; streams of gore had flowed into sticky pools along the floor.

Subsequent examination by the police pathologist estimated the time of the attack as between 3 and 6 o'clock that morning, and from the position of the body, probably carried out while the victim slept. Small comfort for the heart-broken Shaw; for not only had he the shock of the discovery to contend with, but the inescapable evidence that his Phyllis had obviously returned to plying the trade which he fondly imagined she had rejected out of love for him.

Phyllis, the police soon found, was a popular member of the twilight world she inhabited while Bert was cooking mobile breakfasts, and it proved easy to piece together her movements while 'on call'. For example, she regularly used two local pubs as pick-up venues – The Eagle, and The Rising Sun; they tracked down one of her regular customers, a ship's cook named Robert Roberts. Part, at least, of Roberts's wages had been spent entertaining and being entertained by Phyllis (whose non-professional name, incidentally, was the more homely Emily Jane) on the three nights previous to the murder. In fact he freely admitted that he was prepared to rent the girl's affections for a fourth evening, but that she had protested a prior engagement for the Thursday. He also divulged what was to be vitally important information. On the Wednesday, the last evening that he spent with her, Phyllis had shown the young cook a part of a letter that she had received; he clearly remembered the words 'Dear Phillis, Will you meet me at the bar of The Eagle at Camden Town, 8.30 tonight, Wednesday. Bert.' She then, inexplicably, showed him another communication, a picture postcard, on one side of which was the painting of a mother holding her child, and on the reverse the written message, 'Phillis Darling, If it pleases you meet me 8.15pm at the [here was drawn a cartoon sketch of a rising sun with a winking face on it]. Yours to a cinder. Alice.' Whether reference to cinders provoked the next act we do not know, but she replaced the postcard in a drawer, dropped the letter into the fire grate, and set light to it. Both documents were, in Robert Roberts's opinion, in the same hand.

And the police did indeed find the charred remains of a note in the fireplace at St Paul's Road, the little that could still be read proving a credit to the memory of the ship's cook:

ill . . . you . . . ar of the . . . e . . . Town . . . Wednes
[Dear Phillis, Will *you* meet me at the b*ar of the* Eagle at Camden *Town*, 8.30 tonight, *Wednes*day. Bert]

The second document, the postcard, turned up two days

So you think that Bob's a killer?
Don't be silly he just couldn't.
You can say all night, 'twas Robert Wood,
And I'll say Robert Woodn't.
(Contemporary doggerel)

later when Bertram Shaw decided to pack up and move to a different room. At the request of the Commissioner of Police, the press was invited to display the text on the card in the hope that a member of the public might recognize the hand responsible. Sensing that there might be more to be made out of the story, the *News of the World* offered £100 reward to anybody responding to its caption 'Can You Recognise This Writing?'

Ruby Young recognized it; she recognized it as the handwriting of her occasional boyfriend, a young artist with the extravagant name of Robert William Thomas George Cavers Wood. Ruby liked to describe herself as a 'model' – which was to say, of the same profession as Phyllis Dimmock – and it was in this professional capacity that she had met Robert Wood. Wood, unlike many of the denizens of Ruby's world, was a talented engraver in a respected position with a glass-maker in Gray's Inn Road, earned a modest second income as a freelance cartoonist, and shared a comfortable home with his father in St Pancras. Their worlds met on account of Wood's weakness for the company of inexpensive whores.

The *News of the World* offer must have reminded Ruby of the occasion, less than a week after the murder of Phyllis Dimmock, when Wood had extracted a promise from her to say, if anybody asked, that he always spent Mondays and Wednesdays with her. Now, before Ruby had a chance to claim her £100 bounty for Robert Wood, the man in question presented himself at her door. On being taxed with The Rising Sun postcard mystery, Wood confessed 'Ruby, I'm in trouble', and went on to tell the following story. He had, he said, been drinking in the bar of The Rising Sun, when he struck up a conversation with a young woman who was a complete stranger to him; they got to talking about picture postcards, and Wood impressed the lady by showing her the examples he had brought back from his holiday in Bruges. Phyllis (for it was she) had been particularly attracted by one of a woman hugging a child, and asked Wood if he would write something 'nice' on it for her, and this resulted in the mock invitation embellished with the soon-to-be-famous rising sun cartoon. The signature 'Alice' was supposed to be a device to allay any suspicion that Bert Shaw might entertain about the company Phyllis was keeping. At all events, he confided now to Ruby, the wretched card looked as though it would be big trouble for him. Unless Ruby would tell the lie that Wood had spent the evening of 11th September with her. They rehearsed a complicated itinerary, but it must have seemed suspicious even to the uncomplicated mind of Ruby Young. In fact, it played on her mind so much that she passed the secret on to a 'gentleman friend', a journalist; he in turn shared the secret with Inspector Arthur Neil. Who promptly arrested Robert Wood for the murder of Phyllis Dimmock.

At the police station Wood conveyed his explanation of the postcard's origin in the same words he had used to Ruby Young, ending with his alibi for the night of the crime – spent, as they had agreed, with Ruby. Robert Wood was not to know that she had already betrayed him.

At the two identity parades, the prisoner was positively picked out by a number of people, mostly the prostitutes of The Rising Sun, who associated him with Phyllis Dimmock. Another sighting was provided by Robert McCowan; according to his own statement, McCowan had been walking along the St Paul's Road on the day of the murder, when hearing footsteps behind him he

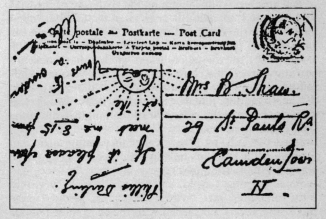

The 'Rising Sun' postcard

turned and saw a man leaving No.29. The time was ten minutes to five; he identified the man as Robert Wood. A coroner's inquest resulted in a verdict of wilful murder, and by the time Robert Wood stood his trial at the Old Bailey on December 12th, his conviction seemed a mere formality.

But that would be to reckon without the fickle, and often inexplicable, sympathies of the general public. For it was the very betrayal by Ruby Young–a prostitute who had turned against her lover for money–that secured for Wood a small place in their hearts. A small place that, as the trial unfolded, and Robert Wood's defence was so ably handled by Mr (later Sir) Edward Marshall Hall KC, developed almost to mass hysteria in his support. Prosecution witnesses were harassed in the street, and the court's public gallery played host to a galaxy of celebrated personalities.

As for Robert Wood, his attitude to the trial throughout was that of a somewhat distant and dispassionate observer, and he spent much of his time sketching the proceedings from the dock. In the witness box he made a good impression, sticking to his original story, and clearly earning the support of Mr Justice Grantham, who summed up to the jury much in Wood's favour.

The jury retired at 7.45pm on the sixth day of the trial, and returned 15 minutes later in order to free Robert Wood from the charge of murder. The court erupted in unrestrained cheers of pleasure and approbation, a jubilant swell that was soon taken up by the thousands waiting outside the court for just such a verdict. While Wood, his family and friends were escorted to a restaurant for a celebration dinner, the reviled Ruby Young was smuggled out of the side door of the building disguised as a cleaning woman.

Robert Wood had been a very lucky young man; and quite possibly a guilty one. But if the jury were right, who did kill Phyllis Dimmock?

'THOU TYRANT, TYRANT JEALOUSY'

The Murder of Hella Christofi by her mother-in-law Styllou Pantopiou Christofi On Thursday, 29th July 1954 at 11 South Hill Park, London NW3

> *Thou tyrant, tyrant, Jealousy,*
> *Thou tyrant of the mind!*
>
> (Dryden, *Song of Jealousy*)

Jealousy is an emotion of limitless strength – as overwhelming as love; as all-consuming as hatred; and more devastating than both.

This is the story of a woman whose intense and unreasoning jealousy caused her to kill not once, but twice; caused her to kill with unimaginable brutality; caused her to kill two members of her immediate family.

The tyrant is Styllou Pantopiou Christofi, and at the time that this episode of her life opens, she is living in a small village in Cyprus. She already looks old beyond her 53 years, wrinkled and dried out by the heat of the sun and overwork. With little help from her reluctant husband, she spends most of her waking life squeezing a small and indifferent existence from a small and indifferent olive grove. She has suffered enough of that relentless, debilitating poverty to have become a sour, envious old woman. And beyond this, Mrs Christofi carries in her heart a terrible guilt.

At the time this episode in her life opens she has already committed one horrible crime – in 1925, when two fellow-villagers had held open the mouth of the victim while Styllou Christofi rammed a blazing torch down her throat.

The victim died. She was Styllou's mother-in-law. Incredibly, Styllou Christofi was acquitted at her trial.

Styllou Christofi's only son Stavros, has long since left the claustrophobic, bitter atmosphere of the village; left the unproductive olive grove, and walked all the way to Nicosia where he worked as a waiter while he saved the money for his boat fare to England. By 1953, he has been in England for twelve years. During this time he has made a happy match with a 36-year-old German girl named Hella, a daughter of the Ruhr. The couple have three healthy children, and live in South Hill Park, a stone's throw from Florence Nightingale's former home. The street, the house, the family, all fit easily into the civilized, very English life that is lived here on the edge of Hampstead Heath. To complete their contentment, Stavros holds a respected post as wine waiter at the internationally renowned Café de Paris in London's West End.

That life of contentment is about to end abruptly and explosively. The peace is about to be shattered by the arrival of Stavros's mother.

Were it not for the mean, intractable nastiness that characterized Styllou Christofi's personality, one could go some way to sympathizing with her position. An ignorant peasant woman set down in the sophistication of London, unable to speak a word of English – illiterate, even, in her native Greek – confronting a daughter-in-law and three young grandchildren for the first time, without the means to communicate directly. It would overwhelm anyone. And Stavros understood this; Hella understood it too; the whole family spared no effort to make the recently arrived member of their family as welcome as they were able.

But the old woman had been wrapped up in her own resentment for too long; the bitterness allowed to take too firm a grip. The mother began to cling to her son like an emotional limpet; began to develop a fanatical and jealous hatred of her daughter-in-law. She developed a hatred for the house; for Hella's stylish way of dressing, and her 'extravagance' in buying make-up; for the way Hella brought up her children. All this and more Styllou Christofi hated, and was not slow to say so – to shout it, in

Greek, often. So oppressive did life become at South Hill Park, that Stavros twice arranged for his mother to live elsewhere; where Styllou rendered herself so objectionable that she was asked to leave on both occasions.

By now, the July of 1954, even the good-natured Hella felt that she had endured enough. 'Next week', she told her husband, 'I am going home to Wuppertal for a holiday. I am taking the children, and when we get back your mother must be gone.'

'But where can she go?'

'Back to Cyprus!'

It cannot have been easy for Stavros to break the news to his mother; harder still for her to accept it. To her it must have sounded like the announcement of the end of her world. She must surely have thought, this is all the fault of that girl; without her, I could be living here happily with my son.

When Stavros kissed his wife goodbye as he left for work on the evening of 29th July, he had no idea of the horror that was to greet his return.

The children in bed, alone at last with the woman who was destroying her family, Styllou Christofi struck. Struck from behind, smashing the cast iron ashplate from the kitchen stove down on to Hella's skull. Struck again, winding a scarf around the unconscious woman's throat, twisting, pulling.

Dragging Hella's now lifeless corpse into the area behind the house, Styllou Christofi, insane in her revenge, made mad with jealousy, soaked the body and a pile of newspaper in paraffin and lit a match. It is just possible that she remembered another fire, twenty-nine years before.

At this time, John Young, a neighbour, happened to be looking in the direction of No.11, and saw the sudden blaze followed by the red glow of the fire. Thinking that the house might have caught light, he went to investigate. What he saw when he looked over the garden fence must have seemed so incredible that Young's mind refused to register the obvious truth. Instead, to him, it looked as though someone was trying to burn a 'wax dummy': 'All I could see was from the thighs down, and the arms were raised and bent back at the elbow like some of the models you see in shop windows. There was a strong smell of wax.' At that point it was about 11.45pm; Mrs Christofi reappeared to stoke up the fire, which seemed to reassure Mr Young, and he returned home.

Shortly before one o'clock, a local restaurateur named Burstoff and his wife were returning home when they were forced to halt by a gesticulating figure in the road, shouting incoherently 'Please come, fire burning, children sleeping.' By the time they had got Mrs Christofi back to the house the fire was out, but the body was still there, just like a charred shop-window dummy, on the paving slabs of the area.

Wisely, Mr Burstoff decided to telephone for the police.

Three months later, Styllou Christofi stood in the dock at the Old Bailey listening, through a court interpreter, to the catalogue of evidence painstakingly collated by the police in support of their prosecution. The bloodstained kitchen, the petrol-soaked rags and papers, the fractured skull, the marks of strangulation around the neck. Most damning of all, the discovery of Hella's wedding ring, carefully wrapped in paper and hidden in the old woman's bedroom.

Styllou's defence was as pathetic as the rest of her life had been. As desperate an attempt to survive as had been her cultivation of the obstinate olive grove.

She had gone to bed before Hella, she claimed, leaving the girl to 'do some washing' (it had been a never-ending source of puzzlement to Styllou that her daughter-in-law washed her body every day – clearly not a feature of her previous experience in the village). The next thing she was aware of was waking to the smell of smoke; she recollected going to the bedroom door, looking out and noticing that the street door was open: remembered going to Hella's room and not finding her there; rushing downstairs where the kitchen door was open revealing the body of her daughter-in-law lying on the ground in the yard, flames licking around her and blood staining her face. She had splashed water on the girl in an attempt to revive her, and when this failed to get a reaction had run in search of help

– which was how she met the Burstoffs.

The trial did not last long. Had Styllou Christofi pleaded insane – as she almost certainly was – it might have been even shorter. In the event, in a final defiant gesture of dignity, she had claimed, 'I am a poor woman, of no education, but I am not mad woman. Never. Never. Never.'

And so Styllou Christofi, on the 13th of December 1954, gave herself up to be the first woman to be executed in England since Edith Thompson thirty years before. And she was nearly the last woman to hang, but Ruth Ellis, who also committed murder in South Hill Park a few months later, was to earn that distinction, [see page 49].

THE POISON PEN

The Murder of Matilda Clover by Dr Thomas Neill Cream
On Wednesday, 21st October 1891 at
27 Lambeth Road, London SE1

Not a very great deal is known about the early life of Thomas Neill Cream, beyond his having been the eldest of eight brothers and sisters, born of William and Mary Cream on 27th May 1850. Four years after this event the family left their home at 61 Wellington Lane, Glasgow, for the new land of opportunity – Canada; here both William and young Thomas became actively involved in the shipbuilding trade, the father managing one firm, the son being apprenticed to another.

By November 1872 Thomas had forsaken trade for a profession, and on the 12th of the month registered at McGill College, Montreal, as a student of medicine. Apart from a rather extravagant life-style (at the expense of his father), and the fact – extraordinary in hindsight – that he taught in Sunday School, little is recorded of significance in this period of Cream's development, but that he graduated with merit on 31st March 1876.

This is the point at which Thomas Cream set his sights on notoriety.

He had already, in the month of September 1874, been provident enough to insure the contents of his lodgings at 106 Mansfield Street for the sum of $1000 with the Commercial Union of Montreal. Little more than a fortnight after graduation, Cream clearly decided it was time to cash in on his investment. At any rate, there was a mysterious fire resulting in a claim from Cream for

$978.40, this despite the fact that almost no damage had been done. The Company smelled a rat, and refused to part with a single cent. Eventually a mutually face-saving compromise was reached, and Cream pocketed $350. The career of Thomas Cream, crook, had begun.

It was around the same time that he met Miss Flora Elizabeth Brooks, the daughter of a prosperous Waterloo (Canada) hotelier. Miss Brooks shortly became pregnant, was aborted by Cream, and nearly died as a result. The furious Brooks senior would settle for nothing less than marriage, and on 11th September Thomas was dragged, unenthusiastic, down the aisle to wed his Flora. However, avoiding the wrath (and shotgun) of Brooks was one thing; bestowing all his worldly goods, etc., was quite another, and on the day following the wedding Cream walked out of the house bound for England. The Brooks family were to hear no more of their errant son-in-law until the unfortunate Flora died of consumption just short of a year after her wedding. It was then that Thomas Cream got in touch; he got in touch to demand the sum of $1000 – claimable, he insisted, under the marriage con-tract. In the end he settled for $200!

In this intervening year, Cream had enrolled as a post-

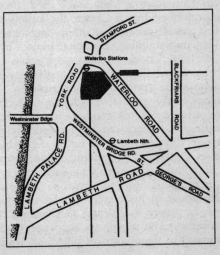

graduate student at St Thomas's Hospital, London, and rounded off his education with a qualification from the Royal College of Physicians and Surgeons at Edinburgh. Thus did Thomas Neill Cream become one of the few genuinely competent medics to turn murderer.

The killings, though, began in a comparatively modest and clumsy manner. Cream had returned to Canada, and was acquiring a lucrative, if unsavoury, reputation as an abortionist, operating out of Dundas Street, London, Ontario. It was during this occupancy that a young chambermaid named Kate Hutchinson Gardener was found dead in the privy behind Cream's rooms; beside her body was a bottle of chloroform. The girl was known to have been visiting Cream for the purpose of securing an abortion, and despite the strength of evidence offered against him, the doctor avoided prosecution for murder. His odious practice, though, was ruined, at least in Ontario.

Chicago fared little better from Cream's attentions, and his newly opened abortion surgery at 434 West Madison Street claimed its first fatality in August 1880. On the 23rd of that summer month, Cream was taken into custody on a charge of causing the death of Julia Faulkner; but luck was with him, and the slippery rogue again escaped his just reward. In December a Miss Stack died after taking medicine prescribed by Dr Cream; the latter's response was the first manifestation of an utterly incomprehensible need to draw unfavourable attention to himself by writing abusive, libellous letters. In this case a series of letters trying to blackmail Frank Pyatt, the perfectly innocent chemist who made up the Stack prescriptions.

A comparatively profitable sideline undertaken by Cream to supplement his earnings from abortion was the marketing of a quack remedy for epilepsy. Whether the treatment did any good or not is debatable, but it appeared at least to do no harm, indeed attracting a number of faithful 'patients'. One such was a railway agent named Daniel Stott, who was so impressed with the improvement in his health that he sent his pretty young wife in person to Chicago, to Thomas Cream, for regular supplies. The inevitable happened, and Cream availed himself of the favours of Julia Stott while taking her husband's money. When Stott became an inconvenience to the liaison his medicine was pepped up with an additional ingredient. On 14th June 1881 Daniel Stott died in great agony, the sudden seizure being attributed to his epilepsy, so that Cream's nostrum would never have been suspected had it not been for the mad medic's inexplicable communication to the coroner of Boone County, claiming that Stott's death had been the result of a blunder on the part of the pharmacist in overdoing the strychnine, and demanding an exhumation. The coroner dismissed the letter as the fantasy of a madman (which at least was true), and paid it no attention. Not so the recipient of Cream's next letter. The District Attorney *did* order an exhumation, *did* find strychnine in the stomach of Daniel Stott, and *did* eventually send prisoner 4374 Thomas Neill Cream to spend the rest of his life at the Illinois State Penitentiary at Joliet.

On 12th May 1887, Thomas's father died at Dansville, New York, and the family began to agitate for the son's release from prison, with the result that Cream's sentence was commuted to seventeen years and, with allowance for good behaviour, he was released on 31st July 1891. Diverting to Canada only for as long as it took to collect his inheritance of $16,000, an unchastened Cream boarded the *Teutonic* for Liverpool, England. Four days later, on 5th October 1891, the deadly doctor was in London, a guest of Anderton's Hotel at 162 Fleet Street.

Having arrived, Cream wasted no time in familiarizing himself with the seedier activities that London had on display. On Tuesday, 6th October, he met a prostitute – Elizabeth Masters – at Ludgate Circus. After drinking wine at the King Lud they went back to her rooms in 9 Orient Buildings, Hercules Road (a turning off Lambeth Road), and thence to Gatti's Music Hall, Westminster Bridge Road.

On the following day, Wednesday the 7th, Cream took lodgings at 103 Lambeth Palace Road, in the heart of South London's slums, an area in which he was to commit a series of indiscriminate murders which were to rival Jack the Ripper's reign of terror in the East End three years before.

On 9th October Cream acquainted himself with the talents of Matilda Clover, a follower of the same calling as Elizabeth Masters, and ironically they were seen by Masters and her friend Elizabeth May entering No.27 Lambeth Road. At about this date, possibly the following day, Thomas Cream purchased from Mr Priest's chemist shop at 22 Parliament Street, a quantity of nux vomica, of which one constituent is the alkaloid poison strychnine. He subsequently bought a box of empty gelatine capsules and a further supply of nux vomica.

Things were about to take a dramatic turn.

The evening of 13th October found James Styles standing outside *The Wellington* in Waterloo Road, doing nothing in particular, when he saw a young prostitute who had been patrolling her beat stagger and collapse onto the pavement. Styles managed to carry her to the address she gasped out (8 Duke Street, now Duchy Street), whence her condition made removal to a hospital necessary. On the journey poor Ellen Donworth confided that a man she had met in the York Hotel in Waterloo Road; 'A tall gentleman with cross eyes, a silk hat and bushy whiskers' had given her a couple of draughts from a bottle of 'white stuff'. She died before reaching the hospital; of strychnine poisoning. Thomas Cream – or 'Fred' as he was known to Ellen Donworth – was away clear. Out of the limelight, that is, until he chose (for what reason God only knows) to make himself obvious in an extraordinary pair of letters. The first was addressed to George Wyatt, who in his position as deputy coroner had presided over the inquest on Donworth: 'I am willing to say that if you and your satellites fail to bring the murderer of Ellen Donworth, alias Ellen Linnell, to justice, I am willing to give you such assistance . . . provided your Government is willing to pay me £300,000 for my services.' It was signed 'A. O'Brien, detective.' The second letter, dated 6th November, was received by Mr W.F.D. Smith, one of the newsagenting family of W.H. Smith and Son, at their offices at 186 Strand. The letter was signed 'H. Bayne, barrister', and the contents read to the effect that Ellen Donworth had been found in possession of two notes that incriminated

Smith in her murder. 'Bayne' was willing to be retained as 'counsellor and legal adviser'.

But this is to take events out of their strict chronology: for on 20th October, Matilda Clover met once again with the man she had been seen with on the 9th. Now the encounter had a less happy conclusion. On this second evening Matilda brought her client 'Fred' back to 27 Lambeth Road where he was seen by the maid, Lucy Rose, as he was leaving. Some hours later Matilda died, writhing and screaming with agonized convulsions. She was buried in a pauper's grave in Tooting on 27th October; believed cause of death: delirium tremens as a result of alcoholism. Cream was in the clear again. Indeed, there was not even a suspicion of murder attached to Matilda Clover's death. Not, that is, until Thomas Cream sent a letter to the Countess Russell at her suite in the Savoy Hotel accusing her husband, Lord Russell, of poisoning Clover. Nor was his Lordship the only one to have a finger pointed in his direction. Dr William Henry Broadbent, an outstanding physician, received a letter dated 28th November, and signed by 'M. Malone'; it began: 'Miss Clover, who until a short time ago lived at 27 Lambeth Road, S.E., died at the above address on 20th October (last month) through being poisoned with strychnine'. 'Malone' went on to accuse Dr Broadbent of the murder outrightly, and threatened to expose him if £2,500 did not change hands.

Dr Thomas Neill Cream now took a brief – albeit very brief – respite from the rigours of murder and correspondence. In fact he found the time to fall in love (at least in his version of that emotion), and to become engaged to be married.

The object of these affections was Laura Sabbatini, a highly respectable young woman who lived with her mother at Berkhamstead. On 7th January 1892 Cream sailed for Canada, leaving Laura waiting.

While in Canada Cream committed one of the most totally gratuitous acts in the annals of crime. He had printed 500 copies of what came to be known as the 'Metropole leaflet'. They were acknowledged by Cream in writing, but never circulated [see illustration page 46].

Title page of a contemporary account of the Lambeth murders

Cream returned to England via New York on 23rd March, a passenger aboard the *Britannic*. He reached London on April 2nd, and arrived back at Lambeth Palace Road via Edwards' Hotel, 14 Euston Square. The brief respite was over.

It was over most specifically for 21-year-old Alice Marsh and 18-year-old Emma Shrivell, two street girls up from Brighton, and currently lodging at 118 Stamford Street, in south London. At about 1.45am on 12th April, PC George Cumley was on his Stamford Street beat when he saw a man being shown out of the door of No.118 by a young woman. The picture was to remain in his memory, for not two hours later behind those same doors, two young women died with great suffering from strychnine poisoning.

Thomas Cream's madness must have struck him again now, for he lapsed into a series of unaccountable and slanderous attacks upon the reputation of one of his neighbours. There happened to be lodged at 103 Lambeth Palace Road one Walter Joseph Harper, a medical student at nearby St Thomas's and son of the respected Dr Joseph Harper of Barnstaple. To their mutual landlady, Miss Sleaper, Cream suddenly broke the news that young Harper was the author of the Stamford Street atrocities. Miss Sleaper's reaction was that Cream was a lunatic (how close she was to the truth would probably have frightened the good woman half to death), and the matter lapsed. Until 26th April, when Dr Joseph Harper received a letter (accompanied, inexplicably, by a newspaper cutting relating to Ellen Donworth's death) declaring that the correspondent. 'W.H. Murray', held incontestable proof that his son Walter had poisoned the Misses Marsh and Shrivell, and that for the consideration of £1,500 the writer was prepared to suppress it. 'Murray' further made it plain that if Harper was unwilling to find the money, the 'evidence' would be offered to the police on the same terms. Quite rightly, the doctor ignored this ludicrous threat and apparently Cream lost interest in the possibility of a transaction.

We now find Thomas Cream returning to Miss Sabbatini in Berkhamstead, where he persuades her – without a word of explanation – to write three letters for him. Had she known even a fraction of the true reason, she would have run a mile; as it was, love prevailed over her apprehensions and she sat down with pen and paper. The missives themselves, signed 'W.H. Murray', were all accusations against Walter Harper, and were sent to

---

Ellen Donworth's Death

To the Guests,

of the Metropole Hotel.

Ladies and Gentlemen,

I hereby notify you that the person who poisoned Ellen Donworth on the 13th last October is to day in the employ of the Metropole Hotel and that your lives are in danger as long as you remain in this Hotel.

Yours respectfully,

W. H. MURRAY.

London April 1892

The extraordinary letter addressed by Cream to the residents of the Metropole Hotel

Coroner Wyatt, presiding over the Marsh/Shrivell inquest, to the foreman of the jury sitting on the same inquest, and to Mr George Clarke, a detective of Cockspur Street.

Whether driven by clinical insanity or by a desperate, illogical desire to be associated with his own crimes, Cream began now to boast about his familiarity with the murders. To one man, John Haynes, he not only revealed far more than he should reasonably have known of the events, but actually took Haynes on a guided tour of the murder spots. To another acquaintance, McIntyre, Cream's uncommon knowledge proved of even greater interest – because his full title was Police Sergeant McIntyre, and he promptly set a watch on the doctor's movements. On 12th May, and quite by chance, Constable Cumley saw Cream and recognized him as the man he saw leaving the scene of the Stamford Street murders, and he too put a tail on Cream.

May 26th and Cream complained through his solicitors to the Chief Commissioner of Police, saying that his business was being adversely affected by the very obvious police shadow. But time was running out for Thomas Cream, and it was not many more days before he had talked himself into police custody. The attempt to blackmail Dr Harper came to light, and with Harper's co-operation in pressing charges, Cream was picked up.

At 5.25pm on 3rd June, Inspector Turnbridge confronted Cream in Lambeth Palace Road and put him under arrest. Cream's response was typical of the irritating arrogance that was to tell so heavily against him at his trial: 'You have got the wrong man', he said, 'but fire away!'

By the time Cream was ready to be charged with attempted blackmail, Matilda Clover's body had been lifted from the soil and analysed. At the inquest on her death, the jury brought in the following verdict: 'We are unanimously agreed that Matilda Clover died of strychnine poisoning and that the poison was administered by Thomas Neill with intent to destroy life'.

Cream stood upon his trial at the Old Bailey on 17th October 1892 before Mr Justice Hawkins charged with the murder of Matilda Clover. Three days later 'The Hanging Judge'* added another capital sentence to his long record: 'The jury . . . have felt it their bounden duty to find you guilty of the crime of wilful murder, of a murder so diabolical in its character, fraught with so much cold-blooded cruelty, that one dare hardly trust oneself to speak of the details of your wickedness. What motive could have actuated you to take the life of that girl away, and with so much torture to that poor creature, who could not have offended you, I know not. But I do know that your cruelty towards her, and the crime that you have committed, are to my mind of unparalleled atrocity. For the crime of which you have been convicted our law knows but one penalty – the penalty of death.'

Still unable to believe that he could be so badly used, Thomas Neill Cream stepped on to the scaffold at Newgate on 15th November to drop into eternal infamy, leaving behind one of the greatest enigmas of his crime: what was the motive?

* 'No human being has the right to take the life of another human being and my business is to make this abundantly clear in the cases that come before me in Court.' (Mr Justice Hawkins, called 'The Hanging Judge')

'THE WOMAN WHO HANGS THIS MORNING'

The Murder of David Blakely by Ruth Ellis
On Easter Sunday, 10th April 1955 outside the
Magdala Tavern, South Hill Park, London
NW3

A great number of words have been written about the murder by Ruth Ellis of her boyfriend David Blakely, but it is as 'The Last Woman to be Hanged in Britain' that she is most often remembered.

Ruth was the unremarkable, rather brassy manager of The Little Club, a London drinking house – and a not very salubrious place even by the standards such establishments set themselves. It was in 1953 that Ruth met Blakely – a good-looking, if somewhat degenerate youth with a generous manner, a romantic occupation – he was a racing driver – and an above average appetite for drink; they were instantly attracted, and for nearly a year (during which time Ruth found time to become pregnant and have an abortion) all seemed to be going as well as such a match might reasonably be expected to go. And then things began, perhaps inevitably, to sour. Blakely had started seeing other women. Ruth had started objecting; Blakely had begun to make his escape. He moved in with friends at 29 Tanza Road in London's Hampstead district for a few days; Ruth tracked him down and smashed all the windows of his car.

Two days later Ruth intercepted David Blakely coming out of the Magdala Tavern in South Hill Park, a stone's throw from Tanza Road. On this Easter Sunday, 1955, Ruth Ellis emptied the chamber of a Smith and Wesson handgun into the body of her former lover.

THE WOMAN WHO HANGS THIS MORNING
By Cassandra

It's a fine day for hay-making. A fine day for fishing. A fine day for lolling in the sunshine. And if you feel that way – and I mourn to say that millions of you do – it's a fine day for a hanging.

If you read this before nine o'clock this morning the last dreadful and obscene preparations for hanging Ruth Ellis will be moving up to their fierce and sickening climax. The public hangman and his assistant will have been slipped into the prison at about four o'clock yesterday afternoon.

There, from what is grotesquely called 'some vantage point' and unobserved by Ruth Ellis, they will have spied upon her when she was at exercise 'to form an impression of the physique of the prisoner'.

A bag of sand will have been filled to the same weight as the condemned woman and it will have been left hanging overnight to stretch the rope.

Our Guilt . . .

If you read this at nine o'clock then – short of a miracle – you and I and every man and woman in the land with a head to think, and a heart to feel will, in full responsibility, blot this woman out.

The hands that place the white hood over her head will not be our hands. But the guilt – and guilt there is in all this abominable business – will belong to us as much as to the wretched executioner paid and trained to do the job in accordance with the savage public will.

If you read this after nine o'clock, the murderess, Ruth Ellis will have gone.

The one thing that brings stature and dignity to mankind and raises us above the beasts of the field will have been denied her – pity and the hope of ultimate redemption.

The medical officer will go to the pit under the trap door to see that life is extinct. Then, in the barbarous wickedness of this ceremony, rejected by nearly all civilised peoples, the body will be left to hang for one hour.

Dregs of Shame

If you read these words of mine at mid-day the grave will have been dug while there are no prisoners around and the Chaplain will have read the burial service after he and all of us have come so freshly from disobeying the Sixth Commandment which says thou shalt not kill.

The secrecy of it all shows that if compassion is not in us then at least we retain the dregs of shame. The medieval notice of execution will have been posted on the prison gates and the usual squalid handful of louts and rubbernecks who attend these legalised killings will have had their own private obscene delights.

Two Royal Commissions have protested against these horrible events. Every Home Secretary in recent years has testified to the agonies of his task, and the revulsion he has felt towards his duty. None has ever claimed that executions prevent murder.

Yet they go on and still Parliament has neither the resolve nor the commitment, nor the wit, nor the decency to put an end to these atrocious affairs.

When I write about capital punishment, as I have often done, I get some praise and usually more abuse. In this case I have been reviled as being 'a sucker for a pretty face.'

Well, I am a sucker for a pretty face. And I am a sucker for all human faces because I hope I am a sucker for all humanity good or bad. But I prefer the face not to be lolling because of a judicially broken neck.

Yes it is a fine day.

Oscar Wilde, when he was in Reading Gaol, spoke of 'that little tent of blue which prisoners call the sky.'

The tent of blue should be dark and sad at the thing we have done this day.

(Daily Mirror, July 13, 1955)

She made no attempt to escape, and scant effort to defend herself at her Old Bailey trial. The jury were in retirement for only fourteen minutes before finding Ruth guilty. There was no appeal and, petitions having been rejected, Mrs Ellis became the last woman to hang in Britain; at 9am on Wednesday the 13th July, 1955.

THE FULL 'RIGOR' OF THE LAW

The Murder Of Maxwell Confait by a Person or Persons Unknown
On Friday, 21st April 1972 at 27 Doggett Road, London SE6 and the Trial and Wrongful Imprisonment of Colin Lattimore, Ronald Leighton, and Ahmet Salih

---

A Fire and a Body

At 1.21 in the early morning of Saturday, 22nd April 1972, the Fire Brigade was called to 27 Doggett Road, Catford, the house at the end of a block which ran alongside the railway line near Catford Bridge Station. The basement and ground floor of the house were ablaze and the fire seemed to be spreading upward. Three firemen entered the house to search for occupants; Station Officer Speed went upstairs and, finding the back bedroom locked, broke into the room. It was full of smoke, but Speed felt his way across the room and, just past the bed on the floor, came upon the prone form of a man. There was no pulse. Reaching the window, Speed flung it open to let out the smoke and hurried downstairs to help douse the fire. By 1.31am it was out, and at 1.45 the police arrived, followed at 2.00 by divisional police surgeon, Dr Angus Bain.

The dead man was a half-caste in his twenties and, on physical examination, a 'possible homosexual'. He was wearing tight fawn-coloured trousers and a long-sleeved T-shirt with a large ace of clubs motif on the chest. His lips were blue and swollen and there was a mark where flex or cord had been twisted round his neck. Cause of death was asphyxia from this ligature. Dr Bain did not take the rectal temperature, the normal procedure for calculating the time of death, for fear of destroying any evidence of recent sexual activity. Nevertheless, he noted that rigor mortis was almost complete and estimated that death had occured at between eight and ten o'clock the previous evening. At 3.45am, the distinguished pathologist, Dr James Cameron, arrived to view the body. He also avoided taking the rectal temperature, and noted that the body was cool to the touch, but that, in his opinion, rigor mortis had only just begun. The time of death he put at between 7.45pm and 11.45pm. By 6.30 in the morning, the body had been removed to

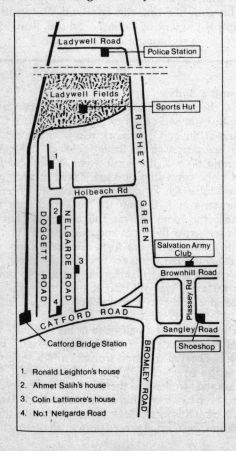

1. Ronald Leighton's house
2. Ahmet Salih's house
3. Colin Lattimore's house
4. No.1 Nelgarde Road

Lewisham Mortuary and Dr Cameron proceeded with the post-mortem. During the morning the police began a careful search of the house. The fire appeared to have been started deliberately by igniting a petrol can in a cupboard under the stairs in the basement. Just before 11 o'clock a length of electrical flex with a lamp holder at one end a switch at the other was discovered in a drawer of the dressing table in the dead man's room. There was no sign of a struggle in the room and no fingerprints. Meanwhile Detective Chief Superintendent Alan Jones had been put in charge of the inquiry and a murder HQ had been set up at Lee Road Police Station.

The First Suspect

The dead man, identified as Maxwell Confait, was 26 years old; he was a homosexual prostitute and a transvestite, and preferred to be called 'Michelle'. The first task for Superintendent Jones was to trace and interview Michelle's friends, acquaintances and clients. He began with his landlord, Winston Goode, a West Indian who had been the first person to discover the fire. Goode and Michelle had first met at the Black Bull public house, Lewisham, in 1970, when Goode had just broken up with his wife. The two became friends and Goode began to hang about the same haunts as Confait, even aping Michelle's fondness for wearing women's clothing. In February 1972 Confait moved into a room in Goode's house in Doggett Road at a rent of £2.50 per week. Confait cooked for the two of them, while Goode was out working as a labourer in Charlton. Goode's behaviour on the night of the fire had given the police some reason to view him with suspicion; he had, he said, been asleep in his room in the basement when he was awakened by the crackling of the flames. He ran up to the ground floor to alert his wife and children, who were still living in the house, and then shouted upstairs to Confait. His wife thought he seemed uncommonly wild-eyed and distraught, and after he had set off for Catford Bridge Station to phone the Fire Brigade she sent a neighbour after him. Goode was still fumbling with the dial when the neighbour arrived and had to be relieved of the receiver.

Goode was interviewed by the police throughout Saturday the 22nd, and during the course of the day he let slip that Confait had been intending to leave Doggett Road to live with another lover. Goode admitted to feelings of jealousy, while denying that he had a homosexual relationship with Michelle. At 5.50pm, samples of hair and semen were taken from Goode, who was then temporarily released. He was interviewed again on the Monday, but by then the police were changing their approach to the inquiry. Some days later, Goode was admitted to Bexley Psychiatric Hospital, confused and unable to remember the traumatic events of the previous few days.

Three More Fires and Three Confessions

On Monday, 24th April, there was a rash of small fires in the area around Doggett Road. A minor fire was started on a grassy railway embankment behind Doggett Road; a small hut containing sports equipment was burnt down in near-by Ladywell Fields; and a blaze was started in No.1 Nelgarde Road, an abandoned house in the next street. At 5.20pm, a young lad of eighteen called Colin Lattimore was stopped by PC Roy Cumming, who was driving his Panda car along Nelgarde Road. He was asked about the spate of fires, and Lattimore (who was educationally subnormal with a mental age of eight) quickly admitted his involvement. PC Cumming then said, 'If I mention Doggett Road, last Friday, can you tell me anything about that?' The reply, as reported in his notebook, was, 'I was with Ronnie. We lit it, but put it out. It was smoking when we left.' Ronnie was 15-year-old Ronald Leighton. Lattimore was then accompanied by police officers to Leighton's home in Doggett Road, where they found Ronnie with 14-year-old Ahmet Salih. All three were taken to Lewisham Police Station and after preliminary questioning by temporary DC Peter Woledge, were driven to the murder HQ at Lee Road to be interviewed by Superintendent Jones and DI Graham Stockwell. Colin Lattimore was interviewed between 6.00pm and 6.55pm, Ronnie Leighton between 7.00pm and 7.35pm and Ahmet Salih between 7.40pm and 8.05pm.

These interviews took place with neither a solicitor nor a parent being present, although Judges' Rules state that, 'As far as practicable, children (whether suspected of a crime or not) should only be interviewed in the presence of a parent or guardian, or, in their absence, some person who is not a police officer and is of the same sex as the child'. Lattimore and Salih also later claimed that they were hit by DC Woledge, so that Lattimore had a nosebleed and Salih cried. Leighton claimed he had been pushed around.

At 9.00pm Lattimore's parents and Leighton's mother arrived at the police station and were told that their sons were ready to make a statement which they were requested to witness; an irregular procedure. Both lads admitted to the murder of Maxwell Confait and to starting the fire at Doggett Road. A little later Mrs Salih arrived, but, because of her poor command of English there was a delay while a Turkish interpreter was contacted. Ahmet's statement was taken at one o'clock in the morning. He admitted to helping start the fire, but said he only observed the killing of Confait. All three were charged with murder. By early on Tuesday, 25th April, Detective Chief Superintendent Jones had wrapped up the case to his satisfaction.

Alibis and Experts – The Trial

In May the charge of murder against Ahmet Salih was dropped and he was allowed bail on the lesser charges he faced. On 2nd June, 1972, Lattimore, Leighton and Salih appeared at Woolwich Magistrates' Court. At this preliminary hearing the prosecution rehearsed its case, which relied almost entirely on the confessions of the three boys. Nevertheless, this was easily sufficient to commit them for trial. Ahmet was allowed bail again and Colin and Ronnie were returned to Ashford Remand Centre.

At this stage the boys' parents and their legal representatives were quite confident of gaining an acquittal at the trial. At the Woolwich hearing the medical experts, Dr Bain and Dr Cameron, had restated their early assessment that Confait had been killed between 6.30 and 10.30 on the Friday evening. All three boys had an alibi for this period. Colin had spent the day at the remedial day centre he attended and after going home for his tea had spent the evening with his brother Gary at a Salvation Army Youth Club until 11.30. He had come home with his brother, being seen by several people, and had watched television with his parents before going to bed. Even after this, he had made sufficient noise for his father to shout down to him to be quiet. This was at 12.35am.

Ahmet and Ronnie had spent the day together at Ronnie's house. They were joined there by two girls, Ahmet's sister Perihan and Deborah Ricketts, who they walked to the bus stop outside the ABC Cinema at 9.15pm. While out they had reconnoitred a shoe-repair shop in Sangley Road, with an eye to breaking in. They returned home for a screw-driver, then set about 'doing' the shop, stealing some goods and £4.50 from the till. They arrived back at Ahmet's house and watched television until 12.55am, popping out for a few minutes to buy a hot dog at one point. They then decided to 'do' the shoe shop again, being arrested as they left the shop at 1.30am by two policemen. So how could any of the boys have been responsible for Maxwell Confait's death if the medical experts were right? The defence had reason to feel confident.

The trial of Colin Lattimore, Ronnie Leighton and Ahmet Salih began on 1st November, 1972, at the Old Bailey. Mr Justice Chapman presided, Mr Richard Du Cann, brother of the politician Edward, led for the prosecution and the defence team consisted of John Marriage QC, Cyril Salmon QC and Brian Watling, representing Lattimore, Leighton and Salih respectively.

The crucial element of the trial was clearly the medical evidence, and the defence team were in for a shock. Dr Bain and Dr Cameron had had second thoughts. They now said that Confait could have died as late as 1.00am. The contention was that the heat of the fire had speeded up the onset of rigor mortis. Then it was suggested that the act of strangulation could add to that process. Alcohol was also mentioned as a contributory factor. The result of this, of course, was to throw the whole question of the time of death into confusion and effectively to invalidate the alibis of the three boys. The defence attempted to introduce the curious behaviour of Winston Goode, but this was quickly quashed by the judge. Mr Justice Chapman finally sealed the matter in his summing-up with a general homily on the evils of hooliganism.

On Friday, 24th November, the jury retired. They took three and a half hours to reach a verdict. Colin Lattimore was found guilty of manslaughter, on grounds of diminished responsibility, and also guilty of arson at Doggett Road and Ladywell Fields. He was ordered to be detained under the Mental Health Act without limit of time and was sent to Rampton Hospital. Ronnie Leighton was found guilty of murder and of the lesser charges of arson at Doggett Road and Ladywell Fields and burglary at Sangley Road. He was sentenced to life imprisonment and sent to Aylesbury Prison. Ahmet Salih was found guilty of arson at Doggett Road and Ladywell Fields and burglary at Sangley Road. He was sentenced to four years in prison to be spent at the Royal Philanthropic School, Redhill, in recognition of his age.

Leave No Stone Unturned

On Thursday, 26th July 1973, the three boys were refused leave to appeal. The law had run its course, and for the authorities, the matter was settled. George Lattimore, Colin's father, was not, however, a man to give up easily and he believed in his son's innocence. A complaint against DC Woledge for assaulting his son in Lewisham Police Station was quickly dismissed. He then began to write letters to the Queen, the Prime Minister, the Home Secretary and anyone else he could think of. Two of these letters bore some fruit. His local MP, Mr Carol Johnson, took up the case in October, writing to the Home Office. Ministers and officials were not over disposed to reconsider matters which, if true, involved misconduct by the police and a breakdown of the judicial system. Their replies were unspecific and evasive, citing the need for new evidence to reopen the case. The reaction of the National Council for Civil Liberties was much more hopeful. They were sufficiently interested in the case to contact one of the most experienced and prestigious pathologists in the country, Professor Donald Teare. In April 1974 he forwarded to them his written opinion of the medical aspects of the Confait case. He discounted any appreciable effect on the onset of rigor mortis from the heat of the fire, the effects of strangulation, or of alcohol. He unequivocally stated that, on the evidence presented, Maxwell Confait had died between 6.30 and 10.30 in the evening.

Meanwhile in February 1974 the General Election brought a change of government. The new Home Office team, Roy Jenkins and Alex Lyons, were committed to reviewing the procedures covering miscarriages of justice. At the same time the new MP for Lewisham, Christopher Price, an educational journalist, became involved in the case and began to mobilize his journalistic contacts. On 22nd May 1974, Winston Goode, the first suspect in the Confait case, committed suicide by swallowing cyanide which he obtained from his new employment as a metal stripper in Catford. Under pressure a police inquiry was set up into the death, led by Detective Chief Superintendent 'Pop' Hemsley.

The appeal committee had also begun to compile a dossier on the controversial Detective Chief Superintendent Alan Jones. Even before his involvement in the Confait case, his name had featured in the law books; he had confiscated the passports of a number of the family of Mastoora Begum, while investigating her disappearance. The Court of Appeal had declared his action illegal and ordered the return of the documents. Subsequently he led the investigation in the Kristen Bullen baby snatch case, arresting an epileptic girl and extracting a confession when it was later proved that she had an irrefutable alibi. Then Jones ran the rather eccentric inquiry into the 'Slag Heaps' affair, in which Ronald Milhench was discovered to have forged the Prime Minister's signature. His assistant in that inquiry was Inspector Davis, who was simultaneously working on the matter of Goode's death. The inquiry into that death reached no helpful conclusions, but it did add to the growing pressure for action.

Christopher Price had also been active. In March 1974 he had introduced a Ten Minute Rule Bill in the House of

Commons, to air the evidence in the case. This was followed by a series of newspaper articles in the *South London Press*, the *Guardian* and the *New Statesman* and an item on BBC2 television news. Then, on November 6th 1974, by a full-scale half-hour documentary on the issues in the Confait case in the This Week slot on ITV television. It was called 'Time for Murder'.

The first fruits of a new attitude at the Home Office had been a secret report, commissioned from another great contemporary pathologist, Professor Keith Simpson, on the medical aspects of the Confait case. Simpson's conclusions were broadly in line with those of Donald Teare. One of the problems in getting the case reconsidered by the Court of Appeal was that new evidence was needed to enact the procedure. The death of Winston Goode had been argued as constituting this, but it was a moot point whether it really constituted new evidence. On 14th January 1975, however, Home Secretary Roy Jenkins announced that the unspecific phrase 'other considerations of substance' had been added to the regulations. It became obvious that the Home Office were at last actively reviewing the case. In fact, during the spring of 1974 the case was unofficially examined by Lord Chief Justice Widgery. On 18th June 1975, Roy Jenkins finally announced in Parliament that the Confait case had been sent back to the Court of Appeal.

The Courts Turned Upside Down
The Court of Appeal case at last opened in the Royal Courts of Justice in the Strand on Monday 6th October 1975, with Lord Justice Scarman, Lord Justice Ormond and Mr Justice Swanwick on the bench. Richard Du Cann QC again represented the prosecution and the three boys were this time collectively represented by Lewis Hawser QC. It was immediately clear that the new hearing would be a very different affair from the original trial. Lord Justice Scarman early on insisted that the Court should accept any evidence it felt was relevant to the case, and the judge himself took a very active role in questioning witnesses to clarify the evidence. It was not so much the three boys as the medical experts, the Director of

Public Prosecutions, the police and the judicial system itself which were on trial. The fire expert at the original trial, Mr Arthur Craven, was allowed to give evidence which questioning had not previously disclosed. This included his assessment of the heat in Confait's room, which was slight, and some inconsistencies in Winston Goode's account of the fire, which indicated that he cannot have tried to alert Confait when he left the burning house. Then Professor Donald Teare appeared in the witness box and impressively demolished the red herrings which had blurred the medical evidence at the trial. This was underlined by written evidence from Professor Keith Simpson, who was too ill to attend the Court in person. Professor Cameron was then allowed the opportunity to rebut this opinion, but ended up by magnanimously concurring with Professor Teare's assessment.

The Court adjourned for a week, and on Friday 17th October, Lord Justice Scarman began to read the judgement. The three boys – now young men – Colin Lattimore, Ronnie Leighton and Ahmet Salih, were exonerated from any involvement in the murder of Maxwell Confait. It was also stated that there was insufficient evidence for the main arson charge and that the other minor offences had been only worthy of a probation order. All three were promptly freed.

Postscript

In his judgement, Lord Scarman put forward a theory not previously advanced, that as there were no signs of a struggle, Maxwell Confait must have known his killer. This was further embellished by the comment that his Lordship had known of cases where half-strangling was used as a stimulus to the homosexual act. Was Maxwell Confait killed by a lover in a tragic accident?

The Court of Appeal judgement led to the setting up of an inquiry into the wider ramifications of the case, which was headed by an ex-judge, Sir Henry Arthur Fisher. The whole question of the Judges' Rules on police questioning of suspects, and of children and the educationally subnormal in particular, was palpably in need of review.

This inquiry was itself delayed when lawyers sifting

through the papers thought they might have found evidence which could yet lead to a successful prosecution. Another investigation of the original case was carried out by Peter Fryer, Assistant Chief Constable of West Mercia. However, no arrests were made.

HANGED BY A FINGERPRINT

**The Murder of Mr Thomas Farrow and his
wife Ann by Alfred and Albert Stratton**
On Monday, 27th March 1905 at 34 Deptford
High Street, London SE8

The early morning of Monday, 27th March 1905 was
characteristic of that season's generally inclement
weather. To one young man named William Jones, already soaked through by the penetrating rain, the oil and
colour shop where he worked offered the welcome opportunity at least of warmth and shelter. It was before 8
o'clock, but the boy was familiar with old Mr Farrow's
habit of opening up early to supply painters and decorators starting their day's work. So he was surprised and not
a little irritated to find the shutters still up and the door
locked. Even more unusually, Jones could not raise anybody by knocking, and so he set off for Greenwich where
George Chapman, who owned the small chain of shops of
which Farrow managed the Deptford branch, had his own
business. Chapman sent one of his assistants back with
Jones, and together they forced an entry at the back of the
shop.

It was a badly shaken pair of lads who rushed back out
the door just minutes later and sped through the rain to
the nearby police station.

There was nothing at all impressive about No. 34
Deptford High Street – indeed, there still isn't; it was a
small rather run-down shop, with rooms above in which
Thomas Farrow, manager of the business for over fifty
years, lived with his wife Ann. Farrow was nearing 70,
Mrs Farrow just a little younger.

It was Mr Farrow that the police found first when they accompanied the shop-boys back to the High Street; found him beaten to death in the shop's back parlour. In the bedroom they found his wife, still alive, but with such dreadful injuries that she died in the Seamen's Hospital at Greenwich three days later without once regaining consciousness.

It was clearly a case for Scotland Yard's Murder Squad, and it was no time before Chief Inspector Fox was taking command of a group of experienced detectives in a thorough search of the scene of the crime. This exercise yielded two vital clues: one of them would change the whole course of the criminal identification procedure.

Near the doorway through which the murderers were presumed to have fled were found two crude homemade masks which had been fashioned from the top of a lady's silk stocking. To the experienced reasoning of Fox this indicated that almost certainly the criminals were local men, men whose faces were familiar enough to need hiding.

But it was the second clue that was to elevate this simple, sordid crime into national headlines and, more

Alfred (left) and Albert Stratton

important, to introduce a completely new feature to future crime investigation. The police found a cash box close to the body of Thomas Farrow. The box had obviously been forced by the robber/killer and plundered of its contents, in the course of which, it was discovered, the impression of a right thumb had been left on the metal tray. When comparisons had eliminated those persons known to have handled the cash box it became clear that the print belonged to the killer.

A simple enough deduction, and one which today would bring speedy retribution to the criminal careless enough to leave fingerprints at the scene of his crime. But this was 1905, and Scotland Yard's small Fingerprint Department had been founded only four years previously. Besides, there was no precedent for such evidence being acceptable in a capital case. It had been difficult enough for the pioneers of the new system to convince scientists of the remarkably individual characteristics of fingerprints – what chance with a jury of twelve ordinary people?

With this doubt in mind, the enquiry continued to focus on finding Deptford-based criminals with no alibi for the night of 26th–27th March. It was not long before the names of Alfred and Albert Stratton began to crop up with sinister regularity. The brothers were already known to the police as housebreakers, thieves with a vicious enough known record to make them suitable candidates for the murderous attack on the Farrows. Subjected to police questioning, Hannah Cromerty, with whom Alfred had shared a room in Brookmill Road, revealed that he and his brother had not been home all night on the 26th, and that when he returned the next morning, Alfred burned the coat that he had been wearing. Albert's partner, Mrs Kate Wade, recalled that he had recently asked her if she had an old pair of stockings he could have.

Both men were arrested and taken to Tower Bridge police station where Detective Inspector Charles Collins of the Fingerprint Department was waiting to take samples of both men's prints. It was established beyond doubt that the thumb-print on the cash-box tray belonged to Alfred Stratton.

Now, although the police knew with certainty that they had the culprits in custody, it was still necessary to convince a court; and when the case opened at the Old Bailey before Mr Justice Channell in May 1905 it was not only the brothers Stratton that were on trial but the credibility of the technique of fingerprint identification.

It was for this reason that the Crown led with one of the greatest counsels of his time, Sir Richard Muir. It was

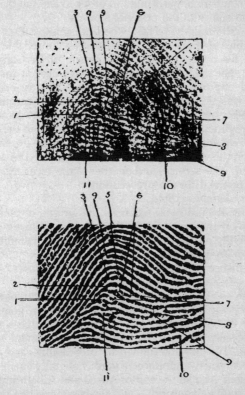

The fingerprints that made legal history. Top, the thumb-print left by Thomas Farrow's murderer on the cash-box that he robbed. Below, the thumb-print of Alfred Stratton. A convincing eleven points of similarity prove beyond any doubt that they were made by the same person.

Muir, in partnership with Collins in the witness box, who patiently inducted the jury in the technicalities of finger-printing. With the aid of giant enlargements, they were shown how comparisons were made, and in particular the conclusive eleven points of similarity between Alfred's thumb-print and the impression left at the scene of Thomas Farrow's murder. The jury, clearly impressed with their newly acquired information, had one of their own members fingerprinted in order to test the theory in comparison with the prisoner's prints.

For Stratton, Mr H.G. Rooth dismissed the whole principle of fingerprint evidence as 'unreliable', and called his own witness, in the person of Dr Garson, to swear that the print on the cash box was not made by Alfred Stratton. When his turn came to cross-examine, Muir was able in a stroke to completely undermine the credibility of this 'expert' witness: 'Did you,' he demanded of the witness, 'when you read of this case in the press, write two letters offering your services as an expert? Did you, on the very same day write one letter to the defence offering your services and another to the Treasury asking to be retained for the prosecution?'

'Yes,' barely audible.

'How, then, do you reconcile the writing of those two letters on the same day? One offering to swear to the infallibility of the system, and the other to its fallibility?'

'I am an independent witness.'

Mr Justice Channell: 'A very unreliable witness I should think, after writing two such letters.'

Even so, it could not be said that the judge himself was entirely convinced by this new-fangled system, going only so far in his summing up as to acknowledge a strong resemblance between the two fingerprints under consid-eration. The jury entertained no such doubts, and after a brief retirement announced a verdict of guilty against both prisoners. And so the end of Alfred and Albert Stratton – hanged by a fingerprint – was the beginning of a new era in the fight against crime.

THE ABHORRENT ALTERNATIVE

The Assassination of Prime Minister Spencer Perceval by John Bellingham
On Monday, 11th May 1812 in the Lobby of the House of Commons, London SW1

On the evening of 11th May 1812 a furtive figure took up position in the House of Commons, just behind the folding-doors which lead into the body of the House. At 5 o'clock the Right Honourable Spencer Perceval, Prime Minister and First Lord of the Treasury, advanced up the lobby; as he did so the shadows parted and the hidden assassin stepped out and aimed a pistol squarely at Perceval's heart; his aim was perfect and the Prime Minister staggered and fell, moaning in a low tone, 'Murder!' Just behind him were Lord Osborne and Mr W. Smith, Member for Norwich, who lifted their senior into the office of the Speaker's secretary, where the injured man expired.

The shot had attracted a strong body of people into the lobby, and a cry rose 'Shut the door; let no one out!', 'Where's the murderer?' 'Who was the rascal that did it?'

At that moment the stranger, still holding a pistol in his hand, advanced through the crowd and calmly announced, 'I am the unfortunate man', and surrendered himself into the hands of a group of Members, who searched his person to reveal another pistol, loaded and primed, and a bundle of letters and papers.

When he had been conveyed to the bar of the House before the Speaker and Members for interrogation, it was General Gascoyne, Member for Liverpool, who identified the villain: 'Is your name not John Bellingham?' The man nodded assent, and continued in his silence. The inquiry discovered that Bellingham had lately been a frequent visitor to the Commons, lurking in the corridors and public galleries, making inquiries as to the names of various Members, and scrutinizing the assembled House through a pair of opera glasses. Gascoyne gave evidence that his knowledge of the prisoner was as the result of receiving a number of petitions and memoranda from him, outlining a catalogue of grievances against the Government as the result of some real or imagined injustices suffered in Russia.

In his early working life, Bellingham had travelled in the service of a Russian merchant to the town of Archangel, where he remained for three years. On his return he married a Miss Nevill and, being a man ambitious for his future, he shortly afterwards, in 1804, removed once again to Archangel on business, taking his new bride with him. As the result of a complicated commercial dispute – for which he appears to have carried no special blame – Bellingham's anticipated short-term trip ended with the

John Bellingham

confiscation of his exit visa, and his virtual imprisonment during the succeeding five years. To complicate matters, the unlucky man also had an award made against him of two thousand roubles to be paid to the other party in the dispute. Whether at the request of the British ambassador, or whether the Russians finally gave up the prospect of ever getting their two thousand roubles, Bellingham was repatriated in 1809. Back in Liverpool he commenced in the business of insurance-broker; it appears, however, that his experiences in Russia continued to haunt him, and eventually unbalanced his reason. He began to write letters of accusation to the Privy Council, demanding compensation for what he saw as the misconduct of Lord Granville Leveson Gower, the ambassador in Russia, for not defending his rights as a British subject. These letters were ultimately passed on to the Treasury and the attention of Spencer Perceval. That gentleman presumably detected a hint of madness in the matter and, unwisely for him as it turned out, decided to ignore it. Bellingham's next line of attack was via General Gascoyne, his local MP, who took his precedent from the Chancellor and refused to have anything to do with it. The Prince Regent referred his correspondence back to the Treasury, and it was once more made clear that neither the government nor the monarchy were inclined to positive action.

These futile fusillades had now occupied three years and Bellingham determined upon a singular and unprecedented mode of attack; he wrote to the police magistrates at London's Bow Street court:

Sirs, – I much regret it being my lot to have to apply to your worships under most peculiar and novel circumstances. For the particulars of the case I refer to the enclosed letter of Mr Secretary Ryder, the notification from Mr Perceval, and my petition to Parliament, together with the printed papers herewith. The affair requires no further remark than that I consider his Majesty's Government to have completely endeavoured to close the door of justice, in declining to have, or even permit, my grievances to be brought before Parliament for redress, which privilege is the birthright of every individual. The purport of the present is, therefore, once more to solicit his Majesty's Ministers, through your medium, to let what is right and proper be done in my instance, which is all I require. Should this reasonable request be finally denied, I shall then feel justified in executing justice myself – in which case I shall be ready to argue the merits of so reluctant a measure with his Majesty's Attorney-General, wherever and whenever I may be called upon to do so. In the hopes of averting so abhorrent but compulsive an alternative I have the honour to be, sirs, your very humble and obedient servant,

John Bellingham

9 New Millman Street,
  March 23, 1812.

The assassination of the Prime Minister

And indeed, John Bellingham was compelled to the abhorrent alternative, and did have his opportunity to argue the merits of his case. It took place at the Old Bailey on 15th May, 1812, before Lord Chief Justice Mansfield. In terms of the quantity and quality of attendance at the Court, Bellingham could not have asked for a better audience; a contemporary describes how 'The judges at ten o'clock took their seats on each side of the Lord Mayor; and the recorder, the Duke of Clarence, the Marquis Wellesley and almost all the aldermen of the City of London occupied the bench. The Court was crowded to excess, and no distinction of rank was observed, so that Members of the House of Commons were forced to mingle with the throng. There were also present a great number of ladies, all led by the most intense curiosity to behold the assassin, and to hear what he might urge in defence or palliation of his atrocious act'.

But John Bellingham's cause was, as it always had been, a lost one; even his counsel's last-ditch defence of insanity was dismissed by a judge who – anticipating the M'Naghten Rules a generation away – asked the jury to consider whether the prisoner possessed the facility to distinguish good from evil, right from wrong.

After only fourteen minutes the jury came to the conclusion that Bellingham knew quite well what he was about when he assassinated Spencer Perceval; and he was ordered for execution on the following Monday.

It is recorded that Bellingham ascended the scaffold 'with rather a light step, a cheerful countenance and a confident, calm, but not exulting air'; he descended with rather more speed and a little less grace, and his body was carried in a cart, 'followed by a crowd of the lower class', to St Bartholomew's Hospital for private dissection.

THE MOST INTIMATE RELATIONS. . .

The Death of Edwin Bartlett
On 1st January 1886 at 85 Claverton Street
(now demolished), London SW1 and the Trial
of his wife Adelaide and her lover the
Reverend George Dyson for his Murder

The cruel exposure of private lives and intimate relationships that occurs when a murderer is brought before the courts has always been a source of fascination to the watching public. The revelation of what goes on behind the door across the street, especially if it is behind the facade of outward respectability, is irresistible. The Victorians, who are held (for no very good reason) to have been the guardians of popular morality were neither better nor worse than ourselves in this respect.

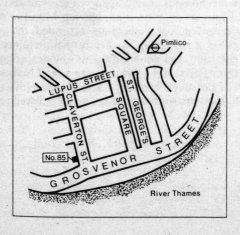

The Bartlett case contained all the ingredients of a classic scandal in plentiful measure, for the relationship that developed between Edwin Bartlett, his wife Adelaide, and the young Methodist minister George Dyson was a truly curious one.

Adelaide Blanche de la Tremouille was born in Orléans in 1856, the natural daughter of a wealthy Englishman then living in France, and was brought over to England as a child. The year 1875 found her lodged in Kingston, in the same house as a young man named Frank Bartlett. There she and her father met Frank's elder brother, Edwin, a grocer who owned a chain of six shops in South London. Within a very short time a marriage had been arranged by Adelaide's father between herself and Edwin, who was ten years her senior; the prospective husband being offered financial help with his business as a part of the settlement. Like many self-made men, Edwin Bartlett had an overdeveloped respect for the value of education and determined that his young wife should have the benefits that he had lacked. Consequently, Adelaide was dispatched to a school in Stoke Newington for the next three years and thence to a convent in Belgium for twelve months, undertaking the duties of a wife during her holidays.

Adelaide's education completed, at least temporarily, the Bartletts moved into a flat above one of Edwin's shops in Station Road, Herne Hill, being joined there by the husband's recently widowed father. It transpired that this combination did not lead to a happy household, Mr Bartlett senior considering Adelaide rather too forward in her behaviour, even accusing her of being over-familiar with Edwin's brother, Frank. The outcome of this was Frank's departure for America, a formal written apology from the old man to Adelaide at Edwin's insistence, and a change of accommodation to a flat above another grocer's shop in Lordship Lane, Dulwich, where there was no room for father.

On the face of it, the Bartletts seemed a happy couple, with Edwin an indulgent, even doting, husband. From the evidence that later came out in court, it appears that Edwin held rather eccentric views on marriage. He believed, for example, that a man should have two wives, one for intellectual companionship and the other for what he termed 'use'. Adelaide's position it was to serve the former function, and she subsequently claimed that she only had sexual contact with her husband on one occasion. This led to an uncomfortable pregnancy and miscarriage in 1881, and she was not encouraged to try the experiment again.

In 1883 the couple decided to move to what was then the country, to a house in Phipps Bridge Road, Merton. There they met the young minister of the local Wesleyan Chapel, the Reverend Mr George Dyson. All three seemed to get on famously and it was quickly decided that Dyson should visit the house to give Adelaide some further tutoring in history, geography, mathematics and Latin. Adelaide and Dyson were thus thrown together alone for large parts of the day, with the predictable result that an inappropriate degree of affection soon grew between the two of them. Dyson was even moved to compose senti-mental verses to send to his love.

> Who is it that hath burst the door
> Unclosed the heart that shut before
> And set her queenlike on its throne
> And made its homage all her own –
>
> My Birdie.

Edwin Bartlett for his part seemed positively to encourage the relationship, going so far as to write to thank Dyson for sending his wife a love letter. It appeared to please him that the couple should kiss in his presence, go for walks together in public and spend long hours in each other's company. In August 1885 the Bartletts took a holiday at Dover. Mr Bartlett paid for a 1st class return ticket for Dyson to join them. During the holiday Edwin went up to London and made a will; Dyson was a joint executor, Adelaide the main beneficiary without the stipulation which was then common about her not re-marrying. Bartlett told them both what he had done, and that he would be pleased to think they might marry if anything should happen to him. They were, it would seem, more or less engaged.

In October the Bartletts decided to move again, this time back into the centre of London, taking rooms in the house of Mr and Mrs Dogget at 85 Claverton Street, Pimlico. Though it was more difficult for Dyson to visit from Merton, he was still in fairly regular attendance. Soon afterwards, however, Dyson moved his ministry to a Methodist church in Putney, a far more convenient location, and Edwin paid for his season ticket up to Pimlico.

Bartlett had always been blessed with the most robust health, apart from a little tooth trouble, but on 8th December 1885, he was taken ill and the local medic, Dr Alfred Leach, was summoned. The symptoms were perplexing; he had a pain in his side, intermittent diarrhoea and intestinal haemorrhaging and, most curiously, a blue line round the edge of his gums. He was also very exhausted and depressed. This caused the perceptive doctor to consider mercury poisoning, but after learning that his patient had taken a mysterious pill a week previously he concluded that, if poisoned it was, then

The Reverend George Dyson

Bartlett must have been accidentally. In the next few days Edwin seemed gradually to improve and Leach arranged for him to visit a dentist to have several abscessed teeth, which could not have been helping his condition, removed.

During this period Adelaide had been nursing her husband with the utmost devotion, staying by his bedside, sleeping in a chair next to him at night and holding his toe, a curious comfort which seemed to calm Mr Bartlett. The Rev Dyson continued to call regularly, each time dropping in to pay his respects to the patient. On one visit Mrs Bartlett made the unusual request that he should obtain some chloroform for her, which she said she used to relieve her husband's pains and was embarrassed to ask the doctor for. This Dyson agreed to, obtaining the drug in small quantities from three separate chemists in Putney and Wimbledon, with the excuse that he needed it to remove stains from some clothes, decanting the supply into one large bottle to give to Adelaide.

On Thursday, 31st December, Edwin Bartlett again visited the dentist and seemed generally to be in better spirits. At four o'clock the next morning, however, Adelaide was knocking wildly on the door of her landlord, Mr Dogget – who by coincidence was the local Registrar of Deaths – explaining that she thought her husband had expired. The doctor was called and the fact confirmed. Edwin Bartlett had been dead for more than two hours. Adelaide's story was that she had fallen asleep at his bedside and awoke to find him lying face down and apparently dead. She had turned him over and tried to revive him with brandy, then ran for help. Edwin's father was sent for, and took an understandably suspicious view of developments, demanding that a post-mortem be carried out.

The results left little doubt as to the cause of death. Edwin Bartlett had been murdered; he had been poisoned with a large dose of chloroform.

Now chloroform is a strong poison, but it has rarely been the cause of death, and certainly not of murder, because it inflames and burns the internal organs and would be excruciatingly painful, not to say impossible, to drink. The inexplicable fact about Edwin Bartlett's death was that while his stomach reeked of chloroform, his throat and digestive passages were not in the least inflamed. To this day no satisfactory explanation has been put forward as to how this could be achieved; it remains the enigma of the Bartlett case.

At this point the activities of Adelaide Bartlett and George Dyson became highly suspicious. Adelaide took the bottle of chloroform that Dyson had obtained for her from where it had stood on the bedside table at Claverton Street and tipped its contents out of the window of a train between London Bridge and Peckham Rye. Dyson disposed of the three small bottles in his possession somewhere on Wandsworth Common.

At the inquest into Edwin Bartlett's death the jury, no doubt scandalized by what they would have seen as the immoral goings on within the Bartlett household, were predisposed to take a stern view of events, and returned a verdict that Bartlett had died of chloroform administered by his wife for the purpose of taking his life, and that George Dyson had been an accessory before the fact.

The trial of Adelaide Bartlett and the Reverend George Dyson opened at the Old Bailey on 12th April 1886, before Mr Justice Wills. The prosecution was led, as is customary in poisoning cases, by the Attorney-General, Sir Charles Russell. Dyson was defended by Mr Frank Lockwood, and Adelaide had a team of counsel led by Mr Edward Clarke. There was an immediate sensation when the Crown decided to offer no evidence against George Dyson and he was formally acquitted. It is true that the evidence against him was weak and circumstantial, but the main consideration had been that a defendant could not at that time give evidence; and the prosecution badly needed Dyson's evidence to convict Adelaide Bartlett.

The trial, predictably, created considerable public interest, mainly due to the curious relationship that had existed between Edwin Bartlett and his wife. Much was made of the only book that was found in the flat in Claverton Street, a medical manual on the sexual relations between man and wife and family planning. Then there was the discovery of six contraceptive devices in Edwin Bartlett's

ESOTERIC

ANTHROPOLOGY

(THE MYSTERIES OF MAN):

A COMPREHENSIVE AND CONFIDENTIAL TREATISE ON THE
STRUCTURE, FUNCTIONS, PASSIONAL ATTRACTIONS, AND
PERVERSIONS, TRUE AND FALSE PHYSICAL AND
SOCIAL CONDITIONS, AND THE MOST INTIMATE
RELATIONS OF MEN AND WOMEN.

ANATOMICAL, PHYSIOLOGICAL, PATHOLOGICAL,
THERAPEUTICAL, AND OBSTETRICAL;

HYGIENIC AND HYDROPATHIC.

From the American Stereotype Edition, Revised and Rewritten.

BY T. L. NICHOLS, M.D., F.A.S.,

Principal of the American Hydropathic Institute; Author of "Human
Physiology the Basis of Sanitary and Social Science."

MALVERN:
PUBLISHED BY T. L. NICHOLS.

*The sex manual found at the Bartlett house in Claverton Street. Until
well into the second quarter of the present century, such books were
forced to masquerade under the description 'Anthropology', and
were invariably credited to a medical doctor.*

trouser pocket and Adelaide Bartlett's quite desperate last-gasp explanation that she had obtained the chloroform to cool her husband's unwelcome ardour. This was to say nothing of her unconventional relationship with the Reverend Mr Dyson, over which the judge seemed particularly outraged.

Nevertheless, there were many inconsistencies in the Crown's case. They could not explain, for example, how the poison could have been administered. Mrs Bartlett had been more than devoted in nursing her husband and he was aware of, and seemed to approve of, all the so-called scandalous goings-on in the household. Edward Clarke made a memorable six-hour speech in Adelaide Bartlett's defence, which seemed to seal the matter. When the jury returned the foreman did not answer yea or nay to the clerk's traditional inquiry, but read a statement.

> 'Although we think that there is the gravest suspicion attaching to the prisoner, we do not think there is sufficient evidence to show how or by whom the chloroform was administered.'

Adelaide Bartlett had been found not guilty.

In popular fiction Adelaide would no doubt have married George Dyson; but she did not. She changed her name, and was heard of no more. The final epitaph to the case has to be left to the famous surgeon Sir James Paget, who attended the trial. 'Mrs Bartlett', he declared, 'was no doubt properly acquitted. But now it is to be hoped that, in the interests of science, she will tell us how she did it!'

THE CHARING CROSS TRUNK MURDER

The Murder of Minnie Alice Bonati by John Robinson
On Thursday, 5th May 1927 at 86 Rochester Row, London SW1 and the depositing of her body in a trunk at Charing Cross Station

---

It was a common enough transaction. An everyday occurrence; all in a day's work for Mr Glass. The trunk that was passed to him across the counter of the left-luggage office at Charing Cross station was ordinary enough as well – round-topped, of wickerwork covered with black canvas, and bound with a business-like leather strap.

The date was 6th May, a Friday in 1927; the respectable-looking owner of the trunk, who looked to Glass as though he might have seen military service abroad, had arrived in a taxi-cab, and in a taxi-cab he had departed, leaving strict instructions for the safe keeping of his piece of luggage.

By Monday morning the trunk was seeming less ordinary, more . . . noticeable. It became difficult to escape the offensive, all-pervading smell that seemed to originate from within it. And when a policeman was summoned to oversee the closer investigation of the trunk and its contents, it proved to be a very unusual item of baggage indeed. Unlike most of its kind, this trunk had, wrapped up among the usual clothing, five brown paper parcels. Each of these five parcels contained a dismembered part of a female body.

According to strict – though in this case rather inappropriate – procedure, a police surgeon was summoned to certify that the woman was dead before her remains could be removed to the mortuary, and thence into the capable hands and experienced analytical mind of Sir Bernard Spilsbury, pathologist to the Home Office. Despite the onset of putrefaction, when Spilsbury had pieced together the remains in the trunk he had most of the body of a short, plump woman of about thirty-five. She had been dead for perhaps a week, and the cause of death had been asphyxia. Extensive bruising on the body suggested that she had been beaten unconscious before being suffocated.

Armed with such clues as they could gather from the trunk and its grisly contents, the police began their laborious search – first for the identity of the victim, and then for that of her killer. The initials 'FA' and the label 'F Austin; to St Leonards' referred to a previous – and quite innocent – owner of the luggage. There was more success, though, with the name-tag 'P. Holt' on a pair of knickers found in the trunk.

Although Mrs Holt had no personal connection with the tragedy, there was some likelihood that one of her many previous employees had stolen the undergarment; which proved to be the case, Mrs Holt identifying the remains as a woman known to her as Rolls, in reality Minnie Alice Bonati, 36 years old, a prostitute, and last seen alive in Chelsea in the late afternoon of 4th May.

Meanwhile the publicity which such cases inevitably attract was now beginning to produce favourable results in terms of hard evidence. The trunk itself had been recognized by a Brixton second-hand dealer who remembered selling it to a well-dressed military-looking gentleman. A shoe-shine boy had turned up with a left-luggage ticket which he had seen dropped out of a taxi window; and the taxi driver himself came forward to add the information that some time after midday on Friday the 6th he had deposited two young men at Rochester Row police station, SW1, and on the return had been hailed by a gentleman standing with a heavy trunk in the doorway of No. 86 Rochester Row, just opposite the police station. Both man and trunk were destined for Charing Cross station.

A routine investigation of the offices at 86 Rochester Row revealed that one of the occupants of the rather run-down office suites – John Robinson, trading as 'Edwards and Co. Business Transfer Agents' – had not been seen around for several days. He had disappeared from his lodgings in Kennington too, though by one of those pieces of luck on which even the most experienced detectives rely, they found a telegram addressed 'Robinson, Greyhound Hotel, Hammersmith'. The Robinson named was not John himself, but his bigamously married wife (the bigamy was a fact of which she was unaware, and understandably not overjoyed to learn) from whom he was now estranged, and who worked at the Greyhound. The man who accompanied 'Mrs Robinson' when she next met her husband was Chief Inspector George Cornish; the same gentleman who then took Robinson back to Scotland Yard with him to stand in an identity parade.

Thirty-six-year-old John Robinson, of course, denied all knowledge of Minnie Bonati let alone of her murder, and as if to lend credence to his story, neither the taxi driver, the railway porter, nor Ward, the second-hand dealer from Brixton, were able to pick him out of the parade.

However, the police had not left the Robinson trail yet. In the wake of the senior officers, the more painstaking job of combing the Rochester Row office was taking place, and the search produced a bloodstained match caught in the wicker work of the waste basket. It proved to be the one clue necessary to break Robinson's confidence; enough to force him to make a statement which, however untrue it was in detail, associated him with the death of Minnie Bonati. Minnie, he told the police, had propositioned him at Victoria railway station. Back at the office, she had become abusive, demanding money and threatening violence. They struggled, the woman fell knocking herself senseless on a coal-bucket, and Robinson in a panic fled the building. No-one was more shocked next morning, he said, to find the body of Minnie Bonati still lying where it had fallen the previous afternoon. Robinson now realized that she must be dead, and that he must do something to get rid of the corpse. He made no denial at all of the trunk business, or of the dismemberment, only of the killing.

John Robinson's trial at the Old Bailey began on Monday 11th July. It was not one of the most spectacular trials; the defence, though ably led by Mr Lawrence Viney, failed to convince judge and jury that Minnie was the victim of an unfortunate, and in many senses self-provoked, accident. When Mr Justice Swift asked Robinson why he did not seek help for the unconscious woman lying on his office floor, why, when he realized that she was dead, he did not summon the police to explain matters, the prisoner replied 'I did not see it in that light.'

He was convicted and sentenced to death on 13th July and executed at Pentonville prison one month later.

A MURDER FROM THE 'YIDDISHER' QUARTER

The Murder of Leon Beron by Stinie Morrison (alias Morris Stein)
In the early hours of Sunday, 1st January 1911 on Clapham Common, London SW4

A Body on the Common

On Sunday, 1st January 1911, PC Joseph Mumford was patrolling his regular beat on Clapham Common. At 8.10am, he was walking along a path leading north-west from the bandstand when he noticed, about twelve feet from the path in the bushes, what appeared to be a body. It was a short, stocky, middle-aged man, smartly dressed in an overcoat with an astrakhan collar and patent-leather boots. He was undoubtedly dead, and not from any natural cause. A black silk handkerchief had been folded over his face and tucked into his collar and the top of his coat and his sleeves were splattered with blood. Looking back to the path, there was a pool of blood and a trail across the ground to where he had evidently been dragged. Near by lay a bowler hat, and there were footprints in the soft earth. PC Mumford carefully left the body undisturbed and ran to Cavendish Road Police Station for help.

Later that morning the body was removed to Battersea Mortuary, stripped and photographed and a post-mortem carried out on it. The cause of death was immediately obvious, a large horseshoe-shaped wound on the forehead, the result of a blow with a blunt instrument (a jemmy was later suggested). There were further blows to the head, three stab wounds in the chest and a number of superficial scratches and cuts on the face, including a curious 'S'-shaped cut on either cheek. The victim was noted as being Jewish in appearance and in his pocket was a small account book containing a list of Polish and French women's names with various sums of money placed against them. In the front of the book was an address and the name 'Mr Israel Inglazer'. Divisional Detective Inspector Alfred Ward, who had been put in charge of the inquiry, decided early in the case to call on the services of Detective Inspector Frederick Porter Wensley of the Whitechapel Police, the area in which the address was situated.

Wensley was at that time involved in the 'Houndsditch' inquiry; three policemen had been shot dead during a robbery by people believed to be East European anarchists. Just two days after the discovery of the body on Clapham Common, this case was to culminate in the notorious 'Siege of Sydney Street'. Frederick Wensley was an experienced policeman, with an unsurpassed knowledge of the local Jewish immigrant underworld, and it did not take him long to locate the mysterious 'Mr Inglazer'. By that evening the two detectives had burst into the shabby second-floor room at 133 Jubilee Street, Stepney, which the dead man – real name Leon Beron – shared with one of his brothers.

The 'Quaint Little Jew'

Leon Beron was a 48-year-old Polish Jew who had first arrived in the East from Paris in 1894. In the seventeen years he had lived in London he had never held down a legitimate job. He was, nevertheless, a man of some means. He owned some slum property which was mainly rented by prostitutes, and he was known as a womanizer and a regular client himself of the oldest profession. It was further rumoured that he was a financial backer of burglaries and a fence for stolen goods. Beron had come to the attention of the police two years previously when two men had attempted to rob him of his gold watch, which he wore on a chain with a £5 gold piece, and of a leather pouch containing twenty sovereigns. These same coveted articles were noticeably missing from the battered body on Clapham Common.

The police were here confronted with a delicate situation. Since the 'Houndsditch Murders' the Press had generated a widespread and irrational fear of anarchist revolution, so that there existed considerable popular feeling against the immigrant Jewish community which was popularly supposed to spawn such 'excesses'. The previous week a Stepney councillor had declared that . . . 'the borough has been inundated by a swarm of people fitly described as the scum of Central Europe'. If the murder on Clapham Common were to be connected in the public mind with this agitation there was no knowing where it might end. The early press reports had already made the inevitable connection with the Houndsditch murders and had gleefully suggested that the 'S'-shaped scratches on Beron's face stood for *'szpieg'*, *'spic'* or *'schlosser'* and were an anarchist device to publicly brand an informer. The police badly needed to damp down any rumours of this sort. The scratches were dismissed as the figment of a lurid imagination. Beron's criminal connections were also carefully avoided; he was calculatedly portrayed as an eccentric, a figure of amusement and pity, a 'mad landlord' and 'a quaint little Jew'.

A Most Convenient Suspect

The first priority of the police investigation was to learn more about Beron's daily habits and his movements up to the date of the murder. They discovered that he spent a great deal of his time at Snelwar's Warsaw Restaurant at 32 Osborn Street in Whitechapel. At Snelwar's, Polish immigrants were served, for eighteen pence a day, with lunch, dinner and as many drinks as they required to carry out their business, reminisce about the old country and generally while away the day. Beron had been seen frequently in the previous month with a tall, elegantly dressed stranger who variously called himself Moses Tagger, Morris Stein and Stinie Morrison. Beron's brother Solomon and other regulars at Snelwar's Restaurant had all pointed the finger of suspicion in this direction, and a glance at Morrison's past record more than justified the police interest.

Stinie Morrison was born in the Ukraine and had

journeyed to England at the age of eighteen in 1898.
Within a few months of his arrival he received his first
prison sentence – one month's hard labour for theft. This
was followed by further periods in prison, culminating in
a sentence of five years' hard labour for burglary in 1901.
On being released on licence in 1905, he once again fell in
with a gang of burglars. In 1906 he was arrested and
sentenced to five years on Dartmoor. Morrison proved a
moody and uncooperative prisoner, and during this time
became involved in a brawl and was given twenty strokes
of the 'cat', a humiliating experience which left a permanent impression on him. In September 1910 he was again
released on licence, and seemed to be making a genuine
attempt to go straight. He got a job in Pither's Bakery at
213 Lavender Hill, close by Clapham Common, using the
skill in bread-making he had learned in prison; the bakery
was directly opposite Lavender Hill Police Station. After
just six weeks he was warned off by the local police who,
knowing his record, wanted him off their patch. From
here, Stinie Morrison returned to his old haunts and his
old friends in Whitechapel.

On New Year's Eve, the day leading up to the murder,
Beron had left his lodgings at midday and spent the
afternoon collecting his rents. At just after seven o'clock
he entered Snelwar's Restaurant in the company of Stinie
Morrison. Stinie held under his arm a brown paper parcel
containing, he said, a flute, which he entrusted to the
waiter, Joe Mintz, to store behind the counter. Mintz
subsequently told the police that the parcel was heavy
and could have been an iron bar. Stinie and Beron were
talking throughout the evening, though each left the
restaurant at some point, Beron being seen by his brother
Solomon outside Cohen's restaurant in Fieldgate at
10.45pm. Beron and Morrison finally left Snelwar's at a
quarter to twelve, Stinie having repossessed his brown-
paper parcel. They then parted, Stinie returning to his
lodgings at 91 Newark Street, where he was seen by his
landlady, Annie Zimmerman, who locked up after him.
This, however, would have been no barrier to an experienced burglar like Stinie if he had wanted to go out again.
The police also found a witness, Mrs Deitch, a brothel

keeper, who claimed to have seen Morrison and Beron together in Commercial Road at 2.15am.

Stinie's behaviour on the morning after the murder was no less suspicious. Setting out from his lodgings, he deposited a package in the left-luggage office at St Mary's Station, Whitechapel, under the name 'Banman', before crossing the river to exchange £10 in gold sovereigns for banknotes with a disreputable Jewish jeweller called Max Frank, in the Walworth Road. After this he went to stay with a prostitute of his acquaintance, Florrie Dellow, in York Road, Lambeth, for the next few days, well away from the attentions of the police.

'You Have Accused Me of Murder'

The police now followed two lines of inquiry. First, they placed a discreet watch on Stinie's lodgings and his regular haunts. Secondly, there was the question of how Beron and Morrison, if he was the murderer, had reached Clapham Common and how Stinie had returned. Police visited likely taxi ranks to interview cab drivers, and a reward of £1 was offered for useful information.

The Press had begun to sniff out that the police had a suspect and, following several broad hints that his name began with an 'S' or an 'M', pictures of Stinie appeared in the newspapers of the 6th of January. At the same time the offer of a reward began to bear fruit. A hansom-cab driver, Edward Hayman, had picked up two passengers at 2.00am on the corner of Sidney Street and taken them to Lavender Gardens, Clapham. This would have taken Beron and Morrison to the scene of the crime. A second hansom-cab driver, a shady character called Alfred Stevens, claimed to have taken a tall man whom he identified as Morrison from Clapham Cross to the Hanover Arms near Kennington Church at 3.10am. A taxi-cab driver, Alfred Castling, then stated that he had transported two men, one of them tall, from Kennington, back across London, to Finsbury Gate at 3.30am. The weakness of this evidence was that Stinie Morrison's picture had already been published in the newspapers by the time he was identified by the witnesses.

On 8th January the patient vigilance of the police finally

paid off. Stinie reappeared at his lodgings and, after asking his landlady to take his washing to the public laundry, strolled down the street to Cohen's Restaurant. At 9.30am he was arrested inside the restaurant, initially on a charge of failing to register his address as a prisoner on licence, and bundled out and dragged down the road to Leman Street Police Station, pursued by a cat-calling, rowdy mob. In the police station, confronted by Inspector Wensley, Stinie was reported as saying 'You have accused me of serious crime. You have accused me of murder.' This was taken to be an unprompted admission of knowledge of a crime which had not yet been mentioned, though it seems unlikely that he hadn't heard the shouts of the crowd which had surrounded him in the street even if he had not seen a newspaper containing his photograph.

The police next visited his temporary abode in Lambeth, where they discovered a left-luggage ticket in the lining of a billycock hat. At St Mary's Station they recovered a parcel containing a pistol and 44 rounds of ammunition. Sorting through Stinie's washing, officers also found a shirt with spots of blood on the collar, cuffs and sleeves, though why he should have kept such supposedly incriminating evidence for a week is difficult to understand.

On 9th January, Stinie Morrison was charged with murder and appeared at the South West London Police Court at Lavender Hill to be remanded to Brixton Prison until his trial.

The Palace of Varieties

The trial of Stinie Morrison opened in Court No.1 at the Old Bailey on 6th March 1911. It must surely stand as one of the most curious and chaotic dramas to be acted out in that celebrated courtroom. Stinie stood throughout the trial, sharply dressed and erect, with one hand on his hip, affecting an attitude of disdain and moral outrage towards the proceedings going on around him. Many of the witnesses were East European immigrants, with an unsteady grasp of English and little understanding or respect for the rituals of the court. To the judge, Mr Justice Darling, who delighted in impressing any court with his clever witticisms, this was a heaven-sent opportunity. Solomon Beron, the deceased's brother was particularly wild-eyed, excitable and incoherent and shortly after giving his evidence had to be removed to Colney Hatch Lunatic Asylum, where he remained for the rest of his days. The foreman of the jury also continually interrupted the testimony to ask questions, an almost unprecedented break with the etiquette of the court that juries should hear but not be heard.

The prosecution was pressed strongly by Sir Richard Muir, though its weakness was that the evidence was entirely circumstantial, and Sir Richard used every opportunity to blacken Stinie's character and bring out his criminal past. The defence, led by Mr Edward Abinger, sought to impugn the honesty of many of the witnesses and the victim of the crime. Beron, it was hinted, could have been a police spy who had 'shopped' the Houndsditch murderers. The greatest disaster for the defence, however, was Stinie's appearance in the witness box with a plainly preposterous account of his movements on the night before the murder. He claimed he had been selling imitation jewellery during the day before dining in Snelwar's Restaurant at eight o'clock. He had then visited the Shoreditch Empire between 8.45 and 11.10pm to watch Gertie Gitana, Harry Champion and Harry Lauder. After this he returned to the restaurant to pick up his flute, where he saw Beron but didn't talk to him, leaving at 11.45pm to return to his lodgings. He added that he had passed Beron on the corner of Sydney Street on his way home. One of Stinie's many girlfriends, 16-year-old Janie Brodsky, and her sister Esther were called to verify Stinie's jaunt to the Varieties. This was all a patent fabrication, though why Morrison should go to such trouble to fix an alibi for a time that was irrelevant to the crime is incomprehensible; it certainly cannot have made a good impression on the jury.

It was evident from his summing up on 15th January that Mr Justice Darling, while he might have thought Stinie guilty, was very unhappy about the reliability of some of the prosecution evidence. Unfortunately, the effect of his rather confusing remarks and the fact that he sent the jury out to consider their verdict at the

unusually late hour of eight o'clock in the evening was the opposite of his intention. The jury took just thirty-five minutes to reach a verdict of guilty. When Mr Justice Darling intoned the infamous words ending 'and may God have mercy on your soul' Stinie replied, 'I decline such mercy. I do not believe there is a God in Heaven either.' He was then taken down and removed to the condemned cell in Wandsworth Prison.

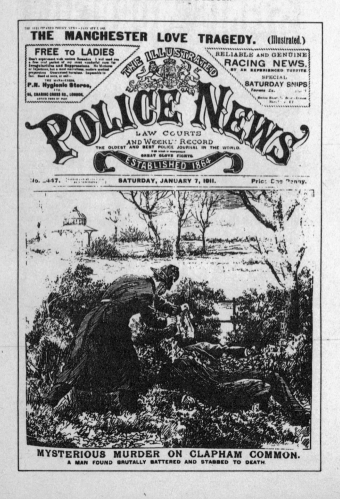

Reprieved but Tortured

Stinie's appeal was heard on 27th April, 1911. Although there was some criticism of the prosecution's presentation of the case, this was insufficient to declare a mistrial and the appeal was dismissed. Stinie did, however, have determined supporters, and a petition for a reprieve containing 75,000 signatures was sent to the Home Secretary. One person who refused to sign it was Stinie Morrison. Nevertheless, the unease felt by the trial judge was shared by others and, on 13th April, the Home Secretary, Mr Winston Churchill, commuted the death sentence to one of life imprisonment.

Stinie Morrison was transported to Dartmoor by train. At Waterloo station, as he was being transferred from a police van to the train, he momentarily shook himself free of the warders and shouted to the crowd of curious onlookers: 'This is the way they treat a prisoner. I am a gentleman. You see how they treat me. Leave me alone!'

After his arrival at Dartmoor, Stinie proved no more co-operative. He was surly, often violent and at once began a hunger strike, the first of many during the years of his imprisonment. He further occupied his time with a volley of letters and appeals. He still insisted on his innocence, but his persistent demand was to be allowed the death penalty rather than continue the hopeless rigours of prison life. One petition was even composed in rather undistinguished verse:

> *I had enough of convict life,*
> *My heart is getting chilly*
> *Enough of bread-and-water strife*
> *And officers to knock me silly.*
>
> *Rt. Hon. Sir, I beg you hear my humble plea*
> *And send – 'Granted' – in reply!*
> *If you will not give me my liberty*
> *I pray you let me die.*
>
> *My Freedom or my Death*
> *Nothing else will satisfy me!*

While Stinie was petitioning for his own death, his supporters on the outside were still pressuring for his release. The committee was now led by Baroness Hilda Von Goetz, a wealthy society lady with a passion for penal reform, with the ever faithful Janie Brodsky, the defence lawyers at the trial and a number of radical journalists providing strong support. In 1913 they managed to organize another petition, this time with 42,000 signatures, and published a number of pamphlets airing the facts of Stinie's trial and imprisonment. The issue was only pushed aside by the understandable distraction of the First World War, though Stinie, isolated in his prison hell, continued his protests. In December 1912 he had been transferred to Parkhurst Prison, on the Isle of Wight, but the petitions, the fits of violence, the suicide attempts and the hunger strikes continued, gradually sapping his physical strength and depriving him of his reason.

At the beginning of 1921 Stinie was again on hunger strike and being force fed with a feeding cup. At 2.15pm on 21st January warders entered his cell to find that he had suffered a heart attack. At 4.30pm he died. Stinie Morrison was finally laid to rest in Carisbrooke Cemetery on 27th January, 1921.

I am grateful to Andrew Rose for the permission to use information from his book *Stinie: Murder on the Common* (Bodley Head 1985) in this chapter.

THE REAL RONALD TRUE

The Murder of Gertrude Yates (also known as Olive Young) by Ronald True
On Monday, 6th March 1922 at 13a Finborough Road, London SW10

Insanity has always been a difficult condition to define legally, and the question of criminal responsibility in the issue of murder has been a continuing cause for controversy. The M'Naghten Rules, developed by the Law Lords during the nineteenth century provide a conservative definition which has become considerably out of line with medical opinion. The case of Ronald True in 1922 provided an opportunity for many of the main arguments in this controversy to be aired.

True's mother was 16 and unmarried when he was born, but when he was 11 she married into wealth, and thereafter his circumstances were always comfortable. Ronald showed inescapable early signs of delinquency – petty theft, cheating, and lying, which did not seem to abate as he got older. Leaving school at 17, he was sent abroad, to New Zealand, Argentina, Canada and then Mexico, in the hope that this would improve his behaviour, but successive employers dismissed him once his dishonesty, boastfulness and incompetence became apparent. It was during this period that True first became addicted to morphine.

The outbreak of the First World War gave him an opportunity to return to England, and in 1915 True somehow acquired a commission in the Royal Flying Corps, where his eccentricity and incompetence were again evident, resulting in a serious flying accident while still training at Farnborough. This eventually led to his being invalided out of the service in 1917. Ronald True then went to New York for a period, where he posed as an injured air ace and married Frances Roberts, an actress. Although his behaviour was never less than peculiar, and complicated by bouts of depression, True could nevertheless be charming – the life and soul of a party; especially when he had access to morphine. Returning to England with his new wife, Ronald was again dispatched abroad by his family, this time to the Gold Coast. The results were predictable, and inside six months he was back in England and palpably unemployable.

The family now decided that something needed to be done, at least to curb his drug addiction, and he was sent to various nursing homes. The treatment met with little success, though this is unsurprising as True would periodically absent himself to London on a morphine binge, leaving a string of unpaid bills, gambling debts, forged cheques and petty thefts in his wake. To complicate the syndrome, his bouts of moodiness had become increasingly violent, and he had begun to take against his wife. The family had finally resigned themselves to the conclusion that he must be permanently institutionalized when Ronald disappeared for one last time, claiming that he had found a job in Bedford.

He was, of course, on another binge in London, moving from hotel to hotel as the time came to pay the bill. He became friendly with a man called James Armstrong and contrived to buy a pistol from him, the bullets for which he proceeded to file down. He needed the gun, he said, to protect himself from a man, also calling himself Ronald True, who followed him around issuing cheques in his name and was bent on killing him. This had begun as a harmless delusion to rationalize the thefts and debts, these were all the doing of 'the other Ronald True'. It was now, however, developing into full-scale paranoia. True had also developed a fixation for a call-girl named Gertrude Yates, who worked under the name of Olive Young. He had visited her once at her basement flat at 13a Finborough Road, Fulham, distinguishing himself by stealing £5 from her purse. She was clearly scared and wanted nothing more to do with him, but he continued to pester her with phone calls. At this time True began to drop garbled hints about a final showdown with 'the other Ronald True' at Finborough Road and mentioned a girl called Olive, who was somehow involved.

True had hired a car and chauffeur, and for three nights running he was driven with James Armstrong to the end of Finborough Road where they parked; True explained that he wanted to see if some friends were in and wandered off. Each time he returned to the car and drove Armstrong home. On the third night, Sunday, 5th March 1922, he returned and dismissed the car and chauffeur, walked back and was let into the flat by Olive Young.

All must have gone well until the morning. True rose at 7.30 to make tea, and returning to the bedroom unexpectedly hit Miss Young three times over the head with a rolling pin as she innocently sipped from her cup. He then stuffed a towel down her throat, strangled her with the girdle of her dressing gown and dragged her body into the bathroom. Returning to the blood-spattered bedroom, True put two pillows under the bedclothes to simulate his victim's body, took £8 from her handbag and selected the best of her jewellery; after which he sat down on the bed and waited for the domestic servant, Emily Steel, to arrive at nine o'clock. As Emily was preparing her breakfast of fried sausages, 'Major' True appeared in the kitchen, asked her not to disturb Miss Young as they had bedded down rather late and, pressing a half-crown into her hand, left. Minutes later, Emily Steel discovered the body of her mistress in the bathroom.

True's next extraordinary action was to visit a gents' outfitters, where he bought an off-the-peg suit and had his own bloodstained clothing tied into a bundle. He excused their state as being the result of a flying accident. He had, it seemed, just flown over from Paris! He then pawned the jewellery stolen from Olive Young before setting off for an afternoon's drive to Hounslow with Armstrong as chauffeur.

In his deluded state, True had made no attempt at all to cover his tracks, and it was with minimum expenditure of effort that the police located and arrested him that evening in the Hammersmith Palace of Varieties.

Ronald True was later lodged in the Prison Hospital at Brixton, where medical staff lost little time in concluding that he was insane. At one point, he escaped into the next ward, where the murderer Henry Jacoby was housed. Slapping him on the back, True quipped, 'Here's another for our Murderers' Club. We only accept those who kill outright!'

At True's trial at the Old Bailey, his counsel, Sir Henry Curtis Bennett, sought to prove that Ronald could not be held responsible for his actions. Opposing for the Crown, Sir Richard Muir contended that, while the prisoner might be deranged, he knew the difference between right and wrong. Mr Justice M'Cardie's summing-up was favourable to the prosecution and True was found guilty.

From the evidence, the Home Secretary was bound to appoint the customary panel of three medical men to pass judgement on True's sanity, and on the basis of their report commuted the sentence to life imprisonment, committing True to Broadmoor Criminal Lunatic Asylum. A great furore arose in the Press because two days previously Jacoby, a pathetic criminal from a far less exalted background, had been hanged. It was suggested that influence had been used to secure True's reprieve, and the Home Secretary was eventually forced to defend his position in the House of Commons before the matter was allowed to rest.

Ronald True remained in Broadmoor for twenty-nine years, eventually dying from natural causes in 1951. He was said to be a popular inmate and very active in all sports and social activities.

THE RATCLIFFE HIGHWAY MURDERS

The Murder of the Marr Family and James Biggs, and the Williamson Family by John Williams
On 7th and 19th December 1811 on the
Ratcliffe Highway (now The Highway),
London E1 as recounted by Thomas De Quincey

Never, throughout the annals of universal Christendom, has there indeed been any act of one solitary insulated individual, armed with power so appalling over the hearts of men, as that exterminating murder, by which, during the winter of 1811, John Williams, in one hour, smote two households with emptiness, exterminated all but two entire households, and asserted his own supremacy over all the children of Cain.

Yet, first of all, one word as to the local scene of the murders. Ratcliffe Highway is a public thoroughfare in the most chaotic quarter of eastern, or nautical, London; and at this time, when no adequate police existed except the detective police of Bow Street, admirable for its own peculiar purposes, but utterly incommensurate to the general service of the capital, it was a most dangerous quarter. Every third man, at the least, might be set down as a foreigner. Lascars, Chinese, Moors, Negroes, were met at every step. And apart from the manifold ruffianism, shrouded impenetrably under the mixed hats and turbans of men whose past was untraceable to any European eye, it is well known that the navy of Christendom is the sure receptacle of all the murderers and ruffians whose crimes have given them a motive for withdrawing themselves for a season from the public eye . . .

Williams was a man of middle stature (five feet seven-

and-a-half to five feet eight inches high), slenderly built, rather thin, but wiry, tolerably muscular, and clear of all superfluous flesh. A lady, who saw him under examination, assured me that his hair was of the most extraordinary and vivid colour, viz., bright yellow, something between an orange and a lemon colour.

In other respects, his appearance was natural enough; and, judging by a plaster cast of him, which I purchased in London, I should say mean, as regarded his facial structure. One fact, however, was striking, and fell in with the impression of his natural tiger character, that his face wore at all times a bloodless ghastly palor . . .

Into this perilous region [Ratcliffe Highway] it was that, on a Saturday night in December, Mr Williams forced his way through the crowded streets, bound on business . . . He carried his tools closely buttoned up under his loose roomy coat . . .

Titian, I believe, but certainly Rubens, and perhaps Vandyke, made it a rule never to practice his art but in full dress – point ruffles, bag wig, and diamond hilted sword: and Mr Williams, there is reason to believe, when he went out for a general compound massacre always assumed black silk stockings and pumps; nor would he on any account have degraded his position as an artist by wearing a morning gown. In his second great performance it was particularly noticed . . . that Mr Williams wore a long blue frock, of the very finest cloth, and richly lined with silk. Amongst the anecdotes which circulated about him, it was also said at the time, that Mr Williams employed the first of dentists, and also the first of

chiropodists. On no account would he patronise any
second-rate skill. And beyond a doubt, in that perilous
little branch of business which was practised by himself,
he might be regarded as the most aristocratic and fasti-
dious of artists.

But who, meantime, was the victim, to whose abode he
was hurrying? For surely he could never be so indiscreet
as to be sailing about on a rowing cruise in search of some
chance person to murder? Oh, no: he had suited himself
with a victim some time before, viz., an old and very
intimate friend. For he seems to have laid it down as a
maxim – that the best person to murder was a friend; and,
in default of a friend, which is an article one cannot always
command, an acquaintance: because, in either case, on
first approaching his subject, suspicion would be disarmed: whereas a stranger might take alarm, and find
in the very countenance of his murderer elect a warning
summons to place himself on guard . . .

Marr was the name of that unhappy man who had been
selected for the subject of this present Saturday night's
performance . . . The minutes are numbered, the sands of
the hour-glass are running out, that measure the duration
of this feud on earth. This night it shall cease. Tomorrow is
the day which in England they call Sunday, which in
Scotland they call by the Judaic name of 'Sabbath'. To both
nations, under different names, the day has the same
functions; to both it is a day of rest; so it is written;
thou, too, young Marr, shalt find rest – thou, and thy
household, and the stranger that is within thy gates. But
that rest must be in the world which lies beyond the grave.
On this side of the grave ye have all slept your final sleep.

The night was one of exceeding darkness; and in this
humble quarter of London, whatever the night happened
to be, light or dark, quiet or stormy, all shops were kept
open on Saturday nights until twelve o'clock, at the least,
and many for half an hour longer . . .

Marr's position in life was this: he kept a little hosier's
shop, and had invested in his stock, and the fittings of his
shop, about £180. Like all men engaged in trade, he suffered
some anxieties. He was a new beginner; but, already, bad
debts had alarmed him; and bills were coming to maturity

that were not likely to be met by commensurate sales. Yet, constitutionally, he was a sanguine hoper. At this time he was a stout, fresh-coloured young man of twenty-seven. The household of Marr, consisting of five persons, is as follows: First, there is himself, who, if he should happen to be ruined, in a limited commercial sense, has energy enough to jump up again, like a pyramid of fire, and soar high above ruin many times repeated. Yes, poor Marr, so it might be, if thou wert left to thy native energies unmolested; but even now there stands on the other side of the street one born of hell, who puts his peremptory negative on all these flattering prospects. Second in the list of this household, stands his pretty and amiable wife, who is happy after the fashion of youthful wives, for she is only twenty-two, and anxious (if at all) only on account of her darling infant. For, thirdly, there is in a cradle, not quite nine feet below the street viz., in a warm, cosy kitchen, and rocked at intervals by the young mother, a baby eight months old. Nineteen months have Marr and herself been married; and this is their first-born child. Grieve not for this child, that it must keep the deep rest of Sunday in some other world; for wherefore should an orphan, steeped to the lips in poverty, when once bereaved of father and mother, linger upon an alien and murderous earth? Fourthly, there is a stoutish boy, an apprentice, say thirteen years old; a Devonshire boy, with handsome features, such as most Devonshire youths have; satisfied with his place; not overworked; treated kindly, and aware that he was treated kindly. Fifthly, and lastly, is a servant girl, a grown-up young woman; and she, being particularly kind-hearted, occupies (as often happens in families of humble pretensions as to rank) a sort of sisterly place in her relation to her mistress.

To this young woman it was that suddenly, within three or four minutes of midnight, Marr called aloud from the head of the stairs – directing her to go out and purchase some oysters for the family supper. Upon what slender accidents hang oft-times solemn life-long results! Marr occupied in the concerns of his shop, Mrs Marr occupied with some little ailment and restlessness of her baby, had both forgotten the affair of supper; the time was now narrowing every moment, as regarded any variety of choice; and oysters were perhaps ordered as the likeliest article to be had at all, after twelve o'clock should have struck. And yet, upon this trivial circumstance depended Mary's life. Had she been sent abroad for supper at the ordinary time of ten or eleven o'clock, it is almost certain that she, the solitary member of the household who escaped from the exterminating tragedy, would not have escaped; too surely she would have shared the general fate. It had now become necessary to be quick. Hastily, therefore, receiving money from Marr, with a basket in her hand, but unbonneted, Mary tripped out of the shop. It became afterwards, on recollection, a heart-chilling remembrance to herself – that, precisely as she emerged from the shop-door, she noticed, on the opposite side of the street, by the light of the lamps, a man's figure; stationary at the instant, but in the next instant slowly moving. This was Williams . . .

It was indispensable that the [shop's] shutters should be accurately closed before Williams could safely get to work. But as soon as ever this preliminary precaution had been completed, once having secured that concealment from the public eye, it then became of still greater importance not to lose a moment by delay, than it had previously been not to hazard anything by precipitance. For all depended upon going in before Marr should have locked the door.

Williams waited, of necessity, for the sound of a passing watchman's retreating steps; waited, perhaps, for thirty seconds; but when the danger was past, the next danger was, lest Marr should lock the door; one turn of the key, and the murderer would have been locked out. In, therefore, he bolted, and by a dextrous movement of his left hand, no doubt, turned the key, without letting Marr perceive this fatal stratagem . . .

Let us [now], in vision, attach ourselves to Mary; and, when all is over, let us come back with her, raise the curtain, and read the dreadful record of all that has passed in her absence. The poor girl roamed up and down in search of an oyster shop; and finding none that was still open, within any circuit that her ordinary experience had made her acquainted with, she fancied it best to try the chances of some remoter district. Lights she saw gleaming or twinkling at a distance, that still tempted her onwards; and thus, amongst unknown streets poorly lighted, and on a night of peculiar darkness, and in a region of London where ferocious tumults were continually turning her out of what seemed to be the direct course, naturally she got bewildered. The purpose with which she started, had by this time become hopeless. At length by his lantern she recognised a watchman; through him she was guided into the right road; and in ten minutes more, she found herself back at the door of No.29 in Ratcliffe Highway . . .

Mary rang, and at the same time very gently knocked. She had no fear of disturbing her master or mistress; them she made sure of finding still up. Her anxiety was for the baby, who being disturbed might again rob her mistress of a night's rest. And she well knew that, with three people all anxiously awaiting her return, and by this time, perhaps, seriously uneasy at her delay, the least audible whisper from herself would in a moment bring one of them to the door. Yet how is this? To her astonishment, but with the astonishment came creeping over her an icy horror, no stir or murmur was heard ascending from the kitchen.

One person might have fallen asleep, but two – but three – that was a mere impossibility. And even supposing all three together with the baby locked in sleep, still how unaccountable was this utter, utter silence!

Most naturally at this moment something like hysterical horror overshadowed the poor girl, and now at last she rang the bell with the violence that belongs to sickening terror. Listen therefore, poor trembling heart; listen, and for twenty seconds be still as death. Still as death she was: and during that dreadful stillness, when she hushed her breath that she might listen, occurred an incident of killing fear, that to her dying day would never cease to renew its echoes in her ear. She, Mary, the poor trembling girl, checking and overruling herself by a final effort, that she might leave full opening for her dear young mistress's answer to her own frantic appeal, heard at last and most distinctly a sound within the house. Yes, now beyond a doubt there is coming an answer to her summons. What was it? On the stairs, not the stairs that led downwards to the kitchen, but the stairs that led upwards to the single storey of bed-chambers above, was heard a creaking sound. Next was heard most distinctly a footfall: one, two, three, four, five stairs were slowly and distinctly descended. Then the dreadful footsteps were heard advancing along the little narrow passage to the door. The steps – oh heavens! whose steps? – have paused at the door. The very breathing can be heard of that dreadful being, who has silenced all breathing except his own in the house. There is but a door between him and Mary. What is he doing on the other side of the door? A cautious step, a stealthy step it was that came down the stairs, then paced along the little narrow passage – narrow as a coffin – till at last the step pauses at the door. How hard the fellow breathes! He, the solitary murderer, is on one side of the door; Mary is on the other side. Now suppose that he should suddenly open the door, and that incautiously in the dark Mary should rush in, and find herself in the arms of the murderer . . . But now Mary is upon her guard. The unknown murderer and she have both their lips upon the door, listening, breathing hard; but luckily they are on different sides of the door; and upon the least indication of unlocking, or unlatching, she would have recoiled into the asylum of general darkness.

What was the murderer's meaning in coming along the passage to the front door? The meaning was this: separately, as an individual, Mary was worth nothing at all to him. But, considered as a member of a household, she had this value, viz., that she, if caught and murdered, perfected and rounded the desolation of the house. The case being reported, as reported it would be all over Christendom, led the imagination captive. The whole convey of victims was thus netted; the household ruin was thus full and orbicular; and in that proportion the tendency of men and women, flutter as they might, would be helplessly and hopelessly to sink into the all-conquering hands of the mighty murderer. He had but to say – my testimonials are dated from No.29 Ratcliffe Highway, and the poor vanquished imagination sank powerless before the fascinating rattlesnake eye of the murderer.

Mary began now to ring the bell and to ply the knocker with unintermitting violence. And the natural consequence was, that the next door neighbour, who had recently gone to bed and instantly fallen asleep, was roused.

The poor girl remained sufficiently mistress of herself rapidly to explain the circumstance of her own absence for an hour; her belief that Mr and Mrs Marr's family had all been murdered in the interval and that at this very moment the murderer was in the house.

The person to whom she addressed this statement was a pawnbroker; and a thoroughly brave man he must have been; for it was a perilous undertaking, merely as a trial of physical strength, singly to face a mysterious assassin. A brick wall, 9 or 10 feet high, divided his own back premises from those of Marr. Over this he vaulted; and at the moment when he was recalling himself to the necessity of going back for a candle, he suddenly perceived a feeble ray of light already glimmering on some part of Marr's premises. Marr's back door stood wide open. Probably the murderer had passed through it one half minute before. Rapidly the brave man passed onwards to the shop, and there beheld the carnage of the night stretched out on the floor, and the narrow premises so floated with gore, that it was hardly possible to escape the pollution of blood in picking out a path to the front door.

By this time the heart-shaking news involved in the outcries of Mary had availed, even at that late hour, to gather a small mob about the house. The pawnbroker threw open the door. One or two watchmen headed the crowd; but the soul-harrowing spectacle checked them, and impressed sudden silence upon their voices, previously so loud. The tragic drama read aloud its own history . . .

Vain would be all attempts to convey the horror which thrilled the gathering spectators of this piteous tragedy . . . Suddenly some person appeared amongst the crowd who was aware that the murdered parents had a young infant; this would be found either below stairs, or in one of the bedrooms above. Immediately a stream of people poured down into the kitchen, where at once they saw the cradle – but with the bed-clothes in a state of indescribable confusion. On disentangling these, pools of blood became visible; and the next ominous sign was, that the hood at the head of the cradle had been smashed to pieces. It became evident that the wretch had found himself doubly embarrassed – first, by the arched hood at the head of the cradle, which accordingly he had beat into a ruin with his mallet, and secondly, by the gathering of the blankets and pillows about the baby's head. The free play of his blows had thus been baffled. And he had therefore finished the scene by applying his razor to the throat of the little innocent; after which, with no apparent purpose, as though he had become confused by the spectacle of his own atrocities, he had busied himself in piling the clothes elaborately over the child's corpse.

On the Sunday se'ennight (Sunday the octave from the event), took place the funeral of the Marrs: in the first coffin was placed Marr; in the second Mrs Marr, and the

The escape of John Turner by means of knotted sheets

baby in her arms; in the third the apprentice boy. They were buried side by side; and 30,000 labouring people followed the funeral procession, with horror and grief written in their countenances.

As yet no whisper was astir that indicated, even conjecturally, the hideous author of these ruins – this patron of gravediggers. Had as much been known on this Sunday of the funeral concerning that person as became known universally six days later, the people would have gone right from the churchyard to the murderer's lodgings, and (brooking no delay) would have torn him limb from limb.

De Quincey then treats at length a second bloody multiple murder that appeared to be committed by the same hand. The victims were the elderly publican of the King's Arms at 81 Gravel Lane (now Garnet Street), his wife Catherine, and their ageing maid-servant. It happened that the Williamsons had at the time a lodger in the house, 26-year-old John Turner who, having been aroused from his sleep and overseen the intruder crouched over the bodies, had lowered himself from his window by means of knotted sheets, into the arms of a passing watchman:

> '. . . a short consultation was held by the people assembled, and it was at once resolved that an entry should be forced into the house by way of the cellar flap . . . On looking round the cellar, the first object that attracted their attention was the body of Mr Williamson, which lay at the foot of the stairs, with a violent contusion on the head, his throat dreadfully cut, and an iron crow by his side. They proceeded upstairs into the parlour, where they found Mrs Williamson also dead, with her skull and throat cut, and blood still issuing from the wounds, and near her lay the body of the servant-woman, whose head was also horribly bruised, and her throat cut in a most shocking manner.'
>
> (*The Newgate Calendar*)

This time the police found a vital clue at the scene; a sailor's maul, which eventually led to the Pear Tree tavern in Cinnamon Street and one of its habituees, John Williams. Williams aroused sufficient suspicion under interrogation that he was remanded to Coldbath Fields prison pending further investigation.

On December 28th, John Williams cheated justice and the executioner by hanging himself from a beam in his cell:

> 'On the last day of this fatal year [1811] the remains of this sanguinary assassin were privately removed, at eleven o'clock at night, and conveyed to St George's watch-house, preparatory to interment.

FIFTY POUNDS
REWARD.

Horrid Murder !!

WHEREAS,

The Dwelling House of Mr. **TIMOTHY MARR,** 29, Ratcliff Highway, Man's Mercer, was entered this morning between the hours of Twelve and Two o'Clock, by some persons unknown, when the said Mr. **MARR, Mrs. CELIA MARR,** his wife, **TIMOTHY** their **INFANT CHILD** in the cradle, and **JAMES BIGGS,** a servant lad, were all of them most inhumanly and barbarously Murdered ! !

A Ship Carpenter's Pœn Maul, broken at the point, and a Bricklayer's long Iron Ripping Chisel about Twenty Inches in length, have been found upon the Premises, with the former of which it is supposed the Murder was committed. Any person having lost such articles, or any Dealer in Old Iron, who has lately Sold or missed such, are earnestly requested to give immediate Information.

The Churchwardens, Overseers, and Trustees, of the Parish of St. George Middlesex, do hereby offer a Reward of FIFTY POUNDS, for the Discovery and Apprehension of the Person or Persons who committed such Murder, to be paid on Conviction.

By Order of the Churchwardens, Overseers, and Trustees,

JOHN CLEMENT,

Ratcliff-highway,
SUNDAY, 8th, DECEMBER, 1811.

VESTRY CLERK.

SKIRVEN, Printer, Ratcliff Highway, London.

The procession advanced slowly up Ratcliffe Highway, accompanied by an immense concourse of persons . . . When the cart came opposite the late Mr Marr's house a halt was made for nearly a quarter of an hour. The procession then moved down Old Gravel Lane, along Wapping, up New Crane Lane, and into New Gravel Lane. It then proceeded up the hill, and again entered Ratcliffe Highway, down which it moved into Cannon Street, and advanced to St George's Turnpike, where the new road is intersected by Cannon Street. Here a grave, about six feet deep, had been prepared, immediately over which the main water-pipe runs. Between twelve and one o'clock the body was taken from the platform and lowered into the grave, immediately after a stake was driven through it; and, the pit being covered, this solemn ceremony concluded.'

CATCH ME WHEN YOU CAN

The Murder of Mary Ann Nichols, Annie Chapman, Elizabeth Stride, Catherine Eddowes, and Mary (or Marie) Jane Kelly by an Unknown Assassin called Jack The Ripper
During the months of August to November 1888 in the Whitechapel area of East London

For the three months from the end of August to the beginning of November in the year of 1888, the Whitechapel area of the East End of London was witness to a series of vicious – and still unsolved – murders. The slayings were characterized by an unparalleled savagery; each of the five victims – all prostitutes – had been attacked from behind and their throats cut; the bodies were afterwards subjected to such mutilation and dissection as to suggest a perverted sexual motive.

The enduring mystery of these, probably the world's most celebrated crimes, has resulted in a Ripper bibliography itself a bulkier tome than most of the volumes it lists*, and this present book is not an appropriate place in which to enter the forum on Jack's true identity.

There follows instead a graphic, if gruesome, account of the murders themselves, described with texts and illustrations contemporary with the gaslight times of the Ripper's London. And though the capital's East End has changed dramatically in the past hundred years, there are still desolate corners to be found in which lurk the vestiges of Jack's reign of terror.

* *Jack the Ripper: A Bibliography and Review of the Literature,* **Alexander Kelly.**

1. Friday 31st August 1888. Buck's Row (now Durward Street). Mary Ann 'Polly' Nichols, aged 42

No murder was ever more ferociously and more brutally done. The knife, which must have been a large and sharp one, was jabbed into the deceased at the lower part of the abdomen, and then drawn upwards, not once but twice. The first cut veered to the right, slitting up the groin, and passing over the left hip, but the second cut went straight upward, along the centre of the body, and reaching to the breast-bone.

. . . The throat is cut in two gashes, there is a gash under the left ear, reaching nearly to the centre of the throat. Along half its length, however, it is accompanied by another one which reaches around under the other ear, making a wide and horrible hole, and nearly severing the head from the body.

(*The Star*)

2. Saturday 8th September 1888. 29 Hanbury Street. Annie Chapman called 'Dark Annie', aged 47

The revolting tale of the Whitechapel murders has been further embellished by the astounding statements which the coroner [Mr Wynne Baxter] deemed fit to make public at his summing up of the case of the unfortunate woman Chapman. The public have supped full of horrors, and now there is added thereto a suggestion which, in spite of its plausibility, is almost too horrible to be credited . . . it supplies a motive for the deed [and] in the presence of this suggestion it is futile to discuss any other hypothesis until this had been thoroughly probed . . .

Mr Phillips [Dr George Bagster Phillips, surgeon], being recalled to add further facts to his previous evidence, he stated that the mutilation of the body was of such a character as could only have been effected by a practised hand. It appears that the abdomen had been entirely laid open: that the intestines, severed from their mesenteric attachments had been lifted out of the body, and placed by the shoulder of the corpse; whilst from the pelvis the uterus and its appendages, with the upper part of the vagina and the posterior two-thirds of the bladder, had been entirely removed. No trace of these parts could be found, and the incisions were cleanly cut, avoiding the rectum, and dividing the vagina low enough to avoid injury to the cervix uteri. Obviously the work was that of an expert – of one, at least, who had such knowledge of anatomical or pathological examination as to be enabled to secure the pelvis organs with one sweep of a knife, which must therefore, as Mr Phillips pointed out, have been at least five inches long.

The theory based on this evidence was coherent enough. It suggested that the murderer, for some purpose or other . . . had committed the crime for the purpose of possessing himself of the uterus.

The similarity between the injuries inflicted in this case and those upon the woman Nichols, whose body was found in Buck's Row a few days before,

gave from the first the idea that they were the work of the same hand. But in the Buck's Row case the mutilation did not extend so far, and there was no portion of the body missing. Again, this is explained by those who think that the possession of the uterus was the sole motive, by assuming that the miscreant had not time to complete his design in Buck's Row . . .

In the face of these facts, the statement made by Mr Wynne Baxter [the coroner] presents a great *prima facie* probability, but we must deprecate strongly any tendency to jump at a conclusion in a matter which may admit of another interpretation. Mr Baxter said:

'Within a few hours of the issue of the morning papers containing a report of the medical evidence given at the last sitting of the Court, I received a communication from an officer of one of our great medical schools that they had information which might or might not have a distinct bearing on our enquiry. I attended at the first opportunity, and was informed by the sub-curator of the Pathological Museum that some months ago an American had called inquiring of the organ [uterus] that was missing from the deceased. He stated his willingness to give £20 apiece for each specimen. He stated that the object was to issue an actual specimen with each copy of a publication on which he was then engaged. He was told that his request was impossible to be complied with, but he still urged his request. He wished them preserved not in spirits of wine, the usual medium, but in glycerine, in order to preserve them in a flaccid condition, and he wished them sent to America direct.'

Although this statement seems to afford a satisfactory explanation of the motive for the deed and mutilation of the corpse, it is impossible to read it without being struck with certain improbabilities and absurdities that go far to upset the theory altogether . . .

Does it not exceed the bounds of credibility to

imagine that he would pay the sum of £20 for every
specimen . . . [and that] his object was to issue an
actual specimen with each copy of the publication
on which he was engaged . . . [this] is too grotesque
and horrible to be for a moment entertained . . .

The public mind – ever too ready to cast mud at
legitimate research – will hardly fail to be excited to
a pitch of animosity against anatomists and curators,
which may take a long time to subside.

(*The Lancet*, 30th September 1888)

**3. Sunday 30th September 1888. Berner Street (now
Henriques Street). Elizabeth Stride called 'Long Liz',
aged 45**

**4. Sunday 30th September 1888. Mitre Square. Catherine
Eddowes, aged 43**

Two more murders must now be added to the
blacklist of similar crimes of which the East End
has very lately been the scene. The circumstances of
both of them bear a close resemblance to those of the
former atrocities. The victim in both has been a
woman. In neither can robbery have been the motive, nor can the deed be set down as the outcome of
an ordinary street brawl. Both have unquestionably
been murders deliberately planned, and carried out
by the hand of some one who has been no novice to
the work. It was early yesterday morning that the
bodies of the two women were discovered at places
within a quarter of an hour's walk of one another,
and at intervals of somewhat less than an hour. The
first body was found lying in a yard in Berner-street,
a low thoroughfare running out of the Commercial-
road. The discovery was made about 1 o'clock in the
early morning by a carter who was entering the yard
to put up his cart. The body was that of a woman
with a deep gash on the throat, running almost from
ear to ear. She was quite dead, but the corpse was
still warm, and in the opinion of the medical experts
who were promptly summoned to the place, the
deed of blood must have been done not many

minutes before. The probability seems to be that the murderer was interrupted by the arrival of the carter, and that he made his escape unobserved, under the shelter of the darkness, which was almost total at the spot . . . The body has been identified as that of Elizabeth Stride, a widow according to one account, according to another a woman living apart from her husband, and by all accounts belonging to the 'unfortunate' class. Her movements have been traced up to a certain point. She left her house in Dean-street, Spitalfields, between 6 and 7 o'clock on Saturday evening, saying that she was not going to meet anyone in particular. From that hour there is nothing certainly known about her up to the time at which her body was found, lifeless indeed, but not otherwise mutilated than by the gash in the throat, which had severed the jugular vein and must have caused instantaneous death . . .

. . . Not so the corpse of the second victim. In this case the purpose of the murderer had been fulfilled, and a mutilation inflicted of the same nature as that upon the body of Annie Chapman. It was in the south-western corner of Mitre-square, in Aldgate, that the second body was found. It was again the body of a woman, and again death had resulted from a deep wound across the throat. But in this instance the face had also been so slashed as to render it hard for the remains to be identified, and the abdomen had been ripped up, and a portion of the intestines had been dragged out and left lying about the neck . . . The deed of blood had been the work of a practised hand. The body bore clear proof of some anatomical skill, but the murderer had been in a hurry, and had carried out his design in a more rough fashion than that with which Annie Chapman's body had been mutilated. The best chance of identification seems to be from the victim's dress, of which a minute description has been put out . . . Beyond this we are unable at present to go.

(*The Times*, 1st October 1888)

5. Friday, 9th November 1888. 13 Miller's Court (now demolished). Mary (or Marie) Jane Kelly, aged 25

The throat had been cut right across with a knife, nearly severing the head from the body. The abdomen had been partially ripped open, and both of the breasts had been cut from the body, the left arm, like the head, hung to the body by the skin only. The nose had been cut off, the forehead skinned, and the thighs, down to the feet, stripped of the flesh. The

abdomen had been slashed with a knife across and downwards, and the liver and entrails wrenched away. The entrails and other portions of the frame were missing, but the liver, etc., it is said, were found placed between the feet of this poor victim. The flesh from the thighs and legs, together with the breasts and nose, had been placed by the murderer on the table, and one of the hands of the dead woman had been pushed into her stomach.

(*Illustrated Police News*)

'AN EVIL, CYNICAL AND DEPRAVED MAN'

The Abduction of Keighley Barton
On Saturday, 10th August 1985 from near her
home in Sebert Road, London E7 and her
subsequent Murder by her stepfather Ronald
William Barton

Most contemporary murders attract little more than a mention in the newspapers. It is only the exceptional case, exceptional in the personalities involved or the sequence of circumstances which catches the headlines and enters the public imagination. There are also occasionally crimes which encapsulate a social dilemma, which seem somehow to be crimes of their time. The abduction and murder of 14-year-old Keighley Barton is not a pleasant story, but it did represent a very particular and far-reaching social dilemma. It helped to bring into the public consciousness a very painful and emotive subject which people would prefer not to entertain – the sexual abuse of children within the supposed 'safe haven' of the family.

Ronald Barton was 45 years old when he was arrested in 1985, and had been a minicab driver, though he was unemployed at that time. For the origins of the crime, however, it is necessary to go back fourteen years to the time when Barton began to live with his 22-year-old girlfriend, Theresa, and the 5-month-old baby girl, Keighley, that she had borne by another man. Two years later, in 1974, the couple were married and subsequently had two other children, both boys. What Theresa Barton was not aware of when she married was that her husband already had a long police record of sexual offences. The full list gives some idea of the potential danger that young Keighley was placed under in the family home.

```
1959 – Unlawful sex with a girl, aged 14 – Absolute
        Discharge
1961 – Indecent assault on a girl, aged 15 – Condi-
        tional Discharge
1962 – Indecent assault on a girl, aged 16 – Six Months
        in Gaol
1963 – Indecent assault on a girl, aged 16 – One Year
        in Gaol
1965 – Grievous bodily harm to a girl – Nine Months in
        Gaol
1966 – Assault with intent to rob – Eighteen Months in
        Gaol
1968 – Indecent assault on a girl
1970 – Indecent assault on a girl, aged 15 – Twenty-
        one Months in Gaol
```

It cannot be known exactly when Ronald Barton began to interfere with Keighley, but the first time that the matter came to the attention of the authorities was in 1980, when, with both Keighley and her mother giving evidence against him, Ronald Barton was given a 1 year suspended sentence for acts of gross indecency with Keighley. Keighley Barton was just 8 years old.

Barton was later to claim that he took medical advice about his problem after this incident, but if he did it had little effect. It may be wondered why Mrs Barton, now aware of the full extent of her husband's 'tendencies', continued to live with Barton and subject herself and her daughter to the inevitable risks. Ronald Barton was a very violent, aggressive and domineering man. He thought nothing of keeping his family in a constant state of fear with threats of injury and worse; indeed, he seemed to positively enjoy it. Mrs Barton later stated that on a number of occasions both she and Keighley were forced to submit to sexual acts under the direct persuasion of a gun barrel. It must have taken a great deal of courage in the first place to inform the authorities of Barton's behaviour. It took even greater courage to accuse him again, as Mrs Barton did in 1982, though at the last minute Keighley refused to testify under the direct threat once more of a gun placed to her head. This did, however, alert the authorities sufficiently for them to place her in care in a council hostel.

Unfortunately, Keighley was unhappy at the hostel and soon ran away, back to her home, to her mother whom she loved and was very worried about; but also back to the brutalities of Ronald Barton. In 1984 Mrs Barton finally decided that something drastic needed to be done. A court order was obtained, banning Barton from going within a quarter of a mile of the family home at Sebert Road, Forest Gate. At the same time Mrs Barton and Keighley together held the threat over his head that they would testify to his indecent assaults on the young girl if he caused any more trouble. And this was a serious threat to make to Barton, who had been in prison before and knew well the kind of 'treatment' he could expect inside as a molester of young girls. So he moved out and took a flat in Mildenhall Road, Clapton. Mrs Barton took a new 'friend', Eric Cross, into the family home and Keighley was sent back to the council hostel. When Barton visited her there she stood up to his bluster and told him that he must give up the idea of living with her mother or he would go to prison for a long time.

This seemed at first to be a workable solution to the tragedy, but it did not take account of the bruising that Barton's massive ego had suffered. Apart from the frustration of his libidinous urges, Barton also felt a bitter resentment at his humiliating dismissal from the family home and the separation from his own two sons. As he immersed himself in this anger and hatred, a vicious plan of revenge began to form in his mind. If Keighley were removed from the scene the principal witness to his unnatural crimes would be silenced, and at the same time he would pay back his wife for defying him. Much later, in prison, he told the police: 'She took my two boys away from me. I took her girl. Now she can suffer. I hate her. She has ruined my life.'

Keighley had again run away from the council home

and returned to live with her mother, her two brothers and her mother's new boyfriend. Barton began to spy out the land. On 5th August 1985 he again confronted his wife. He warned her that he had a gun and assured her that he would take somebody with him if he ever had to use it; he told her that he would put her ten feet under if she ever testified against him. On the evening of the 9th he was again spying on the family, watching Mrs Barton, her boyfriend, Keighley and his sons through the back window as they looked at television. At 11.30pm Keighley had a row with her mother about going to bed, which ended in her running upstairs and locking herself in her room. On the morning of Saturday, 10th August 1985 it was raining, but Keighley decided to take the family Alsatian, Rex, out for a walk on a piece of waste land near the house. Later in the morning the dog returned alone. Keighley Barton would never be seen alive again.

Ronald Barton was immediately suspected of being responsible for his stepdaughter's disappearance. His circumstances gave him the obvious motive; and then there was his inescapable record. When he was questioned he denied all knowledge of the matter, but in such a surly and uncooperative fashion that the suspicions of the police were merely heightened. On 17th August he was arrested, but then bailed. There was, after all, no real proof that Keighley was dead. Returning to his flat, Barton asked a neighbour if the post had arrived, as he was expecting an important letter. In the next few days two important letters did arrive, one for Barton, the other for Mrs Barton. They were both in Keighley's handwriting. In both she said that she had lied when she had made allegations against Barton. In her mother's letter she also called the new boyfriend a 'creep'.

For some time no new evidence emerged, despite extensive publicity about Keighley's disappearance. There were the inevitable crop of possible sightings, but none of them seemed to lead anywhere. The police became convinced that she was dead, and had been dead since soon after her disappearance. She would have remained alive only as long as it took Barton to coerce her into writing those very convenient letters.

On 23rd October Ronald Barton was officially charged with the abduction and murder of Keighley and remanded in Brixton Prison. He now made the great mistake of boasting of his cleverness to a fellow prisoner. Barton was under the common misapprehension that a man cannot be convicted of murder without the evidence of a body. He bragged that he had paid £50 to have his old Peugeot car crushed, with Keighley's body inside it. He said that when the metal was melted the corpse 'would come to the top as dross and there would be no other trace of her'. He also tried to persuade another prisoner to give him a false alibi. Every word of this went straight back to the police.

Ronald Barton's trial was set for 25th February 1986, but evidence was immediately brought by Mr Henry Grumwald for the defence that Keighley had been sighted by several witnesses over the past six months; the case was necessarily adjourned. Monster he may be, but society could hardly take the responsibility of trying Barton for the murder of a child who was alive and apparently well.

The case finally came to court at the Old Bailey on 7th October 1986, with Mr Justice Turner presiding, Mr Michael Worsley QC for the prosecution and Mr Robin Gray QC defending. It opened with the unusual step of the judge himself summoning two witnesses, Mrs Linda Jackson, a teacher in Keighley's school, and her young son, who thought they had seen Keighley in Walthamstow Market in July 1986. The main case then proceeded. The prosecution's evidence was necessarily circumstantial, with no body as proof, and they were further hampered by being unable (under the rules of evidence) to present Barton's previous history as a sex offender. The defence response was twofold. Their strongest card was the slimness of the evidence that Keighley was actually dead. Then Barton put forward a most unlikely alibi to cover his movements on 10th August, the day of Keighley's disappearance. According to him he had gone up to London to watch the Changing of the Guard and had then spent the rest of the day just walking around aimlessly because, he said, he was brooding and needed to be around people. Unfortunately, he was unaware, when cross-examined, that Central London was teeming with football fans on that particular morning, up for the Everton versus Manchester United Charity Shield game.

The jury were out for nearly two days, but returned on 30th October and, by a verdict of ten to two found Ronald Barton guilty on the two counts of the abduction and the murder of Keighley Barton. Mr Justice Turner, passing sentence, said, 'I am satisfied that you for many years abused a girl who should have been entitled to regard you as her father. You started to gratify your unnatural desires when that girl was only eight years old . . . You not only debased Keighley, but you were prepared to commit the ultimate crime of murder against that poor girl, in an effort to avoid the punishment which awaited you . . . There is no question that you are an evil, cynical and depraved man, whom society – including your wife and family – are entitled to be and will be protected from for many years.'

The judge then sentenced Barton to life imprisonment, to last a minimum of 25 years. As Ronald Barton was taken down Mrs Barton screamed at him from the gallery, 'I hope you rot, you bastard.'

The very day after he was sentenced, Barton requested to see the Assistant Governor of Wormwood Scrubs, where he was held. He admitted to the murder of Keighley Barton and then rebutted his earlier assertion that he had disposed of the body in a car crusher. He now said that the body had been buried in Abney Park Cemetery, Stoke Newington, near to his flat in Clapton. Whether this was a last minute fit of remorse, an attempt to draw attention to his cleverness, or a piece of enlightened self-interest is impossible to know. As a convicted child abuser and killer he was certainly in need of the co-operation of the prison authorities to protect him from the rough justice that awaits such despised offenders behind prison walls.

A police team led by Detective Superintendent Charles Farquhar instituted a search of the old overgrown cemetery grounds. In the last sweep of the day a young woman police cadet discovered a skirt, a cardigan and a piece of shoe in the undergrowth. Beneath these sad relics was buried a decomposed body. On the finger was a cheap, fake Mexican ring that Keighley always wore. At the inquest, on 18th February 1987, the pathologist, Dr Peter Vanezis, was able to state that she had been stabbed five times in the chest. The six defence wounds on her left arm bore witness to the spirited attempt she had made to ward off the murderous attack.

On 25th February the body of Keighley Barton was finally laid to rest in Manor Park Cemetery, Forest Gate, just at the end of the road where she had lived out most of a frightened and brutalized existence that had lasted just fourteen years.

THE HANGMAN HANGED

**The Murder of Elizabeth White by hangman
John Price
In the year 1718 on Bunhill Fields, London EC2**

In the year 1718, while George I ruled Great Britain and
Ireland, John Price, ex-sailor and confirmed villain,
reigned as Common Hangman. His occupancy of this
throne was a short one, culminating in his ignominious
death at the end of his successor's rope – hanged for the
murder of a woman whose audacious crime was to resist
Price's attempt to assault her.

It is recorded of John Price that he 'first drew his breath
in the fog-end of the suburbs of London, and, like Mercury, became a thief as soon as ever he peeped out of the
shell. So prone was he to vice, that as soon as he could
speak he would curse and swear with as great a passion
and vileness as is frequently heard round any gaming
table. Moreover, to this unprofitable talent of profaneness
he added that of lying.'

Sentenced to death the first time by the Chelmsford
magistrate, he was reprieved on the recommendation of
his former master, whose position of High Sheriff of the
County of Essex, entitled him to such gratuitous – and in
this case undeserved – kindness.

On his way once more to London, Price was next
apprehended as a pickpocket, and cast into the Bristol
Newgate and flogged. He fared little better at sea, discovering that life on board a man o' war, far from leading
him out of temptation, encouraged him to pilfer from his
fellow seamen, a habit which even such characteristically

JACK KETCH ARRESTED
and taken into Custody, when attending a
Malefactor to the place of Execution

nautical punishments as whipping at a gun, pickling with brine, and keel-hauling failed to break by the time the ship re-entered Portsmouth harbour two years later.

Price's career in crime was marginally more successful on dry land – at least in so far as he tended to get caught less often, though the good times finally came to an end and, chastened by a spell in Newgate and another flogging at the cart's tail, Price endeavoured to change his fortune by marriage.

His wife, Betty, was employed at Newgate Gaol – where probably they met – in the capacity of a run-around; that is, she ran errands for such of the prisoners as had money to pay for the service. It was through his wife's contacts that John raised himself to the position of hangman for the county of Middlesex.

Bunhill Fields Burial Ground. It is said that Bunhill is a corruption of 'Bone Hill' through 'Bonhill', and derives from the transfer here, in 1549, of 1,000 cartloads of bones to ease the congestion in St Paul's Cathedral charnel-house. It later became the main burying-ground for the Non-Conformists

Nevertheless the new hangman, shiftless by nature, could not long stay out of trouble, and despite a salary approaching £40 per year, and the customary perquisite of the condemned man's clothing to sell, John Price soon found himself in the Marshalsea Prison, and out of a job as executioner.

When we next encounter the fortunes of John Price, he has been released from the Marshalsea, and is about to slip into even deeper trouble:

> 'What brought him to this end was his going one night over Bunhill Fields in his drunken airs, when he met an old woman, named Elizabeth White, a watchman's wife, who sold pastry-ware about the streets. He violently assaulted her in a barbarous manner, almost knocking one of her eyes out of her head, giving her several bruises about her body, breaking one of her legs, and wounding her in the belly. Whilst he was acting this inhumanity two men came along at the same time, and hearing dreadful groans supposed somebody was in distress, and having the courage to pursue the sound as well as they could, at last came up to the distressed woman, which made Price damn them for their impudence. However, they secured him, and brought him to the watch-house in Old Street, from whence a couple of watchmen were sent to fetch the old woman out of Bunhill Fields, who within a day or two died, under the surgeon's hands.'
>
> (*The Annals of Newgate*)

Newgate. Enter Price yet again.

> 'At length the fatal day came wherein he was to bid adieu to the world, which was on a Saturday, the 31st of May, 1718. As he was riding in the cart he several times pulled a bottle of Geneva out of his pocket to drink before he came to the place of execution, which was in Bunhill Fields, where he committed the murder. Having arrived at the fatal tree, he was, upon Mr Ordinary's examination, found so ignorant on the ground of religion that

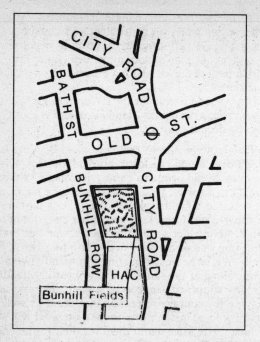

he troubled himself not much about it; but valuing himself upon his former profession of being hangman, styled himself finisher of the law, and so was turned off the gibbet, aged upwards of forty years.'

(*The Annals of Newgate*)

THE PROBLEMS OF 'REGGIE NO-DICK'*

The Murder of Mrs Ethel Christie and others by her husband John Reginald Halliday Christie

Between 1943 and 1953 at 10 Rillington Place, London W11

Some 40 years ago, in the summer of 1953, the visitor to Notting Hill might have stumbled upon a cul-de-sac named Rillington Place. Almost certainly he would have felt inexplicably chilled by the look of its grim rows of terraced houses, one of which – No.10 – was being discussed in tones of horrified disbelief throughout Britain.

No.10 Rillington Place had little about it to justify a second glance; like its neighbours, the house told a tale of the gradual decline of a once respectable district from the time when such dwellings would have been home to a single Victorian family; they had long since been divided into smaller apartments. John Christie and his wife had occupied the ground-floor flat at No.10 for some years, and he was looked upon by the neighbours as a rather superior sort of fellow, with pretensions to education. To look at, Christie could be mistaken for any one of thousands of ordinary Englishmen. He dressed soberly, his thinning hair and studious-looking horn-rimmed spectacles did not attract any special attention, and his observable life-style was in perfect accord with this anonymous appearance.

---

* This unflattering jibe at Christie's physical shortcomings attached to him in youth, where his unsatisfactory performances with his female peers resulted in several such unfortunate nicknames; 'can't-make-it-Christie' was another that stuck.

The house, and Christie himself, had already enjoyed one brief period of notoriety some years before. The Christies at that time shared the house with a Mr Kitchener, and a young couple named Evans who had a baby daughter and occupied the top floor. On 30th November 1949 Timothy Evans walked into a police station in Wales and confessed to 'disposing' of his wife. Subsequent investigation of the Evans home in Rillington Place revealed the body not only of Mrs Evans, but that of baby Geraldine as well. Christie had been witness-in-chief for the prosecution, and it was in large part his evidence which subsequently hanged Evans.

But this moment of glory had faded, and life at No.10 resumed its unremarkable tempo, so unremarkable that the lives of its residents once again became part of the city's grey background. Then two things happened to draw attention to the ground-floor occupant of No.10. Around December, Mr Christie's wife stopped being seen about her domestic activities. Questioned by neighbours, Christie said that Ethel had 'gone to the Midlands on medical grounds' to have a special operation. This expla-

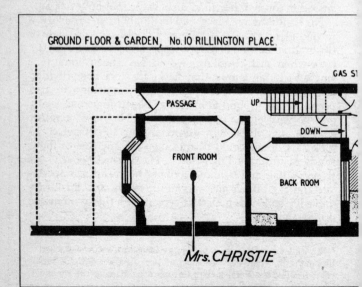

GROUND FLOOR & GARDEN, No.10 RILLINGTON PLACE.

GAS ST

PASSAGE   UP

DOWN →

FRONT ROOM

BACK ROOM

Mrs. CHRISTIE

nation was readily accepted because Christie was something of a self-promoted authority on health matters, always willing to advise when the need arose. The second occurrence was the disappearance of John Christie himself.

Such comings and goings, though, have a limited interest in a large city, and the Christies' rooms were eventually absorbed into the household of Mr Beresford Brown. Exploring his new territory on 24th March 1953, Brown was struck by a strange concoction of smells; at first it was the disinfectant that held the attention, but after a while another, less definite odour could be detected. These smells were at their strongest in the kitchen, and seemed to originate behind a section of wall that was hollow to the knock, and which on further investigation proved to be a papered-over door. Tearing off the paper from over a cut-out section of the door, Brown illuminated the inside with a torch. What he saw were the legs of a woman.

The local police took Mr Brown's discovery very

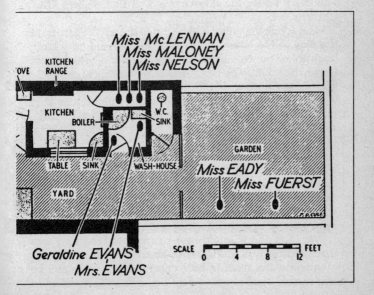

seriously indeed, and reported it straight on to the higher authority of Detective Chief Inspector Griffin of Scotland Yard, who in company with Dr Francis Camps the pathologist was soon at the premises.

The woman had been placed in a sitting position, with her back towards the room. The body was leaning, and would have fallen had it not been secured by a fastening attached to the back of the brassiere. The wrists had been tied with a handkerchief. Upon removal of the body, another girl was found hidden in the cavity, wrapped in a blanket with a pillow-case tied over her head. When this body was being removed, an incredible third was revealed, also covered with a blanket. A fourth victim was uncovered from rubble beneath the floorboards.

By the date of the inquest, 30th March, the following information had become available: Body Number One was identified by Robert MacLennan as his 26-year-old sister, Hectorina; the second body was Kathleen Maloney, aged 26; and Number Three had been identified by Mrs May Langridge as her sister Rita Nelson, aged 25. The body under the floorboards was that of Mrs Ethel Christie.

Meanwhile the police had begun to dig up the garden at the rear of the house, unearthing as they did so a large quantity of bones – many of them human – which were later to be built up by Dr Camps into two almost complete skeletons. Another significant find was a tobacco box in which had been arranged four lockets of pubic hair; one of these relics matched the hair on the body of Ethel Christie. The hunt was now under way for the absentee Christie himself.

By the end of the month of March the manhunt had been intensified; many people had been picked up for questioning, had proved to be other than John Christie, and had been released. The police were trying to keep up with the hundreds of reported sightings of their quarry, from John O'Groats to Land's End.

What the police would have dearly loved to know was that Christie was still lurking about London, using his own name and making little effort to lay low. In fact he had merely booked into a doss house. On the morning of

Tuesday 31st March, Christie made his way from his lodging in Rowton House to Putney Bridge, where he stopped briefly to gaze into the Thames below. Whatever his thoughts were at that moment, they were interrupted by the words 'You look like John Reginald Christie'. Christie straightened up and faced PC Thomas Ledger; he was no longer the clean, well-groomed man who had left Rillington Place; hunger and lack of money, dossing down into an irregular and troubled sleep had all taken their toll of him. 'You are quite right, officer. I am Christie.' The two men walked quietly towards Putney Police Station.

Later that day Christie was faced by Chief Inspector Albert Griffin and Inspector Kelly. Informed that the body of his wife had been uncovered from the front room floor of 10 Rillington Place, Christie began to weep, saying 'She woke me up; she was choking; I couldn't stand it any longer . . .' The prisoner was then cautioned and made the first of several statements embodying his recollections of the murders:

> 'I'll tell you as much as I can remember, I have not been well for a long while, about 18 months. I have been suffering from fibrositis and enteritis. I had a breakdown at the hospital. I got better by September 1952, but kept having attacks after. My wife had been suffering a great deal from persecution and assaults from the black people in the house No.10 Rillington Place* and had to undergo treatment at the doctor for her nerves. In December she was becoming very frightened from these blacks and was afraid to go about the house when they were about and she got very depressed. On December 14th I was awakened by my wife moving about in bed. I sat up and saw that she appeared to be convulsive, her face was blue and she was choking. I did what I could to try and restore breathing but it was hopeless. It appeared too late to call for

---

* This is quite untrue, though the Christies almost certainly entertained the same prejudices as the rest of a generation adjusting to the newly arrived immigrants from the West Indies.

assistance. That's when I couldn't bear to see her, so I got a stocking and tied it round her neck to put her to sleep. Then I got out of bed and saw a small bottle and a cup half full of water on a small table near the bed. I noticed that the bottle contained 2 Phenal Barbitone tablets and it originally contained 25. I then knew that she must have taken the remainder. I got them from the hospital because I couldn't sleep. I left her in bed for two or three days and didn't know what to do. Then I remembered some loose floorboards in the front room . . . I thought that was the best way to lay her to rest.'

Christie then related his financial position, and described selling the furniture. The next significant recollection is of the meeting with Rita Nelson:

'On the way back, in Ladbroke Grove, a drunken woman stood in front of me and demanded a pound for me to take her round the corner. I said, "I am not interested and haven't got money to throw away" . . . She then demanded thirty shillings and said she would scream and say I had interfered with her if I didn't give it to her. I walked away as I am so well known round there and she obviously would have created a scene. She came along. She wouldn't go, and she came right to the door still demanding thirty shillings. When I opened the door she forced her way in. I went into the kitchen, and she was still on about this thirty shillings. I tried to get her out and she picked up a frying pan to hit me. I closed with her and there was a struggle and she fell back on the chair. It was a deck chair. There was a piece of rope hanging from the chair. I don't remember what happened but I must have gone haywire. The next thing I remember she was lying still in the chair with the rope round her neck. I don't remember taking it off. It couldn't have been tied. I left her there and went into the front room. After that I believe I had a cup of tea and went to bed. I got up in the morning and went to the kitchen and washed and shaved. She was still in the chair. I believe I made some tea then. I pulled away a small cupboard in the corner and gained access to a small alcove . . . I must have put her in there. I don't remember doing it . . .

. . . Some time after this, I suppose it was February, I went into a cafe at Notting Hill Gate for a cup of tea and a sandwich. The cafe was pretty full, and there wasn't much space. Two girls sat at a table, and I sat opposite at the same table. They were talking about rooms, where they had been looking to get accommodation. Then one of them spoke to me. She asked me for a cigarette and then started conversation. During the conversation I mentioned about leaving my flat and that it would be vacant very soon and they suggested coming down to see it together in the evening. Only one came down [she was Kathleen Maloney]. She looked over the flat. She said it would be suitable subject to the landlord's permission. It was then that she made suggestions that she would visit me for a few days. She said this so that I would use my influence with the landlord as a sort of payment in kind. I was rather annoyed and told her that it didn't interest me. I think she started saying I was making accusations against her when she saw there was nothing doing. She said that she would bring somebody down to me. I thought she meant she was going to bring some of the boys down to do me. I believe it was then that she mentioned something about Irish blood. She was in a violent temper. I remember she started fighting. I am very quiet and avoid fighting. I know there was something, it's in the back of my mind. She was on the floor. I must have put her in the alcove straight away.

Not very long after this I met a man and a woman coming out of a cafe at Hammersmith [Alexander Pomeroy Baker and Hectorina MacLennan] . . . It was in the morning. The man went across the road to talk to a friend and while he was away she said they had to give up their diggings at the week-end. He was out of work. Then I told her that if they hadn't found anywhere I could put them up for a few days. They both came up together and stayed a few days. They said they had been thrown out of their digs. I told them they would have to go as he was being very unpleasant. He told me that police were looking for her for some offence. When they left the man said that if they couldn't find anywhere could they come back for that night. The girl came back alone. She asked if he had called and I said "No", but I was expecting him. She said she would wait, but I advised her not to. She insisted on staying in case he came. I told her she couldn't and that he may be looking for her, and that she must go, and that she couldn't stay there alone. She was very funny about it. I got hold of her arm to try and lead her out. I pushed her out of the kitchen. She started struggling like anything and some of her clothing got torn. She then sort of fell limp as I had hold of her. She sank to the ground and I think some of her clothes must have got caught round her neck in the struggle. She was just out of the kitchen in the passage-way. I tried to lift her up, but couldn't. I then pulled her into the kitchen on to a chair. I felt her pulse, but it wasn't beating. I pulled the cup-board away again and I must have put her in there . . .'

This was the way Christie remembered the last hours of the three victims boarded up in the kitchen. Or rather, it is Christie claiming not to remember what happened. He 'forgets', for example, that in each case he had sexual intercourse with the victim, during or immediately after killing them. Christie's next statement is dated 5th June, and relates to the murders, some ten years previously, of Ruth Fuerst and Muriel Eady:

'When I was in the Police War Reserve I met an Austrian girl in the snack bar at the junction of Lancaster Road and Ladbroke Grove . . . It was the summer of 1943. I was living in the ground-floor flat at No.10 Rillington Place, and my wife was away in Sheffield . . . The Austrian girl told me she used to go out with American soldiers and one of them was responsible for a baby she had previously.

I got friendly with her and she went to Rillington Place with me two or three times.

I have seen a photograph in a newspaper recently of a girl named Ruth Fuerst. I do not recognise the photograph now shown to me . . . One day when this Austrian girl was with me in the flat at Rillington Place, she undressed and wanted me to have intercourse with her. I got a telegram while she was there, saying that my wife was on her way home. The girl wanted us to team up together and go right away somewhere together. I would not do that. I got onto the bed and had intercourse with her. While I was having intercourse with her, I strangled her with a piece of rope. I remember urine and excreta coming away from her. She was completely naked. I tried to put some of her clothes back on her. She had a leopard skin coat and I wrapped this round her. I took her from the bedroom into the front room and put her under the floorboards. I had to do that because of my wife coming back. I put the remainder of her clothing under the floorboards too . . . during the [next] afternoon my wife went out. While she was out I pulled the body up from under the floorboards and took it into the outhouse. Later in the day I dug a hole in the garden and in the evening, when it was dark, about ten o'clock I should say, I put the body down in the hole and covered it up quickly with earth. It was the right-hand side of the garden, about half-way along towards the rockery. My wife never knew. I told her I was going to the lavatory. The only lavatory is in the yard. I buried all the clothing in the garden. The next day I straightened the garden up and raked it over . . .

. . . I was released from the War Reserve in December, 1943, and started work at Ultra Radio, Park Royal. I got friendly with a woman named Eady, who was about thirty. She used to live at Putney. I took this woman and her man friend to Rillington Place and introduced them to my wife. They came several times together and had tea, and

on one occasion we all went to the pictures together. . .
. . . On one occasion she came alone. I believe she
complained of catarrh, and I said I thought I could
help her. She came by appointment when my wife
was out. I believe my wife was on holiday. I think I
mixed some stuff up, some inhalants, Friar's Balsam
was one. She was in the kitchen, and at the time she
was inhaling with a square scarf over her head. I
remember now, it was in the bedroom. The inhalant
was in a square glass jar with a metal screw-top lid. I
had made two holes in the lid and through one of the
holes I put a rubber tube from the gas into the liquid.
Through the other hole I put another rubber tube,
about two feet long. This tube didn't touch the
liquid. The idea was to stop what was coming from
smelling of gas. She inhaled the stuff from the tube. I
did it to make her dopey. She became sort of
unconscious and I have a vague recollection of
getting a stocking and tying it round her neck. I
am not too clear about this. I have got them confused. It may have been the Austrian girl that I used
the gas on. I don't think it was both. I believe I had
intercourse with her at the time I strangled her. I
think I put her in the wash-house [outhouse]. That
night I buried her in the garden on the right-hand
side nearest the yard. She was still wearing her
clothing.'

In a further statement made on 8th June, Christie confessed at length to the murder of Mrs Beryl Evans – the
crime for which her unfortunate husband had been executed – though it is uncertain what happened to the Evans
baby. In this same statement he acknowledges that the
collection of pubic hair was his and that the samples 'came
from the three women in the alcove and from my wife'.

Christie's trial was a formality, and despite his confession to multiple murder he was charged only with the
killing of his wife. On the bench sat Mr Justice Finnemore,
prosecuting Christie was Sir Lionel Heald QC, and defending him Mr Dereck Curtis-Bennett QC. The court took
four days to examine the prisoner's defence of Not Guilty

by reason of insanity, and his catalogue of self-confessed crimes did much to confirm the plea – that and Curtis-Bennett's frequent references to his client as 'mad as a March hare', and 'hopelessly and utterly mad'. In his summing-up the judge acquainted the jury with the finer points of the M'Naghten Rules and invited them to measure Christie's behaviour against them. The jury took one hour and twenty minutes to decide that the prisoner was guilty, and Christie was sentenced to death. There was no appeal, and the statutory inquiry into his mental condition concurred with the jury's verdict.

John Christie was hanged at Pentonville prison on 15th July 1953. Too late to save poor Timothy Evans, who even then had to wait until 1966 to be granted a long-overdue free and posthumous pardon.

THE MAN WHO SHOT A GHOST

The Murder of John Millwood by Francis Smith
On Tuesday, 3rd January 1804 at the churchyard in Black Lion Lane, London W5

One of the capital's most celebrated hauntings was once associated with the churchyard at Hammersmith, which in the year 1803 was just one of the many small villages skirting London. The restless spirit first displayed its malevolent nature to an unfortunate local who was quietly making her way home across the graveyard at ten o'clock at night. Half-way through the tombstones, she was accosted by something 'very tall and very white', rising as though from the grave. Understandably terrified, the poor woman fled as fast as her legs could carry her; the ghost was quicker, overtaking its prey and enveloping her in its spectral arms. She remained on the cold ground in a faint until discovered and carried home by neighbours to her bed; a bed from which she never again rose.

Though this is the only record of a fatal encounter, enough people were sufficiently badly frightened for there to be formed an ad-hoc watch committee determined at least to discover whether the nuisance was caused, as some said, by the shade of a suicide who had cut his throat a year earlier or, as the cynics had it, by a misguided prankster.

Numbered among the brave band of watchers was one fated to be the only man to appear before the bench at the Old Bailey charged with murdering a ghost.

At about half-past ten on the night of 3rd January 1804,

Mr John Locke met Mr Francis Smith. Smith, in agitation, confided to Locke that he had just killed the Hammersmith Ghost, and summoning a watchman, the trio made off up Limekiln Lane to Black Lion Lane, where lay a white figure, motionless on the ground. The figure proved to be human, and the reason for its immobility was a bullet from Smith's pistol lodged in its jaw.

It is not now, nor was it then etiquette to shoot a man, however much like a ghost he may look. And this, poor fellow, was the victim's only crime; for John Millwood was a bricklayer, and as a bricklayer he was accustomed to wear the traditional clothing of his trade – white trousers, white apron, and a white linen jacket! Perhaps, though, his death could have been avoided if only he had listened to the advice of his mother-in-law; when she gave evidence at Smith's trial it transpired that 'on the Saturday evening before his death, [Millwood] told her that two ladies and a gentleman had taken fright at him as he was coming down the terrace, thinking he was the ghost. He told them he was no more a ghost than any of them, and asked the gentleman if he wished for a punch in the head.' Upon which the mother-in-law recommended that he wear a greatcoat to avoid future trouble.

As to Francis Smith, although he was able to call a number of character witnesses in his defence, each describing him as a mild and gentle man in the extreme, the Lord Chief Baron, in his address to the jury, said that however disgusted they might feel in their own minds with any abominable person guilty of the misdemeanour of terrifying the neighbourhood, still the prisoner had no right to construe such misdemeanour into a capital offence, or to conclude that a man dressed in white was a ghost. It was his own opinion, and was confirmed by those of his learned brethren on the bench, that if the facts stated in evidence were credible, the prisoner had committed murder.

The jury took a more lenient view, as juries often do, and returned with a verdict of 'guilty of manslaughter'.

On hearing this verdict the bench responded that 'such a judgement can not be received in this case, for it ought to be either a verdict of murder or of acquittal. In this case there was a deliberate carrying of a loaded gun, which the prisoner concluded he was entitled to fire, but which he really was not; and he did fire it, with a rashness which the law did not excuse.' Chastened, the jury reconsidered their verdict. 'Guilty of Murder.'

And so it was that the man who shot a ghost was himself sentenced to die. Happily, history has provided a less austere conclusion, for Francis Smith earned a last-minute reprieve, and was sentenced to one year's imprisonment.

MANHUNT

**The Murder of PC Geoffrey Fox,
DS Christopher Head and DC David
Wombwell by Harry Roberts, John Duddy
and John Witney**
On Friday, 12th August 1966 in Braybrook
Street, London W12

On Friday 12th August 1966, Police Constable Geoffrey Fox, Detective Sergeant Christopher Head and Detective Constable David Wombwell were on the 9am to 5pm shift in 'Q' Car Foxtrot Eleven, an unmarked police car. They had just been stood down from the gruesome 'Jack the Stripper' inquiry and the main job of the morning had been to ferry DI Coote to Marylebone Magistrates Court. After lunch at the Beaumont Arms, Uxbridge Road, there was little to do before a call came through at about three o'clock to pick up DI Coote again. They set off up Wood Lane, turning left into Western Avenue and eventually reaching Braybrook Street, East Acton, a road that runs along the perimeter of Wormwood Scrubs prison. At this point they sighted a battered, blue Standard Vanguard Estate Car. For some reason, maybe a combination of its disreputable appearance and its proximity to the prison, they decided to stop it and check on the driver.

Inside the blue car were three smalltime criminals, John Witney, Harry Roberts and John Duddy. Witney, the owner and driver of the car, was a 36-year-old unemployed lorry driver with a number of previous convictions for petty theft. About a year before, Witney had teamed up with Harry Roberts and together they had done a number of jobs stealing lead and other metals. Roberts, aged 30, had a similarly long criminal record, but was a much harder man, having done his National Service in Malaya, which had taught him guerrilla warfare and jungle survival techniques. He had recently served a four-year stretch and had resolved that he'd do almost anything to avoid getting caught again. John Duddy was a heavy drinker and had a history of petty theft, but had always avoided violence. He'd joined the other two more recently and they had begun to carry out a series of small robberies on betting shops and rent collectors. For this purpose they had decided to get 'tooled up' with firearms to use as a 'frightener'. Between the two front seats of the estate car was a canvas hold-all containing three guns.

It was about 3.15. The police car overtook the Vanguard Estate and flagged it down. Sergeant Head and DC Wombwell got out of their car and walked back to the driver's window of the Estate. Head asked to see the Road Fund Licence and Witney replied that he was awaiting his MOT Certificate. This was followed by a request for Witney's driving licence and insurance, the details of which Wombwell wrote down in his notebook. Head then moved round to inspect the rear of the car, and Witney said 'Can't you give me a break. I've just been pinched for this a fortnight ago.' As Wombwell inclined his head towards the driver's window to reply, Roberts drew a gun and shot him in the left eye. DC Wombwell fell to the ground and Roberts and Duddy clambered out of the car in pursuit of Sergeant Head. Head ran back towards the Q Car and Roberts fired a shot, which missed. The Sergeant was trying to crouch behind the bonnet of the Q Car as Roberts shot him in the back. Meanwhile Duddy had run up to the Q Car and fired three shots through the driver's window at PC Fox, one of them hitting him in the left temple and killing him instantly. This released the brake pedal of the police car which, horrifyingly, ran over the body of the dying Sergeant Head, trapping him against the rear wheels. The two criminals then turned and ran to their car, which reversed back down the road in a panic and, turning, sped away past a surprised young couple driving in the opposite direction. Thinking that this might be a prison escape, they took the number of the van, PGT 726, and drove on to be faced by the scene of bloody devastation.

By nine o'clock that evening, the number of the car had been traced to Witney and the police had organized a raid on his house, where they found him and immediately took him into custody. His first story was that he had sold the car that lunchtime to a man in a pub for £15. That evening a description of the car was put out over the TV and radio, which was heard by a man who had seen it parked outside a lock-up garage in Tinworth Road, Vauxhall. Again the police pounced and discovered the car in the garage, complete with three .38 cartridges and Duddy's .38 gun on the back seat. On the Sunday Witney was formally charged with the three murders. Deciding that he had nothing to gain and an awful lot to lose by holding out any longer, Witney confessed to his part in the murder and named Roberts and Duddy as the main perpetrators of the crime.

Meanwhile, Roberts and Duddy had met up on the Saturday morning and, after burying the remaining guns on Hampstead Heath, decided they should separately make a run for it.

Duddy made for Glasgow, his home town, and was arrested several days later in a Carlton tenement. On his way back to London by plane, he confessed his part in the murders.

Roberts thought that his best chance of survival was to

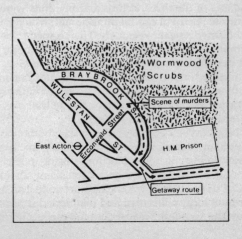

lay low for a while until the heat died down. He decided the safest way of achieving this was by living rough, a technique in which the Army had so thoughtfully trained him during his National Service. Accompanied by his common-law wife, Mrs Margaret Perry, he bought the camping gear he required in Tottenham Court Road and caught a bus from Camden Town to The Wake Arms in Epping. There, Mrs Perry left him, to return to her flat and the waiting attentions of the police. Roberts struck out into Epping Forest.

On 16th August a picture of Roberts was issued to the media and the biggest and most sustained manhunt in criminal history had begun. A reward of £1000 was offered for information leading to his capture and 16,000 posters containing his picture were distributed. For three months Harry Roberts was the most famous face in Britain. Over 6,000 reported sightings had to be followed up and the police were nearly swamped by the sheer volume of mainly useless information they had to check.

On 31st August the three unfortunate policemen were buried, and on 6th September a memorial service was held for them in Westminster Abbey, attended by the Prime Minister, Harold Wilson, and many other dignitaries. Fifty thousand people sent money to a fund set up for the dependants of the three victims and petitions were circulated for the return of capital punishment, which had only been abolished a year previously. This seemed to be all the proof that the retentionists needed of the anarchy which would prevail without the ultimate sanction.

Still nothing substantial had been heard of Roberts. The authorities decided that they must go ahead with proceedings against Witney and Duddy, and the trial was set for 14th November at the Old Bailey.

On 14th November 1966 a gypsy farm labourer, John Cunningham, came across a man living in a tent in Thorley Woods, Bishop's Stortford. Being no friend of the police, he crept away and kept silent about it. A couple of days later he was being questioned on another matter by a local policeman and mentioned it in passing. The sighting was followed up and the camp site found. It was empty, but fingerprints found there matched those of Harry Roberts. The area was surrounded by 100 policemen and at dawn the next day a systematic search was begun. Just before noon Roberts was discovered hiding in a disused hangar on the edge of nearby Nathan's Wood. He gave himself up without a struggle.

It was decided to suspend the trial of Witney and Duddy so that Harry Roberts could join them in the dock. The new trial began at the Old Bailey on 6th December, with Mr Justice Glyn-Jones presiding, the Solicitor-General, Sir Dingle Foot, representing the Crown and Mr W.M. Hudson, Mr James Comyn QC and Mr James Burge QC representing Witney, Duddy and Roberts respectively. Witney and Duddy pleaded not guilty to all the charges and Roberts pleaded guilty to the murder of DC Wombwell and DS Head, but not guilty to the killing of PC Fox. All three were found guilty on all counts. Witney and Roberts appealed, but their appeals were dismissed. The sentence was life imprisonment, with a recommendation from the judge that they should each serve a minimum of 30 years. John Duddy died in Parkhurst Prison in February 1981. Witney and Roberts are still serving their sentences.

THE FACE OF CRIME

**The Murder of Mrs Elsie May Batten by
Edwin Albert Bush**
On Friday, 3rd March 1961, at 23 Cecil Court,
London WC2

The Identikit system of identification was the culmina-
tion of research and development carried out by the
Los Angeles Police Department, notably by Hugh McDonald. At its inception the 'kit' comprised a set of inter-
changeable transparencies of drawings. These depicted
the variations on facial features – eyes, noses, ears, etc. –
which in a collaboration between the police operator and a
witness could be assembled to give a composite picture of
the wanted person. In theory it was possible to combine
the components into thousands of millions of likenesses;
in practice the system proved rudimentary and inaccurate,
even, as in the case of the 'A6 Murder', a possible
hindrance to the course of justice.

In 1959 the concept of Identikit was introduced to the
investigating officers of Scotland Yard, but it was not until
1961 that the system was put to practical use . . .

Britain's first Identikit Face was that of 21-year-old
Edwin Albert Bush, author of a senseless and lacklustre
crime in the heart of London's theatreland. Bush, obligingly enough for the launch of Identikit, was a fairly
distinctive half-caste Indian who had walked into Louis
Meier's antiquities shop in Cecil Court on 2nd March 1961
– the day before the murder – and made inquiries as to the
cost of a dress sword. He had been told £15, and went
from here across the pedestrian court, to the shop of a
gunsmith named Roberts who replied to his question that,

yes, he did occasionally buy swords, but would need to see it before agreeing a price.

On the following morning Edwin Bush returned to Louis Meier's shop, where he stabbed to death Meier's assistant, Mrs Elsie Batten, wife of the President of the Royal Society of Sculptors Mark Batten, and helped himself to a dress sword. At 10am, he re-opened his transaction with the gunsmith, leaving the ill-gotten blade in the care of his son Paul Roberts, suggesting a price of say £10. He never returned to hear the gunsmith's verdict, but Bush (as prime suspect in the murder) could now be reliably identified by three people. This enabled a fairly accurate Identikit portrait to be made; accurate enough, anyway, for Police Constable John Cole to iden-tify and arrest the subject while on patrol in Old Compton Street, Soho, on 8th March.

At Bow Street police station where he was interviewed by Detective Chief Superintendent John Bliss, Bush ex-pressed the opinion that the Identikit looked like him, but denied any connection with the killing of Elsie Batten. However, it was not long before Edwin Bush was making

Edwin Bush's Identikit likenesses, the first time the system was used in Britain

his statement: 'I went to the back of the shop and started looking through the daggers, telling her I might want to buy one, but I picked one up and hit her in the back . . . I then lost my nerve and picked up a stone vase and hit her with it. I grabbed a knife and hit her once in the stomach and once in the neck.'

But aside from his confession, Edwin Bush's catalogue of carelessness had not ended at regularly showing his face in the area where he had committed murder; he had also left behind in the shop an identifiable footprint. There was blood on his clothing, and two fingers and a palm print on the sheet of paper he had used to wrap the sword.

Edwin Bush stood trial at the Old Bailey on 12th and 13th May. In his evidence he admitted going into Mr Meier's shop with the intention of stealing a ceremonial sword; he was then, he said, going to sell the sword to Mr Roberts in order to buy an engagement ring for his girlfriend. Bush then began to haggle over the price and: 'She let off about my colour and said, "You niggers are all the same. You come in and never buy anything", I lost my head . . .' he then repeated his previous account of the killing.

Bush had the benefit of Mr Christmas Humphreys QC as his defender, but at the end of the trial he was convicted, sentenced to death by Mr Justice Stevenson, and hanged. Of PC Cole's part in the apprehension of Mrs Batten's killer, the judge commented: 'You deserve the congratulations and gratitude of the community for the great efficiency you displayed in recognizing Bush. You have been the direct instrument of his being brought to justice. Your vigilance deserves the highest praise, and I hope it will be clearly recognised by the highest authority.'

SOUTH-EAST ENGLAND

Hampshire

Kent

Surrey

Sussex

'A SMALL HOT BIRD'*

**The Murder of Lieutenant Hubert George
Chevis by an Unknown Assassin**
On Sunday, 21st June 1931 at his home on
Blackdown Camp, Aldershot, Hampshire

Any man who has risen to the rank of lieutenant in the
professional Army, and is part of a long family
military tradition, must have some awareness of his
own mortality, the reluctant acceptance that the nature
of his calling may demand from him the ultimate sacrifice
on 'some foreign field'. But to be struck down by a silent
and unknown assassin in the middle of a family dinner
within the security of an Army camp at Aldershot is the
least of his expectations. Nevertheless in one of the most
baffling crime mysteries of the century, that is exactly
what did happen.

In June 1931, Lieutenant Hubert George Chevis, a
young Artillery officer, was occupying a bungalow on
the Blackdown Camp, near Aldershot. He also kept a
family house in London in which his wife and two
children resided during the week while he was on
duty, and the family was reunited at the bungalow for
weekends. On the 21st of the month the Chevis cook, a
Mrs Yeomans, took delivery of the brace of partridges
which Mrs Chevis had ordered from a local poulterer as
the basis for a modest celebration dinner. It was the
weekend of the annual Aldershot Tattoo – always a

---

* 'When I demanded of my friend what viands he preferred, He
quoth: 'A large cold bottle and a small hot bird.''

(Eugene Field, *The Bottle and the Bird*)

special date for military personnel in the area – and the Chevises had planned to take the children with them to see the spectacle.

The cook hung the birds in the ventilated meat safe outside the house, and there they remained until mid-afternoon, when they were transferred to the oven to roast while Lieutenant and Mrs Chevis entertained friends to late-afternoon cocktails. When their guests had left the couple sat down in anticipation of their evening treat, served, in accordance with quaint military protocol, by the Lieutenant's batman, Private Nicholas Bulger. Mrs Chevis took command of the carving, and with their accompanying vegetables the partridges looked a meal fit for a king – or a general, at least.

Hubert Chevis lifted a forkful of bird to his lips expectantly; chewed; swallowed; and grimaced: 'It tastes horrible!' Mrs Chevis was less adventurous, and merely touched a piece of partridge flesh with her tongue: 'Fusty!' was her verdict, and with evident annoyance and disappointment Chevis ordered his batman to dispose of the rest of the meal somewhere where the dogs couldn't get it.

Within minutes Hubert Chevis was feeling more unwell

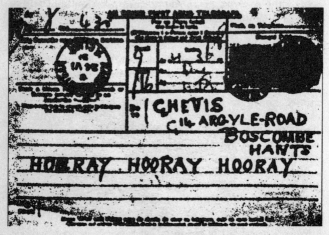

Telegram received by Sir William Chevis on the day of his son's funeral

than angry; within fifteen minutes he had lost the use of his legs and was in the grip of strong convulsions: within the hour he was in a military hospital fighting for his life. The battle was lost in the early hours of the following morning. Mrs Chevis, who had also had contact with the evidently contaminated poultry, suffered milder symptoms and eventually responded to treatment.

According to procedure in cases of violent or inexplicable death, the police were informed, a post-mortem examination ordered, and a coroner's inquest convened. The inquest was formally opened on 23rd July, but immediately adjourned pending the analyst's report.

On the following day Sir William Chevis – Hubert's father – was preparing for his son's funeral when a telegram boy delivered a message. It read, simply: 'Hooray Hooray Hooray', and was signed on the back 'J. Hartigan, Hibernia [a Dublin hotel]'. The police, to whom Sir William immediately communicated the telegram, took a very grave view indeed; for sick though the message was at the time and under the circumstances of Sir William's recent bereavement, it was highly suspicious in view of the fact that no mention of the tragedy had yet been made public, and assuming, as was natural, that the words 'Hooray' celebrated Lieutenant Chevis's death, the sender could only be acting on first-hand knowledge.

Developments in Eire came swiftly; the Garda had interviewed the staff and guests of the Dublin hotel named on the cable, and eliminated any connection between it and anybody named Hartigan. They had seen

the Post Office clerk who took the telegram, and he was able to give a useful description, which happened – and now the investigation seemed to be making progress – also to fit a man who had purchased a quantity of strychnine from a local chemist. Here, however, the trail went cold, and when the inquest on young Chevis was resumed in the West Surrey Coroner's Court on 11th August, there was little more to add.

The coroner opened by recapping on the known facts of the case: that the partridges had been the vehicle for a poison – strychnine – which had been responsible for the death of Hubert Chevis and had been near fatal for his wife; that the grieving parent had received an unfortunately worded telegram, which was subsequently investigated by the Irish police.

The coroner next took time to admonish the *Daily Sketch* for having published – without consultation or permission – a facsimile of the 'Hooray' telegram. This publicity made it impossible for the police to determine whether a series of subsequent messages – all purporting to come from J. Hartigan – were genuine or hoaxes. One of these was a postcard, mailed in London, to the editor of the *Sketch*; it read 'Dear Sir, Why do you publish a picture of the Hooray telegram? J. Hartigan.' This was followed by a further telegram to Sir William Chevis, this time postmarked Belfast and bearing the portentous message: 'It is a mystery they will never solve. J. Hartigan. Hooray.'

Witnesses were then called to elaborate, for the benefit of the jury, their part in the story of the Lieutenant's mysterious death.

Hubert's brother, Captain Chevis, testified that he had seen the telegram on the day of the funeral, and that he did not know anybody of the name or description of the sender.

Mrs Chevis confirmed that her husband had no Irish connections, or any friends or relatives named Hartigan. The rest of her evidence was a simple relating of the sequence of events which led to the tragedy of her husband's death.

Of more significance was the testimony of Dr J.H. Ryffel, Home Office analyst in charge of the Chevis case. Tests on the stomach contents of the deceased, and on the vomit and faeces of Mrs Chevis revealed abnormal quantities of strychnine hydrochloride; in Hubert's case easily sufficient to cause his death, though not enough to cause the rapid death associated with this kind of alkaloid poisoning. He accounted for Mrs Chevis's survival by one of two possibilities – either her contact with the meat had been mercifully brief, or only one of the brace of birds had been poisoned – Mrs Chevis's portion suffering only from secondary contamination during the cooking. This latter theory could not be verified due to the efficient carrying out of the Lieutenant's order to destroy the meal. There had been traces of poison in the dripping and gravy left in the pan, indicating that the partridges had been interfered with before cooking – most likely when they were in the cold safe outside the house. Furthermore, by the nature of the poison, it would need to have been injected into the bird(s) for the flesh to be so heavily impregnated as to cause death from such limited contact with the meat. Dr Ryffel concluded by saying that three birds from the same batch had been randomly selected from the poulterer's stock, tested and found to be 'clean'.

Neither Bulger the batman nor Mrs Yeomans could add significantly to the story, both stating in answer to the now familiar question that they knew nobody who went by the name of Hartigan. There was, though, a small ripple of interest when Nicholas Bulger admitted he was born in Ireland. But everything that could have been said had quite obviously been said, and it remained only for the coroner to sum up the evidence for the benefit of the jury.

He emphasised that the only conclusion it was possible for him to reach, was that Lieutenant Hubert Chevis had died from asphyxia following strychnine poisoning. The poison had been administered in the flesh of a partridge which had been eaten by the deceased, but no evidence was yet available to indicate how or by whom the birds were poisoned. He could therefore form no opinion as to whether death had been accidental or murder.

This might seem an over-cautious conclusion to present to the jury, but it was quite in keeping with the responsibility of the coroner's inquest to consider only the indisputable evidence presented to it. To the layman, of course, it is quite obvious that Hubert Chevis was murdered – the telegram from 'Hartigan' indicates that. But, as Hartigan had pointed out earlier, 'it is a mystery they will never solve'.

The jury took just five minutes to return an open verdict, which is where the case still stands: an unsolved and apparently motiveless killing.

THE GARDENER'S TALE

**The Murder of Michael Robertson by
Timothy John Funge-Smith**
On Friday, 7th October 1984 at Hayling Island,
Hampshire

On the night of Friday, 7th October 1984, Mrs Yianoulla Robertson reported finding the battered body of her husband Michael in the grounds of their home at Salterns Lane, Hayling Island.

Forty-one-year-old Robertson, an executive with the IBM company, was rushed to the Southampton General Hospital suffering severe head injuries from which he died on the 9th, without regaining consciousness.

The police investigation, led by Detective Chief Superintendent John Wright, the head of Hampshire CID, first concentrated on piecing together Mr Robertson's movements during the evening hours leading up to his death. According to Greek-born Mrs Robertson, her husband went out earlier in the evening to collect a take-away meal, and police believed that the victim may have visited several public houses in the seafront area of Hayling Island; subsequently, an appeal was made for witnesses who saw Robertson on that evening.

Events began to move quickly then, and by the morning of the 11th October, a man was in custody and officers were about to arrest the victim's wife. At a brief sitting of the Havant magistrates court, 37-year-old Yianoulla Robertson was charged that 'on a date unknown, between 1st January and 10th October, 1984, [she] solicited Timothy John Funge-Smith to murder her husband'. Mrs Robertson was remanded in custody to appear again before the court in eight days.

Funge-Smith, 41, with an address at The Seafront, Hayling Island, appeared in court the following day, Wednesday, and was remanded in custody on the charge of murdering Michael Robertson, for whom he had worked as a general gardener.

When Timothy Funge-Smith came to trial at the beginning of March 1985 it was before Mr Justice Tudor Evans at the Winchester Crown Court. The jury heard how when the prisoner had first been interviewed by the police he invented the alibi that he had been drinking in a local public house at the time of the attack on his former employer. But, revealed Mr Roger Titheridge QC prosecuting, when he learned that investigating officers had found the murder weapon – a 3ft galvanised pipe – and furthermore that it bore his palm print, Funge-Smith had telephoned the murder incident room and confessed to the crime. Also appearing in the dock was 37-year-old David Stacey, who admitted attempting to pervert the course of justice by giving the prisoner an alibi.

Sentencing Funge-Smith on 5th March, Mr Justice Tudor Evans told him: 'Whatever your motives, this was a brutal murder for which the sentence is prescribed by law'; that sentence was imprisonment for life. In an

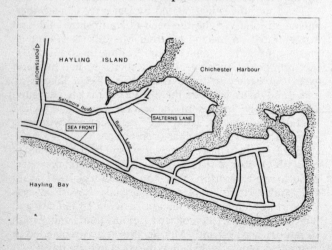

unusual move from the Bench, the judge imposed an order under the Contempt of Court Act prohibiting publication either of the prisoner's motive, or of a conversation he is said to have had with the dead man's widow, who had also been charged.

A month later, on 25th March, Mr Christopher Leigh, representing the Director of Public Prosecutions applied for this order to be rescinded; its original purpose – to ensure an unbiased trial for Mrs Robertson – being redundant as there was insufficient reliable evidence on which to pursue the case against her.

A VERY STRANGE PASTIME

The Murder of Miss Phyllis Oakes by Arthur Charles Mortimer
On Thursday, 8th August 1935 on the Railway Bridge outside Winchfield, Hampshire

---

There can be few more extraordinary stories than that of the killing of poor Phyllis Oakes; and few more extraordinary killers than Arthur Charles Mortimer.

Arthur, you see, had a very strange and anti-social pastime – his greatest pleasure derived from driving his motorcar at women cyclists, knocking them off their mounts, and subjecting them to such further indignities as circumstances permitted, or fancy led.

It was on the morning of 7th August 1935 that Mrs Alice Series, a lady in service, had her unfortunate meeting with Arthur Mortimer, a 27-year-old lance-corporal stationed with the 1st Welch Regiment at Aldershot. It took place at Stratfield Saye, in the Hampshire countryside between Basingstoke and Reading. Having forced Mrs Series into the side of the road with such suddenness to hurl the luckless woman into the ditch, Arthur reversed, wound down his window, smiled, and apologized: 'So sorry, trouble with the steering, Look!' He pointed to the steering wheel. As Alice Series staggered up and neared the open car window, Arthur Mortimer landed her such a punch on the head as to loosen several of her teeth; after thumping her several times more as she lay stunned on the ground, Mortimer made off in a puff of exhaust. Under the circumstances it seems purely incidental to say that the car was a stolen one.

Before abandoning the vehicle to its rightful owner,

however, Arthur Mortimer felt inclined to indulge his hobby once more. The victim this time was Nellie Boyes – another domestic servant as it later transpired. The location was Hartley Whitney, the *modus operandi* was the same. The plucky Nellie, though, was a more equal match and, after giving her assailant the rough edge of her tongue, frightened him off with threats of the police.

On the following morning Arthur Mortimer was out and about early in Farnborough. He was stealing another car.

Driving through Winchfield, the prospect of sport manifested in the persons of 20-year-old Phyllis Oakes and her sister Betty, who were cycling in single file along the road where it bridges the railway line. Riding ahead of her sister, Betty Oakes was horrified to hear a crash from behind, and turned in time to see Phyllis bouncing off the bonnet of Arthur Mortimer's car.

That afternoon brought fresh prospects of pleasure in the neighbouring county of Surrey, where Mrs Lilian Rose

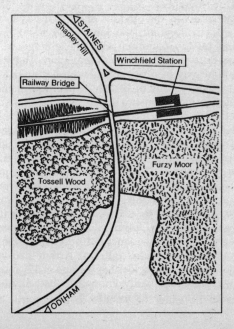

Harwood (unbelievably, another servant) was cycling at Crastock, near Knaphill. Mortimer left her unconscious where she had fallen into the ditch; minus her handbag and the 30 shillings that it contained.

Such very peculiar behaviour could not long escape the notice of the police, not least since Phyllis Oakes was in a serious condition in hospital and her sister was crying vengeance. The law caught up with Arthur Mortimer just outside Guildford, and despite a chase dignified by heroic endeavour, he eventually crashed into a police roadblock set up specifically for that purpose. He emerged shaken and bruised, but in a great deal better bodily condition than most of his victims. On the passenger seat of his car was Lilian Harwood's handbag; in his pocket was Lilian Harwood's 30 shillings.

A charge of grievous bodily harm against Miss Oakes was quickly changed when that unfortunate young woman succumbed to her injuries, and Mortimer faced trial for murder before Mr Justice Finlay at the Winchester Assizes in November.

The defence was the obvious one – that Phyllis Oakes' death was an accident; the kind of accident that was becoming all too common with the emergence of the motorcar as a popular form of transport. But it was a defence that may in retrospect have been unwise.

It is a characteristic of British justice that in the main everything is done to ensure that an accused gets a fair and unbiased trial. For example, only one charge is presented against a prisoner at a time – which means that other crimes, other convictions, are kept from the jury, lest they be unreasonably prejudiced against him. However, with a defence of 'accidental death' it is possible for the prosecution to call 'Evidence of System'; that is to say that evidence of similar crimes committed by the prisoner may be introduced to show whether the death was accidental or designed. And in Arthur Mortimer's case it was very damaging evidence indeed. In mitigation of his behaviour, it was pointed out that Arthur had suffered epileptic fits since an accident at the age of 12, and that at 17 he was suffering badly enough to be admitted to a mental institution for six months.

But after a three-day trial, Arthur Mortimer was found guilty of murder and sentenced to be hanged by the neck. . . But there was no punishment that would really have made much difference to Mortimer. Clearly as mad as a hatter, he was reprieved on the evidence of the statutory medical enquiry that followed all capital sentences since the Criminal Lunatics Act of 1884, and spent the rest of his days in prison under medical supervision; well out of temptation's way.

ANOTHER NOTCH FOR FOUR-DAY JOHNNY

The Murder of Hubert Roderick Twells Buxton and his wife Alice by Hendryk Niemasz
On Friday, 12th May 1961 at Pantile Bungalow, Frith Road, Aldington, Kent

---

Among all the sights that the milkman is traditionally supposed to enjoy on his early rounds, corpses do not often feature. Which is probably why David Pilcher will never forget that spring morning of 13th May 1961. It was 8 o'clock as he whistled his way up the back path through the trim garden of the Pantile Bungalow carrying the daily two pints. It had been a morning much like any other. But that was about to change; change very much for the worse.

As he approached, David Pilcher saw lying across the porchway where he was accustomed to leave the milk the almost naked body of a woman. He needed no close examination to tell him that she was dead; the still, staring eyes, the savagely battered body, and the blood, everywhere. If he had been able, Pilcher would have fled back to his milk float, but it was all he could do to force his numb legs to turn around, his appalled brain to direct him back down the path into Frith Road.

Summoned by the terrified roundsman, Police Constable Allen arrived on the scene with all the haste demanded by such a dramatic and ghastly event. Though no less shocked than David Pilcher, Allen was nevertheless able to bring his police training to bear on the situation, his more developed sense of observation taking in details that had been lost to the milkman. Beneath the drying blood, PC Allen recognized the features of Mrs Buxton; Alice Buxton. She was lying twisted on to her back, dressed as if she had got out of bed in a hurry, naked but for a pink slip and a hastily pulled on cardigan. Beside the body the policeman's eye took in the blood-stained double-barrel section of a broken shotgun, and recognized its potential as a murder weapon.

The constable's dazed concentration was at once broken by the noise of a dog whimpering somewhere inside the house, and by following the sound he discovered the second corpse. Lying on the scullery floor was the man he knew as Mr Hubert Buxton. He too was partly dressed, and by the condition of the man's head Allen knew that he had been shot to death.

In no time the Pantiles Bungalow was playing host to some of the great luminaries of forensic investigation – Detective Chief Superintendent James Jenner, head of Kent CID, Detective Chief Superintendent John Du Rose, whose legendary speed in solving crimes resulted in the nickname 'Four-day Johnny' and Detective-Sergeant Roy Habershon, both of Scotland Yard's Murder Squad, and Professor Francis Camps, pathologist to the Home Office.

While Camps took charge of the post-mortem arrangements, Habershon and Du Rose set about piecing together a background to the double murder and its unlucky victims.

It is often only when confronted with such a tragedy that we realize how little we really know about the people who go quietly about their business on the periphery of our lives. So it was with the Buxtons; what could their neighbours tell police about the couple who had occupied the Pantile Bungalow for the past two years?

He was Hubert Roderick Twells Buxton, a 35-year-old gardener employed in the extensive grounds of the de Pomeroy estate – Pantile House – here in the village of Aldington, between Ashford and Hythe. He seemed an agreeable fellow, but beyond that nobody could add anything. His wife (or more correctly, his common-law wife) was called Alice. She had been born in Belgium and was thought to be a couple of years older than Hubert. The couple had always seemed happy and devoted to each other; and that was the sum total of personal facts on the late Mr and Mrs Buxton.

It was Du Rose's painstaking search of the bungalow that provided the first and most significant clue to the killer's identity, and to a possible motive. On the floor of the bedroom he found the scraps of what looked like a torn-up letter, most of them under the bed. Realizing the potential importance of such evidence, Du Rose and Habershon pieced the scraps together to find the letter had been written to Alice Buxton at an address in Belgium. Despite the hesitant use of the English language, it was clear that this was a love letter of some passion; it was signed 'bye bye, Hendryk, kiss you. XXX'. The date suggested that the letter had been posted on 8th May, five days previously.

Du Rose now set about the task of supplementing the sketchy portraits he had of Hubert and Alice Buxton, in

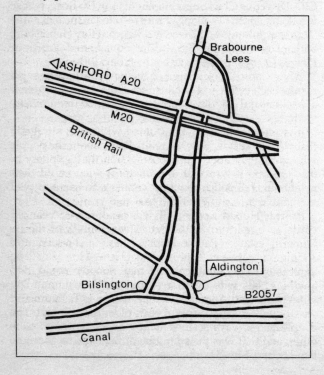

the hope that it might shed light on the effect of Hendryk's letter. From Buxton's employer, Miss Gladys Etta de Pomeroy, he learned that the man had taken up the post of gardener – and the tenancy of the bungalow, which came with the job – in April 1959. He was by her account an excellent gardener, a man of quiet temperament and sober habits. Miss de Pomeroy had also employed Alice Buxton for a short period, but that arrangement came to an end in November 1959. Since then Mrs Buxton had held a number of modest positions – in a local factory as an assembler, as a chambermaid in the Sutherland House Hotel in Hythe, and at The Kings Head nearby as a waitress.

In piecing together details of the 24 hours leading up to the discovery of the bodies, the detectives learned that Hubert Buxton had signed for the registered letter forwarded from Belgium and addressed to his wife from 'Hendryk' on the morning of the 12th. That evening, Alice was positively identified by the driver as having alighted from his bus at 4.50pm from Hythe. Three hours later Hubert had been seen by his employer still at work on the flower beds of Pantile House. At 9.15pm a local farmer noticed a light-coloured car parked on the verge in Frith Road, just down from the bungalow.

At the same time information was coming in from Belgium about Alice Buxton's earlier life. She had been born Alice Gyesel in February 1923 and had been an apprentice dressmaker. During the liberation of Belgium in 1944 she had met a driver in the Royal Engineers named Richard Bateman whom she later married. After demobilization they moved to Evesham, where Bateman set up as a market gardener. Hubert Buxton became not only the Batemans' lodger, he became Alice's lover and, some said with no complaint from Bateman, ran away with her, eventually settling in Aldington. This much she had confessed to her mother on a trip home.

It was about a year after their arrival in Aldington that the lives of the Buxtons and the Niemasz family became entwined. Alice had met Mrs Grypa Niemasz on a bus on her way to work, and had invited her and her husband round to the bungalow for supper; his name was Hendryk

Niemasz, and the two couples began going out together.

DCS John Du Rose was beginning to feel himself making progress. He had almost certainly identified the Hendryk of the letter, and he had the bare bones of a motive. He now began to find people who could confirm his theory; people who remembered seeing Alice Buxton in the company of a man who answered Niemasz's description. They had been seen drinking in pubs together. And Hendryk drove a cream Hillman Husky – was this the car seen parked in Frith Road on the night of 12th May?

On the following day, when the detectives ran Niemasz to ground at his home, the Polish refugee protested that he had been at home in bed on the night of 12th May. Mrs Buxton, he said, was just a family friend: 'I have wife! I want no Alice or other woman!' And the letter to Belgium? Well, he had just written to ask her on what date she returned to Dover so that they could all go down and meet her; so his English was not so good! And the kisses at the end of the letter? 'Everyone put kisses!'

Hendryk Niemasz remained dubiously in the clear for a further couple of days until, acting on instinct, Du Rose, Habershon, and some local detectives returned to the Niemasz house, more particularly to the smallholding at the rear, and more specifically still, to the shed which contained the hay which was the pigs' bedding. When they found the broken stock of a shotgun buried in the hay alongside some live cartridges it was the one piece of tangible evidence the Yard men needed for an arrest: the arrest of Hendryk Niemasz. John Du Rose had lived up to his nickname once again!

By the time it reached Lewes Assizes the case against Niemasz was watertight. Not only did the concealed shotgun stock match exactly with the broken part found next to Mrs Buxton's body, but it also bore her killer's fingerprints. Mrs Niemasz broke down after the arrest and confessed that her husband's alibi was false, that he had been out of the house late on the night of the murder. A pair of bloodstained trousers were found – in the pocket was Alice Buxton's address in Belgium, and the receipt for the registered letter Niemasz sent to that address.

In the face of overwhelming evidence, Hendryk Niemasz's defence seemed a paltry and futile gesture. He had nothing to do with the murder, he pleaded; he had paid a man he knew simply as 'George' to commit the crime, a man he had met in a pub in Gillingham and had bought for £60. A hunt was mounted for the shadowy 'George', but it was to nobody's surprise that he was never found. Throughout the 4-day trial the prisoner listened and spoke through Mrs Jadwiga Sutton, the Polish interpreter appointed by the court for his benefit; but when the black silk square was placed on Mr Justice Pilcher's wig Hendryk Niemasz needed no translation.

Quite why Niemasz felt that it was necessary to slaughter the Buxtons is uncertain. In a statement made by Grypa Niemasz, her husband had told her that Alice was demanding that he run away with her, and threatened to tell the police that he had promised to kill Hubert if he didn't. Hendryk himself told the police another version – that Alice Buxton had given him a pistol and insisted that he shoot not only her husband but Grypa as well. The exact truth of what went on in Hendryk's mind we will never know; he was hanged at Wandsworth Prison on Friday, 8th September 1961.

THE FAIRY FELLER'S MASTER STROKE

**The Murder of Robert Dadd by his son
Richard**
On Monday, 28th August 1843 at Cobham
Park, Cobham, Kent

Born the fourth of seven brothers and sisters, Richard Dadd first saw the light of day on 1st August 1817. The boy's father, Robert, was a native of Chatham, and in the business of apothecary and chemist in the High Street of that town; his mother was the former Mary Ann Martin, of whom we know little beyond the fact that she did not live to see Richard's seventh birthday.

The Dadds were a cultured, moderately prosperous, middle-class Victorian family, and their fourth son received his education at Rochester Cathedral Grammar School, supplementing his classes with drawing lessons from William Dadson, whose Academy was situated not far from Robert's shop in the High Street.

In 1834, in furtherance of a new career as a carver and gilder, Robert Dadd removed his family to London, where they took up residence at number 15 in respectable Suffolk Street, Pall Mall East. In January 1837 Richard entered into full-time study at the Royal Academy School of Art; here he embraced the painterly principles of the exclusive 'Clique', and became a member in such company as Augustus Egg, William Powell Frith, John Phillip, and H.N. O'Neil. His artistic promise was recognized by the award of three silver medals, and his subsequent exhibitions with the Society of British Artists, and the Royal Academy established for him a small reputation and several commissions. He also began to receive the private patronage of Sir Thomas Phillips, a solicitor of Newport, and a former mayor of the town.

It was as companion and draughtsman to Sir Thomas that Richard Dadd departed England on 16th July 1842, following that requisite of Victorian middle-class pursuits – The Grand Tour. During the remainder of 1842 and the early part of 1843, the couple travelled through France, Greece, Italy, and the Middle East. Despite the onset of mental disturbance (aggravated, some say, by sunstroke from the fierce Egyptian sun), Richard managed to complete many estimable watercolours and drawings throughout the trip. Unfortunately, by the time our travellers began the return journey, by way of Malta, Naples, and Rome, Richard had become convinced that he was pursued by devils; the more disturbing since one of the chief of these emissaries from Hell he imagined to be his companion Thomas Phillips. It may or not have been some comfort to Phillips to know that a fellow-demon took the shape of the Pope, whose assassination Dadd seriously considered until he saw the pontiff so heavily guarded.

It says a great deal for family loyalty that although Richard arrived home in May clearly very seriously disturbed, nobody felt that the situation demanded any urgent remedial action. The after-effects of sunstroke, avowed his father, would pass with rest and quiet. Any invocation of that 19th-century bugaboo 'insanity in the family' was strenuously resisted. Indeed, the painter had resumed his work; locking himself in his studio with the vast quantity of eggs and ale which lately formed his diet, Richard began to make a number of portraits of his friends, likenesses to which had been added a deep red gash across the throat.

By the month of August Richard's behaviour could be ignored no longer; his manic flights from imagined persecution had become a public as well as a family embarrassment. On Saturday, 26th August, he was examined by Dr Alexander Sutherland, physician at St Luke's Asylum. The doctor advised that Richard was no longer responsible for his actions, and that he should be confined.

Still unconvinced of the urgency, Robert Dadd allowed himself to be persuaded to take a trip with his son on the following day; a trip during which Richard promised to 'unburden his mind'. Cobham had always been a favourite haunt of the Dadds, and father and son arrived in the village at about 6 o'clock in the evening, alighting at The Ship Inn, where they supped and arranged for lodging for the night. In the following hours Richard was frequently overheard pestering his reluctant father to take a stroll, to which the latter finally acceded, the pair walking off through the darkening acres of Cobham Park. Close by a large chalkpit (called Paddock Hole then, but subsequently renamed Dadd's Hole), the young man made a frenzied and murderous attack on his father and after a desperate struggle left him dead.

The remains of Robert Dadd were found next morning by a butcher passing on his way to Wrotham Market; examination revealed the corpse to be a bloody mess of stab wounds and razor cuts, and the hunt began for his killer . . . his son.

But dishevelled and bloody though he was, Richard Dadd was on his way to France, fleeing via Rochester, through Dover and in a hired boat over the Channel to Calais, and south towards Paris. Meanwhile in London a paper had been found written in Richard's hand. The document comprised a list of names of several eminent people – headed by Robert Dadd, and including the Emperor Franz Ferdinand I of Austria. It proved to be Richard's assassination list.

Though hardly a tragedy of national importance, the case did receive some attention from the local press, and beneath the heading 'Murder at Cobham Park', the *Illustrated London News* reported:

> 'A rumour was prevalent during the week that the wretched parricide Dadd (the particulars of whose atrocity appeared in our late editions last week) had been arrested at Calais by one of the old Bow-street officers, on Monday last; but we regret to state that this is not the fact, and that the savage maniac is still prowling about in quest, perhaps, of other victims.'
>
> (9th September 1843)

The fugitive might have remained undetected for some time longer, had he not made an incomprehensible – and fortunately incompetent – attempt to cut the throat of a fellow passenger on the stage-coach which they shared at Fontainebleau. As a result Richard was arrested by the French police, and in accordance with their customary treatment of the criminally insane, committed to an asylum without benefit of trial. It would probably have been better for all concerned if the unhappy fellow had been allowed to remain confined in Clermont – certainly his family approved, and had even made arrangements for special food to be provided for Richard's comfort. But for complicated, and rather vague, 'political' reasons the Home Office was unwilling to let things remain as they stood, and Richard Dadd was extradited to England, taken before the Rochester magistrates, and remanded by them to the Assize at Maidstone, where:

> 'No doubt can remain in the mind of anyone who was present at the examination that the unfortunate young man is altogether irresponsible for his own acts. While in the presence of the bench his demeanour underwent various and instantaneous changes. The opinion of the bench was unanimous and decided as to the state of his mind, and there is little doubt that the last public scene in this melancholy tragedy has closed, and that this once promising artist will be removed to a place of permanent safe-keeping without coming to trial.'
>
> (*Illustrated London News*, August 1844)

He was indeed found unfit to plead his case in a court of law and – in the manner of his times and class – quietly relegated to the roll of inmates of the Bethlehem (or Bethlem; or Bedlam) Hospital at Southwark.

More fortunate than many in his position, Richard came to the enlightened notice of Dr Edward Monro, who encouraged him to take up painting again, and in collaboration with Dr W.C. Hood, Resident Physician at Bethlem from 1853 and a great admirer of Dadd's work, was responsible for promoting the most brilliantly productive four decades of the painter's life. Here in the hospital, and later in the newly instituted Broadmoor Asylum for the Criminally Insane, the academic achievement of Dadd's youth was transformed into intense and obsessive allegories, crowded with the unreal denizens of his fantasies – the fairies, goblins, and spirits of his most popular works such as the celebrated *Fairy Feller's Master Stroke*. At the end of 1885, Richard Dadd became fatally ill with consumption; on 8th January of the following year he died, and was buried in the small cemetery at Broadmoor.

IT'S THE WAY YOU SAY IT . . .

The Murder of Caroline Ellen Trayler by Gunner Dennis Edmund Leckey
On Whit Sunday, 13th June 1943 in an empty shop at 94 Foord Road, Folkestone, Kent

---

Pretty Caroline Trayler was a member of that generation whose young lives were fated to be lived in the disruption and uncertainty of 1940s wartime Britain. The majority survived the bombs, and the blackouts, and the irritating personal privations; but for Caroline there was to be one blackout too many.

In 1943 she was 18 years old, already a bride of six months, with a husband on active service with the British Forces in North Africa. And like many lively youngsters in her peer-group, Peggy was bored; the war had been going on just too long. She had a part-time job as a cinema usherette which gave her a small financial independence, but there was little enough in those days of austerity on which to spend her well-earned wages.

It might have been just another familiar Sunday evening spent with her mother behind the black curtains which kept their modest private lives from the searching eyes of the Luftwaffe's bombers. But this was Whit Sunday, and Caroline Trayler was determined to find some pleasure in the weekend holiday. Which is probably why she ended up at the Mechanic's Arms; and it would be kindest to her memory to suggest that it was a combination of drink and boredom that resulted in her leaving the pub at closing time on the arm of an off-duty soldier. The darkness swallowed them up; Caroline never returned from it.

When her anxious mother reported Caroline's disappearance, the police moved into a now-familiar wartime routine – first search the considerable area of bomb-damaged Folkestone buildings. It took them four days, but it had been the right decision – Caroline Trayler's body was found in a blitzed shop, and a cursory glance at the body indicated strangulation compounded with violent sexual assault.

The unenviable job of forensic pathologist was to be undertaken here, as in so many cases during those war years, by the late Professor Keith Simpson, who arrived at the scene of the crime with other Scotland Yard specialists within hours. Simpson's reconstruction suggested that the 'rape' almost certainly began with Caroline Trayler's consent – the dirtied state of her calves was consistent with her lying with her legs wide apart and flat on the floor. Whether she changed her mind or found herself the unwilling consort of a sexual sadist we will never know. The bruising around Caroline's throat indicated that her killer had tried unsuccessfully to strangle her from the front, then turned her over and completed the job from behind. The pathologist then began the gruesome task of scavenging such clues as the body could offer to the identity of its attacker. Simpson found a half-dozen dark body hairs stuck to Caroline Trayler's thighs which contrasted sharply with her own auburn colouring and almost certainly came from her killer. The girl's fingernails had also become torn and broken in her last brave struggle, and scrapings from the nails contained rusty-brown fibres, in all likelihood from the assailant's clothing. All that was needed was a suspect to match the clues.

If Dennis Leckey, a serving Artillery gunner, had not gone absent on the day that Caroline's body was found, it is possible that the trail would never have led to him. As it was, his evident panic caused the Folkestone police to issue a nationwide description and a request for his apprehension. Gunner Leckey was picked up by an observant London Bobby named Briggs ten days later. Formally arrested, the prisoner was required to surrender samples of his body hairs which Professor Simpson was pleased to confirm matched those left behind in the assault on his victim. Furthermore, the couple had 'exchanged' hairs, one of hers being found on Leckey's uniform trousers. The fibre taken from beneath Caroline's fingernails matched those of his uniform shirt. Not conclusive proof, it is true, but it was strong enough evidence to take Dennis Leckey to trial on. And it was enough to convince the jury of his guilt; to convince the presiding judge, Mr Justice Singleton, who without the least hesitation pronounced the sentence of death upon Leckey.

Now, we must remember that English law has built into it – and rightly so – certain safeguards for the protection of persons accused of committing a crime. One of these basic rights is that to remain silent – not to be obliged to say anything that may incriminate him until he has the benefit of legal advice. An extension of this is the right of an accused not to give evidence at his own trial. And it must not be inferred from a prisoner's silence in either of these circumstances that he is making an admission of guilt.

At the conclusion of the Leckey trial, in a legal error that was as damaging to the prosecution case as it was inexplicable from so experienced a judge, Sir John Singleton not once but three times in his summing-up gave utterance to the sentiment that the prisoner's reluctance to make a statement to the police at the time of his arrest could be seen as an indication of guilt – 'Of course, he is not bound to say anything – but what would you conclude?' he asked the jury. Anyway, it was enough to force the Court of Appeal to overturn the conviction, and allow Dennis Leckey – without dispute the brutal killer of poor Caroline Trayler – to walk free. Society had, on this thankfully rare occasion, become victim to its own impeccably fair legal system.

THE BRIDES IN THE BATH

The Murder of Beatrice ('Bessie') Mundy by
George Joseph Smith (alias Williams)
On Saturday, 13th July 1912 at 80 High Street,
Herne Bay, Kent

Mrs Margaret Lloyd looked up from the letter she was struggling to write and gazed adoringly at her brand-new husband. How exciting, she thought, to be married and living in London after all the dull old years at home in Bristol. And it had all happened so romantically, so quickly, she could hardly believe it was real. She studied her husband's profile carefully as he sat reading his newspaper. True, she thought, he wasn't exactly handsome, but there was certainly something about him – something so magnetic, so stylish; and with a little thrill of possessiveness she remembered the way other women blushed or lowered their eyelids when John Lloyd spoke to them. He might not be what Mother called a 'proper' gentleman, but he could quote line upon line of divine poetry, and he played the piano, and drew the sweetest, most flattering portraits of her; and his manners were beautiful. So what were a few rough edges and dropped aitches she reflected petulantly, compared to the riches of such a character. Margaret Lloyd – or Margaret Lofty as she had been until only the day before – was completely happy and in love.

She took a deep breath, 'I must not get over-excited,' she reminded herself, 'or I might find myself in the middle of another strange attack like yesterday.' She had known nothing about it until she came round with dear John patting her hand and asking, 'Margaret, are you all right, my dear? You blacked out for a moment.' He had insisted on taking her to the local doctor, who luckily could find nothing wrong with her. She sighed; it would be too awful if anything should happen now to spoil the joy of their first few days together.

Reluctantly she refocused her thoughts on the half-filled sheet of paper in front of her. It was not an easy letter to write, telling Mother, and her sister, that she had eloped with a man whose very existence they had never even suspected. She would have to confess how she had written to him in secret, and arranged to marry behind their backs. She had been so afraid they would disapprove and spoil everything. Well, it was too late now; they would just have to get used to it.

During the evening, after she had walked down to the postbox, John Lloyd suggested that a 'nice warm bath' might relax his wife; he still thought she looked a little pale from the previous day's upset. He summoned Miss Blatch, the landlady, who was soon bustling around with hot water, soap and towels. The tub in the bathroom was tiny, and Margaret rather tall, but still she climbed gratefully into the steaming water and tried to relax, soothed by the sound of her husband playing the harmonium in the downstairs room.

She was still sitting in the bath when she became aware that the music had stopped; that the bathroom door was slowly opening. Margaret blushed as her husband crossed the room and gently put his hand on the top of her head, but as she tried to turn and smile his grip tightened; the next instant his arm was under her knees and before she even had a split second to wonder he was pushing her down, down into the bath; the water was filling her eyes, her nose, her mouth . . . then there was nothing but total swirling blackness.

Fifteen minutes later Miss Blatch was startled when a knock at the front door revealed John Lloyd holding a brown paper bag. 'Oh, Mr Lloyd', she greeted him, 'you did give me a start. I didn't even know you'd gone out.' 'Just popped along the road to get some tomatoes for Mrs L's supper,' he told her with his engaging smile. 'Is

The History and Fate of the Seven Brides of George Joseph Smith

Name	Bride	Place of Marriage	Date	Fate of Bride	Possessions gained by Smith	Inquest	Exhumation
Oliver Love	Caroline Thornhill	Leicester	January 17th, 1898	Emigrated to Canada 1900	–	–	–
George J. Smith	Edith Pegler	Bristol	July 30th, 1908	Survived	–	–	–
George Rose	S. A. Faulkner	Southampton	October 1909	Deserted at National Gallery	£300	–	–
Henry Williams	Bessie Mundy	Weymouth	August 26th, 1910	Separated 1910–1912 Drowned in bath at Herne Bay, July 13th 1912	£2,500	July 15th, 1912 Drowning in epileptic fit	February 18th 1915 Herne Bay
George J. Smith	Alice Burnham	Portsmouth	November 4th, 1913	Drowned in bath at Blackpool, December 12th, 1913	£140 plus Life Assurance for £500	December 13th. 1913. Accidental drowning	February 9th 1915 Blackpool
Oliver James	Alice Reavil	Woolwich	September 17th, 1914	Deserted September 23rd, 1914, at Brockwell Park	£78, piano and furniture and clothes	–	–
John Lloyd	Margaret Lofty	Bath	December 17th, 1914	Drowned in bath at Highgate. December 18th, 1914	£19 plus Life Assurance for £700	December 22nd, 1914 and January 1st, 1915 at Islington. Accidental drowning	February 4th, 1915 Finchley

she out of her bath yet?' 'Haven't heard a squeak from upstairs for ever so long,' the landlady confided. Lloyd called up the stairs, and getting no reply, turned a face dark with concern towards Miss Blatch, 'Oh dear, I do hope nothing's amiss', he said, 'she has these fainting fits; she's not terribly strong, you know. I wonder, would you be so very kind and come upstairs with me . . . just in case . . .' Miss Blatch would be delighted, and they mounted the stairs together.

The sight that greeted them in the bathroom was one of horror. Margaret Lloyd's face was completely submerged beneath the water in the three-parts full tub; her knees were raised, and she was terribly still. Between them they lifted her from the bath and summoned help from the police and from Dr Bates – the physician who had so recently attended Mrs Lloyd's fainting fit.

Miss Blatch was still telling and retelling the story to her fascinated neighbours three months later – 'There was nothing they could do for the poor soul – stone dead she was; the inquest said it was a fainting fit due to the 'flu and the hot water sort of overcoming her. Poor man, he was beside himself when he saw she was dead. Mind you,' she added with smugly relished disapproval, 'she hadn't played straight with him, you know; told him she was all alone in the world, she did. And then that solicitor turning up and saying her mother and sister had asked him to investigate. Mr L told him straight – "My wife told me she had no surviving relatives", he said, "I know nothing of any letter she might have written, or of any family to whom it might be written". That put the legal nosey-parker in his place all right . . .'

After the funeral, Mr Lloyd (alias Smith, alias Love, Rose, Williams, James, and more) collected the £700 life assurance he had taken out on this, his sixth bigamously married wife, emptied her savings-bank account of its remaining £19, and quietly disappeared.

So ended the last in a series of fraudulent, bigamous and – in three cases – murderous episodes in the life of George Joseph Smith – the man who used the power of his charm for women to such cynical and profitable effect. And, but for a long chance, Smith might well have continued to prosper in his horrible career, claimed even more victims to his insatiable greed.

Smith's story started in Bethnal Green in 1872 born the son of an insurance company agent. A troublesome child, at 9 years old he was sent to one of the harsh and brutalizing reformatories that characterized the era; at 18 he was serving 6 months for stealing, and in 1896, after two years' service with the Northamptonshire Regiment, he was sentenced, in the name of George Baker, to 12 months' hard labour for larceny, followed by another 2 years in 1901. By this time Smith, under the alias Oliver Love, was already married to his first wife, Caroline Beatrice Thornhill, a domestic servant. 'Love' shortly persuaded her to act as his accomplice in a series of break-ins in London and along the prosperous south coast, though it is unlikely that she needed much persuading; at any rate, all good things coming, as they do, to an end, Caroline was caught in 1899 and sentenced to 3 months' gaol; he managed to escape. On her release Mrs Love evidently decided that she had had enough not only of the life of crime into which she had been introduced, but of Oliver Love as well and she made a strategic escape to Canada.

Smith flirted with several occupations before finding his true vocation – he was a baker and a gym instructor among other things, and in his spare time he was an enthusiastic writer of letters on such subjects as Manners, Objectionable Literature, and other social dilemmas, a number of which were published in the *Bath and Wilts Chronicle*.

In July 1908, disregarding his previous marriage, Smith 'married' Edith Pegler in Bristol under his own name, and of all his subsequent marriages and affairs, Edith alone seems to have been the woman for whom he had any real or lasting affection. Time after crime he would return to her welcoming arms, and it was to her that he sent his last farewell as he faced death.

Although Smith had proved that he could earn his living, he found work of the sort for which he was qualified uncongenial, and he hungered for more lavish rewards. He could not help but be aware that women of nearly all stations and ages found him inexplicably attractive, and the bright idea occurred to him to maximize this gift into a positive asset. So, with what were to be horrendous consequences, George Joseph Smith set about perfecting the art of living off his charms . . .

In 1909, as George Rose, he married a Miss Faulkner at Southampton, and on her he developed a technique that was to become something of a trademark. He persuaded the poor woman to make over to him any money that she had, and then one day, during a pleasant walk in the park or, in Mrs Rose's case, a visit to the National Gallery, he excused himself on some pretext and while the unfortunate woman was waiting, hastened to her home, stole everything of value – in one case going so far as to take the furniture and a piano – and disappeared for ever, leaving the lady without even a change of clothing to her name.

However, horrible as the crime against Mrs Rose had been, the fate of Smith's next wife was incalculably worse – for she was to be robbed of her very life. Bessie Mundy married 'Henry Williams' in Weymouth in August 1910, and although he robbed and deserted her soon after the ceremony they ran into each other again in 1912, and Bessie, silly girl, forgave him. They set up home once again, this time at No. 80 High Street, Herne Bay. Her forgiveness was rewarded when Smith accorded her the distinction of becoming the first of the 'Brides in the Bath', the one on whom he perfected his silent and ingenious slaying technique. The format never varied – from the preliminary visit to the doctor (in Bessie's case for an 'epileptic fit') through to his appearance at the street door with 'something for my wife's supper' after he had committed his victim to a watery grave.

After his success with Miss Mundy, Smith was ready to murder again. He met Alice Burnham at a Congregational Chapel and, greatly against her father's wishes, married her – as George J. Smith – in Portsmouth on 4th November 1913. A month-and-a-half later, in Blackpool, he was collecting £500 life assurance on her, after a verdict of 'accidental drowning' had been pronounced by the Coroner's inquest.

Then came Alice Reavil – who became Mrs 'Oliver

James' in Woolwich in September 1914. She escaped with her life, but not much else; using the classic desertion technique – this time in South-East London's Brockwell Park – Smith got away with what was left after he had already relieved Alice of her life's savings.

In between the 'marriages', George Smith was also finding the time to practise his love-'em-and-leave-'em-penniless tricks on several other ladies to whom he clearly felt no constraint to offer his hand in marriage; and he was also returning each time to the unsuspecting Edith Pegler, explaining his extended absences as 'business trips', an excuse made thinly credible by their ownership of an antique shop in Bristol.

The beginning of the end came for the vile Smith when Charles Burnham – father of wife number five, Alice – saw an account of the inquest on Margaret Lloyd in the *News of the World*. The circumstances of the death were identical to those in which his own daughter has so tragically and unexpectedly lost her life, and Burnham's deep dislike and mistrust of his daughter's husband immediately galvanized him into action. He was convinced that this John Lloyd was one and the same person as the George Smith who had coolly collected life assurance on the late Alice.

He instructed his solicitor to contact Scotland Yard, and so a long and painstaking investigation was launched into the activities of George Joseph Smith. Chapter by chapter, the story was fitted together; the first link was an examination of the circumstances in which Mrs Williams (poor Bessie Mundy) had also died in her bath at Herne Bay in 1912. It was then that police came to the awful realization that Lloyd, Smith, and Williams were the same gruesome killer. And so the manhunt for Smith began, and just as police were beginning to think that their quarry might have escaped abroad he was run to ground and arrested in a solicitor's office in Shepherd's Bush. As a holding measure, Smith was initially charged with the bigamy at Bath (Edith Pegler). The next step was to exhume, one by one, the bodies of the three dead 'brides'; and this time the medical experts were of the unanimous opinion that accidental death in baths of the size of the three murder tubs was virtually impossible. With no reason to suppose

Left to right: Alice Burnham, Bessie Mundy and Margaret Lofty

that all three women suffered from suicidal tendencies, they concluded that the deaths were therefore homicidal. Forensic experts later unravelled the silent murder technique used by the ingenious Smith, and demonstrated it in court.

At an identity parade, a large number of witnesses successfully picked out Smith as the man they knew under one or another of his soubriquets. Among them, triumphant in avenging his daughter, was Charles Burnham. Smith's hearing at Bow Street Magistrate's Court, where he was charged with the murder of his three 'wives' took six weeks and, six weeks after that, on 22nd June 1915, he came to trial at the Old Bailey charged with the murder of Mrs Williams (née Mundy) at Herne Bay – incidentally, the most lucrative of his 'transactions'. One hundred and twelve witnesses filed before the court during the eight-day trial, and the proceedings were nearly brought to a nasty, if wryly appropriate, close when an over-zealous young detective nearly drowned a swim-suited nurse who had volunteered to help in the reconstruction of the murder method; it proved necessary to give her artificial respiration on the courtroom floor!

The story broke in the middle of the Dardanelles campaign of the Great War, and the grey pages of the national Press, devoted almost entirely to military news, gratefully accepted the spicing of the terrible tale of 'The Brides in the Bath'. Smith became the monster anti-hero almost overnight, and women fought for places in the public gallery to catch a shuddering glimpse of the creature whose reputed magnetism had lured susceptible members of their own sex to ruin and even to violent death.

On 1st July, after retiring for only twenty-two minutes, the jury brought in their verdict, and Mr Justice Scrutton passed sentence in accordance with that verdict. Friday, 13th August was an unlucky day for George Joseph Smith; they hanged him at Maidstone Prison.

THE MISDEEDS OF A LOVELY BOY

**The Murder of Mrs Rosaline Fox by her son
Sidney Harry Fox**
On Wednesday, 23rd October 1929 at the
Metropole Hotel (now demolished), Margate,
Kent

Sidney Harry Fox was a blackguard, and a very successful blackguard at that. In fact he may have been born
a crook, at least if one believes that such traits are
inherited, because his mother, Rosaline Fox, was known
to travel a fairly crooked path herself.

Mrs Fox had been born at Great Fransham around the
year 1866, the daughter of a Norfolk agricultural labourer.
She married early to a railway signalman and bore him
three sons before walking out of the matrimonial home to
live on what wits and good looks nature had been kind
enough to bestow on her. Rosaline soon took up with
another railwayman, a porter this time (perhaps it was the
uniform!), and the union was blessed in 1899 with little
Sidney Harry.

Sidney grew apace, and before anyone had time to take
breath he was starting his own career, supplementing his
meagre income as a page boy with rather more profitable
pickings from other people's pockets and houses. Like all
beginners he made a few mistakes, and repaid his debt to
society in the time-honoured way. By the outbreak of the
Great War in 1914, with Sidney in his middle teens, he
seemed to have life in the palm of his young hands. For a
start, he had dicovered that his brand of boyish charm and
vivacity was attractive both to women and to men of a
certain age and appetite; Sidney had discovered his
homosexuality early, and took great pride in it. There

was a phrase current in those days to describe just such a lad as Sidney; he was a 'lovely boy'. And when he was not being entertained by some generous host or hostess, he was being boarded by His Majesty's prison service.

A brief and undistinguished military career embraced a term of imprisonment for forgery and some time in the sick bay recovering from an epileptic fit. For these services to King and Country, Sidney was pensioned off with a weekly stipend of eight shillings. His not entirely unprofitable contribution to the war effort behind him, Sidney Fox went back to what he did best – living off people gullible enough to let him get away with it.

Time having taken its toll of Rosaline Fox's 'assets', mother and son formed a partnership that was to last until Sidney's decision to convert his mother into a realizable asset. Between them they travelled from town to town, from hotel to hotel the length and breadth of the country. The Foxes never stayed very long in one place – if they had it might have meant paying their bills, and that would have offended the family principles; they had plenty of cheques to spread around, but sadly no credit at the bank with which to honour them.

In 1928 Sidney was engaged in a romantic encounter with a Mrs Morse, a lady who at the time of her infatuation with young Fox was involved in a divorce from her husband – in this Sidney was, however unwittingly, to make the only generous gesture in his life – he provided Captain Morse with a co-respondent. In moved the Foxes to the Morse residence in Southsea; and they could almost certainly have ended their days there in comfort and tranquillity had not two circumstances mitigated against this sensible option. The first was Sidney's pride. The thought of a life fulfilling his sexual obligations to Mrs Morse offended, as he saw it, the dignity of his homosexuality. The second was the knowledge that the good lady had made a will of which Sidney Fox was the sole beneficiary; unfortunately it required that Mrs Morse should die first, and with commendable self-interest Sidney obliged as best he could.

Was it his fault that the victim woke from her sleep before the open gas tap in her bedroom had done its worst? But Sidney's impatience also made him careless, and his subsequent blatant theft of Mrs Morse's jewellery earned him 15 months in prison, and his white-haired old mother was removed to the workhouse.

When Fox was released from gaol in March 1929 he rescued his mother from the care of the parish and together they went on the road again, scrounging and deceiving as of old. But time and illness had tired Mrs Fox, and she began to dwell on the happier world to come; she made her will on 21st April, leaving her worldly goods to her devoted son. To Sidney's chagrin he knew exactly how pathetically few those worldly goods were; but he was a resourceful young man, and as an investment for the future he took out a few thousand pounds' worth of accident insurance policies in his mother's name to supplement the worldly goods. Was it purely academic interest that caused Sidney to ask the insurance agent 'Would this policy cover the case of drowning in the bath? Would it apply supposing a person was poisoned, say in a restaurant?'

During the following six months the Foxes travelled through London, Canterbury, and Folkestone, leaving in their wake a flurry of unpaid bills, stolen cheques, and unredeemed pawn tickets. When they arrived at the Metropole Hotel in Margate on 16th October 1929 they had no more than the clothes they stood up in, and a few solitary coins rattling in the corners of their pockets. Six days later Sidney borrowed the money for his fare to London and visited the insurance company; with his last few shillings he had the policies on his mother extended to midnight on the following day, 23rd October. Sidney Fox was about to realise his assets.

On the morning of the 23rd, Sidney announced to the hotel management that he and his mother would be checking out on the following day, and he would be obliged if his bill could be made up. That evening Mrs Fox and her son dined together in the hotel restaurant, and as a special treat Sidney ordered half a bottle of port for his mother as a nightcap.

Shortly before midnight Sidney Fox was rushing madly around the hotel corridors shouting 'Fire!' Summoned to room 66, the manager was in time to see the partially clad body of its occupant being dragged from the smoky interior. Still hopping about in the background was the victim's son – Sidney Fox.

Police and medical assistance soon arrived, though the latter were unable to render any assistance to the silent figure of Mrs Rosaline Fox. Dr Austin certified the cause of death to be shock and suffocation through smoke inhalation. On the following day a verdict of death by misadventure was returned at the coroner's inquest. Clutching an advance of £40 on his imminent insurance claim, Sidney accompanied the remains of his mother to her final resting place at Great Fransham. On the morning of the funeral Sidney was in negotiation with the manager of the Norwich branch of his insurance company. Three days later he was back in Margate in police custody – blackguard to the end, he had walked out of the Metropole without paying his bill.

But it was two months before Sidney was called to account for his greater crime. Police suspicion had resulted in a Scotland Yard presence in the person of Chief Inspector Walter Hambrook, and a forensic presence in the person of Sir Bernard Spilsbury, being despatched to Great Fransham where an order for exhumation had been made. The conclusion of Spilsbury's examination was that Mrs Fox had not died from suffocation as had been supposed, but from manual strangulation; as the basis for this opinion he gave the small bruise at the back of the larynx. Unfortunately the rapid decomposition that set in once the body had been exposed to the air rendered this tell-tale mark unrecognizable to later observers – a fact that was to have serious repercussions in court.

The trial of Sidney Harry Fox opened on 12th March 1930, before Mr Justice Rowlatt. The Attorney-General, Sir William Jowitt, led for the Crown and Mr J.D. Cassels had the difficult task of making Fox appear innocent.

Much of the early evidence concerned the fire itself, and the mysterious way in which everything pointed to the fire originating under a heavy armchair which stood between the gas fire (ostensibly the source of the blaze) and the bed on which Mrs Fox lay. In his evidence the Chief Officer of the Margate Fire Brigade testified that the only way in which he had been able to start a fire with similar characteristics was with petrol. Petrol like that in a bottle found in Sidney's room which he claimed to have bought to clean his suit! With the death occurring only minutes before Mrs Fox's accident policies ran out, and the ample proof of Fox's poverty there was enough evidence of motive to convince the most stubborn of jurors.

But the prosecution did not have all its own way. When it came to refuting Spilsbury's medical testimony the defence was ready to fight back. As we have noted, the decomposition of the corpse of Mrs Fox had rendered Sir Bernard's strongest proof – the bruise to the larynx – unobservable to later examiners. Examiners like the great Professor Sydney Smith, a forensic pathologist every bit Spilsbury's equal in experience and reputation. It was Smith's contention that Mrs Fox had died of a heart attack, and that Spilsbury's 'bruise' was a sign of putrefaction: '. . . if there was a bruise there it should be there now; it should be there for ever'. Unmoved, Sir Bernard maintained: 'It was a bruise, and nothing else; there are no two opinions about it!'

On the seventh day of the trial Sidney Fox had the star billing; he was in the witness box for the greater part of the day, though he did himself little credit. His contribution to his own defence can be summed up in his answers to the Attorney-General on the subject of the night of the fire:

> *Sir William Jowitt*: Did you realise when you opened the communicating door [between Fox's room and his mother's] that the atmosphere in the room was such as would probably suffocate anybody inside? – *Fox*: If I had stayed in three or four minutes, I should have been suffocated.
>
> So that you must have been greatly apprehensive for your mother? – I was.
>
> Fox, you closed that door? – It's quite possible I did.
>
> Can you explain to me why it was that you closed the door, instead of flinging it wide open? – My

explanation for that now is that the smoke should not spread into the hotel.

Rather that your mother should suffocate in that room than that smoke should get about in the hotel? – Most certainly not, sir.

Why, at the moment when you believed that your mother was in that room, did you trouble one twopenny bit about the smoke getting into the hotel? – I have not admitted that I did shut the door. I very much doubt that I did.

Does it not strike you now as an inconceivable thing to have done? – Not in the panic I was in; I don't think it was.

I suggest the communicating door was closed. You don't dispute that? – I don't know.

Before rushing down you closed the door of your room? – I don't remember closing the door.

And then you passed the door of No.66? – I must have done so to get down.

Did you open that door? – Not then. What would have been the use?

Will you swear you did not? – Yes.

So that you left your mother, as you say, with the communicating door closed, and with the door of room 67 closed; you passed the door of No.66, but you did not open that, and you knew that your mother was inside that room? – Yes, I did not stop to open the door. I rushed downstairs to get help, which I think is a reasonable explanation.

Don't you think that before rushing down for help you might have flung the doors open as wide as you could? – No, I don't.

Why not? – Because I wanted to get help as quickly as possible.

Do you say you do not remember whether you closed your mother's door? – I hardly know what I did. It is all very well to try to pin me down to details, But I don't hardly remember what I did do. I was agitated at discovering the hotel on fire.

Discovering the hotel on fire? That was what made you agitated was it? – Yes.

I should have thought that what would have made you agitated was your mother being in that room? – Certainly.

Which is it now? – I do not remember. You cannot pin me down to detail. I cannot remember all that happened that night.

I suggest that if you had wanted to preserve your mother's life you would have flung open the doors. – I tried to get in, and when I could not, I dashed downstairs.

There was one thing between. You closed the door? – I do not remember.

Sidney was found guilty of the murder of his mother Mrs Rosaline Fox and sentenced to death. Although he consistently maintained his innocence he must have realized that the game was up; or perhaps it was just another example of his arrogance that he refused to apply to the Court of Criminal Appeal. Sidney Fox was hanged at Maidstone prison on 8th April 1930; he was 31 years old.

THE PLUCKLEY ENIGMA

The Murder of Miss Gwendoline Marshall
On Tuesday, 7th October 1980 at her home,
Enfield Lodge, Pluckley, Kent and the
Imprisonment of Peter Luckhurst for the Killing

Until 1980 there was nothing to distinguish Pluckley from dozens of similar villages that dot the uneventful landscape of Kent. The population has risen steadily over the decades, and like many villages around which large towns have grown that population has become diversified in recent years. The top of the village is much as it ever was with its substantial houses and stone cottages clustering around the picture-postcard Norman church; it is the image that the mind's eye creates in response to the words 'country village'. But Pluckley has a newer, quite different type of resident occupying the rather drab post-war council estate at the bottom of Forge Hill. It too is an archetype, representative of a rash of 1950s housing programmes.

Miss Gwendoline Marshall was a member of the 'upper' village class, though her spacious house, Enfield Lodge, stands at a distance from the main residential centre in its own six acres. A short, slight woman, Miss Marshall could also be said to be an archetype, for she typified that kind of elderly eccentric whose habits are validated by the possession of money. A fiercely independent person, Gwendoline Marshall was a virtual recluse, rarely going out into the village and having what necessities she could not grow in her vegetable garden delivered, paying the bills by post. Her one regular outing was the weekly trip to London. The villagers speculated wildly about these visits, which were in fact to a property in Bloomsbury which had been left to her by her parents. Miss Marshall's art-student tenants there provided her with a comfortable income on which to live and indulge her own hobby of painting. Enfield Lodge had also come to Miss Marshall from her father, who had built it in the 1930s.

Gwendoline Marshall encouraged only one visitor to the Lodge, young Peter Luckhurst from the council estate. Until her premature death from tuberculosis, Peter's mother had been Miss Marshall's only regular visitor in her capacity as cleaner. This meeting of distant generations seemed conspicuously successful – for Peter his elderly friend was like a mother-substitute, a sympathetic ear to which he could tell his troubles; more practically, the boy was given the freedom of the orchard and, uniquely, the privilege of shooting rabbits on the six acres. From Miss Marshall's standpoint Peter was not only a lively young companion for whom she seemed to entertain a genuine affection, but was useful at light jobs around the house and gardens. In all a more satisfactory relationship than many in the village would have thought.

But something was about to go terribly wrong.

At three o'clock on the afternoon of Tuesday, 7th October 1980, Miss Marshall's nearest neighbour, Mrs Lucy Wilson, was disturbed in her garden by a young woman in evident distress who begged her to come to Enfield Lodge. It transpired that the woman and her husband, Alan, had been given a rare invitation to pick apples in the Marshall orchard, and when they arrived could not raise the mistress of the house to announce themselves. Now, led by Alan Dryland, his wife and Mrs Wilson went round to the side of the house. Lucy Wilson called through the open kitchen door, and when there was no reply stepped into the room and called again. While wondering over Miss Marshall's unaccustomed absence the search party noticed a pool of fresh blood on the floor. They looked further and found another patch in the lounge; in the dining-room Miss Marshall's ransacked handbag lay on the table. Nervously following the bloodstains upstairs Dryland and Mrs Wilson were horrified to see the trail lead from one room to another of the upper floor. Leaving the house in a state of shock the party began a search of the grounds and outbuildings, all except for a garden shed which had been padlocked. Fearing the worst, Mrs Wilson summoned the police. When PC Coulson arrived it was apparent to his trained eye that this was no matter for a village bobby and he called in the resources of the Ashford force.

As more police officers arrived a systematic search of the house and grounds was put under way in the hope of finding Miss Marshall – dead or alive. At around 6 o'clock in the evening Sergeant Eric Peacock approached the garden shed and ordered the padlock cut off . . .

. . . There on the floor lay the twisted body of Gwendoline Marshall, her hands tied tightly behind her back, her face and head terribly mutilated, her throat cut, and worst of all, a hay fork had been thrust through her neck pinning her to the wooden floor.

Within the hour Detective Superintendent Earl Spencer, head of the East Kent CID had taken charge and ordered immediate house-to-house inquiries. By 8 o'clock detectives had spoken to a local ne'er-do-well named Nikki Mannouch about his activities that day. Mannouch claimed to have been in company with Peter Luckhurst who he placed at the scene of the murder at 2.30 that day. On the following afternoon both Mannouch and Luckhurst were taken to Ashford for routine questioning; nobody could have anticipated the extraordinary statement that was about to be made by Peter Luckhurst. After initially denying that he was at the Lodge at all on the day of the murder, Peter simply looked up and in a quiet voice said: 'I hit her with a log. I wanted some money. I had too much to drink.' Later that day Peter Luckhurst wrote his statement:

> 'I had known Miss Marshall a long time but only through my mother. I left the Spectre Inn at around two o'clock. From there I went into my house got my bike and went to Enfield Lodge where I left my bike and entered the house. On entering I saw Miss Marshall and I grabbed a log and hit her. I asked

have you got any money. She replied no. So I hit her again on the head trying to knock her out but failing this I got angry and forced her around upstairs and downstairs of the house, but I could find no money at all except a cheque book which was no use so I left it. I hit her again this time knocking out the lady. While unconscious I got her to the shed and tied her hands and pushed her on the floor and kicked her and I went all weird and started hitting her with a [garden] fork. On recovering from the funny turn I locked the door and ran like hell. I got on my bike and went home and into my shed. From my shed I saw Nick Mannouch walking past. I asked him where he was going. He said up to the village so I went with him to get his bike which he'd left there and we then went back to my house where I ate my tea and then left for Smarden.'

A subsequent search of the Luckhurst home was rewarded by the discovery, in a kitchen drawer, of a knife stained with blood of the same group as Miss Marshall. In addition, minute spots of blood were found on Peter's clothing, though it proved insufficient to provide an accurate match.

Peter Luckhurst's trial at Maidstone Crown Court in June 1981 was all but a formality. By now he had withdrawn his confession which, he claimed, had been made under pressure. His defence was as predictable as it was unsuccessful; he had simply been visiting Miss Marshall, and found her already dead. His uncannily accurate description of the crime was simply conjecture. Why then, having stumbled innocently upon this ghastly scene, did he not immediately summon the police? Luckhurst's reply was hardly calculated to endear him to the jury: 'I won't give them assistance for nothing!'

After a five-day trial and a two-hour jury retirement Mr Justice Stocker sentenced Peter Luckhurst to be detained during Her Majesty's pleasure.

And there might have been an end to a tragic but by no means unique killing.

But that would be to reckon without the good citizens of

Pluckley – from both ends of the village. Peter, they had decided, was innocent. It was not that the boy was universally approved of – he had been a difficult young-ster, particularly after the death of his mother; he rarely attended school and managed to get himself into more than the average number of scrapes – petty theft, vand-alism, lying . . . But never, the village agreed as one, was there any hint of violence; indeed, quite the reverse.

The result of this overwhelming dissatisfaction with the outcome of the trial was the Peter Luckhurst Defence Committee, and under this umbrella new moves were made towards reassessing the evidence. The Committee appointed a solicitor to press for a revision of the case with a view to appeal; the main grounds for the Committee's unease could be resolved into a number of questions to which no satisfactory answer could be given that would implicate Peter in the murder of which he had been convicted:

1. Why, for example, in his crucial statement did he not make any mention of cutting Miss Marshall's throat? Which in turn exposes the enigma of the knife – would he really have been naive enough to leave the bloody weapon hanging around in the kitchen for his family to find? And how did he get it home without it staining his clothes?

2. There was never any question that the clothes in which Peter was picked up by the police were the same as he wore on the day of the murder; nor had there been any attempt to clean them. But despite the pathologist's stated opinion that the killer would have been 'covered with blood', Peter's clothing was stained with so little that it was impossible to make a comparison with the victim's group.

3. How was it possible for Peter Luckhurst to carry out such an extended crime without leaving a single finger-print. He denied wearing gloves, and this is consistent with the recollections of people who saw him that day.

4. In his interview with the police Peter gave an accurate description of his tour around the house, pulling and shoving Miss Marshall with him – with one exception. He omitted the downstairs toilet, indeed when questioned

he had no knowledge of its existence. It was, however, smeared with the victim's blood.

All these points and more were to be welded into the case with which to overturn Peter's conviction.

In addition, one of the *Kentish Express* journalists, Dudley Stephens, began a newspaper campaign under the headline 'The Unanswered Questions of the Pluckley Murder'. A private detective, Brian Ford, even left his Hastings 'practice' to pursue his theory that Miss Marshall had been the victim of what he called 'a Ritual Killing'.

But Peter's case became the inevitable victim of fickle hearts and empty pockets as people lost interest and the solicitor's fees overstretched the modest Defence Fund. The appeal faded into memory, and while few villagers believe to this day that Peter is guilty, there the matter rests.

But if Peter Luckhurst did not kill Gwendoline Marshall, who did? And why did Peter confess; and how did he know so much about the crime and yet leave out crucial details that cast suspicion on that confession?

On the basis of their own first-hand researches Justine Picardie and Dorothy Wade advance a theory that offers so far the most plausible explanation of the unanswered questions:

Say Peter Luckhurst was not alone. Say he was merely an accomplice in Miss Marshall's murder, possibly even only a 'bystander'. This would explain how he knew so much about the crime, but had so little blood on his own clothes. It would explain the absence of fingerprints, and if he were not the protagonist himself, he could easily not have seen or registered the contact with the downstairs lavatory. Furthermore, if he ran away before the killer had completed his task Peter would have known nothing about the cutting of Miss Marshall's throat. But for this to be true it would mean that the murderer must be somebody that Peter knew well (and obviously feared, accounting for his silence); and besides, in a village community a stranger gets noticed. So the killer must have been known to a great many people – may be living at one end or the other of Pluckley to this day.

A footnote apropos of Peter Luckhurst's readiness to confess is the story that is told of the time when a car was vandalized in the village. Despite that fact that most of the village knew who the culprit was, a completely innocent Peter Luckhurst confessed to the crime, was taken before a juvenile court, and fined.

'NOT ALL A DREAM'*

The Murder of Eric Gordon Tombe by Ernest Dyer
In the month of April 1921 at 'The Welcomes',
Kenley, Surrey

When they left the Service at the end of the First World War, the two young Army officers remained close friends – like many others whose relationships had been cemented by the mutual hardships of active service in a war notable for its privations. It was to prove the great irony that one of these young men was to achieve what the Kaiser's army could not – the shooting of his friend.

For 25-year-old Eric Tombe and 27-year-old Ernest Dyer the world made free by the blood of their comrades was their oyster. Tombe had a healthy bank balance, and Dyer knew some ways to manipulate it. Their first business partnership – a motoring venture – quickly ran into difficulties, as did a second attempt to make a fortune out of the new mode of transport. Learning from this, they exchanged four-wheeled vehicles for four-legged ones, and in 1920 Eric's money bought them a horse-racing stable and stud farm at Kenley, in Surrey. The farmhouse was called 'The Welcomes', a name Ernest Dyer clearly took to heart when he moved in with his wife and children.

The proposition was no great success, which was in large part due to Dyer's preference for backing horses over breeding them; and there can be no doubt that this

---

* 'I had a dream which was not all a dream'

(Byron, *Darkness*)

financial instability was behind the mysterious fire which damaged 'The Welcomes' in April 1921. Dyer's claim for £12,000 was summarily rejected by the insurers, and he prudently let the matter drop. But it was no curb to Ernest's passion for spending money – he had already been borrowing heavily from Tombe, and now began to forge the young man's signature on cheques. Not unreasonably, Eric saw this as a decidedly unfriendly gesture, if not treacherous, and appropriately unfriendly words were exchanged. They may have been the last words the unlucky Eric Tombe ever uttered; it was certainly the last time that anybody remembered seeing him alive.

Although it was not a particularly intimate family, the Tombes had always enjoyed each other's company and confidence. Tombe senior was a clergyman, and both he and Eric's mother were of those advancing years when the presence of a son can be a great comfort; the sort of parents who fret when filial duty was not felt to be done. And when Eric seemed to have disappeared out of their, and everybody else's, lives without leaving a word of explanation, the family was rightly worried. The ten weeks dragged into several months and still there was no word from the errant son. A man of action, albeit eccentric, the Reverend Gordon Tombe began to insert a series of advertisements into the personal columns of newspapers: 'Anyone knowing the whereabouts . . .' etc. When these proved unproductive of the result so anxiously awaited, Tombe came to London in person and scoured the West End haunts so familiar to Eric and Ernest, the two young men-about-town; but with no conspicuous success. Then Gordon Tombe recalled a letter that he had once received from his son praising his hairdresser who operated in an establishment in London's fashionable Haymarket. Yes, the barber remembered Eric, he had been a regular, though not seen for some months now. The man also remembered Eric's pal – Dwyer was it, Eric called him? Lived somewhere down in Surrey at a place called 'The Welcomes'.

Dyer was not at home when the old clergyman called, but his wife was able, she thought, to shed some light on the disappearance of his son. Mrs Dyer recalled her husband saying he had received a telegram from Eric, excusing his absence with: 'Sorry to disappoint. Have been called overseas.'

The Rev. Tombe next felt he might benefit from an interview with young Eric's bank manager, and that gentleman received him with the consideration and sympathy that the old fellow's obvious anxiety deserved. Anxiety which, the manager assured Tombe, he could dispel that instant. Eric Tombe had been in regular touch with the bank by correspondence, and a letter had been received only recently instructing them to allow power of attorney to his partner Ernest Dyer.

The old man's relief lasted no longer than it took him to read to the bottom of the page. 'This is not my son's signature, it is a forgery.' And a consequent investigation of the bank's file on the Tombe account revealed a whole series of such forgeries – one, for example, had transferred a sum in excess of £1,000 to a Paris bank 'for the use of Ernest Dyer'. Indeed, the man Dyer seemed to have quite milked the account dry, and more besides. That the villain had fleeced his son clean was bad enough, but it began to occur to the tenacious old cleric that Dyer might also be privy to his son's disappearance. But where was Ernest Dyer? He seemed to have vanished quite as completely as Eric Tombe.

It was not until many months later, in November 1922, that the question was answered; and then only by the intervention of chance. A man calling himself Fitzsimmons had been advertising in a local Scarborough newspaper, up in Yorkshire. It was one of the oldest confidence tricks in the book – 'Contact advertiser for employment with outstanding prospects; small financial investment asked . . .' – and the district police force had tracked 'Fitzsimmons' to the Bar Hotel, Scarborough. On 16th November a detective entered the hotel and asked to see Mr Fitzsimmons, and as the man in question was escorting the policeman to a room he occupied on the upper floor he made a fatal, for him, movement; a movement that called to the detective's mind those words beloved of Hollywood – he was 'going for his gun'. The officer lunged; there was a struggle; the gun went off; and, true to movie scenario, Fitzsimmons fell limply to the floor . . .

But he wasn't Fitzsimmons at all. He was Ernest Dyer; and a search of his room uncovered a treasure trove of incriminating evidence – not least among which were a pile of cheques bearing the forged signature 'E. Tombe', and a suitcase bearing the initials 'ET'.

And what of Eric Tombe? We might suppose that the one key to his whereabouts was now beneath six feet of earth. But that would be to reckon without the supernatural: to ignore those powers which are neither explicable nor controllable – the unknown secrets of the mind.

Mrs Tombe, until now but a sad and silent bystander in this family tragedy, began to dream. She dreamed such nightmares as to wake her shouting and shaking with fear. The vision was always the same, she saw the dead body of her son lying at the bottom of a well.

It was some days before Gordon Tombe's persistence succeeded in persuading the hard-headed Francis Carlin of Scotland Yard's Murder Squad to take the dreams seriously. But before Carlin and his handful of diggers left 'The Welcomes' they took them very seriously indeed. At the bottom of a well, beneath a covering of rubble, they found the body of Eric Tombe, the back of his head removed by the blast of a shotgun.

PORTRAIT OF MURDER

The Murder of Margaret Rose Spevick by William Sanchez de Pina Hepper
Between Wednesday, 3rd and Sunday, 7th
February 1954 at Western Road, Hove, Sussex

Margaret Rose Spevick, Pearl Hepper; two names on a school register; two normal, healthy 11-year-olds whom fate had chosen to bring together in a bond of friendship. Margaret and Pearl both attended the same school in Victoria, in south-west London; they lived in the same area, not far from the school – the Spevicks at Embankment Gardens, Chelsea, the Heppers at Ormonde Gate in the same Royal borough: the Hepper family also had a seaside flatlet at Hove.

What more natural, then, than that Mrs Spevick should receive a letter on 17th January 1954, from Pearl's father, inviting Margaret down to the coast to convalesce after an unfortunate fall had resulted in a simple fracture of her arm?

William Hepper was 62, and had a modest local reputation as an artist. One of his reasons for inviting young Margot (as she was affectionately known) to stay in Hove was to paint her portrait. He had assured her mother that all Margaret's medical requirements would be attended to, and there were fond farewells when Hepper collected her from her on 3rd February, and returned to the South Coast.

On the following day Mrs Spevick received a postcard: 'Enjoying myself. Having a splendid time . . .' On Sunday of the same week, Mrs Spevick arrived, as arranged, to visit her daughter in Brighton; she had expected to be met at the station, not least because she did not know the

Heppers' address, but after two hours wait she was obliged to return on the London train, promptly visiting the Ormonde Gate house on her return. Finding no-one at home, Mrs Spevick began to feel twinges of anxiety, and with commendable sleuthing discovered the Hove address and sped back to the south coast. There she waited outside the one-room flatlet as she had previously waited at the station – in vain, and with mounting misgivings. So long did she wait that a neighbour, the tenant of another of the flats, a Mrs Holly, took pity on her evident distress and together they enlisted the help of the caretaker to get into Hepper's flat.

It was Mrs Holly's misfortune to find Margaret. She had been first into the room, first to see a child's foot sticking out from the edge of the bed: 'I pulled back the blankets,' she wept, 'and saw the little girl lying naked. She was dead.' The pitiful sight was made the more macabre by the presence, next to the bed, of an artist's easel. Propped on it was the unfinished portrait of Margaret Spevick.

The police lost little time in putting together evidence of this unhappy child's last days. Margaret had been seen with Hepper two days previously by the same Mrs Holly who had found her corpse. On that same Friday, in the evening, a Major Davey had visited Hepper and talked with the girl. Hepper had spoken of going to Gibraltar. The local police checked town and port transport along the coast, while their counterparts in London sought Hepper in his known haunts in the capital. The newspapers carried Hepper's portrait, as did the cinemas; and for only the second time in that medium's existence, police collaborated with BBC television in broadcasting the wanted man's description, the announcement being made by popular broadcaster Donald Gray.

But it was from abroad that the clue came to William Hepper's hiding-place. Friends in Gibraltar had received a card from him postmarked 'Irun', the little Spanish border town where Hepper had spent the past three days sightseeing. It was Detective Inspector Reginald Bidgood of the Hove CID who negotiated Hepper's extradition, and escorted him back from the gaol at San Sebastian where he had been detained.

On 19th July 1954 William Sanchez de Pina Hepper appeared on his trial before Mr Justice Jones. The brutal rape and murder of a child will always, and rightly, arouse public anger; add a touch of xenophobia – Hepper was half-Spanish – and a reputation as an artist (always synonymous with 'weirdos') and William Hepper must have felt a very lonely man standing there in the dock of the historic Lewes Assize court. But he had one champion: his defence was in the more than capable hands of Mr Derek Curtis-Bennett, the great Sir Henry's son.

Hepper's defence had originated as far back as the time of his extradition (if not before), when he told DI Bidgood in San Sebastian on February 20th, in reply to a request to explain Margaret's death: 'That is impossible. I cannot remember since I lost my memory in Brighton until I come round a few days ago.' On his behalf, Curtis-Bennett submitted to the court that Hepper was the victim of a mental disorder known as paranoia. Indeed, Hepper's father had died in confinement in a Madrid asylum.

Hepper's story was that, on arriving in Hove with Margaret on the evening of 3rd February, he found a letter bearing the news that his brother was dangerously ill in Spain and he would have to rush to his sick bed. Both he and Margaret were terribly unhappy that their holiday should be so truncated. He gave her a spare key, and a 10-shilling note for her fare home if she left while he was abroad. On the following evening Hepper suffered a severe attack of asthma, and went walking on the beach to take in the sea air; when he returned he took some tablets with a glass of brandy and fell into a deep sleep. What follows is Hepper's recollection of that night as he told it in the witness box:

Hepper: I had a terrible dream; I saw my wife coming into the room with a man I know very well and I got up from the chair and followed almost in the dark to the corridor outside my room.

Mr Justice Jones: Whom did you follow?

Hepper: The man. My wife stayed in the room. The man disappeared in the dark. I went back into the

room and had a discussion with my wife and
accused her of infidelity.
Mr Justice Jones: This is still a dream, isn't it?'
Hepper: Yes, my Lord . . . Then we had like a fighting, and she fell on the floor, suffering from pain
because we had a fight. Later, I woke up and found
nobody in the room. It was about six o'clock in the
morning. I took the first train to Victoria, where I
buy a ticket as far as Paris. I don't remember
reaching Spain.

Hepper's quite irrational accusations of his wife's infidelity were not entirely new to his paranoia. While he was
incarcerated in San Sebastian two months previously he
had written a very eccentric letter to the Spanish Ambassador in London, which contained the passage: 'On the
night of my wedding I bore an enormous disillusion. She
[Mrs Hepper] was not what I believed before. I continued
to love my wife madly as on the first day, but she treated
me coldly . . .' He claimed she later told him, 'My heart
always belonged to another man whom I loved with
passion. I always hated you.' Hepper had also sent a
similar letter to Dr Hugh Gainsborough, his physician
at St George's Hospital in London, which the doctor
testified he thought an untrue and scurrilous slight on a
devoted and long-suffering wife.

There was a minor drama in court the next day when
the prisoner collapsed on the ground when his name
was called. A doctor, summoned to attend him, told
Mr Justice Jones: 'I cannot find any physical cause for his
collapse. His pulse is normal. He is just lying down and
will not speak to me, and will not even co-operate to the
extent of taking smelling salts.' A genuine psychotic
attack, or a cynical attempt to give credence to his
defence?

There next followed a succession of physicians and
psychiatrists arguing for and against William Hepper's
legal culpability. Dr Alexander Willson Watt, a specialist
at the Royal County Hospital, testified that he thought
Hepper was a paranoiac; 'It is my belief', he said in
evidence, 'that on the night of February 4th, and the

morning of February 5th, Hepper was the prey of his delusions.'

This medical opinion was rebutted by prosecution witness Dr Matheson, principal medical officer at Brixton Prison, where he had had ample opportunity to examine the accused and members of his family during Hepper's remand awaiting trial. He had concluded that the prisoner was not, at the time of the crime or since, legally insane.

The jury took just under an hour and a half to find Hepper guilty of Margaret Spevick's murder. Asked if he had anything to say before sentence was passed, the prisoner replied: 'I think it is quite unfaithful – I mean, incorrect, I did not do it.'

On 11th August, William Hepper, the man who, according to his own account, had been a successful wool merchant, a translator for the BBC, a spy for the United States Intelligence Service, a key figure in the International Brigades during the Spanish Civil War, and an exhibiting artist of at least passable talent, was hanged at Wandsworth Prison. There is no doubt that he was the killer of little Margaret Spevick. What is in doubt, perhaps, is his mental accountability for the crime; for if he was not insane, then he could have convincingly added acting to his list of creative achievements.

NORMAN'S WATCHWORDS

**The Murder of Elsie Cameron by John
Norman Holmes Thorne
On Friday 5th December 1924 at his Wesley
Poultry Farm, Crowborough, East Sussex**

———————————

They say that it is always a mistake to trifle with the affections of women, and that many men throughout history have discovered it to their cost.

At the time he paid for his mistake, in 1924, Norman Thorne was 24 years of age. He left the Services, where he had enlisted as a mechanic in the Royal Naval Air Service at the end of the Great War, and took similar civilian employment with a firm of engineers. The business failed in 1922 and Norman found himself in the dole queue, with plenty of time on his hands but precious few prospects. He was living with his father at this time on the outskirts of London, and whiling away a great deal of his life in the company of Miss Elsie Cameron, a girl about his own age with whom he shared an enthusiasm for God's more eccentric manifestations in the form of Wesleyan Methodism and the Band of Hope. It was with her characteristic enthusiasm that Elsie embraced Norman's proposal of marriage.

But marriages, made in Heaven though they may be, still require at least a basic earthly funding. And it may have been with this in mind that Norman embarked upon his rather basic enterprise. Buying a small field in Crowborough with £100 of his father's money he set himself up as the Wesley Poultry Farm, eschewing the comforts of the parental home for a seven-by-twelve wooden hut in the middle of the chicken runs. With Norman, all his belongings, and probably a few chickens strayed off-course the hut was less basic than squalid, a domestic disaster that was to serve as Norman's fortress for two years. With the blindness of true love, Elsie Cameron became a regular guest at the hut: she was filled with an unreasoning optimism that found expression in one of the many letters exchanged by the couple:

> 'Our courtship is like a fairy-tale and will it end with "they lived happily ever after"? . . . Oh my treasure, how I adore you' . . . if only we could get married. Oh pet, lets try to do so this year . . . We can manage in a little hut like yours: your Elsie is quite well now and there is no fear of any children for three or four years . . .'

By November she was making claims of impending motherhood, and began to press Norman with greater urgency to fulfil his vows.

He resisted. She insisted.

Norman, you see, had found a new passion. It came in the person of a young dressmaker named Bessie Coldicott whom he had met at a local dance and who had occupied his heart and his bed frequently since. But if chapel had taught Norman one thing it was honesty. He might be two-timing his fiancée, but he could not conceal it from her. He wrote to Elsie on 25th November 1924 after she had made another attempt to browbeat Norman into wedlock:

> 'You seem to be taking everything for granted . . . There are one or two things I haven't told you . . . it concerns someone else . . . I am afraid I am between two fires.'

Elsie replied by return admonishing her swain for his cruelty, adding that 'this worry is very bad for the baby'. She concluded: 'I really think an explanation is due to me over all this.'

Obligingly, if clumsily, Norman explained:

> 'What I haven't told you is that on certain occasions a girl has been here late at night . . . She thinks I am

going to marry her; of course I have a strong feeling for her or I shouldn't have done what I have . . .'

Elsie's response was understandable if unoriginal:

'You have absolutely broken my heart. I never thought you were capable of such deception . . . You are engaged to me and I have first claim on you . . . Well, Norman, I expect you to marry me, and finish with the other girl as soon as possible. My baby must have a name.'

On 30th November, Elsie took her complaint in person to Crowborough, where Norman, with apologies and further vague promises of wedding bells, managed to get rid of her before his appointment with Bessie.

But Elsie was a persistent girl; stubborn, some might say obstinate. Determined once and for all to get a firm date for matrimony out of her reluctant fiancé she left her home at 86 Clifford Gardens, Kensal Rise, on 5th December en route for Crowborough via Victoria station.

It gives some indication of the laissez-faire attitude of Elsie's parents that it was five days before they began to wonder whether she was all right. It was only on 10th December that Mr Duncan Cameron sent an almost apologetic telegram: 'Elsie left Friday have heard no news has she arrived reply.' Cameron pondered Norman's reply – 'Not here open letters cannot understand' – for a day or so, and then informed the police of his daughter's disappearance.

Despite Norman's evident enthusiasm for showing the investigating officers around his home and estate, and posing willingly for the coterie of press photographers that had joined the bandwagon, the only clue to emerge was the recollection of two nurserymen of seeing a young woman of Elsie's description walking towards the farm at about 5.30pm on the day of her disappearance. Confronted with this, Norman could only reiterate his willingness to help in any way he could, but regretted that the flower-growers must have been mistaken.

Meanwhile, when he was not offering useful hints to the

police, it was Bessie Coldicott who was receiving the best of Norman's attentions. On New Year's Eve he wrote:

> 'My darling Bessie . . . I have been in love twice . . . [but] Honour bright, darling, I never felt for any girl as I do for you . . . No one knows the struggle that has raged within but, dearest of pals, you have pulled me through. Love, Honour, Bessie; my watchwords for '25.'

Scotland Yard were less gullible than their country counterparts when it came to Norman Thorne, and within days of Chief Inspector Gillan's arrival in Crowborough, Thorne was under arrest. While he was 'helping the police with their inquiries' they were digging up his chicken farm. At 8.30 next morning, 15th January, Elsie's pathetic little attaché case was unearthed. It was sufficient for DCI Gillan to feel confident enough to start putting the frighteners on Norman. That evening he made a statement in which he confided that he had known all along that Elsie was dead; told them where to dig her up. But he emphatically denied having been the instrument of her death. The truth according to Norman went something like this: he was having his afternoon tea when Elsie arrived at the hut (the nurserymen, on reflection, must have been right!) Over tea and bread and butter Elsie had outlined her plans for the immediate future. She intended to stay in the hut until Norman married her! After a few hours of intermittent threats and recriminations, Norman left a very belligerent fiancée in the hut while he went out (probably in search of Love, Honour, and Bessie). When he returned at around 11.30pm he found Elsie swinging from the roof beam on the end of a washing-line.

Cutting her down with trembling hands, Norman realized that Elsie's immortal soul was now in the hands of the angels. His own fate, he came quickly to realize, was somewhat less certain; they had been known to quarrel – indeed, they had spent the better part of that day squabbling – what if people should think he drove poor Elsie to her final desperate act? They might even think that he . . .

Out of sight, out of mind, mused Norman; and hopefully out of trouble too. Using the hut as a makeshift operating theatre, and his handyman's hacksaw, Norman set about rendering Miss Cameron a little less – bulky. The pieces he wrapped in newspaper and interred beneath one of the chicken runs – 'the first pen inside the gate'. Which is exactly where, by lamplight, the police unearthed her.

This, then, was Norman's story; the story to which he stuck throughout his trial; stuck to loyally in the face of the strongest evidence to the contrary.

The trial was held in the historic Assize Court at Lewes, and opened before Mr Justice Finlay on 4th March. Thorne was lucky to have the services of Mr J.D. Cassels KC who, if anyone could, might have been able to help Norman out of this mess. The redoubtable Sir Henry Curtis-Bennett led for the Crown, with a formidable ally in Sir Bernard Spilsbury, the Home Office pathologist who was to present the medical evidence for the prosecution.

If the Thorne version of events were true, pondered Sir Bernard – that Elsie Cameron had been hanging for some time on a rope from a beam – then it must have been a very extraordinary rope indeed to have left no single trace on either beam or neck. There was a more plausible cause of death; Spilsbury was convinced that Elsie had died of shock following a severe beating – evidenced by the bruised state of the head and body; compounded by a savage blow to the forehead which could conceivably have been delivered by one of the Indian clubs found in the hut. At any rate, the jury favoured this explanation and Norman Thorne, to his utter disbelief, was sentenced to hang.

And hang he did, at Wandsworth Prison on 22nd April 1925. Ironically, it would have been Elsie's 27th birthday.

Thorne never confessed, and so for all we may ever know, Elsie Cameron could have had a hand in her own death as Norman had insisted. One thing that we can be sure about is that the dismemberment was no flash of inspiration, for found among the piles of junk in his hut was a collection of newspaper cuttings relating to the case of Patrick Mahon. Patrick Mahon had been tried in the Lewes court only months previously on a charge of murdering and dismembering an inconveniently pregnant girl-friend who was pressing for 'marriage'.

But there was one difference. One fact that had Norman known it might have saved both his own and Elsie Cameron's life. When Sir Bernard Spilsbury examined the remains that had been taken from the earth at the Wesley Poultry Farm, he was able to state categorically that Elsie was not, and never had been, pregnant.

NORTH-WEST ENGLAND

Cumbria

Cheshire

Greater Manchester

Lancashire

Merseyside

POINTS OF LAW

The Murder of Ivy Lydia Wood by Arthur Beard
On Friday, 25th July 1919 at the Carfield Mills, Hyde, Cheshire

---

Arthur Beard was one of those killers for whom no punishment could really have matched his sordid, brutal crime. He had been found guilty of a drunken rape committed on a 13-year-old on 25th July 1919 during the course of which the poor girl was suffocated. When sentence of death was passed on Beard at the Chester Assizes in October there can have been few who felt sorry to lose him, and the whole sad affair should quickly have passed from public notice, leaving only the bereaved with wounds that would not heal so easily.

Beard had been employed as watchman at the Carfield Mills and his shift comprised the twelve hours between 6 o'clock in the evening and 6 o'clock in the following morning; during this period he was the factory's sole occupant.

On the evening of 25th July young Ivy Wood had returned from school only to be sent out again on an errand for her father, a trip that took her to Mr Francis Booth's shop to purchase some umbrella ferrules. She was seen by a youth named Ernest Gosling as she passed through the gates of Carfield Mills, and apart from her killer the boy was the last person to see her alive.

Earlier on the 25th, Arthur Beard had spent his time drinking at the Great War Comrades Club in the company of Charles Jones; when they parted Beard purchased a bottle of whisky. Between 6.30 and 7.00 that evening Jones called at the mill to collect his friend on their way to the Navigation Hotel and a meeting of the Engine and Firemen's Union which Arthur Beard was particularly keen to join.

When Beard emerged a Member at 9.00pm he took a quick drink with a colleague before returning to the mill and the job from which he had taken French leave.

At 1.30am Samuel Bower, the watchman of a neighbouring mill was startled out of his nap by a frantic Arthur Beard, somewhat the worse for drink, mumbling: 'I'm in a mess . . . I have found a girl pegged out . . . I was in the grounds near the dining room . . . I carried her on my back to the lodge.'

Shortly before 2 o'clock police constable Vernon arrived on the scene in response to the watchmen's call. He saw the dead girl, and noted that Beard's trousers were soiled with clay, particularly around the knees; this Beard accounted for by saying that he fell while carrying the dead girl. Later, while Beard was showing the Chief Constable where he had discovered the corpse, the watchman claimed that his trousers had been dirtied when he climbed an embankment to inspect the reservoir behind it.

On 26th July Inspector Neal made a thorough search of the mill and in the cellar found signs of a fierce struggle; some of the tiles were chipped and revealed blood stains to which were attached hairs of the same colour as the late Ivy Woods. Dirt on the girl's clothing and on Arthur Beard's proved to be similar to that coating the cellar tiles, and further incriminating evidence turned up a week later in the form of three metal umbrella ferrules – identified by Mr Booth as those bought by Ivy for her father on the evening of her disappearance.

Meanwhile a post-mortem had been conducted by Dr Smith, who found that death had been due to suffocation; and that Ivy had been sexually violated.

After passing sentence the judge made an unprecedented address to the court:

'I see this court is full of men – young men and old men. I want to say this solemn word to you all. You have just witnessed the trial of a man of good connection and of good upbringing. You can see to what a pass drink has brought him. I want to beg you, with all the force I can put into my words, to take warning by this example, and for God's sake keep away from drink.'

But Arthur Beard was not going to the rope without a struggle, and that struggle was to stir the legal system right up to the House of Lords. The fact was emphasized that Beard was drunk at the time he committed his dreadful crime. Now some might have thought that that was no extenuation – merely aggravating an already unforgivable crime; but for Beard's legal defenders it represented a possible mitigating circumstance; if he was intoxicated, the lawyers argued, how could he be capable of forming the intention to kill? Where was the 'malice aforethought' required to be proved before a person can be convicted of murder? Where indeed, agreed the Court of Criminal Appeal, and reduced the conviction to one of manslaughter, and the sentence to one of 20 years.

Perhaps echoing the unspoken feelings of an outraged nation the Crown, in the persons of Beard's prosecutors led by Sir Gordon Hewart KC, MP, the Attorney-General, and Sir Ernest Pollock KC, MP (the Solicitor-General), took the matter still higher – as high, in fact, as it could go. On 5th March 1920 Arthur Beard once again sat on trial, a wretched and insignificant figure in the awesome splendour of the highest court in the land, the House of Lords: a man barely aware that some of the finest legal minds in the country were debating the continuance of his miserable life.

From the Woolsack the Lord Chancellor, Lord Birkenhead, voiced the Court's ruling: that Arthur Beard may well have been too drunk to form the intention to kill, but he was clearly and provably not too drunk to intend to rape, and as death was the direct result of an intended felony then Beard must be guilty of murder. Ironically, Lord Reading (who had upheld Beard's appeal in the Court of Criminal Appeal), now effectively reversed his previous judgment by concurring with the Lord Chancellor's decision.

In the event, even the unworthy Arthur Beard was the recipient of mercy; the Home Secretary ordered a reprieve, and 31-year-old Beard was returned to his long term of imprisonment.

THE PEAT BOG MYSTERY

The Killing of Lindow Man (called 'Pete Marsh') by Assassins Unknown
Around 300BC-AD100 on Lindow Moss, Cheshire

The investigation which follows does not conform to the familiar pattern of most of the murders which comprise this book. For a start there are no names, and there is no date for the crime – at least no date accurate within a couple of centuries; there is no provable motive, no accused, no trial, and no retribution.

But there is forensic detective work to rival the greatest cases of a Bernard Spilsbury, or a Francis Camps. This is the strange case of Lindow Man – called affectionately 'Pete Marsh' after his place of discovery.

Finding the Body

Lindow Moss is a bleak, scrub-covered marsh in the north-east of Cheshire, below Altrincham. It has been common land since the Middle Ages, and its peat has provided winter fuel for centuries. Large areas of the marsh are now being cut commercially, and it was one of the crews on the mechanical excavators that unearthed the body.

On 1st August 1984 Andy Mould and Eddie Slack were standing by the elevator to the peat-shredding mill when Mould threw off the conveyor what he thought was a block of wood. When its fall to the ground knocked off a covering layer of peat, the block of wood turned out to be a human foot. Both the local police and the county archaeologist were summoned, and both made a priority of locating the rest of the body. By 6th August it had been established that this was no ordinary victim of violence or accident, but another prehistoric corpse,* preserved over centuries by the chemical action of the peat. The valuable find was dug out without delay and removed to the mortuary attached to Macclesfield District Hospital.

It was not long before Pete Marsh was being accorded all the attention to which his venerable age (about two thousand years) and historical importance entitled him. A team of the country's top archaeological specialists was assembled under the benign auspices of the British Museum to extract every last piece of valuable information on the life, death and habits of our ancestors. Among the experts was forensic specialist Dr Ian West.

Discovery of a Murder

As the peat was painstakingly removed from around the body, it became increasingly apparent that Lindow Man had been the victim of a violent death, and although there remains some doubt as to the pre- or post-mortem origin of some of the signs of trauma, there is sufficient corroborative evidence to indicate an overwhelming measure of foul play. Furthermore, there was evidence of a multiplicity of deliberate injuries any one of which could have been responsible for the bog man's death:

1. *Stab wound to the chest:* Forensic examination was unable to confirm absolutely that this was a deliberately inflicted wound, though its straight and clean cut was consistent with the appearance of a stabbing.

2. *Bludgeoning:* After the peat had been cleared from the head, wounds were apparent that indicated a severe battering. Blows from some blunt instrument had split the scalp in two places and had been delivered with enough force to shatter the skull, driving fragments of bone into the brain.

3. *Asphyxia due to strangulation:* The most intriguing

* On 13th May of the previous year the body of a woman – called Lindow Woman – had been unearthed little more than 250 metres from the present discovery. By coincidence it had been found by Andy Mould.

evidence of foul play could be seen when the area around the neck was cleaned and examined. What at first was thought to be a length of root fibre caught in the folds of skin proved to be a ligature made from two twisted and knotted strands of sinew. Rather than a decorative necklace, it was clear from the way in which the thong had bitten into the flesh of the neck that it had been used in the manner of a garrotte. The abnormal angle at which the neck had set, and the two broken cervical vertebrae seemed to lend credence to the strangulation theory.

4. *Cut Throat:* During the examination of the neck region and the thong associated with it, another potentially fatal wound was discovered on the right side of the throat. Certainly there was every evidence to suggest a human agency behind the cut, though whether the intention had been to kill or merely to bleed the victim is uncertain.

If only two of the wounds discovered had been inflicted with the intention to kill, it represents one hundred per cent overkill by comparison with most murderers; but if all four wounds had been deliberately inflicted then a very strange story indeed must lie behind the death of the bog man.

Who and Why?

Who Pete Marsh was we are unlikely ever to know; we can merely conjecture on the basis of what few clues are available. It is likely that the bog victim was a man of some importance judging by the uncommonly neat appearance of his trimmed beard – this kind of shaping is not known on other bog people – and the well-tended fingernails exhibiting rudimentary manicure. Incongruously, Lindow Man was naked but for a fox fur armband, and so unlike many prehistoric burials it is impossible to guess at social status on the basis of the quality or style of clothing.

That Lindow Man was murdered is certain. For what reason he was murdered is a puzzling mystery. Assuming that he was not the victim of Iron Age footpads, each of whom tried to kill him in a different way and then robbed him even of his clothes, what other explanation could fit the bizarre facts on which an explanation must be based?

One plausible theory fitting the known facts is that Pete Marsh was the subject – willing or unwilling – of an elaborate ritual sacrifice; certainly this provides the most comfortable explanation for the catalogue of potentially fatal wounds which he suffered. This hypothesis of ritual murder is one that has been advanced in earlier studies of the bog people, and in particular by the celebrated Danish expert Professor P.V. Glob, to whom we give the final word:

> 'Surveying the vast corpus of finds from Denmark's Early Iron Age and relating to our knowledge of the numerous discoveries of bog people, it emerges clearly that the circumstances of the bog people's deposition shows nothing in common with normal burial customs, but on the contrary have many of the characteristics of the sacrificial deposits. Probably, then, the bog people were offered to the same powers as the other bog finds, and belong to the gods . . . Naturally we must except from this inter-pretation those who ended their days in the bog by accident, such as those who went astray in fog or rain and were drowned one dark autumn day. We must also except those who were murdered and hidden in bogs, away from the beaten track. Several such are known amongst the bog people; but by far the greatest number of the bog people, where proper observations are recorded, bear the stamp of sacri-ficial offerings.'

> (*The Bog People*, P.V. Glob)

Lindow Man is now on permanent display at the British Museum, though ownership has been contested by Manchester University Museum. Despite Manchester's enthu-siastic campaign organized by Barbara O'Brien and supported by a number of northern Members of Parlia-ment, the BM's director, Sir David Wilson, is adamant that Lindow Man remains the capital's treasure trove.

'I WISH I COULD STAY HERE FOR EVER'

The Manslaughter of Mrs Margaret Hogg by her husband Peter Hogg

On Sunday, 17th October 1976 at their home in Mead Road, Cranleigh, Surrey and his disposal of the body in Wast Water lake, Cumbria

---

To 21-year-old Veronique Marré, an agricultural student from Sceaux, near Paris, the English Lakes were a glimpse of paradise. In July 1983, Veronique wrote enthusiastic postcards to her family and friends in France, from Wasdale's youth hostel: 'The country is beautiful. I wish I could stay here for ever'. It was a morbidly prophetic sentiment, for Mademoiselle Marré was never seen again after leaving the village pub and striking off towards Wast Water.

Ironically, Wast Water is not one of Lakeland's more attractive bodies of water, and the four-mile stretch of its bleak surface hides a perilous depth of hundreds of feet of inky darkness. It was the forbidding depth that had prevented police frogmen from searching the bottom of Wast Water for the missing French girl, though they continued to monitor the lake throughout the summer and winter lest a body should be found floating. Then in February 1984 an amateur diver named Nigel Prith reported seeing a bundle lying on a ledge about a hundred feet below the surface of Wast Water. Frogmen returned to the icy waters once again, and on 29th February, a hundred yards out from the shore, they found the 'bundle'.

From the thick deposit of slimy green vegetable matter that was enveloping the bulky parcel, it seemed to have been in the lake longer than the seven months since

Veronique Marré's disappearance, and when officers opened the plastic wrapping and exposed the half-naked body of a woman they knew that this was an unexpected find – not a petite French student, but a plump middle-aged stranger.

It is a comforting fact of police routine that most bodies are identified sooner or later, and with a greater or lesser degree of forensic detective work – even those remains that are so scant as to defy visual recognition. But in the case of the Lady of the Lake it came much sooner than anybody could have hoped. The clue was on the dead woman's finger in the form of a wedding ring; undistinguished on the outside, the inner surface had been engraved with the inscription 'Margaret 11.11.63 Peter'. More than 300 miles to the south, in Guildford, Mrs Gillian Seddon read the first reports of the killing in her newspaper, and was able to tell police that she had once acted as housekeeper to a couple named Hogg – Margaret and Peter Hogg; they had been married on 11th November 1963. Irrefutable corroborative evidence from dental records confirmed the identification of the corpse, and Scotland Yard's Murder Squad under Detective Chief Inspector Timothy Blake set about piecing together the story which ended in the freezing waters of a Cumbrian lake.

Peter Hogg, they learned, was alive and well and living in Mead Road, Cranleigh. When Hogg, an airline pilot, had married Margaret she was an air stewardess, and the couple had lived near Luton Airport; subsequently they moved to Cranleigh, where Margaret gave up the air to run a restaurant that they had bought in the Surrey village. Hogg continued his flying career, and even enjoyed a brief moment of celebrity in 1974 when he 'rescued' 385 British holidaymakers stranded in Nova Scotia when their tour company Court Lines went bankrupt. But while Peter was flying the air lanes of the world his wife was enjoying her own flights of fancy – in the person of a wealthy bank executive whom she had met in Los Angeles. While most women seek to draw a veil of discretion over their indiscretions, Margaret Hogg seemed incapable of keeping her affair with Graham Ryan to herself; least of all was it hidden from Peter Hogg, who was able to keep an accurate diary of his wife's amours.

Then quite suddenly, in the middle of October 1976, 37-year-old Mrs Hogg disappeared. Her husband reported Margaret missing and told the police that she had probably run away with Graham Ryan; he then instituted divorce proceedings naming Ryan as co-respondent and charging his legal costs to the amorous financier.

On 4th March Peter Hogg was arrested and charged with the murder of his wife, the concealment of her body, and making false statements when filing for divorce. At his trial at the Old Bailey Hogg (now aged 57) pleaded not guilty to murder, and through his defence counsel, Mr Patrick Back QC, offered a defence of provocation. Describing the events leading up to the killing on Sunday 17th October 1976, Peter Hogg said that his wife had spent the previous week with Graham Ryan at a cottage in Dorset, had returned the day before (Saturday), and had spent most of that Sunday in Ryan's company. When she returned home her husband was alone – the au pair had a day off, their youngest son was staying with friends and the eldest was away at boarding school. After an angry row which quickly developed into a physical brawl Peter Hogg, in a moment of blind fury, put his hands round his wife's neck and squeezed. Hastily parcelling up the late Margaret Hogg in some plastic sheets bound with wire, Hogg packed the body into the boot of his car. He now approached the dual problem of disposing of the body and establishing an alibi. On Monday, 18th October Hogg telephoned his son's boarding school in Taunton and made arrangements to pick the boy up for the impending half-term, giving the impression that he would stay in Taunton overnight and return the following morning. In reality Peter Hogg drove the 350 miles through the night to the Lake District, rowed a dinghy out into the freezing mist that hung over Wast Water and dumped his wife's body into the deeps weighted with a block of concrete. Had he known it, he need only have rowed another 25ft where the floor of the lake sloped dramatically down into ten black fathoms, and the body would never have been found. Told by police that they

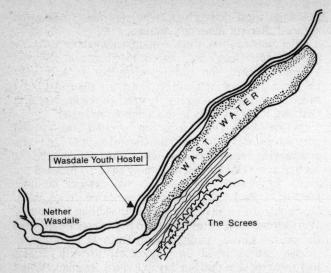

had come upon Margaret's remains by chance while searching for the French girl, Hogg is said to have replied: 'That was unlucky, wasn't it?'

Evidence at the trial – including that of Mr Ryan – was revealing of the gross manner in which Margaret Hogg had flaunted her affair at her husband, and the sympathy of the court was reflected in the reduced verdict of guilty of manslaughter and the comparatively light sentence of 4 years' imprisonment. Even so, Peter Hogg had discovered that it is impossible to run away from justice – even after ten years.

The question is, how long will it be before the mystery of Veronique Marré is solved?

1   Hawley Harvey Crippen: Age 50, 5ft. 3″ or 4″, complexion fresh, hair light brown, inclined sandy, scanty, bald on
top, rather long scanty moustache, somewhat straggly, eyes
grey, bridge of nose rather flat, false teeth, medium build,
throws his feet outwards when walking ... somewhat
slovenly appearance, wears his hat rather at back of
head. Very plausible and quiet spoken, remarkably cool
and collected demeanour.
(Metropolitan Police description of Crippen issued July
1910)
[see 'The Hen-Pecked Killer'. p.7.]

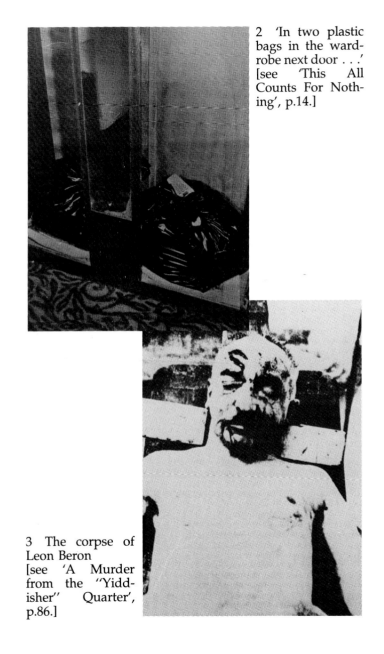

2 'In two plastic bags in the wardrobe next door . . .'
[see 'This All Counts For Nothing', p.14.]

3 The corpse of Leon Beron
[see 'A Murder from the "Yiddisher" Quarter', p.86.]

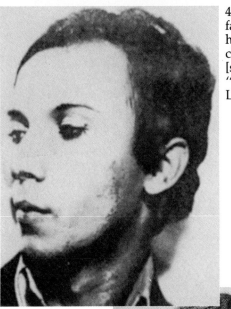

4 Maxwell Confait, *left*, and as his *alter ego* 'Michelle'
[see 'The Full "Rigor" of the Law', p.53.]

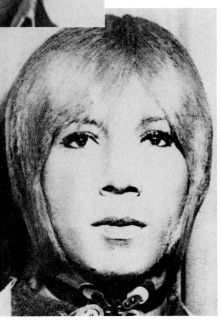

5 The real Ronald True?
[see 'The Real Ronald True', p.97.]

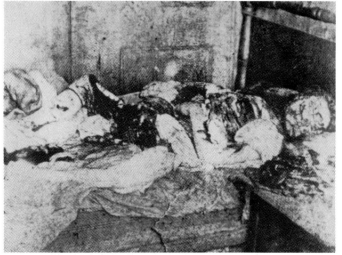

6 Mary Kelly as she was discovered in Miller's Court
[see 'Catch Me When You Can', p.113.]

7 Portrait of John Reginald Christie by Philip Youngman Carter. The artist recorded: 'I would say that the man was the nearest thing I have ever encountered to unadulterated evil . . . Two days' association with [the picture] made me almost physically sick, and the woman cleaning my studio, who had no idea about the subject of the portrait, asked me to put it away whilst she was working because it was frightening . . .'
[see 'The Problems of "Reggie No-Dick".', p.133.]

8 Sidney Harry Fox [see 'The Misdeeds of a Lovely Boy', p.193.]

9 The body of Miss Gwendoline Marshall lying in her garden shed
[see 'The Pluckley Enigma', p.200.]

10 Norman's Castle, the hut at Wesley Poultry Farm
[see 'Norman's Watchwords'. p.216.]

11 Elsie Cameron, Norman Thorne, and (inset) Bessie Coldicott. [see 'Portrait of Murder', p.211.]

12 The body of Olive Balchin lying where it was found in Cumberland Street
[see 'The Innocent that Suffered?', p.241.]

THE LAST TWO TO HANG

**The Murder of John Alan West by Peter
Anthony Allen and Gwynne Owen Evans
(real name John Robson Welby)
On Wednesday, 7th April 1964 at his home at
28 King's Avenue, Workington, Cumbria**

As if to prove that every silver lining has a cloud,
England's justly famous Lake District has Workington. It's not that there is anything intrinsically wrong with
the town – it was once a thriving jewel of industrial
progress. But that glory is past, and has left behind it a
layer of soot that seems indelible. In a word, Workington
is drab. And its suburbs no less so.

Seaton used to be a village; now it is one of Workington's suburbs, and one of the main roads that thrusts a
grey finger through it was named King's Avenue – to
celebrate the crowning of George VI in 1936. The street
that joins it is named Coronation Avenue.

At 3am on 7th April 1964, Joseph Hardon Fawcett, a
retired insurance inspector, and his wife had been sleeping soundly before being awakened by what Fawcett later
described as 'heavy thuds, as though something was
hitting the foundations of the house'. He also recollected
'a shrill scream'; the scream was followed by a couple of
lighter thuds. The noise whatever it was, came from next
door. Joseph Fawcett got up, and as he dressed was aware
of a car engine starting up and the vehicle driving away.

When he got to the porch of No.28 King's Avenue,
Mr Fawcett found the front and then the back door locked,
and he received no reply to his knocking. By this time
another neighbour, Walter Lister, had arrived, and it was

Mr Lister who telephoned through to Workington police station. Shortly after 3.30am Sergeant James Park and Constable John Rogers pulled their police minibus up outside No.28 King's Avenue. In minutes Mrs Fawcett had retrieved the spare key from its hiding-place in a box of nails in the garage, and Sergeant Park and Joseph Fawcett entered the front door. Park was later to write in his report:

> 'I saw the body of a man lying on the floor at the foot
> of the stairs. The body was on its back, dressed only
> in a shirt and vest. The body was at an angle to the
> staircase. There were obvious severe head injuries.
> There was a large amount of blood on the floor, and
> the man was obviously dead. There was also quite a
> lot of blood on the staircase, and it appeared that a
> struggle had taken place.'

After making a quick search of the house to satisfy himself that the intruder had fled, the Sergeant radioed in for assistance.

The victim, John Alan West, was a 53-year-old van driver for the Lakeland Laundry. He was unmarried, and since the death of his mother at the advanced age of 80 some nine months previously, West had lived alone in the house. John West was Workington in microcosm – hard-working and reliable (he was immensely proud of the engraved gold watch with which his employers had rewarded his long service), but unremarkable and a little colourless. Though this could hardly be considered an adequate reason to bludgeon and stab him to death.

At 4.30 Inspector John Leslie Gibson of the Cumberland and Westmorland Constabulary was at the scene of the crime accompanied by Detective Constable Fred Smith. A search of the house revealed a raincoat that clearly did not belong to John West: it had a medallion in one of the pockets inscribed 'G.O. Evans, July, 1961'. With it was a piece of paper with the scribbled name and address of Norma O'Brien of Liverpool.

Soon Miss O'Brien was telling Inspector Gibson who Gwynne (called 'Ginger') Owen Evans was, and where he could be found. And so, less than 48 hours after the murder Ginger Evans was in police custody. So was his friend – the one who was found with a gold wrist-watch in his pocket engraved with the names of John Alan West and Lakeland Laundry, and a message to the effect that the former had served the latter for twenty-five years; his name was Peter Anthony Allen.

When Allen and Evans (who was charged in his real name of John Robson Welby) stood in the dock at Manchester Crown Court in June 1964, there were few who could give them much comfort – not even each other, Evans had already blamed everything on his 'pal'. Ginger, it turned out, had once worked with John West, and with Peter Allen for moral support had gone to his house that night to try to borrow money. They had even taken along Allen's wife and children for the car ride!

A squalid, easily forgettable crime. A crime such as one might, perhaps, expect to take place on the grey outskirts of a faded, industrial town. And it was almost certainly its lacklustre qualities which led to an obvious lack of interest in the final act of the drama: the carrying out of the sentence of death – for Peter Allen at Liverpool's Walton Prison, for Evans at Strangeways, Manchester.

In hindsight the executions of Allen and Evans were of some significance, but on those high-summer mornings of August 1964, it was difficult to find any mention in the Press of the macabre activities taking place behind the high walls of the two prisons.

Ten years previously, in July 1955, the execution of Ruth Ellis ('The Last Woman to Hang') at Holloway Prison for the murder of her lover David Blakely was greeted with howls of protest, and concerted press interest kept her case on the front pages till her last breath. The powerful voice of 'Cassandra' (Sir William Connor) of the *Daily Mirror* whose article headed 'The Woman Who Hangs This Morning' brought half a nation to tears [see page 50], was notably silent on the impending demise of the two Workington killers. Indeed, the *Mirror* recorded the event in nine lines – most of which dealt with the 'silent meditation protest' led by a Preston curate.

For the record, the following 'report' embodies all that

could be found and threaded together from national and northern local newspapers of 13th August 1964:

PROTESTS OVER TWO HANGINGS

The two dairymen sentenced to death at Manchester Crown Court on July 7 for the capital murder of a laundry-van driver were executed today at separate prisons.

Today as Evans was executed at 8am only a handful of people waited outside the main door of the prison in Southall Street, Manchester. There was no demonstration.

THREE CITY VIGIL

An all-night vigil outside Walton Prison was kept by two anti-capital punishment supporters. Mr Robert Burt of Portishead, Somerset, and Mr Roger Moody of Bristol. They carried banners, one reading 'No More Hanging' and the other 'Why Take Another Life?' In Leeds 16 people held a half-hour vigil. Bristol opponents of hanging stood silent and bare headed outside their cathedral.

The mothers of the men yesterday sent a telegram to the Queen at Balmoral pleading for clemency on account of their sons' ages [both were in their twenties].

Although they would never know it, Peter Anthony Allen and Gwynne Owen were making history. They were the last people in Britain to suffer the sentence of death.

On 9th November 1965 a Bill was enacted that suspended capital punishment for a trial period of five years. On 16th December 1969 Parliament re-affirmed its commitment to abolition.

THE INNOCENT THAT SUFFERED?*

The Trial, Appeal, and Execution of Walter Graham Rowland for the Murder of Olive Balchin
Early on Sunday morning, 20th October 1946 at Cumberland Street, Manchester and the confession of David John Ware to the same crime

The people of Manchester had had enough of violence and death by 1946. Parts of the city had been laid waste by the bombs of the Luftwaffe with fatal consequences for hundreds of families; there were few whose lives had not been touched by the tragedy of losing a relative or friend in action. But now with the indomitable good humour and determination of a people fighting a common cause, efforts were being made to get back to some kind of normality; like much of the rest of the world, Manchester was getting on with the job of rebuilding for peace.

One of the most severely war-damaged areas of the city was around Deansgate, among Manchester's best known and busiest shopping streets right in the heart of town. Late on the morning of Sunday, 20th October 1946, a woman's dead body was found on a bomb site in Cumberland Street close to where it joined Deansgate. The body had been found by two young boys who had informed a passer-by, Mr James Acarnley, who in turn summoned the police.

*'It is better that ten guilty persons escape than one innocent suffer.' (*Commentaries on the Laws of England*, Sir William Blackstone, 1769.)

At 11.45pm Detective Inspector Frank Stainton took charge of what was obviously a case of brutal murder; the woman's head had been savagely smashed by repeated blows from a blunt instrument – almost certainly the bloodstained hammer found beside her body. Dr Charles Evans Jenkins, who conducted the post-mortem, described the woman as aged between forty and fifty with yellow hair turning grey; the injuries to her head which in some places had exposed the brain were consistent with the hammer being the murder weapon. It was in Dr Jenkins's opinion 'improbable' that the killer could have escaped extensive bloodstaining. The dead woman was fully dressed and in possession of a ten-shilling note and some loose change and an identity card naming her as Olive Balchin.

The following morning Mr Norman Mercer, the licensee of The Dog and Partridge at 298 Deansgate, reported that on the previous day, Saturday the 19th, he had been walking his dog at around midnight. Almost at the corner of Deansgate and Cumberland Street he saw a man and a woman arguing. Mercer was subsequently able to identify both the body and the coat it was wearing as the woman he had seen. Her companion was 'a man 30 to 35 years of age, 5ft 7ins tall, of proportionate build, full round face, clean-shaven, dark hair, dressed in a blue suit; clean and tidy appearance.'

Police also published details and a photograph of the hammer thought to be the murder weapon, and within hours Edward MacDonald came forward to say that he had sold the hammer from his broker's shop at 3 Downing Street, Ardwick. The tool was identified by MacDonald as of the type used by leather-dressers, and it had been bought for 3/6 at just after 5.30pm on Saturday the 19th. Mr MacDonald had entered into conversation with his customer over the suitability of such an oddly shaped hammer for 'general purposes', and was able to provide a fairly detailed description of the man: '28 to 32 years of age, 5ft 7 or 8ins in height, medium build, very pale face, thin features, clean-shaven, quiet spoken, no hat, white soft collar and shirt, dark tie, dark suit, and a dark fawn cotton raincoat. He was of clean and respectable appearance.'

A few days later, during routine inquiries in the area around Deansgate, officers interviewed Mrs Elizabeth Copley, a waitress at the Queen's Cafe in Queen Street. On the night of Saturday 19th October she was on duty between 10.00 and 11.00pm. She remembered that two women and a man came in together – an old woman, a young woman she identified as Olive Balchin (who, it transpired, was a prostitute), and a young man who she thought carried a small brown paper parcel, thin and about a foot long.

So, the police reasoned, this 'young man' having purchased a hammer which was of no practical use outside the leather trade, picked up (or met if he already knew her) Olive Balchin, a known prostitute, went to the Queen's Cafe for a cup of tea carrying the hammer with him, walked back into Deansgate and across the road to its junction with Cumberland Street. Here they fell into an argument – about what, nobody will ever know – and at some time after midnight the man took Olive on to the bomb site and frantically bludgeoned her to death with the hammer.

It was a strange scenario for which to find a motive. Did the man really buy the hammer just to batter Olive Balchin to death; or had he just killed in a moment of frenzy? – in which case why did he buy the hammer?

It is a characteristic of police work that the officers of a given area get to know their 'clients'; the denizens of the twilight world of crime and violence in which they do daily battle. And odd characteristics will stick in a good policeman's mind.

This was probably the reason that the name Walter Rowland came to mind in connection with the Cumberland Street murder. Rowland was known as a man given to fits of violence – he had been convicted and sentenced to death in 1934 for the murder of his own baby. What was more, he was known to have associated with Olive Balchin. That he looked very little like the description given by Mercer, MacDonald and Mrs Copley was a fact temporarily disregarded.

Exactly one week after the murder, on 26th October at 11.00pm, two police officers collected Walter Rowland from the Services Transit Dormitory where he was staying. At Bootle Street police station Rowland insisted: 'I am admitting nothing because it is only a fool's game to do that. I can account for where I was. I was at home at New Mills when she was murdered. I did not come back to Manchester that night.'

However, he did later give an alibi, and admitted an 8-week-old relationship with the murdered woman. Shown a photograph of Olive, Rowland said: 'Things like that don't happen to decent women, and whoever did it did not do it without a cause. You can't see what you have done in the dark.' [He was then shown a photograph of Olive Balchin as she looked after the murder] 'Yes, that's her, but I have got a fighting chance and I am going to hang on to it. I have got an uncontrollable temper, but that's not evidence is it? I am sure I would not do that. It's possible the hammer was got to do a job with. I was not going to do a job that night . . . I was never near that place on Saturday night.'

Rowland then volunteered a hospital appointment card which showed that he was undergoing treatment for venereal disease: 'I might as well show you this. [You'd] find it. I had pride in my body. It was a blow to find I had VD. I wanted to know where I got it. If I had been sure it was her I would have strangled her. I did think it was her. It's hard to say it was her now. Has she VD? If she gave it to me she deserved all she got.'*

Walter Rowland later made a written statement in which he once again admitted having sexual intercourse with Olive Balchin, and to suspecting that his venereal disease was a direct result of that contact.

Identification parades were set up for the benefit of the witnesses Mercer, MacDonald and Copley who picked out Rowland with greater or lesser degrees of certainty.

Walter Rowland's trial opened at the Manchester Autumn Assizes on 12th December 1948 before Mr Justice Sellers. The case for the Crown was presented by Mr Basil Nield KC, and Mr Bazil Wingate-Saul; Rowland was represented by Mr Kenneth Burke and Mr H. Openshaw.

---

* Olive Balchin was not infected with venereal disease

While the prosecution evidence relied solidly on placing Rowland at the scene of the crime, it was a grave shortcoming to their case that not a single trace of blood could be found on his suit – his only suit.

Rowland's defence attempted to put him as far away from the scene of the crime as possible, and although his previous statements to the police gave a rather hesitant (indeed, improbable) picture of his movements, his counsel had managed to present the alibi with some degree of logical sense. Mrs Agnes Hall, Walter's mother, testified that her son had visited her home at 65 Bridge Street, New Mills at 7.30pm; while there he changed his shirt and underwear and left at 9.20 to catch a bus which arrived in Stockport at 10.09. Now, although there is no direct evidence that Rowland did get the bus, one significant fact points to the truth of his statement. Rowland claimed that he was in the lower storey of The Wellington at Stockport (called the 'bottom Wellington') when he saw two policemen walk down the stairs from the 'top Wellington' and leave by the lower exit. This is a fact attested to by Sergeant Jones of the local force who was one of those two policemen; and he had noted the time – 10.30pm. So at 10.30 Walter Rowland is six miles from Manchester. He next claims to have taken a bus to Ardwick (still a long way from Deansgate) where he stopped at a fish and chip shop on his way to a lodging house at 81 Brunswick Street. He arrived at around 11 o'clock which was verified by the landlord. Rowland had signed the register with his own name and that register was presented as evidence.

After a retirement of two hours the jury found Walter Rowland guilty of murder, and on 16th December he was sentenced to death. Notice of appeal was immediately lodged by Rowland's defence.

At this point there might already have existed in some people's minds an uneasiness at the jury's verdict; an uncomfortable feeling that guilt had not been proved 'beyond all reasonable doubt'. What follows is the beginning of a sequence of events which may have resulted in the hanging of an innocent man.

On the 22nd of January, 1947, the Governor of H.M.

Prison at Liverpool received a letter from one of his guests, prisoner 7305:

Sir,

I, David John Ware, wish to confess that I killed Olive Balshaw [sic] with a hammer, on a bombed-site in the Deansgate, Manchester, on Saturday, October 19th, about 10pm. We had been to a Picture House near the Belle-Vue Stadium earlier in the evening. I did not know her before that night. I wish this to be used in evidence and accepted as the truth.

Signed,
David John Ware.

Two days later Inspector Stainton paid Ware a visit, and after the customary caution, took down his statement:

Liverpool
24th January, 1947.

I, David John Ware, have been told by Detective Inspector Stainton that I am not obliged to say anything unless I wish to do so, but that whatever I do say will be taken down in writting and may be given in evidence.

(Signed) David John Ware

I left Stoke on Friday Oct. 18th 1946 with money I had stolen from the Salvation Army Hostel where I worked as a booking Clerk.

I hurried to Longton where I caught a bus to Uttoxeter & from there by Train to Manchester. Arriving in Manchester about 7.30pm I met a girl & stayed the night with her in some part just outside the City. On Saturday morning I left her & wandered around on my own scheming how I could get some more money. I decided in the Afternoon to by a Hammer for the purpose of committing robbery with violence.

I bought a hammer after some searching near the railway station which is on the road from Piccadilly leading to Manchester Hippodrome. I tried many shops in this area but they could not oblige me.

At six pm I met Olive Balshaw outside the Hippodrome I spoke to her & suggested going to the pictures my idea was to kill time till it got dark.

I went to small Picture House near the Belle Vue stadium with her. We came out at 9.00pm had a cup of coffee opposite the cinema & caught a bus to the centre of the City.

I did not know whether to leave her or not but after finding a dark place not far from Piccadilly I decided to spend a while with her. The spot where we stopped was a place or building that I took to be bombed in this war. We went inside the ruins & stood for a short while near the entrance. We were quite close to each other & being so near she took the opportunity of going through my pockets. I was aware of this but did not show her. I was ate up with hatred & felt immediately that I'd like to kill her. I realised I had the hammer so suggested that I'd like to make water & went further in the building. In there I took the brown paper off the hammer & threw it in the corner.

I went back to her & suggested moving further inside where we could not be seen. She agreed to this & we moved further inside. She was on my left & with my right hand I got the Hammer out of my pocket. While she was still in front & had only a few paces to go before reaching the wall I struck her a violent blow on the head. (I should say the right side). She screamed & before her scream lasted any length of time I struck her again this time she only mumbled. Her hands were on her head protecting it the second time and she fell to the floor up against the wall & I repeated the blows. Blood shot up in a thin spray. I felt it on my face & then I panicked threw the hammer & left everything as it was. I made no attempt to get my money. I ran & ran zig-zag up and down streets I didn't know eventually getting to Salford Station. I was frightened of going on the station so decided to go to Stockport I caught bus to the Hippodrome then another to Stockport, sleeping at a lodging house there. On Sunday I tramped to Buxton & on to Chapel en le Frith where I stayed the night at the institution.

On Monday I Hitch Hiked to Sheffield & surrendered to the Police for the stealing of the money at the Stoke on Trent Salvation Army Hostel.
I have been in custody since.

(Signed) David John Ware

I have read over the above statement.

(Signed) David John Ware.

Witness: (Signed) Douglas Nimmo.
Detective Constable.
Manchester City Police.

(Signed) F. Stainton.
Detective Inspector.
Manchester City Police.

In a further statement to lawyers, Ware takes up the story:

... When I got to Sheffield I took the belt off my mackintosh and threw it away together with my cap. I did this in order to alter my appearance. I later read in the newspapers that the man wanted for killing the woman in Manchester had not been wearing a hat and I realised I had made a mistake in throwing my cap away.

I surrendered myself to the Sheffield police for the Offence I had committed at Stoke as a 'cover up'. I thought I would be safer from possible detection in the hands of the Police or in prison, than I would be if I were wandering about.

Whilst on remand before my conviction I had access to newspapers, I read all about the finding of the woman's body but did not read any report of either the Police Court Proceedings or the trial of Rowland. The last I read was a paragraph which said that an arrest in connection with the Manchester 'Blitz Site Murder' was expected at any moment.

I then purposely avoided reading the newspapers, as I did not want to read anything more about the murder. The first thing I heard of Rowland's conviction was on Saturday the 18th January 1947.

On that day whilst at Exercise in Walton Prison a fellow Prisoner told me that a man who had been

convicted of the Murder of a Woman in Manchester
had Appealed and that his Appeal had been dismissed.

This information worried me a great deal as I
knew that only a short time would elapse before that
man's execution. I thought a great deal about it and
on Wednesday the 22nd January 1947 I asked to see
the Governor of the Prison and I made a statement to
him.

I do not know the man Rowland.

This was clearly seen as a lucky break by Rowland's
defence attorney who made application that this additional evidence be heard by the Court of Appeal – after all,
this was precisely the purpose for which the court had
been established. As it turned out, though, the court
refused to hear anything but evidence on Rowland's
whereabouts on the night Olive Balchin died, and having
heard that evidence dismissed the appeal.

However, there was now sufficient doubt, sufficient
pressure, to persuade the Home Secretary of the wisdom
of holding an official inquiry into 'whether there are any
grounds for thinking that there has been any miscarriage
of justice'. The man appointed to lead that inquiry was
Mr John Catterall Jolly KC. Mr Jolly had a bare five days in
which to reach his informed opinion – after that it would
have been purely academic, Walter Rowland would be
swinging from the hangman's rope.

Clearly the 'further information which may have become available' referred to in the Home Office's directive
to Mr Jolly meant David Ware's confessions; statements
in which he displayed an intimate knowledge not only of
the circumstances of Olive Balchin's decease, but also of
the layout of Manchester's city centre. Further investigation of Ware's statements revealed still further mysteries.
Police had traced the Stockport lodging-house where he
claims to have slept and in whose register Ware's name
could be found. Furthermore, the lodging-house keeper
remembered his guest arriving – at between 11.15 and
11.30 on the night of the murder. So if both Ware and
Rowland were tucked up in bed by 11.30, who was the

man seen by Norman Mercer standing on the corner of Cumberland Street at midnight. Perhaps Mr Mercer had been mistaken altogether. But for reasons not entirely clear Mr Jolly decided that Mercer was right and that Rowland was not in the Ardwick lodging-house at the time he claimed, and that the register had been falsely

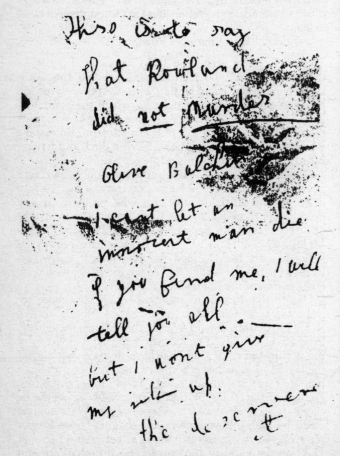

Anonymous letter sent to Walter Rowland's solicitor before David Ware's confession

entered and that, heaven knows why, the lodging-house keeper was lying.

Then quite suddenly, despite prior assurances to the board of inquiry to the contrary, David Ware now claimed that his statements were false – that he had been lying, that he had concocted his story from newspaper reports. The effect of this bombshell was further complicated when the three witnesses from Rowland's trial – Mercer, MacDonald and Mrs Copley failed consistently to pick Ware out of an identification parade. Even when confronted with him face-to-face the trio were emphatic that he was not the man they had seen over the weekend of the murder.

Even so, it might be thought that there were aspects of the case – including Ware's statements – that would have favoured a reappraisal of Rowland's conviction on grounds of reasonable doubt alone. However, John Jolly's report to the Home Secretary concluded: 'Having inquired into the confession made by David John Ware of the murder of Olive Balchin, and having considered further information which has become available since the conviction of Walter Graham Rowland for the murder of Olive Balchin, I report that I am satisfied that there are no grounds for thinking that there has been any miscarriage of justice in the conviction of Rowland for that murder.' This report was received on 25th February, Mr Jolly had made it with time to spare; Walter Rowland was executed on the morning of 27th February.

This is the end of the story as far as Rowland is concerned. But for David John Ware there is a post-script. On 10th July 1951 Ware bought a hammer and attempted to kill an unknown woman in Bristol. When he gave himself up to the police he said: 'I have killed a woman. I don't know what is the matter with me. I keep having an urge to hit women on the head.' He was tried on 16th November and found guilty but insane and re-manded to Broadmoor. On 1st April 1954 David Ware hanged himself.

THE SMASHING OF THE VAN

**The Killing of Police Sergeant Charles Brett
by William O'Meara Allen**
On Wednesday, 18th September 1867 at Hyde
Road, Manchester

On 18th September 1867, two men – who gave their names as Martin Williams and John White – appeared at Manchester Police Court to answer a charge of loitering; White had also been found in possession of a pistol when the two were stopped and questioned. It seemed a perfectly straightforward case, and both men were remanded pending enquiries.

Outside the court a curious incident occurred when police apprehended two further men who were behaving in a suspicious manner. One of them drew a knife and stabbed Superintendent Gee in the eye, though fortunately for the officer, not fatally. The two men were promptly taken into custody.

After their court hearing, Williams and White were put into a police van with other prisoners who had appeared in court that day, and as a precaution in view of the earlier stabbing incident, the police provided an escort for the van. What the forces of law did not know, was that the two prisoners in the van, Williams and White, were in reality Colonel Kelly and Colonel Deasey, both important members of the clandestine Irish Republican Brotherhood.

As the police van reached a railway arch across Hyde Road, a mob of fifty or sixty persons, some carrying firearms, blocked the path of the horse drawn vehicle, surrounding it and separating it from the escort. While most of this mob held off the police and a number of public spirited passers-by who had come to their assistance, the remaining attackers set about the van with hammers, hatchets and stones. Eventually they managed to break through the roof of the van by pounding it with a large boulder. They discovered, however, that the prisoners were locked in individual cells within the van and still could not be released. The leader of the gang, William O'Meara Allen, then stepped forward and shot away the lock on the door of the van, threatening to shoot the police sergeant inside if he refused to hand over his keys to the cells. When Sergeant Brett replied 'I cannot, I must do my duty', Allen shot him in the head, the bullet entering his eye. Allen then took the keys and released Kelly and Deasey, as the dying Sergeant staggered from the van.

Having achieved their aim, the gang, with Kelly and Deasey, scattered across the adjoining fields. In the ensuing melee, a number of the attackers were immediately caught, including Allen, who was tackled by a member of the public called Hunter. In the following few days several more of the gang were apprehended, and a reward of £300

Executioner Calcraft at work

was offered for the recapture of Kelly and Deasey, but without success.

When the trial of the captured Fenians began on 26th October 1867, they were escorted to Manchester Assize Court by no less than three troops of Hussars. In all, twenty-six persons were arraigned in batches before Mr Justice Mellor and Mr Justice Blackburn. Only the first five defendants, Allen, Michael Larkin, William Gould, Maguire and Shore, were charged with the capital offence, the murder of Sergeant Brett. The court was packed with a sympathetic, mainly Irish, audience and the five men defended themselves bravely and passionately, making eloquent speeches in justification of their Irish Nationalist affiliations. After a five-day trial, the jury took just one hour to find all five guilty and the death sentence was pronounced.

There was considerable doubt about the strength of some of the evidence of identification presented at the trial and, after a short enquiry, the Attorney General released first Maguire and then Shore for lack of reliable evidence. The other three defendants, Allen, Larkin and Gould, met their prescribed fate outside the New Bailey Prison, Salford, at 8 o'clock in the morning on 23rd November 1867, at the experienced hands of the official executioner, William Calcraft.

From *The Smashing of the Van*
by Enoch Kent, 1960

Attend you gallant Irishmen
And listen for a while.
I'll sing to you the praises of
The sons of Erin's Isle.
It's of those gallant heroes
Who voluntarily ran,
To release two Irish Fenians
From an English prison van.

On the 18th of September, boys,
It was a dreadful year.
When sorrow and excitement ran
Throughout all Lancashire.

At a gathering of the Irish boys,
They volunteered, each man,
To release those Irish prisoners
Out of the prison van.

Kelly and Deasey were their names,
I suppose you knew them well.
Remanded for a week, they were,
In Bellevue Jail to dwell.
When taking of the prisoners back
Their trial for to stand,
To make a safe deliverance
They conveyed them in a van.

With courage bold, those heros went
And soon the van had stopped.
They cleared the guards from back and front
And then smashed in the top.
But, in blowing open of the lock,
They chanced to kill a man.
So three men must die on the scaffold high
For smashing of the van

THROUGH A MIST OF TEARS

The Murder of June Anne Devaney by Peter Griffiths
In the early morning of Saturday, 15th May 1948 in the grounds of Queen's Park Hospital, Blackburn, Lancashire

---

Chronology of a Murder

12.20am. Twenty minutes past midnight on the morning of Saturday May 15th 1948: ward CH3, a children's ward of the Queen's Park Hospital outside Blackburn: staff nurse Gwendoline Humphreys is making her routine rounds. Of the twelve cots only six have occupants, and the oldest of these small sleeping figures is June Anne Devaney, not yet four. June had been admitted to the ward ten days before with mild pneumonia, had made a good recovery and has been looking forward to being collected by her parents later in the day.

12.30am. Nurse Humphreys thinks she hears a child's voice calling. She looks out of the window on to the grounds and then puts her head round the door of CH3; finding all as it should be, she returns to the kitchen where she has been preparing the children's breakfasts.

1.20am. Gwen Humphreys feels a draught, and going to the porch doors which give access to the hospital grounds she finds them open. The catches of the doors have been faulty for some time, so Nurse Humphreys is unperturbed; she closes the doors and once again goes to check that everything is quiet on her ward.

This kind of pedestrian routine is being carried on all over the country by countless nurses on countless night shifts in countless hospitals. Soon Gwendoline Humphreys and the Queen's Park Hospital are to become the centre of one of the most heartbreaking, most thoroughly vile atrocities in the history of that most atrocious crime, murder.

Nurse Humphreys' heartbeat stops momentarily as she looks down into the empty cot where June Devaney had been sleeping an hour before. Her trained eye takes in the drop side of the cot, which is still in place, and inwardly reasons that even a child as big for her age as June could not have climbed over it; the girl must have been bodily lifted and taken out. With the help of the Night Sister, Gwen Humphreys makes a search of the immediate area, noticing as she does two vitally important clues; beneath June's bed is a large bottle of the type commonly found in hospitals and called Winchester bottles. The last time the nurse had seen this particular example was on her 12.20 round when it was in its proper place on an instrument trolley at the end of the ward. She now also notices some footprints on the highly waxed floor; one pair of them beside June Anne's empty cot.

1.45am. Having failed to locate little June Devaney, the hospital authorities alert the local police, a squad of whose officers carry out a systematic search of the extensive seventy acres of the hospital's grounds.

3.17. The body of June Anne Devaney is found by a police constable close to the boundary wall of the hospital grounds; she has suffered terrible injuries to the head, and first indications suggest sexual interference as well.

4.00am. Blackburn's Chief Constable Mr C. G. Looms, Detective Superintendent Woodmansey of the Lancashire Constabulary and a police surgeon arrive at the scene of the crime. Shortly afterwards Detective Chief Inspector John Capstick is roused from his bed in London by the telephone; on the other end of the line Blackburn's Chief Constable is requesting Capstick as one of Scotland Yard's most experienced officers to lead the hunt for June Devaney's killer. Capstick in his turn rouses Detective Sergeant John Stoneman from his bed.

6.20am. DCI Capstick and DS Stoneman meet at London's Euston station for the train north to Preston. There they are met by a police car which speeds them to Blackburn by early afternoon. They are later joined by

two other Murder Squad detectives, DI Wilfred Daws and
DS Millen.

Marks of Cain
On that bleak, drizzly afternoon of Saturday 15th May,
the Yard officers waited as the waterproof sheeting was
peeled back from the scene of the crime revealing the
tragic body of June Devaney. Jack Capstick recalled that
first glimpse later: 'I am not ashamed to say that I saw it
through a mist of tears. Years of detective service had
hardened me to many terrible things; but this tiny pathetic
body, in its nightdress soaked in blood and mud, was
something no man could see unmoved, and it haunts me
to this day.' While scene-of-crime photographs were taken
and the body removed, the detective team returned to
ward CH3 where they met Detective Chief Inspector Colin
Campbell, head of the Lancashire Fingerprint Bureau.
Campbell had been at the hospital since five in the

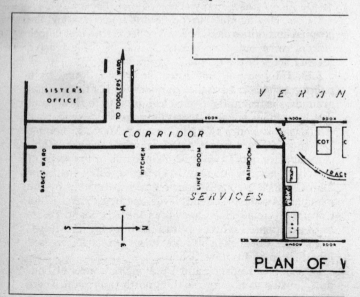

Plan of ward CH3, showing Griffiths' route through the room

morning and had already assembled a catalogue of potentially vital clues. These included a vast number of fingerprints, among them those on the Winchester bottle that had been inexplicably removed from its customary place and stood by June Devaney's cot. There were also the footprints which had been seen by Nurse Humphreys, seemingly made by stockinged feet impressed into the waxed surface of the floor. The trail began at the door leading from an office (see plan) at the north end of the ward (it was later found that the windows of this office were open, and forensic investigation of the sills and ground beneath them indicated that this was the point of entry of the intruder). From the office the prints went first to cot No.1, then to the instrument trolley, to cot No.2, cot No.3, and cot No.4, which was where June Devaney was sleeping. From here the footprints went southward again to within a couple of feet of the door leading into the corridor, turned, and passed back the length of the ward

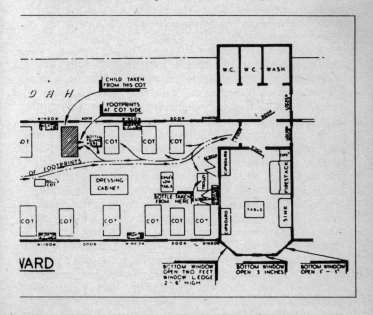

to the door of entry. Colin Campbell ordered photographs to be taken of the prints, and then the wax beneath the prints was carefully scraped off for further forensic tests for microscopic fibres and particles.

As for the fingerprints, it became the task of a team of detectives from the Lancashire Constabulary under DCI Robert McCartney to trace and fingerprint every person who in the past two years could have had a legitimate reason to have been in the children's ward. Within one month they were to find 642 names, 642 sets of fingerprints.

On the matter of the Winchester bottle, Campbell had eliminated all the prints but one set; this, he declared with assurance, was the mark of June Devaney's killer.

But fingerprints are only of any use if there is a suspect whose prints can be compared with them, or if a matching set can be found in one of the police fingerprint bureaux. In this case there was no suspect, and there were no matching prints on file – the person who killed June Anne Devaney had no criminal record.

An Unprecedented Step

This conclusion led to desperate measures. Knowing that their killer was just a fingerprint away the Yard men, in consultation with local forces, decided to take the unprecedented step of fingerprinting every male over the age of 16 who was in Blackburn on 14th and 15th May.

In a massive public relations campaign every possible local resource was mobilized – the Press carried the story and the appeal, the Mayor of Blackburn endorsed the plea, and the Chief Constable gave his solemn assurance that all prints taken would later be destroyed or, if preferred, returned to the donor. Such was the strength of the appeal and of public revulsion at the ghastly murder of little June Anne that police met no resistance to the scheme. Using twenty officers and the electoral register, Inspector William Barton began a two-month trawl of more than 35,000 homes. Chief Inspector Campbell designed a special compact card for the convenience of the 'mobile' fingerprint squad; the cards were 3¼ inches square with spaces on one side for Name, Address, National Registration

Number (a wartime requirement), and the left thumb and forefinger prints; on the reverse the other fingers of the left hand (left hand to match with the prints on the Winchester bottle).

Towards the end of July the fingerprinting had been all but completed but had revealed no apparent lead; it began to look as though, despite the intensity of the coverage, June Devaney's killer had slipped through the net. Then a procedure was tried that would not be possible today. In the immediate post-war years, rationing persisted, and records were kept of the issue of ration books and the Registration Number by which they and their owners were identified. It was a simple, if time-consuming operation to check the local registration officer's file against the numbers on the fingerprint cards, the shortfall representing those individuals who had been missed.

In the event some 200 sets of prints were found to be needed to complete the job. One of those sets belonged to Peter Griffiths, a 22-year-old former soldier then living at 31 Birley Street in Blackburn. At 3.00pm on Thursday, 12th August Chief Inspector Colin Campbell confirmed that Griffiths was the owner of the prints on the Winchester bottle.

The Anti-climax

By comparison with this massive task of superbly co-ordinated police investigative work the arrest of Peter Griffiths was something of an anti-climax. When he left home for work on the night shift at a local flour mill Griffiths was intercepted by John Capstick and DS Millen; following a half-hearted attempt at denial, he made the following statement:

'I want to say that on the night the little girl was killed at the Queen's Park Hospital, it was a Friday night, the Friday before Whitsun. I left home that night on my own about six o'clock. I went to spend a quiet night on my own. I went to the Dun Horse pub or hotel and bought myself about five pints of bitter beer. Then I went to Yates's Wine Lodge and had a glass of Guinness and two double rums. I then had another glass of Guinness and then went back to the Dun Horse again. I then had about six more pints of bitter. I was on my own and came out of there at closing time. I walked down to Jubilee Street off Darwen Street and I saw a man smoking a cigarette sitting in a small closed car with the hood on, with wire wheels, they were painted silver. I did not know him. I had never seen him before. I asked the man for a light as I had no matches to light my cigarette. I stayed gabbing to him for about fifteen minutes. He said to me, "Are you going home?" I said, "No, I'm going to walk round a bit and sober up first." He asked me where I lived and I told him. He said, "Well, get in, open the window and I'll give you a spin." He took me to the front of the Queen's Park Hospital and I got out opposite the iron railings. I don't know what happened to him, I never saw him again. I must have got over the railings, for the next thing I remember was being outside the ward, there were some children. I left my shoes outside the door, which had a brass knob. I tried the door and it opened to my touch and I just went in and heard a nurse humming and banging as if she was washing something so I came out again and waited a few moments.

I went back in again and went straight to the ward like, I think I went in one or two small rooms like, like a kitchen, and then I went back into the ward again. I then picked up a biggish bottle off a shelf. I went half way down the ward with it and then put it down on the floor. I then thought I heard the nurse coming, I turned round sharply, overbalanced and fell against a bed. I remember the child woke up and started to cry, and I hushed her. She then opened her eyes, saw me and the child in the next bed started whimpering. I picked the girl up out of the cot and took her outside by the same door. I carried her in my right arm and she put her arms round my neck and I walked with her down the hospital field. I put her down on the grass. She started crying again and I tried to stop her from crying, but she wouldn't do, like, she wouldn't stop crying. I just lost my temper then and you know what happened then. I banged her head against the wall. I then went back to the verandah outside the ward, sat down and put my shoes on. I then went back to where the child was. I like just glanced at her but did not go right up to her, but went straight on down the field to the delph. I crossed over the path alongside the delph leading into Queen's Park. I walked through the park and came out on Audley Street. I went down Cherry Street into Furthergate, then I went down Eanam to Birley Street and got home somewhere around two o'clock on Saturday morning. It would be somewhere about that time. I went into my house, took my collar and tie off and slept in my suit on the couch downstairs. Mother and father were in bed and did not know what time I came in. I woke up about nine o'clock, got up, washed and shaved, then pressed my suit because I was going out again after I

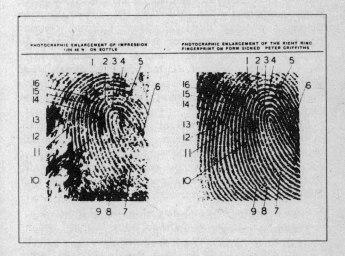

Points of similarity between the print on the Winchester bottle and those of Peter Griffiths

had had my breakfast. I went out then down the town, had a walk round, then went to the Royal Cinema in the afternoon, came out of the pictures at five o'clock, went home and had my tea. I looked at the papers and read about the murder. It didn't shake me, so that I just carried on normally after that. My mother and father asked me where I had been that night and what time I came home and I told them I had been out boozing and had got home at twelve o'clock. This is all I can say and I'm sorry for both parents' sake and I hope I get what I deserve.'

Friday the 13th had proved very unlucky for Peter Griffiths, and shortly before midnight he was formally charged with the murder of June Anne Devaney.

On Friday, 15th October 1948 Griffiths' trial began before Mr Justice Oliver at the Lancaster Assizes. By now the prosecution had considerably more even than a confession and a fingerprint to offer the jury. After retrieving the prisoner's suit from a pawn shop the police forensic laboratory had uncovered two further damning pieces of evidence: fibres taken from Griffiths' clothing proved a perfect match for the fibres adhering to the victim's body and those found on the window ledge where the killer had entered the hospital. Human blood stains were found in several places on both the suit jacket and trousers – blood group A, the same group as June Devaney's.

Such was the solid weight of indisputable scientific evidence that Griffiths' defence of insanity stood little chance of influencing the decision of the jury; they retired for a bare 23 minutes before returning to empower Mr Justice Oliver to pass the only sentence that the law then allowed in the case of murder:

'Peter Griffiths, this jury has found you guilty of a crime of the most brutal ferocity. I entirely agree with their verdict. The sentence of the Court upon you is that you be taken from this place to a lawful prison and thence to a place of execution and that you there suffer death by hanging and that your body be afterwards buried within the precincts of the prison in which you shall have been confined before your execution. And may the Lord have mercy on your soul.'

On Friday morning, 19th November, the sentence was carried out at Liverpool Prison.

On the 3rd of that month the police had honoured their pledge to the citizens of Blackburn; about 500 people took up the option of having their fingerprint record returned to them, while the remaining 46,500 were ceremoniously pulped at a local paper mill observed by the Mayor and a coterie of journalists, photographers and newsreel cameramen.

RED STAINS ON THE CARPET

The Murder of Mrs Isabella Ruxton and Mary Jane Rogerson by Dr Buck Ruxton
On or about Sunday, 15th September 1935 at 2 Dalton Square, Lancaster, Lancashire

Red stains on the carpet, red stains on the knife,
For Dr Buck Ruxton has murdered his wife:
The maid-servant saw it and threatened to tell,
So Dr Buck Ruxton he's killed her as well.

(Contemporary children's song)

The story of Buck Ruxton, the murder, dismemberment and disposal of his wife Isabella and nursemaid Mary Jane Rogerson is brutal enough. The crime ranks, however, as more than Britain's most gruesome dismembering case; its importance rests on some startling achievements in the field of forensic pathology, and was a landmark in the careers of four of Britain's leading medico-legal experts: Dr John Glaister, Professor of Forensic Medicine at the University of Glasgow and a Barrister-at-Law; Dr James Couper Brash, Professor of Anatomy at the University of Edinburgh; Professor Sidney Smith, Regius Professor of Forensic Medicine at Edinburgh University; and Dr Gilbert Millar, also of Edinburgh University, Pathology Department. The case represents the triumph of science and reason.

The case opens, as do most murders, with the discovery of a body in suspicious circumstances; only in this case the victims were in considerably more than one piece, and the circumstances could lead to only one conclusion: murder in its foulest guise.

Gardenholme Linn is a tributary stream of the River Arran, and it runs beneath a bridge on the Edinburgh-Carlisle road about two miles north of Moffat. On 29th September 1935, while crossing the bridge on foot, Miss Susan Haines Johnson saw what she thought was part of a human arm sticking out from some wrapping thrown into the gully below. Miss Johnson relayed these fears to her brother Alfred, and he visited the gully to check for himself; he found not only the arm but various other more or less identifiable human pieces in several packages. The awful finds were reported to the authorities at Moffat, and it fell to the lot of Sergeant Sloane of the Dumfriesshire Constabulary to investigate on behalf of the police. He was later joined by Inspector Strath, and between them the two officers began the grisly job of combing the gully for pieces of flesh and bone. Such fragments as were found were removed to the mortuary of Moffat Cemetery. The search was resumed on the following morning and other portions were discovered, and on subsequent days until 7th October when the use of bloodhounds convinced the police that no more was to be found in the immediate vicinity. On 28th October a roadman found a left foot wrapped in newspaper on the Glasgow-Carlisle road nine miles south of Moffat, and on 4th November a young woman found a right forearm and hand lying by the roadside about a half-mile south of the Linn.

Medical experts later catalogued the finds as follows.

Four bundles: the first was wrapped in a blouse and contained two upper arms and four pieces of flesh; the second comprised two thigh bones, two legs from which most of the flesh had been stripped, and nine pieces of flesh, all wrapped in a pillow-case; the third was a piece of cotton sheeting containing seventeen pieces of flesh; the fourth bundle was also wrapped in cotton sheeting and consisted of a human trunk, two legs with the feet tied with the hem of a cotton sheet and some wisps of straw and cotton wool.

In addition, other parcels contained two heads, one of which was wrapped in child's rompers; a quantity of cotton wool and sections from the *Daily Herald* of 6th

August 1935; one thigh; two forearms with hands attached but minus the top joints of the fingers and thumbs; and several pieces of skin and flesh. One part was wrapped in the *Sunday Graphic* dated 15th September which was subsequently to provide an important clue. All the remains were badly decomposed and infested by maggots.

From this unsavoury shambles the medical experts were required to provide not only identification but legally acceptable proof of identification, plus such other details as time of death and cause of death, and any information that might point to a murder suspect. Preliminary examination had established that the remains were from two bodies, both female, one young and the other in middle age, and a statement was issued to this effect.

Meanwhile another team of experienced detectives were engaged in the detailed police investigation that necessarily accompanies a major murder hunt. Missing-persons inquiries were made over a large area around Moffat, though results were negative, as were inquiries into irregular movements by motor-cars in the area of the Gardenholme Linn bridge. Officers examined closely the materials in which the dismembered remains were wrapped for any clue as to the origin of the victims. The first major breakthrough was in the sheets of the *Sunday Graphic* for 15th September 1935. This was recognized as what in the newspaper trade are called 'slip editions' – issues that celebrate an event of local importance, and are circulated only in that area; this particular 'slip' contained features on the Morecambe festival and was sold only in that town, in Lancaster, and in the immediately surrounding district. Now, by happy coincidence the Chief Constable of Dumfries – under whose expert leadership the investigation was proceeding – saw an article in Glasgow's *Daily Record* which gave an account of the disappearance three weeks previously of a young woman named Mary Jane Rogerson, who had been employed as a nursemaid to the family of a Lancaster doctor named Buck Ruxton. Further investigation acquainted police with the fact that Mrs Ruxton had disappeared at the same time.

A distraught Mrs Jessie Rogerson, resident of More-cambe and stepmother of Mary Jane, was brought in to see if she could identify any of the material which had wrapped the grisly Moffat remains; to her great sorrow Mrs Rogerson immediately picked out the blouse which she had given to Mary after repairing it with a distinctive patch under the arm. Following a direct lead from Jessie Rogerson, the child's rompers were later identified by a Mrs Holme of Grange-over-Sands; she had passed on some children's clothing to the Ruxtons when they had stayed with her as boarders the previous summer.

The connection between the dismembered bodies, the missing Lancaster women, and the family of Buck Ruxton was now established if not proved, and at this point the main thrust of the investigation was taken over by Captain Henry Vann, Chief Constable of Lancaster. The Lancaster force had already had some contact with Ruxton – or rather he with them – on a couple of recent occasions, and in one very excited conversation with Captain Vann he had requested that something be done to stop the spread of gossip linking him with the finds at Moffat: 'This publicity is ruining my practice,' Ruxton complained, 'particularly at a time when I am negotiating a loan on it.' Thus a statement had been issued by the police to the Press which seemed (temporarily, at least) to soothe the Doctor.

Bukhtyar Rustomji Ratamji Hakim was born into a Parsee family of French-Indian extraction in Bombay; it was later in England that he changed his name by deed poll to Buck Ruxton. Young Hakim grew up in the religion of his parents as an intelligent, thoughtful youth, and in 1922 received his Bachelor of Medicine and Bachelor of Surgery degrees from Bombay University. He later served in the Indian medical service in Bombay, Basra, and Baghdad. He attended courses at London's University College Hospital, and in 1930 settled in Lancaster at 2 Dalton Square, where he ran a substantial practice. At the time of the Gardenholme Linn finds Ruxton was 36 years old.

Mrs Ruxton was not strictly speaking Mrs Ruxton, for although up to the time of her disappearance they had

lived together for more than seven years she and Buck
Ruxton had never married. She was born Isabella Kerr in
Falkirk, and in 1919 took the name of her Dutch husband
Van Ess. The marriage did not last and Isabella fell in love
with the man then calling himself Buck Hakim (or sometimes Captain Hakim). There is no doubt that there
remained considerable mutual affection in the relationship, though given Ruxton's explosive nature and his
morbid jealousy it is not surprising that his subsequent
trial brought to light many incidents of ill-use by Ruxton
of his wife – on two occasions resulting in the police being
summoned to defuse his extravagant abuse. But the
quarrels were becoming more bitter as they became more
frequent, and Buck Ruxton's constant and insupportable
suspicions of his wife's fidelity became an obsession.

The Ruxtons had three children: Elizabeth aged 6, Diane
4, and Billie 2 years, and a nursemaid, 20-year-old Mary
Jane Rogerson. Mary was a simple, cheerful girl devoted
to the Ruxton children and to her father and stepmother,
with whom she spent all her spare time. Two charladies,
Agnes Oxley and Elizabeth Curwen shared the heavy-
duty work and much of the cooking, and from August
1935 they were supplemented by Mrs Mabel Smith.

Mrs Curwen was on duty on Friday, 13th September
1935 when Dr Ruxton told her that she could finish up
now and go home and need not return till the following
Monday. Mrs Oxley (who was expected on the Sunday)
received a message via her husband that as Mrs Ruxton
and Mary had gone on holiday to Edinburgh – an annual
occurrence – there was no need to come. During the rest of
that Sunday a succession of delivery people came to the
door about their errands, including the delivery of the
Sunday Graphic. Shortly before midday Ruxton deposited
his three children with the Andersons, close friends of the
family with whom the children were familiar, and where
they would spend the greater part of the next few days.
When Ruxton arrived he complained of a cut hand –
injured, he said, while opening a tin of fruit for the
children's breakfast: he was to make much of this cut to
everybody he met over the following days.

At 4.30 that afternoon Ruxton visited Mrs Hampshire,

one of his patients, and after relating the story of the cut hand persuaded her to return with him to Dalton Square to help 'prepare for the decorators' who were expected to arrive the following morning. He explained that Mrs Ruxton and Mary were away in Edinburgh.

In retrospect, this invitation to Mrs Hampshire (and later to her husband as well) was either grossly arrogant on Ruxton's part, or grossly stupid. This woman's evidence alone could have convicted the doctor at his trial – evidence of carpets soaked with blood taken up and rolled, strange stains on the bath, clothing so stained with blood that she could only burn it, and a similarly stained blue suit which Ruxton had the audacity to offer as a gift to Mr Hampshire.

This is just a sample of the extraordinary trail of clues left about the scene of the crime by Ruxton, which were methodically welded into a completely watertight case by the police forensic laboratory. Scientific investigators, in collaboration with the police, established that other items of stained clothing and carpet had littered the yard at the side of the house, and that fires had been seen blazing at all hours of the day and night; charred fabric identified as having been Mary Rogerson's clothing was found in the ashes. An unwholesome smell had been noticed in the house by the charladies, and Ruxton had been obliged to spray with air freshener and eau-de-Cologne. Scraps of human tissue were found in the drains and waste pipes leading from the bath, and extensive bloodstaining was present on the stairs and stair carpets, bathroom walls and floor and various items of clothing.

In the meantime, Ruxton had obligingly compiled a document entitled 'My Movements' for the benefit of the police, from which it was clear that the doctor had been putting considerable thought into establishing a defence for himself.

The dismembered remains had by now been transferred from Moffat to the University of Edinburgh, where Dr Gilbert Millar undertook their preliminary treatment. This consisted mainly of cleaning off the mass of maggots which were infesting the tissue. The total of parts was seventy, and the extent and type of mutilation displayed immediately suggested that every effort had been made to prevent identification – for example, distinguishing features (particularly of the face) had been cut away, and the fingertips with their tell-tale prints had been severed. Nevertheless, despite the overwhelming circumstantial evidence being assembled by the police that the corpses were indeed Isabella Ruxton and Mary Rogerson, and that Buck Ruxton was responsible for their deaths and dismemberment, it was still necessary to establish identity scientifically.

No detail will be given here of the piecing together of the two bodies and the painstaking investigation by the team of pathologists who carried out the work – a brief description would be misleading and do disservice to their remarkable achievement. However, space must be given to an account of the crowning triumph of the procedure – the 'positive' identification of the heads by means of a comparison of the skulls with known photographic portraits; a technique never before used in criminological investigation.

It had been noticed early on that the two heads – called for convenience Head 1 and Head 2 – were markedly different in shape and size. Photographic portraits of the two missing Lancaster women showed similar marked differences of form. Thus even at this stage it could be stated with certainty that Head 1 could not be Mrs Ruxton and Head 2 could not be Miss Rogerson.

Two photographs were used of each of the women – a studio portrait of Mrs Ruxton (called Portrait A) and a snapshot showing the left-side view of the same woman (Portrait B). Of Mary Rogerson only two photographs could be found (Portraits C and D), both taken by an amateur and consequently losing some clarity of detail when enlarged to life-size. Then the two skulls, by now cleaned of their remaining tissue, were each photographed from four angles – matching as closely as possible the position of the head in the portraits. From the life-size prints of the skulls and the portraits distinctive shapes and features were traced in ink on transparent paper; subsequent super-imposition revealed that Portraits A and B (Mrs Ruxton) fitted very well over the outline of Skull 2.

Similarly, Portraits C and D (Mary Rogerson) were seen to fit Skull 1. Further elaborate photographic techniques were employed to provide positive and negative images from the skulls and portraits which when superimposed also showed a remarkable consistency. It should, however, be emphasized that remarkable though this evidence was, it was not conclusive in the sense required by the court – indeed, the defence objected to the admission of the photographs at all on the grounds that they were 'constructed evidence, so liable to error'.

The Edinburgh team also examined closely for signs of cause of the death in both cases, and their findings may be summarized briefly:

Body No. 1 (thought to be Mary Rogerson): The neck and trunk with its internal organs were never found, and so no cause of death could be established. However, severe bruising to the tissue of the face and arms indicated violence before death, and the swelling of the tongue was consistent with asphyxia.

Body No. 2 (thought to be Mrs Isabella Ruxton): Asphyxia was thought to account for the congested state of the lungs and brain, and the damaged condition of the hyoid bone in the neck indicated manual strangulation.

Both bodies had been successfully drained of blood suggesting dismemberment taking place soon after death.

Buck Ruxton's trial opened at the High Court of Justice in Manchester on Monday, 2nd March 1936 before Mr Justice (later Lord Justice) Singleton. The Crown case was presented by Mr J.C. Jackson KC, Mr Maxwell Fyfe KC (later Lord Kilmuir), and Mr Hartley Shawcross. Defending Dr Ruxton were Mr Norman (later Lord) Birkett KC, and Mr Philip Kershaw KC.

Characteristically Norman Birkett defended Ruxton gallantly and enthusiastically, ever vigilant in challenging prosecution claims which he felt were unsubstantiated. Nevertheless, so strong was the medical evidence, and so expertly presented, that Birkett was defeated almost from the start, and in a long examination and cross-examination in the witness-box Ruxton was unable to cut a convincing figure on his own behalf. In his concluding speech to the jury Norman Birkett tried once more to cast doubt upon the reasoning and the conclusions drawn from it in the Crown case:

'It seems scarcely necessary to have to say to you that if you are satisfied of the fact that in the ravine on that day were those two bodies, identified beyond the shadow of a doubt, it does not prove this case. If, for example, the word of the prisoner was true, "They left my house," there is an end of the case. Even though their bodies were found in a ravine, dismembered, and even though those were the bodies, this does not prove the case against the prisoner. The Crown must prove the fact of murder, and you may have observed how much of this case has been mere conjecture. It is not for the defence to prove innocence; it is for the Crown to prove guilt, and it is the duty of the defence to propound a theory which would be satisfactory to your collective mind . . .

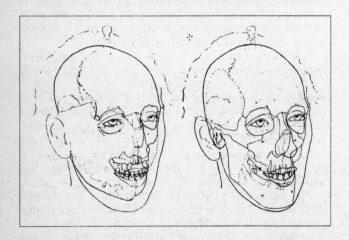

Left: Outlines of Portrait A (Mrs Ruxton) and Skull 1 superimposed and showing that they do not correspond. Right: Portrait A and Skull 2 superimposed and showing a good correspondence.

It is never incumbent upon the prosecution in a charge of murder to prove motive, but they say, "We will show you the motive; here it is – jealousy because of infidelity." I ask you to accept with the greatest reserve evidence spoken to after the event, such as that which has been given in this court from the servants and others . . . The doctor is arrested for murder, and how it colours the mind. This is clear, and I do not seek to deny it, that there were intervals and periods of the greatest possible unhappiness. You will remember that phrase employed by Dr Ruxton, a phrase so revealing and so powerful – "We were the kind of people who could neither live with each other, nor live without each other." Unhappiness was no new thing . . . The Crown said this was a record of marital unhappiness, grievous quarrels; she had left him and under the persuasion of her sister had returned, and there in that family was this canker, this jealousy, and so he would kill her. I suggest to you it is fantastical, and to suggest that was the motive and that was the occasion is, in my submission, not to strengthen this case in any

Lancaster.
14. 10 35.

I killed Mrs Ruxton in a fit of temper because I thought she had been with a man. I was Mad at the time. Mary Rogerson was present at the time. I had to Kill her.

B Ruxton

Dr Ruxton's confession from the death cell

particular but on the contrary to weaken it. For years that unhappiness has subsisted, and there was nothing revealed to you upon the evidence which on that occasion should prompt him to do that which the Crown lay at his charge.'

It was indicative of the complexity of the trial, and the care with which it was conducted, that it took up eleven whole days. The jury, however, needed little more than sixty minutes to return a verdict of guilty. Dr Ruxton's appeal was dismissed, and on 12th May 1936 at Strangeways Prison, Manchester, he was executed.

THE ROCHDALE MUMMY

**The discovery of the body of James Finlay
and the Inquiry into the means of his death**
In August 1975 at 28 Buttermere, Ashfield
Valley, Rochdale, Lancashire

It has been with varying degrees of competence and enterprise that murderers have approached the tricky problem of disposing of the mortal remains of their victims. Some, like Dr Buck Ruxton, take elaborate steps to try to render their handiwork unidentifiable; others simply leave the unfortunate victim where he falls. When a murder has been committed in the killer's own home it has been the general rule to sooner or later remove the noisome remains from their temporary hiding place and 'lose' them elsewhere. This is sometimes done piecemeal – as in the case of Dennis Nilsen – or, under cover of dark, in one piece – like John Reginald Christie. It is only very rarely that a corpse is kept around the house for more than a couple of weeks, and although the strange circumstances of James Finlay's death may not have been considered by the court a matter of murder, it does throw into sharp relief the dilemma of having a dead body on one's hands.

If James Finlay had been told in life that his body would suffer the indignity of being tied up in a sack in a supermarket trolley and dumped in the rubbish bay of a block of flats in Rochdale, he would have been very surprised and almost certainly a bit put out. On the bright side he would by then, of course, be past caring.

On Tuesday, 8th March 1977 a woman and her two daughters, who lived in the block of flats in Ashfield Valley, had noticed a shopping trolley containing a bundle in the refuse area but probed no further on account of the smell. Another resident saw the trolley on the 10th, and he too gave its stinking contents a wide berth. The caretaker was down in the gloomy area on 13th March and stumbled across the carrier and its contents. He instructed the borough Cleansing Department to remove it, and the refuse cart arrived on Tuesday the 15th. Now, rubbish collectors have no particular reason to treat the objects of their occupation with any great delicacy, and when the two men assigned to the trolley gave it a hefty shove across the concrete floor of the rubbish bay it was with no disrespect to James Finlay. Indeed, they were as startled as he would have been when the trolley fell on to its side and his severely decomposed body fell out.

Not that anybody knew that it was Finlay at the time; it required the skill and patience of Detective Chief Inspector Tony Fletcher of Manchester's fingerprint bureau and a team of forensic scientists to uncover the background to the bin-men's bizarre find.

The corpse's head had been enclosed in a plastic carrier bag which had quickly played host to millions of mites and maggots which effectively picked the face clean of any identifying features. The skin of the trunk had been virtually mummified and the comparatively good state of preservation of the internal organs made it possible to identify sufficient traces in the liver to point to barbiturate poisoning. More specifically an overdose of Amylobarbitone, commonly called Amytal.

The hands, which like the feet had been tied together when the body was found, were in a particularly advanced stage of decay, and with the deterioration of the skin any hope of fingerprint identification appeared to have been lost. However, when pathologist Dr Garrett removed the hands and sent them to the fingerprint bureau, Inspector Fletcher was able to reappraise them with the advantage of some very special experience.

Not long before the finding of the 'Rochdale Mummy', Fletcher had been involved with a team of experts at Manchester Museum's department of Egyptology on a scientific analysis of its collection of mummies. This new problem facing Tony Fletcher was similar in almost every detail to what he had faced in trying to fingerprint the mummies; that is, the extreme delicacy of the fingers due to corporeal deterioration making the customary ink-and-roll method impossible. Inspector Fletcher now decided to use the technique he developed at the Museum on the one finger of his corpse – the right middle digit – that might possibly yield a print.

A special quick-drying, fine-grain dental putty was gently applied to the tip of the finger and left a few moments to set. The 'mould' was then carefully peeled off and the inside treated with several coats of acrylic paint; when the paint was dry and had been removed it reproduced an accurate cast of the fingerprint which could be printed in the usual manner. It showed a remarkable sixteen points of similarity with those of James Edward Finlay, whose prints were already on file.

James Finlay was born in 1943 in Southport and had lived in the area for most of his life. In 1971, after six years of unsuccessful marriage, Finlay met Eileen Willan and together they set up home in Rochdale where James worked as a building labourer. Subsequent on James's divorce they married and Eileen produced a brace of children. In February 1975 the family had moved into No.28 Buttermere, a council flat adjoining the block in which the mummified body of James Finlay would be found two years later.

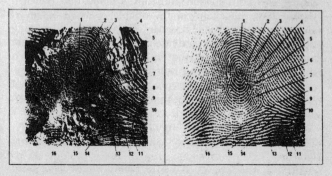

Fingerprints identifying the 'Rochdale Mummy' as James Finlay

When police officers spoke to Finlay's last employers – R. and T. Howarth of Rochdale – they learned that he had last collected wages on 29th August 1975, and had not been seen since. Meanwhile detectives who had spoken to the local council housing department were told that Mrs Finlay had become so badly in arrears with her rent over the two years since her tenancy began that they were obliged to issue an eviction notice. In recognition of this notice Eileen Finlay quitted the property on 5th March 1977.

There was little difficulty in tracing Mrs Finlay's where-abouts, though she insisted that the body found in the shopping trolley was not her husband. Informed that he most certainly was her husband, Eileen Finlay decided to confide what she now assured the interviewing officers was the truth . . .

About eighteen months previously – sometime in August 1975 – she and James had been having one of their periodic fights in which Eileen found herself on the receiving end of her husband's fists. In a fit of anger and desperation James had threatened to kill himself and Eileen had obligingly thrown him a bottle of sodium amytal tablets, and with a parting 'Bloody well get on with it, then!' she had stalked out.

When she returned to the flat several hours and many drinks later, Eileen Finlay found her husband lying dead on the sofa. For some reason never adequately explained, Finlay was bound hand and foot, a contortion which it would have been almost impossible to have achieved alone; but there it is. True, Mrs Finlay admitted having tightened the bonds in order to drag the corpse off the sofa and across the room, but that still leaves the puzzle of why a man should want to tie himself up after taking an overdose.

Tying a carrier bag over his head so that she could not see his face. Eileen Finlay pushed James's body into an airing cupboard, where it remained until March 1977 when force of eviction made its removal necessary. Where better than the rubbish bay of the neighbouring flats?

Despite a suspicion that Mrs Finlay might have been more than a passive participant in her husband's death, there was no concrete evidence on which to bring so serious a charge. Instead she was tried, convicted, and sentenced to two-year prison sentences on each of two obscure criminal charges. The first was concealing a body which had died from unnatural causes and so preventing the coroner from fulfilling his statutory duty to hold an inquest (an offence dating back at least to the Middle Ages); the second charge was not having given James a decent Christian burial.

And so what was the reason for James Finlay's death? Was it a dramatic gesture that went tragically wrong; was it a serious suicide?

Or might it have been murder?

MURDER ON THE HIGH SEAS

The Murder of Andrew Rose by Captain Henry Rogers
In the year 1857 aboard the *Martha and Jane* on the High Seas and his Trial and Execution at Liverpool

---

Captain Henry Rogers, of the *Martha and Jane* was indicted at the Liverpool Assizes, along with his two mates, for the murder of a seaman named Andrew Rose under circumstances, according to the evidence given by the crew, of horrible cruelty.

The serious nature of the charge was emphasized by prosecuting counsel who confirmed that the Crown had undertaken the proceedings in order to show that British subjects were never beyond the reach of British justice, and that seamen were to be protected from such barbarous abuse.

The case against Rogers, William Miles, and Charles Edward Seymour opened before Mr Baron Watson on 19th August 1857. The prosecution was led by the Attorney-General, Mr Bliss QC; counsel for the prisoners were Mr Monk QC, and Mr Aspinall.

For the benefit of the court the Attorney-General opened the case with a dramatic reconstruction of the prisoners' catalogue of crimes against the unfortunate seaman Rose, which resulted eventually in his death:

> 'Gentlemen of the jury, the three prisoners at the bar stand indicted of feloniously and of their malice aforethought killing one Andrew Rose. This offence was committed on the high seas, between 11th May and 5th June [1857]. The prisoner Henry Rogers was

Master of the ship *Martha and Jane*; the prisoner
Miles was the chief mate; and Charles Edward
Seymour, the second mate. Andrew Rose, the deceased, was an able seaman on board, and the means
of death a series of violences and outrages committed by the prisoners upon the deceased, by
beating and ill-treating him. The *Martha and Jane*
is a British ship, owned at Sunderland, and it sailed
from Hartlepool last year to Calcutta, where there
was a change of Masters. From Calcutta it came to
Demerara, and from Demerara to Barbadoes, where
Henry Rogers became the Master, and Andrew Rose
entered on board ship. He entered on the 29th of
April as an able seaman, and signed articles which
stipulated, among other things, for a certain allowance of provisions. When he came on board he was
put to some duty by the second mate, Seymour, who
found fault with him and beat him so severely that
Rose was advised by some of the crew to leave the
ship, and he ran away. About the 9th or 10th of May
he was brought back by the police and was put in
irons. The vessel sailed on the 11th May. The day
after the vessel sailed he was again beaten by
Seymour; the chief mate and the Captain also beat
him on the same day.

From that day until the last outrage, about two or
three days before his death, he was beaten by the
prisoners almost every day with a rope and a whip,
when in irons and out of irons. It is difficult to get the
precise dates; but they all occurred after the sailing
of the ship and before the death of the deceased.
When he came on board he was apparently an able
seaman and in good health; his hair was close
cropped, and there is reason from that and his
conduct to surmise that his intellect had been deranged. He was fond of singing, and he sang "Oh, be
joyful". One Sunday morning the Captain bade him
be silent, and said, "I'll make you sorrowful," and
forced an iron bolt of considerable size into his
mouth, and the other two prisoners tied it with a
rope behind his head, and he was kept with that gag

in his mouth for about an hour and a half. The Captain had a dog on board, and he taught that dog to bite the deceased. He first set him on with a command to "Bite that man", and afterwards, whenever the Captain came forward with his whip, the dog would fly at [Rose] and bite him. Upon some occasions the blood spurted out. The dog bit out a piece of the flesh, and as the deceased put out his hands to protect himself, the dog bit them too. Upon another occasion, when the deceased was sent aloft to furl the sail, he was naked and went up with a bucket of water probably for a cause to which I shall allude presently. The chief mate followed him up, and whipped him so severely that the blood ran in several places. Upon another occasion, when the deceased was in irons, he asked to be allowed to go to the bows to do a necessary act. And I must here mention that the deceased laboured under such an infirmity which prevented him containing his excrement, which came from him involuntarily. When he was in irons he asked leave to go forward for that purpose. He was refused, upon which he relieved himself upon the deck. The mate and the Captain then beat him, and the latter ordered two men to hold the deceased upon his back, and called for a spoon. He took a "fid" – a wooden pin – with which he forced the excrement of the deceased into his mouth, and up his nose, saying, "Isn't it nice?" and "You shall have more of it," until those who were called to assist shrunk away, unable to bear it longer. A day or two after, this was repeated several times.

The Captain ordered the carpenter to knock the head out of a water-cask; but as he was not quick enough, the captain and mates did it themselves. It was the smallest of the water-casks on board the ship; they brought Rose to the cask and put him in. They then rolled the cask backwards and forwards several times over the deck, the only means of getting air being through the bung-hole, which was on the bilge. They lashed the cask to the side of the ship, and there the deceased remained from twelve at noon till twelve at night. While there he begged for water, and uttered great cries of distress. One of the men gave him a little pea soup – poured it into his mouth, at which the Captain was very angry, demanding who had done it, and threatened to serve him the same. Another seaman gave him a little water, when he complained of suffocation and excessive heat. The last act, which terminated the cruelties was upon the occasion the deceased was told by the Captain – "Rose, I wish you would either drown or hang yourself," to which Rose answered, "I wish you would do it for me." The Captain and the two mates then took him to the mainmast. They got a rope and made what was called a "timber hitch". They put it over his neck and hoisted him up, his feet being from one to three feet from the deck. He remained suspended by the neck for about two minutes. His face became black, his eyes protruded from the sockets, and froth came out of his mouth, and they then let him down. The moment his feet touched the deck he fell flat, as if lifeless, and the Captain was heard to say that, had they kept him there half a minute longer he would have been dead. This seems to have been the last outrage he had to endure.

After this his body and mind both gave way. The crew got him down to the forecastle, but he was so crazy they were obliged to tie his hands. He remained in the forecastle a day or two, but on the morning of the 5th June – two or three days after the hanging – they got him up on the deck to wash himself. He could scarcely crawl. He lay down on the deck, with his head towards the forward hatch, and the water came in over his legs, but not over his head, and he died. An hour or two after they came to remove him and found him dead. He had wounds all over his body from the biting of the dog and the whipping. These wounds had festered. There were maggots in some of them, and he was in such a state that the crew were loth to touch him. They dragged

him with a rope aft, and in an hour after that, by
order of the Captain he was thrown overboard. The
ship made land the next morning, and arrived in
Liverpool on the 9th of June. Information was given
and the Captain and mates arrested . . .'

Such was the weight of evidence and the feeling of
revulsion among the general public that the prisoners
were necessarily found guilty, though with a recommendation to mercy from the jury on account of previous good
behaviour. The passions of the mob had been excited by
the revolting disclosures of the crew, and the verdict was
received with vociferous cheering by the crowds which
thronged the streets around the court. It is said that the
verdict took all the professional men engaged in the trial
by surprise, and it was supposed that upon the recommendation of the jury the obligatory sentence of death
would have been commuted. This was done in the case of
the two mates, but the captain was left to the extreme
sentence of the law, and was executed at Kirkdale (now
Walton Gaol) on 12th September.

When public indignation had time to cool it began to be
felt that the grounds for conviction were of a very
ambiguous nature. The crew, it was noted, had been
almost in a state of mutiny during the voyage, and bore
a violent prejudice against the captain. The fact that the
two mates were indicted along with the captain – and so
unable to offer evidence in his defence – deprived Rogers
of all means of rebutting the charges. In such a case a
conspiracy to exaggerate, if not to falsify, evidence was not
difficult to achieve. Outside pressures had a good deal to
do with the verdicts, there having been reported a great
number of atrocious acts of cruelty perpetrated at sea,
especially on board American vessels. A remonstrance
made by the English to the American Government on
this subject was met by the curt rejoinder of Mr Secretary
Marcy 'that we might look at home'. Our Government
then would have been placed in a most awkward position
if, in the very first instance in which a capital conviction
had been obtained, the royal prerogative had been exercised to screen the culprit. There can be little doubt that

captain Rogers was executed to allay the popular thirst for vengeance, and to vindicate the determination of the Government.

In a solitary gesture of selfless generosity, a public subscription was set up for Rogers' widow, which raised the sum of £670.

SHOTS OFF SCREEN

**The Murder of Leonard Thomas and John
Catterall by George Kelly**
On Saturday, 19th March 1949, at the
Cameo Cinema, Webster Street, Wavertree,
Merseyside

The Cameo cinema used to occupy a site in Webster
Street in the broken-down Wavertree district of Liverpool. Shortly after 9.30 on the evening of Saturday, 19th
March 1949, an unmemorable but popular Western was
playing to a packed house.

Behind the office door 44-year-old manager Leonard
Thomas and his assistant John Bernard Catterall – well
known to their Saturday morning matinée audiences as
Uncle Len and Uncle John – had just received the day's
takings from box-office cashier Mrs Jackman, and begun
the familiar routine of sorting the pennies, sixpences,
shillings and half-crowns into their different bags.

Mrs Jackman had got no further than the end of the
corridor when she was startled by the sharp explosions of
six shots fired from a gun in rapid succession. With commendable courage but little common sense both the cashier
and the doorman, Patrick Griffin – who had also been
attracted by the shooting – rushed back to Mr Thomas's
office in time to see a masked gunman retreating down the
emergency stairs and into the wintry night.

In the warmth of the cinema's auditorium seven hundred faces had eyes only for the drama being played out
on the big screen; of the real-life tragedy taking place just
yards beyond the wall they were innocently unaware.

Inside the office Leonard Thomas was dead and John
Catterall lay fatally wounded.

Despite the best efforts of the Liverpool police force – including the interviewing of more than 75,000 people – it was six months before any further information became available on the murders, and when it did, it was in the form of an anonymous letter. The unknown correspondent proposed a 'deal': in exchange for police protection he was prepared to put names to the Cameo murderers, and as requested the police inserted the following advertisement in the next edition of the *Liverpool Echo*: 'Letter received. Promise definitely given.' This was followed up a little later – on 29th September – by a telephone call from a small-time crook named James Philip Northam – called 'Stutty' by his associates on account of a speech impediment. Northam and his girl-friend had been privy to the initial planning of the Cameo job in The Beehive public house in Mount Pleasant.

Resulting information led to the arrest of two men: George Kelly, 28 years old, thug and titular head of the Kelly Gang, a bunch of mainly Irish ruffians dredged from the slums of Liverpool's dockland; and Charles Connolly, 26-year-old member of Kelly's Gang. It emerged later that Connolly had been delegated to act as look-out while Kelly committed the robbery, but that hearing shots – whether from the cinema's auditorium or its manager's office – he had fled in panic.

The unsavoury pair were arraigned before Mr Justice Oliver at Liverpool Assizes in January 1950, and Kelly was ably defended by Miss Rose Heilbron, the first woman to lead a defence in a British murder trial, and subsequently the first female High Court judge. (Predictably Kelly's reaction was 'I want no judy defending me' – an opinion he quickly reversed.) The thirteen-day trial ended in disagreement among the jury and the prisoners were ordered for retrial at the next assize in the following month, February. This time Kelly was tried separately, and despite a spirited second try, Miss Heilbron was unable to convince the jury. It fell to Mr Justice Cassels to don the black cap, and George Kelly went to his Maker at Walton Prison on 28th March 1950.

Connolly's second appearance was also before

Mr Justice Cassels, on 13th February. No evidence was presented this time on the murder charge, of which he was formally declared Not Guilty. On the charges of robbery and conspiracy to rob he pleaded guilty, and was sentenced to ten and two-year sentences respectively, to run concurrently.

THE MIDLANDS

Derbyshire

Gloucestershire

Hereford and Worcester

Leicestershire

Lincolnshire

Northamptonshire

Nottinghamshire

Shropshire

Staffordshire

Warwickshire

West Midlands

THE CARBON COPY MURDERS

**The Murder of William Arthur Elliott and
George Gerald Stobbs by Michael Copeland
On Sunday, 12th June 1960, and Wednesday,
29th March 1961 respectively at Clod Hill Lane,
Baslow, Chesterfield, Derbyshire**

Moor Body Riddle

Tuesday, 14th June 1960: On Sunday, 12th June the
shoeless body of 60-year-old William Arthur Elliott
was found in isolated Clod Hill Lane which crosses the
moor near Baslow. Mr Elliott was believed by the pathologist to have died of severe head injuries. The victim's
'bubble' car containing his shoes was subsequently found
crashed in Park Road, Chesterfield. While police continue
to search the desolate moorland for a possible weapon,
detectives have been making inquiries around Mr Elliott's
home at 9 Haddon Road, Bakewell, in an attempt to piece
together his last hours alive; they are asking anybody who
saw the ivory-coloured bubble car, registration number
KLU 488, to contact them.

Victim's Double tells of Attack

Wednesday, 15th June 1960: 51-year-old bus cleaner William
Atkinson, of Church Lane, North Wingfield, revealed
today that he had been attacked about a week before
the murder of Mr William Elliott in the same area where
the bubble car had been found – Boythorpe Road, which
runs close by Park Road. Mr Atkinson bears a remarkable
physical likeness to the moors victim, and police are
working on the theory that he may have been assaulted
in mistake for Mr Elliott. Furthermore, the two men were
known to each other, being habitués of The Spread Eagle

public house in Chesterfield. The inquiry is being headed by Detective Superintendent Leonard Stretton.

Bubble Car Murder
Tip by Woman

Saturday, 18th June 1960; Mrs Gladys Vickers of Sutton Spring Wood, Chesterfield, told police last night that she may have seen Mr William Elliott attacked the night before his body was found. Mrs Vickers knew Mr Elliott and: 'I saw him being chased along an alley outside The Royal Oak public house. The man chasing him was dark-haired, swarthy, and with thin features, and he caught up with him. Then I heard someone say "Oh" and groan.'

Man Dead in Bubble-Car murder Lane
'Carbon Copy Theory'

Wednesday, 29th March 1961: An unidentified man was found today dead from injuries in Clod Hill Lane, where 9 months ago William Elliott was found murdered. A police spokesman said that they were working on the assumption that it was a 'carbon copy' killing. The inquest on the late Mr Elliott returned a verdict of 'murder by person or persons unknown'; he had been kicked to death.

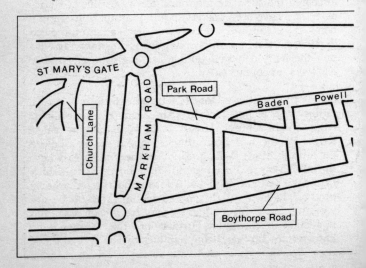

Although more than 100,000 people had been questioned, no arrest resulted. Detective Superintendent Stretton, who led the former inquiry, has taken over the present investigation; he revealed that an abandoned car had been found in exactly the same spot in Park Road that Mr Elliott's blood-stained bubble car had been left.

Carbon Copy Murder
Thursday, 30th March 1961: Victim of what police have called the 'Carbon Copy Murder' has been named as 48-year-old Chesterfield chemist George Gerald Stobbs.

Another Dramatic Similarity
Saturday, 1st April 1961: Police issued a statement today which revealed another startling similarity to the 'bubble-car murder'. It would appear that a man named Gillespie, living near Stubbing Court, and who bears a great resemblance to victim Gerald Stobbs, was attacked shortly before the latest killing – police think that, as in the case of the assault on William Atkinson before the Elliott murder, Dr Gillespie was mistaken for the intended victim. The inquest called by Mr Frederick Nesbit, High Peak coroner, was adjourned to a date to be fixed.

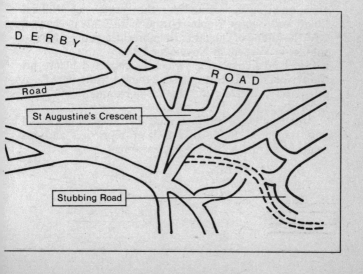

Probe into Double Lives of Victims
Undercover Man in Hunt for Killer

Monday, 3rd April 1961: It was announced by officers investigating the 'Carbon Copy Murders' that they are to give an 'undercover' man the task of infiltrating the circles in which both of the victims moved. Police now believe that both Mr Elliott and Mr Stobbs led double lives of which even their closest relatives were unaware. Both men had acquaintances in common and drank in the same public house – The Three Horseshoes at Chesterfield.

Despite continued investigations by the Derbyshire constabulary, the case remained unsolved over the succeeding months. The only further dramatic incident was the death of 63-year-old Arthur Jenkinson shortly after he had been interviewed by the police. Although the coroner's jury returned a verdict of suicide, there was some persistent rumour that Mr Jenkinson had been murdered – had been overcome and had his head forced into the gas oven.

Month followed month and the likelihood of getting to the bottom of the Carbon Copy Mystery grew more remote. But three years later 26-year-old Michael Copeland, a former regular soldier from St Augustine's Crescent, Chesterfield (near where the two cars had been abandoned) was arrested for the murder of William Elliott and George Stobbs. Furthermore, he was charged with the killing of Guenther Helmbrecht, a young German soldier, in Verden, in November 1960.

Copeland's confession (which he retracted before his trial) explained that 'It was something I really hated' – a reference to the fact that both Stobbs and Elliott were homosexual.

Found guilty of all three murders, Michael Copeland was sentenced to death but later reprieved and his sentence commuted to life imprisonment.

ARSENIC IN THE SHEEP DIP

The Death of Harry Pace from Arsenic Poisoning
On Wednesday, 18th January 1928 at Fetterhill Farm, Coleford, Gloucestershire and the Trial and Acquittal of his wife Beatrice Annie for his Murder

---

It must have seemed like adding insult to injury to Mrs Pace when she was accused of murdering her bully of a husband. Harry Pace had never been easy to live with, and the long-suffering Beatrice would not have been normal if it had never crossed her mind how pleasant life would be without him; especially after one of those periodic outbursts of sadistic rage which always left her scarred and bruised, inside and out, for months afterwards: 'We have been in our present house nearly four years, and on two occasions my husband thrashed me severely, once about two years ago and again in March before I was having my baby. The first time was with a strap and the second time with a stick. In the early part of last year he threatened to shoot me and I called the police.'

But now Harry *was* dead.

The facts of the matter were these. Harry Pace, quarryman and part-time sheep rearer, living at Fetterhill Farm, in Coleford on the edge of the Forest of Dean, had been taken ill while dipping sheep in the early summer of 1927. Pace was clearly suffering so acutely from stomach pains and a burning sensation in his throat that it was thought prudent to confine him to the Gloucester Royal Infirmary for observation. He was discharged in October, but in

December was stricken with a similar attack. On 10th January, 1928, Harry Pace died.

The funeral was arranged for 15th January, and would have proceeded without interruption had it not been for the suspicions of Harry's brother Elton who obtained an order from the coroner, Mr Maurice Carter, to stop the funeral and conduct a post-mortem examination. In many respects it is comforting to be reminded of the degree of power that still rests in the hands of the ordinary citizen to effect this kind of dramatic action. In the case of Harry Pace it would probably have been best left alone.

Nevertheless, Harry's mortal remains were subjected to close medical scrutiny, and in his evidence to the inquest Professor Walker Hall testified that he could discover no signs of natural disease in the body's organs, but that the appearance of the stomach lining suggested the presence of a strongly irritant poison; furthermore, changes in the liver, heart and kidneys pointed to arsenic, the last dose of which must have been taken between 6 and 48 hours before death, but that the poison must have been present in the body at least three weeks before death; the total amount of arsenic found was 9.42 grains. Asked if it would have been possible for Pace to have absorbed the arsenic – which was a major active constituent of sheep-dip – through the skin, Professor Hall excluded the possibility of infiltration to the extent found.

During the inquest which was to span an incredible twenty-two hearings between 16th January and the end of May, Sir William Willcox, a senior medical adviser to the Home Office was summoned to comment on the post-mortem findings, and submitted his report on 23rd March. The symptoms, he confirmed, were indicative and typical of arsenical poisoning, the analyses showing the substance to be present far in excess of a fatal dose. In addition, Willcox felt that the previous illness – in July 1927 – also suggested arsenical poisoning. Other symptoms exhibited by the late Mr Pace – pigmentation of the skin, slight jaundice, inflamed throat, and the retardation of putrefaction in a sample of blood – were all suggestive of the same conclusion.

Dr Ellis gave evidence on the analysis of various preparations of sheep-dip found about the farm, and advanced several theories to the coroner's jury as to how the potentially lethal substance could have been secretly administered.

After the briefest of summations, the coroner emphasised that in his opinion there was no evidence to support the suggestion that Harry Pace had been accidentally poisoned. After an hour's retirement the jury's foreman was able to state that in the opinion of his colleagues and himself: 'Harry Pace met his death by arsenical poisoning administered by some person or persons other than himself, and in our view the case calls for further investigation.'

In a move that was subsequently to be heavily criticized (and quite rightly so), the coroner declined to accept this verdict: 'Only the committal of a person after a coroner's inquiry can bring about an investigation, which cannot take place unless there is some person named. It is necessary for you to name a person if a person is to be charged.' The jury retired for a further twenty-five minutes before returning with the amended verdict 'that Harry Pace met his death by arsenic poisoning administered by Beatrice Pace'.

Within moments Mrs Pace, sitting distraught in the body of the court, was arrested on the coroner's warrant. With cries of 'I didn't do it! I didn't do it!' her pathetic figure was assisted to the cells.

Beatrice Pace was committed for trial at the Gloucester Assizes on 2nd July 1928. Mr Justice Horridge presided, and the evidence for the prosecution, as is traditional in poisoning cases, was led by one of the Law Officers of the Crown – in this instance the Solicitor-General, Sir Frank Boyd Merriman KC. Such was the strength of sympathy for Mrs Pace that a public subscription was sufficient to enable her solicitors, Wellington and Mathews, to retain the services of no less an advocate than Mr Norman (later Lord) Birkett KC.

In his opening address, the Solicitor-General observed that there was no dispute whatever as to the cause of Harry Pace's untimely decease – he had died from a massive 9½ grains of arsenic – more than four times a lethal dose. And that the sheep dip – purchased, he emphasized, by Mrs Pace – contained at least 2,800 grains in a single packet! Mrs Pace, he reminded the court, had made two significant statements to the police: 'I don't think it possible for any person who had visited him to have given him any poison to take'; and 'It is my view, and I am convinced, that my husband poisoned himself and I don't think anyone else could have done it. If they had, I should have known'.

In all, Sir Frank Merriman called seventeen witnesses fairly equally divided between medical experts and relatives of the deceased. Of the latter, Leslie, the 11-year-old son of the Paces, had some of the most damaging evidence to relate. He described the day on which his father, lying on his sick-bed, had asked for a box in which he kept his sheep-dipping materials to be brought to him. After checking the contents he instructed the boy to lock the box away in a chest of drawers in the room. The implication was clear: Harry Pace already suspected that he was being slowly poisoned and was keeping the source under lock and key.

Pace's mother recalled how, two days before his death, her son had complained of the bitterness of the water that was given to him to drink, and asked her to bring a fresh glass from the tap. And then came Elton, whose suspicions had initiated this elaborate legal ritual. He claimed that he

---

Arsenic

No metallic poison has been so much used by criminals as arsenic. In the earliest days it was administered in the form of yellow sulphide, the bright colour of which convinced the ancient alchemists that it must be a source of gold.

The more common white oxide of arsenic was traditionally prepared by roasting the ore slowly and putting the resulting product into a vessel and applying greater heat; the vapours produced condense as a heavy white powder, or a crystalline mass. The vapour, which smells strongly of garlic, is very poisonous, and the greatest care has to be taken to avoid inhaling it.

The symptoms of arsenic poisoning vary a great deal, according to the form and dose which is administered. In a typical case of poisoning by white oxide the patient experiences a feeling of sinking and depression, followed by sickness, and an intense burning pain in the stomach, which is increased by pressure. These symptoms are followed by vomiting and diarrhoea, which is more or less violent, and often accompanied by cramp in the calves of the legs. Collapse rapidly comes on, and the patient dies from exhaustion. One of the most marked external characteristics is cyanosis—blueness of the skin caused by lack of oxygen in the bloodstream. Post-mortem examination reveals the lining membrane of the stomach to be very much inflamed, and in many cases badly ulcerated. Arsenic is a distinct irritant poison.

had heard – 'with his own ears' – Mrs Pace wishing 'the old bastard' was dead; wishing she could poison him. On one of his visits, Elton maintained, he found Beatrice Pace leaning across his brother murmuring 'Harry, you're dying – we shan't see you much longer.'

The medical witnesses in the main reiterated what they had presented to the coroner's court. It was Sir William Willcox that Norman Birkett met in cross-examination:

Birkett: Arsenic may find its way into the body through the mouth?
Willcox: Yes.

Sometimes through the skin? – If the skin is broken.

You have from time to time referred to cases of accidental poisoning from certain preparations such as sheep-dip, which contain arsenic? – Yes.

Also, that there is a danger of suicidal death from this preparation?' – Yes, there is, of course, a risk.

There is a risk of chronic arsenical poisoning to

those who carry out sheep dipping? – Yes.

If the most perfect methods of cleanliness were not followed during the process, some of the arsenic might be absorbed when taking food? – Yes, if the person did not wash his hands, or if there were rashes on the hands.

As the case for the prosecution closed, Norman Birkett rose to take one of the biggest and most successful gambles in the whole of his long career at the bar. He submitted to Mr Justice Horridge, in advance of any evidence being presented on behalf of the defence, that there was insufficient evidence for the trial to continue further; the scientific evidence was, he suggested, as consistent with self-administration as with any other possibility.

Amid general surprise, the judge responded: 'My opinion is that it would not be safe to ask the jury to proceed further with it.' He instructed them to return a formal verdict of 'Not Guilty', and to evident public approbation Mrs Pace was acquitted.

THE MURDERING MAJOR

The Death of Mrs Katharine Armstrong
On 22nd February 1921 at 'Mayfield', Hay-on-Wye, Hereford and Worcs and the Trial and Conviction of her husband Herbert Rowse Armstrong for her Murder

---

'**S**cuse fingers,' mumbled the Major, placing a fresh buttered scone on his guest's tea-plate. Oswald Martin smiled – he was enjoying his visit to Major Armstrong's house; he had almost forgotten what good company the old boy could be when he chose.

Both men shared the profession of solicitor, with offices at either end of the high street in the small town of Hay-on-Wye; but over the past year the relationship had been more than a little strained. In fact they were locked in a legal wrangle which had become so acrimonious that they could scarcely bear to acknowledge each other in the street, and Martin had felt constrained to threaten the Major with legal action for the recovery of a £500 deposit from a client which Armstrong had no right to retain, but which he was nevertheless stubbornly withholding.

The battle was still raging, but the two men had called a brief armistice, and on this agreeable afternoon in late October, they were reliving a happier acquaintance over currant-bread, tea, and scones. They chatted idly about this and that, and Armstrong was soon firmly entrenched in his favourite subject of gardening, and the ceaseless temerity of the dandelions in infesting his rambling lawns. The afternoon was fast fading when Oswald Martin thanked the Major for his hospitality and departed homeward.

As soon as his guest had left, the small, dapper figure of the Major could be seen carefully clearing away the tea things.

Then he crossed to his desk and with deep concentration counted a number of little white-paper packages that he had taken from a drawer. Rubbing his hands with satisfaction, he replaced the packets and drifted into a deep reverie.

Not long after Oswald Martin reached home he began to feel distinctly uncomfortable. Soon the unfortunate man was engulfed by a terrible wave of nausea, vomiting and diarrhoea, which continued to plague him throughout a sleepless night. On the following morning, Mrs Martin called in Dr Thomas Hincks, who diagnosed a bilious attack and confined his patient to bed. It was in no time at all that the village grapevine carried news of Oswald's illness to his father-in-law, Mr John Davies, local chemist, and a fussy old fellow, who soon materialized at the sick-bed's side with questions on recent diet. No sooner had he heard of the tea-party with Armstrong than an unmistakable gleam came into his eye. John Davies scratched his nose reflectively; 'Oswald,' he said, 'I don't want to alarm you, but I very much fear that there's more to this bilious attack of yours than meets the eye. In fact, I'd almost stake my reputation on it being no less than a case of arsenical poisoning!' 'Really, father,' Martin expostulated, 'Armstrong may be a bit of a shark legally, but dash it all, you can't go around saying the chap's a poisoner. There's such a thing as slander, you know. . .' 'Just a minute,' Davies interrupted him. 'You wouldn't know anything about this, Oswald; in fact nobody does, because I've kept it to myself for quite a while now. I've had my suspicions all along – ever since the death of poor Mrs Armstrong. Even before that. If I showed you my ledger . . . that man has bought enough pure arsenic to kill an army . . . always coming in for it he is; says it's for the dandelions. By God, Oswald, the most voracious weeds in Christendom couldn't get through that lot. What's more, he's still buying the stuff when no self-respecting dandelion's shown its head above ground for weeks. You take care, boy, or you could end up like the Major's lady. Have nothing to do with that man, that's the best advice I can give you!' and John Davies strode purposefully out of the sick room. He took with him a determination to action; he was on his way to Dr Hincks' surgery.

Hincks listened carefully to all the grim-faced Davies had to say – including a snippet of information about a certain box of Fuller's chocolates that had been sent anonymously to his son-in-law's house by post in September. The box had shown signs of having been tampered with, and Oswald's sister-in-law had been taken quite ill after eating a chocolate at a dinner party in early October. The postmark on the package had been unreadable, but Davies was prepared to hint at who he thought was the sender! Hincks was understandably alarmed by the accusation of poison; he paid a return visit to his patient and collected a sample of Oswald Martin's urine and (as they were still in the house) the box of suspect chocolates. Both specimens he sent to the Home Office for analysis – the regular procedure where there was a suspicion of poison being present. When the results came back the combined fears of Hincks and Davies were more than vindicated – the urine did indeed contain traces of arsenic, and on the top layer of the chocolates there were two in which had been injected a substantial amount of that same fatal substance.

Dr Hincks was a worried man, and in an attempt to divert his attention for a while from the awful implications of the analyst's report he saddled a horse and set out for an hour's vigorous riding . . . Suddenly he reigned in his horse and sat stationary in the saddle; an awful thought had grown in his mind. 'What about Mrs Armstrong?' He had signed the certificate himself: death from natural causes. But now, going through each symptom and circumstance of her illness, it was impossible for him to overlook the fact that those causes could have been something very far from natural.

Mrs Armstrong had been a strong-willed and domineering woman; some six inches taller than her husband, she had ruled him with a firm hand that brooked no smoking, no drinking, and no answering back. She was also a neurotic and a hypochondriac, dosing herself with prodigious quantities of the most fashionable patent medicines. Hincks had treated her for rheumatism between May and August 1919, and later for bilious attacks, insomnia, and delusions of guilt and inferiority that became so marked that in August 1920 she was admitted to a mental hospital. By December of the same year, however, both her physical and mental condition had improved dramatically, and the Major had insisted that she return home immediately, quite against medical advice. Armstrong obtained his wife's discharge on 22nd January 1921, but no sooner had she returned home than she relapsed into another bout of a serious illness; within a month Mrs Armstrong was dead. Thinking over the final passage of her illness, Dr Hincks became more and more convinced that the certificate should have read 'cause of death – arsenical poisoning'.

The doctor had practised in the same locality for upward of twenty-three years; he was deeply respected – even loved – by his patients, many of whom invested him with an almost saintly infallibility. It thus took more than a little courage now for him to write to the Home Office confiding that he could possibly have been wrong in his diagnosis. But a good doctor will never shirk his responsibility, and Hincks at least aspired to competence in his professional duties; as a result he found himself a few days later on the way to an interview with Hereford's Chief Constable and the Director of Public Prosecutions. On his way to the meeting Dr Hincks's thoughts were completely centred around Major Armstrong. What sort of a man was he? He wore a mask of deep respectability, and yet he was currently undergoing treatment for venereal disease contracted during the period his wife was in hospital. Despite this illness, just three days after Mrs Armstrong's death, the Major had been seen in London in the company of an old flame from his army days; and three months later he had unsuccessfully proposed marriage to a local lady.

With vision clarified by hindsight, Hincks saw a new image of his patient with the anomalies of behaviour that caused the doctor to caution the Chief Constable to conduct his enquiries in the strictest secrecy: 'If he gets to know about it, he might murder himself, his children, and me!' Hincks had by now convinced himself that Armstrong was a homicidal maniac, and recollected with concern that the Major always kept a loaded revolver by his bed. He also remembered vividly the day that Armstrong had casually asked him, 'By the way, doctor, what is a fatal dose of arsenic?'

But there was another reason for the police to tread warily in investigating the case; Major Herbert Rowse Armstrong, TD, MA (Cantab), solicitor, clerk to the local magistrates, and churchwarden, was a clever and educated man, and a highly respected pillar of the community.

During the time that the police were cautiously building their case, the unsuspecting Armstrong was positively bombarding Oswald Martin – now recovered and back at work – with further invitations to tea and dinner. Martin, not surprisingly, found one excuse or another to refuse the Major's 'hospitality'.

The evidence was mounting against Armstrong. The police carefully noted the dates and amounts of arsenic that the Major had purchased and the fact that he owned a tiny spray-gun with which he individually eradicated the hateful dandelions – the nozzle of a similar gun exactly fitted the puncture marks discovered in the contaminated chocolates. It was also known that about six months before Mrs Armstrong's death her husband had drawn up a new will for her, leaving the £2,278 estate and all her personal assets to him, and excluding their three children who would have been joint beneficiaries with their father under the terms of the previous will. The new document had been witnessed by the maid but not, as is legally required, in the presence of Mrs Armstrong herself.

At last the police were confident enough of their case to move in, and on New Year's Eve Major Herbert Rowse Armstrong was arrested in his office at Hay for the attempted murder of Oswald Martin. Armstrong appeared completely composed, and blustered: 'This is not a very serious matter and I will help you all I can.' But the statement that he made later was guarded, and when he was searched two tiny packets were found in his waistcoat pocket – one containing several grams of white arsenic, and the other an arsenic and charcoal mixture. In the Major's desk at home more of the poisonous packets were found. The Major's explanation that he had divided the arsenic up into 20 equal-sized packets 'for convenience in killing the weeds' fell very flat indeed. When he was asked why this method was more convenient than just pushing the stuff straight into the ground he maintained a dignified silence.

At 6.45pm on 2nd January 1922, the icy ground of the local churchyard at Cusop yielded up the exhumed body of Mrs Armstrong, and her organs were removed in a chilly cottage nearby to be sent for analysis. The analyst later reported: 'It is the largest amount of arsenic I have found in any case of arsenical poisoning.' Mrs Armstrong's suffering had been prolonged by constant and systematic dosing over a long period of time, resulting in the terrible mental and physical torment of her last unhappy years.

Armstrong now faced the dual charges of the murder of his wife and the attempted murder of Oswald Martin; ironically he appeared in the very court at Hereford where he himself had acted so many times as Clerk to the Court. On this occasion his place had been taken by an 80-year-old stand-in, to whom Armstrong constantly offered advice.

When the case came to trial – which lasted for ten full days – Armstrong proved a stalwart witness, remaining for over 5 hours in the box; finally, after a deliberation of 48 minutes, the jury found him guilty and sentence of death was passed upon the murdering Major.

He was hanged at Gloucester on Wednesday, 31st May 1922. Perhaps to this day his body lies beneath the triumphant heads of a host of golden dandelions!

STATEMENT MADE BY HERBERT ROWSE ARMSTRONG TO THE POLICE

Broad Street, Hay.

I, Herbert Rowse Armstrong, having been cautioned by Chief Inspector Crutchett that anything I may say may be used in evidence hereafter, wish to make the following statement:

Mr Martin is a brother solicitor in Hay. He had been married in June last but owing to ~~a personal bereavement~~* my wife's death in February last I had been unable to do any entertaining. I asked Mr Martin to have a cup of tea on Wednesday the 26th of October 1921. At that time I had two men working in my garden, which had been allowed to get in a very

---

* These alterations appear on the original document

bad state: their names are McGeorge, who was working in the garden, and Stokes who was erecting a fowl-house. They both live in Bear Street, Hay.

I had no special reason for inviting Mr Martin to tea other than that I had not entertained him since his marriage, and at that time I was not entertaining on a very large scale.

On the day in question Mr Martin arrived at my house about 5pm. I had previously gone home to see that everything was in order. I took him round the garden and showed him the various improvements that I proposed to make. We then entered the drawing room where tea had been laid out by my housekeeper Miss Pearce. As far as I remember the food was placed in three plates on a wicker stand. I ~~can trace~~ remember that wicker stand as I have a more ornate one in brass, and my housekeeper had asked which I preferred. The food consisted of buttered scone, buttered currant loaf in slices, and bread and butter. I handed Mr Martin some scone on a plate. He took some, and I also took some which I ate and I afterwards placed the dish of currant bread and butter by his side on the table and asked him to help himself. I shall be able to ascertain by going to my house where the scone and ~~buttered bread~~ currant loaf were bought. I remember Mr Martin saying that buttered loaf was a favourite dish of his, and I know that he ate heartily and cleared the dish. Afterwards I asked him to smoke, and remember that he was off colour and instead of having a pipe said that he would smoke a cigarette. At the time both Mr Martin and I were working at high pressure on some sales of a Capt. Hope, and probably this was the reason for his being below par. Mr Martin and I discussed general office organisation, and I remember telling him that I was understaffed. I also was feeling the effects of hard work. It was light when we began tea, but it soon became necessary for me to light the gas, and as I did so the globe came off and fell which caused it to break. Mr Martin left about 6pm and drove home in his own car. All the food which

Martin consumed was prepared by Miss Pearce and was waiting for us when we entered the drawing room; and either she or the maid brought the tea and hot water in when we had taken our seats. Miss Pearce had previously asked if the food (which was subsequently placed on the table) would be satisfactory, and I had said 'Yes'.

The following morning I went to Mr Martin's office to get various documents relating to Capt. Hope's sale which was to be completed on the 2nd November. It was a big property sale in which he was acting for several purchasers. I was told ~~that Mr~~ by one of his clerks (I cannot remember which) that he had been taken ill. I think now that it was Preen as I have a recollection of him saying that Dr Hincks had been called and had said that he thought Mr Martin was suffering from jaundice.

Mr Martin's illness was causing a great inconvenience as the completions were fixed for the following Wednesday, and there was a great deal to be done. I sent a message to Mr Martin by one of his clerks (I do not remember which), and said that if I could assist in any possible way, and he would authorise his clerks, that I would carry the matter through if he were not well enough. The next thing that I remember was that he was not down at his office on Saturday. I called at his house on the Sunday morning after church. I saw Mrs Martin, and she told me that he had been very sick but was better, and would be down at his office on Monday. It was not necessary for Mr Martin to accept my offer of assistance as he was able to attend his office and carry through the completions by the stated date. After Mr Martin's illness he told me that he had been very sick and that he had had a thorough clean out. Prior to his illness I had chaffed him about his practice of motoring to and from his office saying that if he did not take walking exercise he would be ill. I always walk to my office, not possessing a car.

I am continually meeting with Mr Martin professionally and he and his wife have a standing dinner invitation to my house when a date can be fixed.

The first time I purchased arsenic was in 1914. I think ~~I have got the receipt in my gardening book~~. At this time I came across a recipe for weed killer consisting of caustic soda and arsenic which was very much cheaper than the liquid weed killer, which my gardener had previously been in the habit of purchasing. I therefore purchased caustic soda and arsenic from Mr Davies, chemist of Hay, and signed the book. I remember him telling me that the arsenic had to be mixed with charcoal and he mixed it accordingly. I made the weed killer at my house by boiling the caustic soda and arsenic in an old petrol tin. I think I put in all I purchased. It might have been in the proportion of equal parts of each but I don't remember. I think Miss Pearce will remember the preparation. It was all used in the garden as weed killer. I have always had considerable trouble with weeds on the path of my vegetable garden.

The purchase of half-a-pound of arsenic in June, 1919, was for the same purpose and was used in exactly the same way.

The liquid and powder weed killer were purchased to my order by Jay of Castle Gardens, Hay ~~(My gardener)~~ who attended to my garden at that time ~~to my order~~. I don't even know how much was purchased and I never saw it. I believe it was kept in the stable.

In January 1922 I made a further purchase of a quarter of a pound of arsenic at Mr Davies's shop. A small amount of this was used as a weed killer after being boiled with caustic soda by myself. It was not a success which explains why I have some left at my house. When I purchased this arsenic it was mixed with charcoal. I am keeping this to make a further trial later on. I remember talking to Mr Taylor, the Bank Manager of Hay, respecting my recipe for weed killer. I remember being pleased at being able to make my own weed killer at a much cheaper rate than the prepared article, which after the war was very dear and I could not afford it. This last preparation I

CERTIFIED COPY OF AN ENTRY OF DEATH

The minutes fee for this certificate is 3s. 9d. Where a search is required to find the entry, a search fee is payable in addition.

Given at the GENERAL REGISTER OFFICE,
SOMERSET HOUSE, LONDON.

Application Number 30 7/54

1922   DEATH in the Sub-district of Gloucester   Northern   in the County of Gloucester C.B.

REGISTRATION DISTRICT   Gloucester

Columns:— (1)	(2)	(3)	(4)	(5)	(6)	(7)	(8)	(9)
No.	When and where died	Name and surname	Sex	Age	Occupation	Cause of death	Signature, description, and residence of informant	When registered	Signature of registrar
483	31st May 1922, H.M. Majesty's Prison, Gloucester U.D.	Herbert Rowse Armstrong	Male	53	of Cusop Herefordshire R.D. Town Solicitor	Executed pursuant to judgment of death	Certificate received from Waghorne Coroner for Gloucester (Upper District) held 31st August 1922, 31st May 1922	Second June 1922	H.A. Barrett Registrar

CERTIFIED to be a true copy of an entry in the certified copy of a Register of Deaths in the District above mentioned.

Given at the GENERAL REGISTER OFFICE, SOMERSET HOUSE, LONDON, under the Seal of the said Office, the 12th day of September 1954.

DA 465350

Death certificate issued after Armstrong's execution

carried out myself as before by boiling the arsenic with caustic soda in a petrol can. Although I have no motor car I use petrol for a petrol gas installation.

From the 2nd September to the 20th September 1921, as far as I can trace, I did not leave Hay, but on the 21st September 1921, I went motoring with Mr Lee, Surveyor of Taxes, of Derby, who took myself and my son to Bath where my son was returning to school. We returned on the Sunday following.

I don't take chocolates myself and have not purchased any of them since I bought a small box for my late wife in August 1920. These I bought in Hay but I can't remember the shop – they were certainly not Fuller's, which I was of the impression were not procurable in Hay.

During the period between the 2nd and 20th September 1921, ~~while~~ I was in Hay transacting business at my office and residing at my house. I did not leave the town. I may have called on friends socially but I do not remember.

I am unable to throw any light upon the finding of arsenic in Mr Martin's urine or as to the cause of his illness after having tea with me on 26th October 1921. I did not touch the food he ate in any way and partook of what was on the same dish. If arsenic got into the food, I cannot account for it being there.

The cupboard where I keep the arsenic at my house contains boot cleaning materials and is unlocked. Nobody in the house as far as I know is aware of the presence of arsenic in the house. This arsenic I speak of is the only poison in my possession anywhere, excepting of course any contained in medicine. I have a medicine chest in ~~my~~ a bedroom.

I make this statement quite voluntarily, and without being questioned.

H Rowse Armstrong

31 December 1921   *Alfred Crutchett (Chief Inspector)*
                          Walter Sharp (Sergeant)

THE GREEN BICYCLE MYSTERY*

The Death of Annie Bella Wright
On Saturday, 5th July 1919 on the Gartree
Road, Nr. Little Stretton, Leicestershire and the
Trial and Acquittal of Ronald Vivian Light for
her Murder

On the evening of Saturday 5th July 1919, a 21-year-old
girl left her home at Stoughton (where her father was
a farm worker), and cycled to Evington to get a stamp at
the post office and to post a letter. She then returned, and
proceeded on the road to Gaulby to visit her uncle, a
Mr Measures.

At about the same time a man of 34, who lived in
Highfield Street, Leicester, went out for a cycle ride and
arranged to be back for supper at around 8pm. He turned
left into London Road and proceeded through Stoneygate
and Oadby to Great Glen. He then turned left and
proceeded to the left turn into Gartree Road. This would
have taken him back to Leicester, but he looked at his
watch just before he reached Great Stretton and realized
that he would be home too soon; so he decided to return
through Houghton-on-the-Hill. He therefore turned right,
and when he came to the cross-roads where the Gaulby
Lane crossed the Houghton Lane he saw a girl bending
over a bicycle. She raised her head as he approached and
asked him if he had a spanner. He replied that he hadn't,

---

* This text has been based on the researches of Mr A.W.R. Mackintosh
into the murder of Bella Wright. With colleague Mr W Richardson,
Mackintosh has for many years pursued the minutiae of the Green
Bicycle Mystery and has opened many new avenues for investigation.
By no means the least of their achievements has been to identify the
spot where Bella was buried.

but asked what the trouble was. She said that her back wheel was loose and while he did what he could to put it right he asked where she was going. When she said 'Gaulby', he thought he might as well go with her as he could easily get to Houghton from there. When the couple arrived at Gaulby she said that she would only be about ten minutes and as that appeared an invitation to wait, he went with her to her uncle's house and waited outside. Mr Measures's daughter and her husband, a Mr Evans, happened also to be on a visit, and they asked about the man who was waiting outside. When she told them of the circumstances they advised her not to go back with him as he looked 'too old' for her. So she prolonged her visit until the man eventually tired of waiting and set off for home. His route took him uphill to Gaulby church, and when he arrived there he found he had a puncture. It took nearly an hour to mend it, and as the girl hadn't passed him during that time he went back to the house and got there just as she was coming out. They then cycled back together the way they had come. When they got to the road junction beyond King's Norton the girl said she would have to bid goodbye to her companion as her route was to the left. He then, according to his subsequent evidence, proceeded directly back to Leicester via Stoughton and Evington.

At about 9.20pm Mr Cowell, a farmer, was going along the Gartree Road when he found a girl lying on the road alongside a bicycle; when he examined her he found she was dead. Returning to his farm at nearby Little Stretton, Cowell harnessed his pony and trap, and after arranging for someone to guard the body, proceeded to Great Glen to report the matter to Constable Hall, the local policeman. From there he phoned Dr Williams at Billesdon, and then returned to Little Stretton. It was dark by the time Dr Williams arrived so he gave instructions that the girl's body be removed to an unoccupied house at Little Stretton. At this point it was assumed that she had died in a cycling accident.

The next day, Sunday the 6th, PC Hall returned to the scene and after a careful search found a bullet on the road. He then went to the house where the body had been deposited, and after washing the congealed blood from the face discovered a bullet wound. Dr Williams was immediately informed and he and another doctor carried out a full post-mortem.

It was subsequently established that the girl's name was Bella Wright and that she lived in Stoughton. When her relatives at Gaulby got to hear of her death the hue and cry went out for the 'Man on the Green Bicycle' as everyone jumped to the conclusion that he must have been the killer.

What Happened to Bella Wright?

Until recently there was a doubt as to where Bella Wright was buried, as there was nothing in the Stoughton Church records to indicate that she had been buried there. A contemporary report of the funeral was recently discovered in the *Leicester Daily Post* of 12th July 1919:

LEICESTERSHIRE MYSTERY

Burial of Murdered Girl:
Impressive Scenes at Stoughton

'Simply and impressively the funeral took place in the pretty little churchyard of Stoughton Parish Church yesterday (Friday) afternoon of Miss Annie Bella Wright, the 21-year-old (she would have been 22 on the 14th July) victim of the brutal crime perpetrated on Saturday night at Little Stretton. The church was filled with people who knew the dead girl – representatives of her workpeople at Bates Rubber Mills, friends at Leicester and the villagers at Stoughton where her father and mother live, all of whom knew her well. The funeral bell tolled as the cortege was starting from an old world cottage at the other end of the village. People lined the route along which the cortege passed, rustic roads lined with grassy banks and over which the foliage of lines of trees hung impressively.

The principal mourners were Mr and Mrs Wright (father and mother), Archie Ward, HMS *Diadem* (the victim's young man), Philip, Tom, and Leonard (brothers), Mr and Miss Beaver (uncle and cousin), Mrs Harrison and Mrs Lambert (aunts), Mr and Mrs Measures (aunt and uncle), Messrs. T. Wright and Len Wright (uncles), Miss Ward, and Mr and Mrs Langley.

The hymn *Peace, Perfect Peace* was sung as the flower-laden coffin was borne up the aisle and many of the women wept silently.

The Vicar of Stoughton, the Rev. W.N. Westmore BA said he wanted to ask each one there why they had come to see the burial. He hoped it was to show sympathy to the relatives of the girl who had been so foully murdered. He trusted it was not a sense of curiosity that brought them to the church that afternoon. Curiosity would not lead forward on the path of righteousness, but they did want to show their sympathy at this poor girl being taken away from them. He wanted to say to those who thought that religion was at a discount, and Christianity had had its day, and that a man need not attend any longer to those things that the church persists in teaching, and that he was taught in childhood – he wanted them to think that in a question of this sort when a girl was suddenly and foully murdered on a country road, that in the midst of civilisation there was a heart of barbarism. Why were murders of this sort not more common? It was because Society in the main was impregnated with the spirit of Christianity. Men may not go to Church, but still the spirit of Christianity enters into their lives and they live with moral courage. The hymn *Brief Life is Here our Portion* was sung, and to the recessional *Rest in The Lord* the murdered girl was borne to her last resting place. Hundreds filed by to take a last look at the coffin and numerous floral tributes, among which was a heart-shaped wreath from the dead girl's fellow-workers. The mother and father broke down at the graveside.'

What Happened to Ronald Light?
Although the identity of the 'man on the green bicycle' was not to be known for many months, his name was

Ronald Light, and at the time of Bella Wright's death he was living in Highfield Street, Leicester. Light was born in October 1885 and the first family home had been in Granville Road, Leicester. It is understood that his father had been the manager of Ellistown Colliery, near Coalville. After graduating as a civil engineer at Birmingham University, Ronald Light was employed as an engineer and draughtsman at the Midland Railway Works at Derby, but he usually returned to Leicester at weekends.

In May 1910 he purchased a green BSA bicycle from a firm named Orton & Co. of Derby. At about that time he also became a member of the Fortress Company, Royal Engineers, whose headquarters were at Buxton. From time to time, Light used to hire a motor cycle from Orton's to enable him to get into Buxton.

The Great War broke out in August 1914 and in February 1915, after undergoing training at Chatham, Newarke and Ripon, Ronald Light was granted a commission as a Second Lieutenant in the Royal Engineers. He was later posted abroad on active service, though for some reason he left the Royal Engineers in August 1916, and in the September he rejoined in the Honourable Artillery Company as a private. After undergoing further training Light was sent overseas again. He eventually suffered badly from shell-shock, and was invalided to a number of hospitals in England before his demobilisation in January 1919.

Sometime in 1916 or 1917 Ronald's father died accidentally at Granville Road, and in May 1917 the home was moved to Highfield Street where Ronald lived with his mother and a maid-servant.

It was not until the Tuesday evening following his encounter with the girl cycling to Gaulby that Ronald Light read of the tragedy in the *Leicester Mercury*, and learned that the dead girl's name was Bella Wright. By this time the public and the press had decided that it was the man on the green bicycle who had been responsible for her death. According to his later evidence. Light was now in a serious dilemma. He worried over the matter for some time before eventually deciding to do nothing

Telephone 357 and 862.

LEICESTERSHIRE CONSTABULARY.

£5 REWARD.

At 9-20 p.m., 5th instant, the body of a woman, since identified as that of ANNIE BELLA WRIGHT, was found lying on the Burton Overy Road, Stretton Parva, with a bullet wound through the head, and her bicycle lying close by.

Shortly before the finding of the body the deceased left an adjacent village in company of a man of the following description :—

Age 35 to 40 years, height 5 ft. 7 in. to 5 ft. 9 in.; apparently usually clean shaven, but had not shaved for a few days, hair turning grey, broad full face, broad build, said to have squeaking voice and to speak in a low tone.

Dressed in light Rainproof Coat with green plaid lining, grey mixture jacket suit, grey cap, collar and tie, black boots, and wearing cycle clips.

Had bicycle of following description, *viz.* :—Gent's B.S.A., green enamelled frame, black mudguards, usual plated parts, up-turned handle bar, 3-speed gear, control lever on right of handle bar, lever front brake, back-pedalling brake worked from crank and of unusual pattern, open centre gear case, *Brooke's* saddle with spiral springs of wire cable. The 3-speed control had recently been repaired with length of new cable.

Thorough enquiries are earnestly requested at all places where bicycles are repaired.

If met with the man should be detained, and any information either of the man or the bicycle wired or telephoned to E. HOLMES, ESQ., CHIEF CONSTABLE OF COUNTY, LEICESTER, or to SUPT L BOWLEY, COUNTY POLICE STATION, LEICESTER.

County Constabulary Office,
Leicester, 7th July, 1919.

T H JEAVS & SONS, PRINTERS 7 ST. MARTINS, LEICESTER.

except remove the bike from where he usually kept it to the attic.

In October 1919, Ronald Light decided to get rid of his bicycle. He filed off the number at the top of the saddle column and took it down to the canal to a point near the Gas Works, and after detaching the back wheel (because it had a distinctive backpedalling brake) he threw the parts separately into the canal.

When he was an officer in the Army Light had a .45 revolver, but when he reverted to being a private and was posted overseas, he took the revolver with him but not the holster. According to his evidence, when he became a casualty, all his belongings, including the revolver, were left behind in France. But he still had the holster and some rounds of ammunition at home which he also threw into the canal.

In January 1920 Ronald Light took up an appointment as a mathematics master at a school in Cheltenham. On 23rd February in the same year a horse-drawn barge was going along the canal when suddenly its tow-rope tightened and up came a green bicycle. The manager of a cycle shop in Leicester, who examined the bicycle, found a number on the inside front fork, the duplicate of one usually stamped at the top of the saddle column. In no time ownership of the bike was traced to Ronald Light.

After the preliminary police-court proceedings, Light's trial was fixed for 20th June 1920, at Leicester Castle. He was defended by the celebrated advocate Sir Edward Marshall Hall, and to everyone's surprise, he was found Not Guilty.

If you ask any of the older generation today, you will almost invariably be told that 'he done it', and it was only through the brilliance of Marshall Hall that he got off. What they don't tell you is that at the inquest proceedings Mr Robert Churchill, the ballistics expert, revealed that a carrion crow which was found dead nearby had also been shot. So it is almost certain that whoever shot the crow also shot Bella Wright. As this evidence was not given at the trial, it would appear that the police were very remiss in not properly following through with this line of investigation.

I, the writer, happen to be 77 years of age; and in that very summer of 1919 I was staying at a farm belonging to a relative of my father in Strathglass in Inverness-shire. I was 14½ years of age at the time and there was a boy, Billy, at the farm who was about my own age.

There was also an older member of the family who had been an officer in the army during the Great War and had later been in the Black and Tans. He had quite an armoury of weapons in the house so Billy got hold of a couple of .45 revolvers with a supply of ammunition and we went about the place firing indiscriminately. At one stage we were going along a road on which you would not be likely to see more than about one person a week. Suddenly we saw someone coming towards us, so we hid our revolvers. I then said to Billy, 'I know who that is.' He said, 'You can't possibly know.' I said, 'It's my uncle Charlie.' The reason I knew him was that he was the only person I had ever seen with a Louis Napoleon beard. He was a civil engineer in London and I lived in Glasgow, so he was as surprised to see me as I was to see him. He said it was the first time he had been to the farm in thirty years. The point is that I could easily have accidentally shot my uncle. There were thousands of service revolvers about after the Great War, and it would have been well within the bounds of possibility for someone like myself to be shooting indiscriminately, and for poor Bella to unwittingly come within the line of fire.

A.W.R. Mackintosh

The matter has never been satisfactorily resolved. After his acquittal, Ronald Light went to stay at the Isle of Sheppey, in Kent, where he lived unobtrusively until his death in May 1975 at almost 90 years of age. His funeral was at Charing Crematorium, near Ashford, and his ashes were scattered in the Garden of Remembrance there.

'THE OLD NURSE, DEATH'*

The Murder of Ada Baguley by 'Nurse' Dorothea Waddingham
On Tuesday, 10th September 1935 at 32 Devon Drive, Nottingham, Nottinghamshire

Dorothea Waddingham had almost as unsalubrious an entry into this world as she was to have a parting from it. She was born to a poor family who eked out an existence in the village of Hucknall, seven miles north of Nottingham. After a brief and undistinguished spell at the village school Dorothy (as she was known) spent a brief and undistinguished spell in a local factory. When she was in her early 20s she exchanged the drudgery of the factory for that of the workhouse infirmary at Burton-on-Trent, where she was taken on as a ward maid. It was while she was at Burton that Thomas Willoughby Leech came into her life. Leech was considerably older than Dorothy – in fact, almost twice as old – and neither wealthy nor physically fit; he was indeed very poor, and a chronic invalid. Nevertheless, for matters that may for all we know have been connected with love, the couple married and set up their first home under the roof of one of Leech's sisters, at Church Gresley, not far from Burton. During their eight years of marriage Dorothy bore three children – Edwin, Alan, and little Mary who was still a baby when tragedy finally struck the sickly Thomas Leech in the form of throat cancer, to which he succumbed. As a final act of unwitting generosity Thomas had provided his widow

* 'The friendly and comforting breast of the old nurse, Death.'

(William Ernest Henley, *Echoes*)

with a new partner. Ronald Sullivan was near to Dorothy's age, and when his marriage had collapsed and his family split up, his friend Tom Leech invited him to share his home, which was by now in Haydn Road, in Sherwood, Nottingham. Now, there is a great deal of difference between a ward maid and a nurse; but for Dorothy it was but a short stretch of the imagination. Rudimentary understanding of nursing care she may have picked up, but despite her own extravagant claims, and despite the fact that she has subsequently become notorious as 'Nurse' Waddingham, she was no more entitled to that distinction than the next ward maid. Not that it prevented her from turning the Haydn Road house into a nursing home.

Following her husband's death, Dorothea Waddingham – now Nurse Waddingham – took a smaller house in Devon Drive, accompanied by Sullivan and the three children. Before long there was another mouth to feed in the person of baby Ronald, and it was as much as the new 'nursing home' could manage to keep those mouths satisfied.

On the afternoon of 5th January 1935, Dorothy was away from the house, so it was Ronald Sullivan who opened the door to Miss Blagg, dynamic secretary ('hon.') of the County Nursing Association. The Waddingham Home had come to the favourable notice of the Association, it seems – which probably meant that it was cheap and not too particular – and Miss Blagg wondered if it might be the suitable accommodation she sought for elderly Mrs Louisa Baguley and her paralytic daughter Ada; the former 'delightful old lady' was nearing 90, the latter somewhere around 50.

The Baguleys were a courageous couple in their own modest way; Ada had since early womanhood suffered with what is known medically as progressive disseminated sclerosis, and popularly as 'creeping paralysis'. She had become worse as the disease had progressed over the past twenty years, and was now unable to walk or to employ her arms and hands to any very useful degree. Mr Baguley had died six years previously, and despite her own great age and frailty, her mother now devoted her time to caring for Ada the best she could. But she was beginning to realize that her best was no longer adequate, and far from being able to sustain the pressure imposed by an invalid's needs, she was feeling the want of care and attention herself.

And so a bargain was struck, pending the approval of Nurse Waddingham; and after visiting the two ladies at their present home in Burton Joyce, Dorothy accepted the rather paltry offer of thirty shillings a week each, and made ready the ground floor back room. On 12th January Mrs Baguley and Ada took up residence.

During the following six weeks the two lady 'patients' settled in comfortably to their new surroundings; and Miss Blagg was delighted to have found so pleasant a refuge for her charges. This too was the impression of Ada's cousin Lawrence, who was subsequently called upon to testify in court as to the great peace of mind now enjoyed by his elderly aunt and cousin.

At the end of February the house went into brief mourning for the passing of Nurse Waddingham's other patient at the time, who had died on the 26th.

Now Dorothea Waddingham was beginning to have second thoughts about the income from the Baguleys; she was frequently to be heard grumbling about the miserable reward for the huge burden of two infirm patients: 'they would have to pay five guineas for no better treatment in hospital; which is really the proper place for them.' In hindsight, it is a pity the ladies had not been put in a five guinea hospital, for they would certainly have had better 'treatment' than that which they were about to receive at Devon Drive. But money was not as plentiful as it might have been, and all that stood between the Baguleys and the dreaded workhouse were Ada's nest-eggs. These comprised a £500 Conversion Loan, about £120 in the bank, and a further £1,000 inherited from her father, of which the interest went to Mrs Baguley during her lifetime. What remained after her death, Ada had willed to Fred Gilbert. Gilbert, although a cousin, was also Ada's fiancé, and but for the devastating effect of her illness they might have been married long before. As it was, the closeness of even their friendship had been put under considerable strain over the years, and by now Fred's visits had all but stopped. In despair, and probably out of pique, Ada made a new will: very much at variance with the advice of her solicitor, Mr Lane. Ada proposed to settle upon Nurse Waddingham the whole of her property in return for an undertaking to look after her and her mother for the rest of their lives. As a compromise, Lane persuaded the petulant Ada Baguley that instead of handing over her property, she should simply make her will in favour of Waddingham and Sullivan, in consideration of their caring for her mother and herself during their lives. The document was signed on 4th May.

A week later old Mrs Baguley died and was laid to rest beneath the earth of Caunton churchyard. Among the mourners, Ronald Sullivan and Ada Baguley and, reunited in sorrow, Fred Gilbert. Fred Gilbert, after all this time; Fred pushing Ada in her wheelchair to the church! In fact, nothing of the old romance seemed to develop, but it may have given Sullivan pause to think on the future of his recently promised inheritance.

Back at Devon Drive, life for Ada, now that her greatest companion had passed away, was a succession of unremarkable days.

One rare excitement was the visit of Mrs Briggs, a friend of the Baguley family for as long as anybody could remember. It was 10th September, and Mrs Briggs's unexpected arrival found Ada in the garden snoozing in the last of the late summer sun. They chatted over tea and ate some of the chocolate drops that Mrs Briggs had brought from her little shop in Alfred Street – The Black Boy Chocolate Shop. At 4 o'clock, after fond farewells and promises of future visits, Ada's guest left. At 2 o'clock the following morning Ada Baguley slipped into a coma; at 9.00, Sullivan phoned and left a message for Dr Manfield to attend urgently. At midday Manfield arrived. Ada was dead.

With the medical certificate reading 'Death through cerebral haemorrhage due to cardio-vascular degeneration'. Nurse Waddingham wasted no time in arranging for Ada's body to be cremated. Which would not be remarkable in 1990: but in 1936 less than 1% of deaths received cremation, and those that did were unusual enough to be noticed. But there were other reasons why Miss Baguley's disposal attracted the attention of Dr Cyril Banks. Banks was the Crematorium referee, and in that capacity had received an extraordinary letter requesting: 'It is my desire to be cremated at my death. And it is my wish to remain with Nurse [Waddingham] until I die. It is my final wish that my relatives shall not know of my death.' The note purported to have been signed by Ada, but had been written by Ronald Sullivan. And it had been addressed from 32 Devon Drive, a house which, in his capacity as Medical Officer of Health for Nottingham, Dr Banks had reason to know was not, as it advertised, a 'registered' nursing home, and was in contravention of the law in describing itself as such.

It was as well that Cyril Banks had his misgivings; for poor Ada Baguley had not died of cerebral haemorrhage at all. That became clear when the Nottingham City Analyst performed his post-mortem examination; after ten days' careful investigation Dr W.W. Taylor found 2.59 grains of morphine in the stomach, 0.37 grains in the spleen and kidneys, 0.14 grains in a portion of the liver, and 0.092 grains in the heart. A convincingly lethal dose of 3.192 grains. Given the speed with which the body tissues break down morphine, the celebrated Home Office analyst, Dr Roche Lynch, was able to state that the original ingestion must have been a very much greater dose than that found.

Clearly Ada Baguley had died from acute morphine poisoning; which gave rise, not surprisingly, to misgivings about the cause of her mother's sudden death. On 30th September, Mrs Baguley's body was exhumed from the churchyard and taken to Leenside mortuary, where Dr Roche Lynch was to perform the post-mortem. Casting aside the medical jargon, the conclusion was dramatically simple – Mrs Louisa Baguley had died of an excessive dose of morphine!

Somebody would have some questions to answer.

On 14th February 1936, Dorothea Waddingham and Ronald Sullivan were put on trial before Mr Justice God-

dard (later Lord Chief Justice). In an unusual switch from
his familiar role as defender, Mr Norman Birkett QC led
for the Crown. On 26th February, Mr Justice Goddard
instructed the jury to formally acquit Ronald Sullivan,
against whom there was no evidence of complicity to
murder. The following day he passed sentence of death
on Dorothea Waddingham in accordance with the verdict
of the jury; she was removed to Winson Green Prison,
Birmingham.

Despite the recommendation to mercy, the Home Office
could find no grounds on which to interfere with the
course of justice, and on the morning of 16th April
1936, Nurse Waddingham walked to the gallows.

OPIUM
(Laudanum, Morphine)

There is no drug so well known as a poison, and, at the
same time so rarely used by the murderer, as opium
and its derivatives. Whether this is due to the slow
action of the poison or to the distinctive smell and
symptoms, we cannot say, but the fact remains that the
poisoner shuns it.

Opium is the juice of *Papaver somniferum*, the opium
poppy. No more beautiful sight can be imagined than to
see the whole countryside ablaze with purple and
white poppies from which the valuable extract is
obtained. The native cultivators guard their fields very
carefully when they see that the flowers are about to
fall. Then, as soon as the petals have been shed,
leaving the familiar capsule containing the seeds,
the time for reaping the harvest has come. Armed
with a slender knife, wrapped round with cotton or
string to within a quarter of an inch of the point, the
ryot passes rapidly from plant to plant, making two little
slits, one on each side of each capsule. The thick white
juice of the poppy oozes out of the slits, and soon dries
to a brownish, gummy matter on the side of the
capsule. That evening the cultivator goes round again

and scrapes the gum off the plants, making more slits for a fresh supply of juice to be ready the following morning. About six incisions in each capsule is as much as the plant can stand, and then it commences to die.

The sticky juice is collected and warmed, and then rolled up into balls which are covered with leaves; this product is crude opium. The refining is effected by means of mixing carefully with water and filtering, then drying the product and treating it with other solvents. It is then ready for conversion into the various forms under which we know it.

The poisoner (and the suicide) at one time principally used Laudanum, which is a tincture of opium, or the purified drug dissolved in spirits, and more recently, Morphine, the alkaloid which gives to opium most of its power.

The characteristics of opium poisoning are as follows: The patient gets drowsy, and is often afflicted by nausea. The face is sometimes swollen and highly coloured, while the pupils of the eyes are contracted, and do not dilate in the dark. Gradually the patient becomes unconscious, as a man who is intoxicated with alcohol. The skin may be cold and clammy, yet bathed in profuse perspiration, although the victim complains of feeling cold. Then unconsciousness sets in, and the muscles get flabby and relaxed in most cases, though occasionally there may be spasmodic contractions. The breathing is slow and noisy, the pulse low. As a rule, there is a strong smell of laudanum if that drug has been taken, but if the victim is suffering from an overdose of morphine there is no smell.

The symptoms of morphine poisoning are precisely similar to those of laudanum (with the exception of the lack of smell). Morphine is a fine white crystalline substance, and as little as one grain has been known to be fatal.

THE BLACK PANTHER

**The Murders of Lesley Whittle, Donald
Skepper, Derek Astin, and Sidney Greyland
by Donald Neilson**
On various dates in 1974 and 1975 at locations
in the Midlands and North of England

By November 1974 the mystery man had notched up
some twenty robberies in seven years with a combined haul of over £20,000. Worse still, the elusive thief
had killed three times and left several other victims
seriously wounded. The *modus operandi* was almost in-
variable: armed with a shotgun the intruder chose the
early hours of the morning to drill through window
frames to release the catches, rouse the still-sleeping
occupants, mainly of sub-post offices, and demand the
keys to the safe. His working uniform was always the
same: black plimsolls, army camouflage suit, white gloves,
and the black hood which earned him his sobriquet of 'The
Black Panther'.

The first to die had been Donald Skepper. On 15th February
1974 the youngest son of this sub-postmaster woke with a
start to find himself looking down both barrels of the
shotgun held by a man demanding keys to the safe. When
the intruder failed to find them where the boy had indicated,
he entered the parents' bedroom with the same demand.
With more courage than forethought Donald Skepper
shouted 'Let's get him', and was immediately shot.

On 6th September in the same year sub-postmaster
Derek Astin tackled an intruder in his post office at
Higher Baxenden, near Accrington; he was shot dead in
front of his wife and two children.

The intense activity on the part of the Yorkshire constabulary obliged the Panther to transfer his activities to a different location, and mid-November found him in Langley, Worcestershire. Here he shot Sidney Grayland, bludgeoned his wife Margaret fracturing her skull, and stole £800 from the cash box.

It was less than two months later that the Black Panther committed the crime that was to move the nation and make him Britain's most wanted man.

'Beech Croft' was the family home of the Whittles in the village of Highley in Shropshire. On the morning of Tuesday, 14th January 1975, Mrs Dorothy Whittle was alarmed to find her daughter missing from the house; 17-year-old Lesley had simply disappeared. In her place were a number of messages pressed out of red Dymo-tape which left the family in no doubt that Lesley had been kidnapped. The ransom demand was for £50,000 and the conditions graphically clear: 'No police . . . You are on a time limit. If police or tricks, Death'. Nevertheless, Lesley's brother Ronald made immediate contact with the West Mercia police force.

Despite the quite obvious need for the police involvement to be kept secret, news of the kidnapping and of the ransom demand was 'leaked' to a freelance journalist who, with a callous disregard for Lesley Whittle's safety that characterizes the worst elements of his profession, sold this information to a Birmingham newspaper and to the BBC; the latter went so far as to interrupt programmes to broadcast the newsflash.

On the same night, an incident took place which provided the Scotland Yard team which had been called in with their first major clues. Gerald Smith was a security officer at the Freightliner container depot at Dudley, and while on a routine patrol had observed a man loitering around the perimeter fence. So strange was the man's behaviour when approached that Smith decided to call the police. Turning his back, the next thing he was aware of was the loud report of a gun and a searing pain in his buttocks; the attacker then emptied the remaining five cartridges into the unfortunate watchman and disappeared. Remarkably, Gerald Smith was able to crawl to a telephone and alert the police.

Subsequently, ballistics experts were able to confirm, by matching the tell-tale ejection marks left like 'fingerprints' on the spent cartridges, that they came from the same gun that had been used in two earlier crimes – crimes known to have been the handiwork of the Black Panther. When investigating officers traced the green Morris 1300 saloon car that had been seen parked at the Freightliner depot they were rewarded with further vital pointers to the identity of the man who had added kidnapping to robbery and murder. Among the items recovered from the car were a number of Dymo-tape messages quite clearly pieces of a ransom trail and identical to those left at the Whittle home. A cassette recorder contained a taped message from Lesley Whittle to her mother. Soon Gerald Smith's description of his assailant had been transformed into a portrait drawing that was to become one of the best known faces in the country and was carried by the television networks as well as by the Press and cinemas.

Just before midnight on 16th January Ronald Whittle received a telephone call from a man claiming to be Lesley's captor. Following a trail marked by further Dymo-tape messages, Ronald arrived at Bathpool Park near the town of Kidsgrove, Staffordshire. Here the kidnapper was supposed to respond to Ronald Whittle's flashing car headlights with a torch. In the event there was no contact and Ronald's 'undercover' police escort were left once again helpless and frustrated.

For reasons best known to themselves, the police took more than a fortnight to get around to a detailed search of Bathpool Park, by which time the developments had received sufficient publicity to prompt a local headmaster to remember that one of his pupils had handed him a strip of Dymo-tape bearing the message 'Drop Suitcase into Hole' which he had found in the park a couple of days after the kidnapping. Another significant clue was a torch found by another schoolboy wedged in the grille of a ventilating shaft to the sewage system that runs beneath Bathpool Park.

Encouraged by these clues, police and tracker dogs began to search the underground culverts; it was during this operation that the naked body of Lesley Whittle was

found at the bottom of one of the ventilating shafts.
Around her neck was a noose of wire attached to the
iron ladder. It was to be almost a year, though, before the
Black Panther was captured.

On the night of 11th December 1975, Pcs Stuart Mackenzie
and Tony White were on a routine Panda car patrol in the
Nottinghamshire village of Mansfield Woodhouse. Seeing
a small shambling man carrying a black holdall the two
officers decided to investigate; the suspect in his turn
produced a sawn-off shotgun and forced White and
Mackenzie back into the car. Taking the front passenger
seat, and with his gun stuck in Pc Mackenzie's ribs the
man issued only one instruction – 'Drive!'
    With a cool professionalism, the more remarkable under
the circumstances, the two officers, using a combination of
verbal and visual signals (via the rearview mirror), con-
spired to disarm and capture the man holding them at
gunpoint. Jamming his foot on the brake at a T-junction
Mackenzie sufficiently surprised the gunman for White to
lunge at the gun now pointed away from his companion.
In the struggle which followed the car became a riot of
smoke and noise as the shotgun exploded into action, and
despite injuries to White's hand from pellets and to
Mackenzie's eardrums which had been perforated by
the explosion, they hung on to their former captor. With
assistance from a member of the public who was queueing
for fish and chips where the car had stopped, the two
officers were able to subdue their prisoner and make an
arrest. Although they did not know it yet, Pcs White and
Mackenzie – with a little public-spirited help – had just
terminated the career of the Black Panther.

The Black Panther; born near Bradford in 1936 and
christened Donald Nappey, he had subsequently changed his name to Neilson to avoid the association with
babies' underwear. This was a characteristic gesture of a
man who, after being conscripted for National Service
with the British forces in Cyprus became obsessed by the
techniques of 'survival' and of guerrilla warfare.
    When the police searched his home at Grangefield

Avenue, Thornaby, Bradford, they found all the evidence they needed to bring four charges of murder against Neilson. For these he was to receive life sentences; for kidnapping he was condemned to 61 years' imprisonment.

Gerald Smith died in March 1976 as a result of his confrontation with Neilson; but the laws of England allow a person only a year and a day in which to die if a charge of murder is to be brought.

THE DEVIL'S WORK

**The Killing of Charles Walton by an
Unknown Assassin
On Wednesday, 14th February 1945 in a field
outside Lower Quinton, Warwickshire**

The calendar proclaims many brief oases in the otherwise monotonous flow of time; days when there is an opportunity to celebrate – or not, as we choose: Christmas, Easter, a number of Bank Holidays, Jewish New Year, Muslim New Year, and the First Day of Ramadan to name a few. In addition there are some more personal dates – birthdays, anniversaries, and a few gratuitous occasions on which shopkeepers can fill their pockets between the major festivals – Mother's Day, Father's Day . . . And there is St Valentine's Day. February the 14th, the day for sending hearts and flowers; lovers' day. In fact the likelihood of St Valentine ever existing was considered to be so remote that his name was removed from the Calendar of Saints long ago. What survives – the sending of 'valentines' – has nothing to do with the saint anyway, but became confused with the Roman fertility festival of Lupercalia when, on 15th February the priests ran around the city waving goatskin thongs; a blow from the thong was said to be a sure cure for infertility in women.

Just an innocent relic of older, more pagan rites, St Valentine's Day has nothing really to do with the mysterious death of Charles Walton – except that it took place on 14th February. But other, blacker, pagan ceremonies might well have been very closely connected.

Charles Walton lived with his niece Edith in the medieval village of Lower Quinton, between Chipping Norton and Stratford-on-Avon. Although he was seventy-four and crippled with rheumatism, Walton exhibited a fierce independence and still earned his own scant living as a hedge-cutter. On Wednesday, 14th February 1945, he left his cottage at 9.00 in the morning as he had done for most of his insular life – slash-hook in hand, double-pronged hayfork over his shoulder, a shambling figure hobbling up Meon Hill to attend to the hedges bordering Alfred Potter's farm about a mile from the Walton home.

When Charlie had not arrived home by 6 o'clock, Edith Walton began to worry – the old man was never later than 4.00, and with his legs as bad as they were she feared he might have had a fall. Summoning company in the person of neighbour Harry Beasley they hiked up the hill to Potter's farm, The Firs. Potter thought that he had seen Charlie Walton earlier in the day – it had been way across the fields, but the figure had been cutting hedges on his land so it could hardly have been anyone else. By torchlight, Potter, Beasley, and Edith Walton picked their way over the fields to the lower slopes of the hill where farmer Potter had caught a sight of the hedger.

Quite suddenly, out of the darkness, the flashlight picked out the figure of a man. One look was enough for Potter, and protecting Miss Walton from the sight before them, he hurried her back home and called the police. Beasley was left the unappetising responsibility of standing guard over a corpse in the middle of a dark field.

When the police arrived at the scene later they could fully appreciate the revulsion felt by Alfred Potter. Walton had been impaled by his own hay-fork, the two prongs of which had been driven with such force through his neck that they had penetrated six inches into the ground beneath; on his cheeks, throat, and body the sign of the cross had been etched with his slash-hook. Close to his body lay the old man's walking stick, bloody from the blows it had dealt to its owner's head.

With commendable foresight the Warwickshire police asked for assistance from Scotland Yard, and were rewarded by the presence of Detective Superintendent

Robert Fabian – famous throughout the country simply as 'Fabian of the Yard'.

At first Fabian and his assistant, Detective-Sergeant Albert Webb acted on the assumption that this was an ordinary murder – if particularly brutal and seemingly motiveless. Understandable war-time xenophobia resulted in the close scrutiny of the several thousand enemy prisoners of war incarcerated in the camp two miles away at Long Marston. But however many deaths they may have been responsible for on the field of battle, the pathetic rag-bag of Italians, Slavs, and Germans were apparently innocent of the death of Charlie Walton.

But events were now, in the parlance of Hollywood, about to take a dramatic turn. Robert Fabian recalled the opening scene:

> 'I climed Meon Hill, a bleak and lonely spot, to examine the scene of the crime for myself. A black dog, a retriever, sat on a nearby wall for a moment. Then it trotted past me. I did not look at it again. Shortly afterwards a farm boy came along.
>
> Looking for your dog? I asked him.
> What dog?
> A black dog . . .
> The lad didn't wait to hear any more. He fled down the hill. Instantly, word spread through the village that I had seen The Ghost.'

Now read this passage from an obscure book entitled *Folk Lore, Old Customs and Superstitions in Shakespeareland* written by an equally obscure Warwick parson named J. Harvey Bloom in 1930:

> 'At Alveston a plough lad named Charles Walton met a dog on his way home nine times in successive evenings. He told both the shepherd and the carter with whom he worked, and was laughed at for his pains. On the ninth encounter a headless lady rushed past him in a silk dress, and on the next day he heard of his sister's death.'

Charlie Walton. The same Charlie Walton.

Regardless of his own feelings at the time about country

superstitions this was clearly a line of inquiry that Fabian could not ignore; especially after Detective-Superintendent Alec Spooner of the Warwickshire C.I.D. drew his attention to another piece of local lore. In his work *Warwickshire*, Clive Holland related the circumstances of a murder which took place in the nearby village of Long Compton in 1875. In this case a simple-minded youth, John Haywood, slew an old woman named Ann Turner who he was convinced was one of a coven of witches meeting at Long Compton. At his trial, Haywood declared: 'Her was a proper witch, I pinned her to the ground [with a hayfork!] before slashing her throat with a bill-hook in the form of a cross.' Long Compton was reputedly still an important centre of witchcraft.

Whether or not the urbane detectives from Scotland Yard believed in the continued existence of the Warwickshire Witches, it was plain that the inhabitants of Lower Quinton were taking no chances; and not a word would they utter, not a gesture would they now make towards helping the inquiry. It was, they declared, best left alone; best left to rest – particularly when the body of a black dog was found hanging from a tree close to where Charles Walton had been murdered.

In the end, even the experience and determination of one of the country's finest detectives found that it had met its match in the stubborn silence of Lower Quinton, and Detective-Superintendent Fabian and Detective-Sergeant Webb retreated to London, and less spooky lines of investigation.

Charlie Walton was buried in the quiet graveyard attached to the village's picturesque Saxon-Norman church. Life resumed its normal pattern.

In retrospect, though, Robert Fabian considered that there was a clear warning to be taken from the Mystery of Lower Quinton, and wrote in his autobiography:

'I advise anybody who is tempted at any time to venture into Black Magic, witchcraft, Satanism – call it what you will – to remember Charles Walton and to think of his death, which was so clearly the ghastly climax of a pagan rite. There is no stronger

argument for keeping as far away as possible from
the villains with their swords, incense and mumbo-
jumbo. It is prudence on which your future peace of
mind and even your life could depend.'

Of course 'Fabian of the Yard' was quite right in warning
the idly curious about embarking on flirtations with the
'occult'. And of course he was quite right in keeping to
himself any unprovable suspicions as to who was responsible for Charlie Walton's murder; the laws of slander and
libel dictate this. But before he died in 1978, Fabian
confided in crime historian Richard Whittington-Egan
that he was sure Alfred Potter had committed the
crime. Potter, who died in 1974, had borrowed a large
sum of money from Charles Walton, and Charlie, it was
said, was demanding to be repaid. Motive for murder?

MURDER BY PROXY

**The Shooting of Gail Kinchin by Detective-
Constable Gerald Richards**
In the early morning of Thursday, June 12th
1980 at 4 Deelands Road, Rubery, Birmingham,
West Midlands, and the Trial for her Murder,
and Conviction of her Manslaughter of David
Pagett

Wives, mistresses and girl-friends have always featured
at the top of any list of potential murder victims,
and while rivalry still supports sexual role play, bleakly
unaffected by the new spirit of liberalism, it is certain to
stay that way. In the main, domestic killings are squalid,
uninspired crimes commonly the pathetic conclusion to
years of less lethal violence.

Such was the death of Gail Kinchin, and the conviction
of David Pagett for her killing. The difference was, Pagett
didn't kill his mistress; she and her unborn child were shot
by a policeman.

The affair started when Gail was only 15 years old and
living with her mother Josie and step-father Eric Wood in
Brandwood Park Road, King's Heath, Birmingham; in a
council flat across the way David Pagett lived with his
common-law wife Sheila. Thirty-one-year-old Pagett was
a mechanic who earned his living mending washing
machines, supplementing bad patches with a little petty
crime; he was a flashy braggart, much given to the
pleasures of women and drink. Young Gail used to
baby-sit for the Pagetts while they went out on the
town, and it was when he returned, full of drink, that
he began to notice that maybe his baby sitter was more
than just the kid over the road. And youngsters being
what they are, Gail responded to the unaccustomed
flattery from an older person, and sat entranced by

Pagett's heavily embroidered tales of heroism with the Green Jackets in Northern Ireland. At once a bond grew between them that was to destroy their two families and ultimately themselves. First, Sheila came home unexpectedly early one day and found her 'husband' on the bed with Gail; Sheila moved out, Gail moved in, so causing great emotional grief to her parents. Mrs Wood was heard to complain to neighbours: 'When kids reach the age of sixteen, they think they know it all!'

So far, this story is not as unfamiliar as we might like to believe; it is being told the world over, every day – grubby, perhaps, but not criminal. What made this relationship so vulnerable was David Pagett himself. Already known to be a bully, Pagett now began to be driven by the blind belligerence that came with an increase in his need for alcohol, and his behaviour towards Gail deteriorated into violence and paranoia. She would be locked up in the flat for days on end while he roamed from pub to club, from girlfriend to girlfriend, coming home only for more sex and to give Gail another cautionary beating.

Inevitably, Gail became pregnant, and equally predictably, Pagett made her condition the excuse for still further indignities – often forcing her to spend nights sleeping on the draughty floor.

The unhappy girl had tried in a half-hearted way to leave several times, but by now her self-confidence had been destroyed, her spirit broken, and she allowed herself to be dragged back – usually physically – to face punishment and further degradation. On the last occasion the physical savagery was accompanied by Pagett's very believable threats against her mother's life.

But of such desperation are desperate means born, and if for no other reason than the safety of her unborn child, Gail Kinchin with the help of her mother secretly plotted the only way they knew to rid themselves of Pagett's constant threat.

He was sitting behind the wheel of a stolen car when police picked him up; they had been acting on an anonymous telephone call! But then the Woods made a foolish, if understandable, mistake.

Instead of waiting for Pagett's case to come to court at

the end of the month, and take advantage of his almost certain imprisonment, Gail fled the flat on the afternoon of 11th June 1980, and travelling via her mother's home, sought refuge in the house of a friend in Masefield Square, in the Northfield district.

Pagett's response was predictably brutal. Loading himself, a double-barrelled shotgun, and a pocketful of cartridges into his car, he raced across town to the home of Gail's parents, smashed his way into the house and raised his gun. In fear for his own and his wife's life at the hands of this lunatic, Eric Wood made a dash for the front door and out into the night to summon the police. It was the burning pain in his back and legs that cut his dash for freedom short as a shower of lead shot burst from the barrel of Pagett's gun, leaving the badly injured man to crawl to safety in a neighbouring house.

Pagett now grabbed Josie Wood by the hair and dragged her screaming, the gun to her head, into his car. Realising she was in the clutches of a madman who, for all she knew had just blasted her husband to death, it is no surprise that Mrs Wood was co-operative; there was only one thing that her captor wanted – an address!

When he reached the 'safe house' in Masefield Square, the crazed gunman grabbed Gail and kicked and punched her down the steps and into the car beside her terrified mother; now driving madly back across Birmingham to his own flat, the shotgun in readiness by his side.

By this time neighbours had alerted the police to the attempted murder of Eric Wood and the abduction at gunpoint of Mrs Wood and her daughter, and a series of road blocks had been set up in the area. It was while Pagett was negotiating one of these – with his gun – that Josie Wood, with immense courage, managed to flee the car; but blind with anger and satisfied that he still had one captive, Pagett sped on seeming not to be concerned. He had Gail. He was going to teach her a lesson she would never forget!

When he reached the first-floor flat, David Pagett bolted the doors as if for a siege. And siege was what the police were preparing for at the same time, for armed police officers were at that moment surrounding the block. Inside the building were Detective Sergeant Thomas Sartain and Detective Constable Gerald Richards, both carrying police issue Smith and Wessons.

It was just after 2.15 on the morning of 12th June when the detectives positioned themselves outside Pagett's front door; the tense atmosphere was made more acute by the darkness imposed by the broken hall lights. Suddenly there was a rattling of locks and a dim silhouette appeared framed in the light from Pagett's doorway; in one arm he cradled the lethal shotgun, the other held Gail tightly in front of him – a human shield. Clearly feeling secure enough from the law, Pagett refused all opportunities to surrender, indeed, he took advantage of his position to force the two officers back up the stairs towards the second floor. To their horror the policemen found themselves trapped – behind was a solid wall, in front a madman with a shotgun and a pregnant hostage. Their only defence – training, experience, and a pair of .38 revolvers.

The shotgun approached; the terrified girl cried for help; there was a momentary scuffle in the darkness below them, then with a deafening roar the shotgun exploded in a flash of fire. Miraculously the deadly spray missed the crouching officers, and with the only reaction they could possibly have shown – self-preservation – Richards and Sartain returned fire; six rounds punched into the dark, followed by an eerie silence that rang in their ears. Still the shadow on the stairs inched forward; but obviously panicked, Pagett loosed the other barrel of his weapon, and with a faltering aim shot high into the ceiling of the stairway. Once again the officers retaliated. This time a body crumpled and fell. Gail lay bleeding on the floor, her unborn child killed instantly by a bullet, its mother was to die before the month was out from two others. Pagett was unmarked, and only being disarmed before he could reload prevented him from continuing the bloody battle.

At his trial in Birmingham's Crown Court, David Pagett at least had what satisfaction could be drawn from creating legal history. To sustain a murder charge against him, the prosecution had to establish that Pagett had used the girl as a shield knowing that when he first fired the shotgun at the police officers they were likely to return fire and possibly kill, or maim, his hostage.

On the two kidnap charges, on the charges of the attempted murder of Eric Wood and the policemen, the jury found David Pagett guilty; they also convicted him of a lesser charge of possession of a shotgun with intent to endanger life. But on the murder charge they were in disagreement, eventually settling for a verdict of guilty of manslaughter.

Sentencing Pagett to seven concurrent 12-year terms of imprisonment, Mr Justice Park observed: 'The use of a hostage by a desperate armed man to achieve safety for himself – and by that use to cause the death of the hostage – is indeed a very grave offence, falling only just short of murder . . .'

THE MAN WHO SAID NOTHING

The Murder of Mona Lillian Tinsley by Frederick Nodder
On Tuesday, 5th January 1937 at 'Peacehaven',
Hayton, Nottinghamshire

The unpleasant looking man who stood in the dock of the Victoria Courts, Birmingham, had been charged in the name of Frederick Nodder. A brutish, squalid drunk, Nodder's crime was as unspeakable as the man himself, and the jury had listened to its details with undisguised distaste.

Nodder had deserted his wife some years previously, and had gone to Sheffield where he lodged with a Mr and Mrs Grimes. For no honest reason he had adopted the name Hudson and claimed to be a car mechanic, though his intemperate habits resulted in his being for the most part unemployable. After a year with the Grimeses, in 1935, Frederick Nodder took lodgings with Mrs Grimes's sister, Mrs Tinsley, at 11 Thoresby Avenue, Newark, where for some unaccountable reason he was a popular figure with the many Tinsley children to whom he became 'Uncle Fred'.

Before long Nodder, alias Hudson, was on the move again; this time as sole occupant of an isolated semi-detached near Hayton; a house inappropriately named 'Peacehaven'. Once there, Nodder seemed to have broken all contact with the Tinsleys. That is, until 5th January 1937. In the late afternoon of this chilly Tuesday, shortly after 10-year-old Mona Tinsley had left her school in Guildhall Street, Newark, she was seen at the bus station near the Robin Hood Hotel in the company of Frederick

Nodder. According to his own statement, Mona had asked Uncle Fred to take her to visit her aunt (Mrs Grimes) and new baby cousin in Sheffield. He had persuaded Mona to spend the night at 'Peacehaven', and the following evening Nodder took his young charge by bus from East Retford to Worksop and then put her on another bus to travel alone to Sheffield.

Little Mona Tinsley was never seen alive again. When he was confronted by the police on his return to 'Peacehaven' (Mona's anxious parents had quite naturally already reported her absence from home), Nodder had at first denied any recent contact with the Tinsley family; in a second statement he gave the story outlined above which was to constitute his defence. During 9th and 10th March, Frederick Nodder stood before Mr Justice Swift at the Birmingham Assizes accused of abducting Mona Tinsley.

The prosecution was conducted by Mr Norman Birkett KC, and despite an enthusiastic plea on his behalf by defence attorney Mr Maurice Healy KC, Nodder's case was not to be believed. In a subsequent reference to the prisoner's reluctance to take the witness stand, Mr Justice Swift in his summing up said: 'Nobody knows what has become of that little girl . . . Whatever happened to her, how she fared, who looked after her, where she slept, there is one person in this court who knows, and he is silent – he is silent. He says nothing to you at all . . . He sits there and never tells you a word.' In passing sentence he added: 'What you did with that little girl, what became of her, only you know. It may be that time will reveal the dreadful secret you carry in your breast.'

And so it was to prove.

Despite the continuing painstaking search undertaken by the police over succeeding months, no trace was found of Mona Tinsley – alive or dead. 'Peacehaven', which had been in as indescribably squalid a state as its occupant, was virtually taken apart brick by brick, stick by stick; the garden was completely dug over, and the area for miles around combed by an army of police officers. Cesspools were opened up, and the five-mile stretch of the Chesterfield Canal where it ran close to Nodder's home was drained. The river Idle was dragged several times.

It was three months into Frederick Nodder's seven-year sentence, on Sunday the 6th of June, that a party of people boating on the Idle just below Bawtry saw the floating bundle which was Mona Tinsley's tiny corpse.

Mona had been strangled, but the advanced state of the body's decomposition made it impossible to state whether or not she had been sexually assaulted.

In November Nodder once again faced the full might of British Justice. Before Mr Justice Macnaghten at the Nottingham Assizes he was charged with Mona Tinsley's murder. Norman Birkett was once again retained for the Crown, and Mr Healy returned to present Nodder's defence. This time, however, the prisoner did go into the witness box. He described how after meeting Mona from the Wesleyan School in Newark, he had taken her by the 4.45pm bus to Retford, and from there to 'Peacehaven'. After supper, he claimed, Mona had been put to bed in his own double room and he had slept downstairs. On the following morning, in a moment of guilt, he had determined to send Mona on to her aunt in Sheffield. Quite why it took all day to put this plan into effect Nodder never adequately explained; after a day during which the girl had played around the house while Uncle Fred was out working in the garden, the couple set off in the blustery darkness of late evening. In evidence, Nodder told how he had given Mona two shillings and instructions on how to get to Sheffield; he also claimed to have given her a note of explanation for Mrs Grimes. He had never seen the child again, and advanced the possibility that she had been lured off the bus and murdered.

It was with no surprise that the court heard the jury's verdict of guilty; and in passing sentence of death upon him, Mr Justice Macnaghten told Nodder: 'Justice has slowly but surely overtaken you.'

At Lincoln Prison on the morning of Thursday the 30th of December, 1937, the degenerate Frederick Nodder took his last breath of air before plummeting, unlamented, into the pit below the scaffold.

THE EASTERN AND HOME COUNTIES

Bedfordshire

Berkshire

Buckinghamshire

Cambridgeshire

Essex

Hertfordshire

Norfolk

Oxfordshire

Suffolk

THE LUTON SACK MURDER

**The Murder of Mrs Caroline Manton by her
husband Horace William 'Bertie' Manton
On Thursday, 18th November 1943 at
14 Regent Street, Luton, Bedfordshire**

It is a platitude that all criminals make one mistake: a
platitude because there are enough unsolved crimes to
attest that, through luck or good planning, some criminals
do not make that one fatal error.

And this might have been the case for Bertie Manton.
Bertie nearly committed the perfect murder – the more
surprising since the victim was his own wife. Certainly the
scrupulous care with which he covered his tracks made
the inquiry one of the most difficult in modern police
history; it was more than three months before investigating officers got even the sniff of a clue. Manton had made
his one mistake.

Friday, 19th November 1943, and a heavy fog has descended over the capital and the nearer reaches of the
Home Counties. Few people under the age of forty will
remember such days, when at noon the streets were dark
as evening with an impenetrable ochre mist. It was on this
particular afternoon that two sewermen were engaged on
measuring the water level of the River Lea where it flows
through Luton. Lying in about 6 ins of water they found a
roughly tied up sacking bundle; closer inspection revealed
that the sacking covered the naked, bludgeoned body of a
woman. Subsequent forensic examination by Dr Keith
Simpson was to determine that the victim had suffered
a violent blow to the head with the edge of some heavy

blunt implement. The blow had split the ear and cheek and had fractured both the upper and the lower jaw; the specific cause of death had been brain haemorrhage. The woman had also been 5½ months pregnant. Time of death was placed at around the evening of 18th November, the day prior to the discovery.

In any investigation into murder the vital first clue is the identity of the victim; from this information it may then be possible to trace his or her movements up to the time of death. In the case of the Luton sack victim Scotland Yard's Chief Inspector William Chapman and Detective Sergeant William Judge were clearly faced with a problem, for not only had every identifiable accessory been removed from the body – jewellery, clothing, even her false teeth – but the injuries suffered had rendered the face unrecognizable.

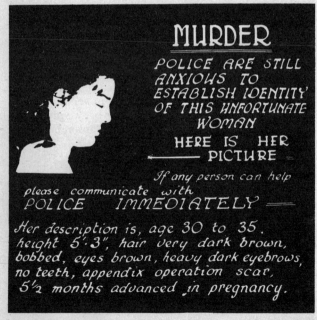

MURDER

POLICE ARE STILL ANXIOUS TO ESTABLISH IDENTITY OF THIS UNFORTUNATE WOMAN

HERE IS HER PICTURE

If any person can help please communicate with POLICE IMMEDIATELY

Her description is, age 30 to 35, height 5'·3", hair very dark brown, bobbed, eyes brown, heavy dark eyebrows, no teeth, appendix operation scar, 5½ months advanced in pregnancy.

Lantern slide shown in cinemas in an attempt to identify the Luton sack victim

Nevertheless, normal procedure was followed and photographs were circulated to the Press and special lantern slides were made for projection to cinema audiences. In fact, thirty-nine people were taken to the mortuary in the hope of identifying a lost friend or relative, but in the end she remained unclaimed. As the news spread, a further distressing complication arose: it was wartime, and literally hundreds of letters were addressed to Scotland Yard from men on active service anxious lest the victim might be their wife or girl-friend.

In the search for the woman's missing clothes the second-hand shops were painstakingly searched and tons of old clothing and scraps of clothing were examined; but the mystery remained, as thick and as impenetrable as the fog out of which it had appeared.

On 21st February, more than three months after the discovery of the body, that fog began to clear. Amongst a heap of old rags that had been retrieved from a rubbish dump, a fragment of dirty black cloth with a shoulder pad attached yielded up the clue that was to be instrumental not only in identifying the victim, but in leading to the

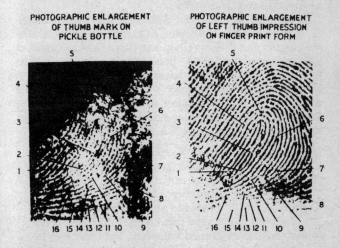

Fingerprint found on the pickle jar compared with that of Caroline Manton

person responsible for her death. On the inside of the pad was a dyer's tag bearing the number 'VI 2247' which a routine check of cleaners' and dyers' shops traced back to the Sketchley Dye Works in Wellington Street, Luton. It was the number of a coat deposited for dyeing by a Mrs Caroline Manton of 14 Regent Street.

Ironically, the police had already been the length of Regent Street showing the photograph of the then mystery corpse. They had called at the Manton house and the two young boys who answered the door had failed to recognise the woman as their own mother. Now Chief Inspector Chapman called in person, where he found Bertie Manton, a former lightweight boxer and now a driver for the National Fire Service.

The story that Manton told was plausible enough on the surface: after months of disagreement – mainly over their mutual infidelity – one final violent quarrel had resulted in Mrs Manton packing her bags and leaving, first to stay with a brother in Grantham and then on to London from where she regularly corresponded with her husband and her mother. Bertie had the letters to prove it! Letters addressed from 'Hamstead'.

So perhaps the clue of the dyer's tag was a red herring? Perhaps they were *still* trying to identify a three-month-old enigma. But William Chapman (though as he confided later he was almost on the point of relegating the case to the 'unsolved' file) was as tenacious as he was perceptive. He just could not take Manton's story at face value. With a stroke of inspiration, he called in Scotland Yard's leading fingerprint expert, Superintendent Frederick Cherrill. In his own account of the case, Cherrill describes his triumph:

'Opening the door of a cellar-like place under the stairs, I found its walls grimed with dust. In the gloom I could make out a shelf on which were stacked quite a number of bottles of all shapes and sizes, from medicine-phials to beer-bottles.

I started to examine them. The walls of the cellar may have been grimed with dust, but there was no dust on these bottles. They had obviously been as scrupulously cleaned as had the crockery in the kitchen. It struck me that somebody had been reading detective stories, and that somebody had gone to great pains to remove any trace of finger-marks. Why?

One by one the bottles were tested, without result. It looked as though my search was to be fruitless. The examination was nearing its end when, lurking in the shadows of the remotest corner of that shelf, I came across the last bottle of all.

It was a pickle-bottle! I handled it carefully – almost lovingly, for it was my last hope. It was the one remaining article in the whole of that house which had not been tested, and it was the one remaining article which the murderer somehow overlooked, when, in his anxiety to remove all traces of his crime, he had carefully performed his cleaning operations.

This bottle had not been cleaned like the others. On its sloping shoulders was a film of dust. I tested it, and knew at once that this prosaic article held the secret which had eluded the police for three months, the secret they were so anxious to discover – the identity of the body in the sack.

On that pickle-bottle I found a thumbmark which corresponded with the left thumb impression of the dead woman, whose fingerprints had been sent for comparison weeks before. This was one of the prints I had been looking for during my search of the house. I had found it in the dingy, ill-lit cupboard at the home of Bertie Horace William Manton, who had so light-heartedly told detectives that his wife had "gone away".'

Chapman was now able to look afresh at the letters supposed to have come from Bertie Manton's 'estranged' wife; and to notice the spelling of 'Hamstead'. He asked Manton to write out the text of the letters from his dictation, and true to expectation Manton left out the 'p' in Hampstead.

Confronted with such evidence Horace William Manton, called Bertie, broke down and confessed: 'I killed her, but it was only because I lost my temper. I didn't intend to.' He went on to explain to Inspector Chapman about the frequent quarrels which finally came to a head on 18th November as they were having their tea. In a moment of rage Caroline Manton had thrown a cup of hot tea in her husband's face: 'I lost my temper. I picked up a heavy wooden stool . . . and hit her about the head and face several times . . . When I came to and got my sense again I see what I'd done. I saw she was dead and decided I had to do something to keep her away from the children. I undressed her and got four sacks from the cellar, cut them open, and tied her up in them. I carried her down to the cellar and left her there. I had washed up the blood before the children came home to tea. I hid the bloodstained clothing in a corner near the copper. After tea Ivy [his daughter] went out with a friend, and the two boys and Sheila [his other children] went to the pictures. After it was dark I brought the wife up from the cellar, got my bike out, laid her across the handlebars, and wheeled her down to Osborne Road. I laid her on the edge of the bank and she rolled into the river.'

Manton repeated his confession from the witness stand at Bedford Assizes before Mr (later Lord) Justice Singleton. He added that he had written a series of letters to his wife's mother purporting to be from Caroline, and taken a number of trips to Hampstead to post them. He had told the children: 'She's gone to stay in London with grandma'.

Mr Arthur Warde, KC, in advancing Manton's defence, pleaded the reduced charge of manslaughter, emphasising the extreme provocation of his wife's behaviour stating that Manton was generally a stable hard-working man devoted to his children and quite incapable of premeditated murder.

But if he had acted on the spur of the moment, what about the calculated disposal of the body; the stripping down even to the false teeth to avoid identification? Mr Justice Singleton in summing up to the jury reminded them: 'The test to be applied in such cases is whether the provocation was sufficient to deprive a reasonable man – as Manton was – of his self-control.'

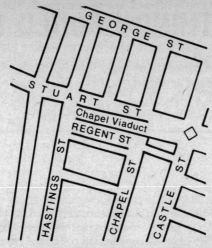

Bertie Manton was found guilty of murder and sentenced to death; but he did not die on the scaffold. After his sentence had been commuted to life imprisonment he was locked away in Parkhurst Prison on the Isle of Wight where he died three years later in 1947.

'NOTHING I COULD DO'

The Murders of Jaqueline Williams and Jeanette Wigmore by David Burgess
On Monday, 17th April 1967 at the Gravel Pit in Admoor Lane, Beenham

F aced with danger it is the instinctive response of all animals to protect themselves; this applies equally to communities of animals, who will collectively combine to ward off the threats of predators. It is an instinct that in humankind has been developed to the degree that we employ separate categories of citizens to undertake professional responsibility for our protection – servicemen and policemen. But when these custodians of the law fail us, when the police fail to apprehend a brutal killer, there is a return to animal fear. Women in particular are vulnerable and tend to keep to their houses after nightfall, as in the case of the spate of killings perpetrated by the so-called 'Yorkshire Ripper' [see page 528]. Children too are at risk, and at such times are rarely allowed beyond the sight of a responsible adult.

And so it had been in the little Berkshire village of Beenham after the savage murder of Yolande Waddington, a 17-year-old nursemaid, in October 1966. But even the ugliest memories fade with time, and within six months children were once again playing outdoors without constant supervision.

Jaqueline Williams and Jeanette Wigmore were two such lively 9-year-olds. Jaqueline and Jeanette had become inseparable – they went to the same school together, and they spent their evenings and weekends playing together.

The evening of Monday, 17th April 1967 was no exception, and when school was over the girls wheeled out their red bicycles and with Jaqueline's 6-year-old sister Caroline were soon engaged in whatever flights of fantasy children indulge. Shortly after 6 o'clock Caroline returned home in tears complaining that the others had left her and ridden off on their bikes. Although she didn't feel it at the time, Caroline was a very lucky little girl.

As dusk descended, the Williams and Wigmore families became justifiably anxious, and over the next few hours the horror of Yolande Waddington's death cannot have been far from their minds. A search party was organised by Terence Williams and Anthony Wigmore and nearly fifty villagers began to scour the countryside between the village and Beenham Stocks, where in Admoor Lane a disused and partially water-filled gravel pit provided and enticing, if forbidden, adventure playground for the neighbourhood children. It was here on this desolate waste-land that the search party found the two familiar red bicycles; a few yards farther on, with unbearably cruel irony, Tony Wigmore found his own daughter in a pool of water. She had been stabbed to death.

The villagers had now been joined by a team of police officers and two hours later a police dog discovered Jaqueline's body lying in 6 ins of mud under a thin covering of leaves; she had been sexually assaulted, half-strangled, and then drowned.

In response to a request from Berkshire's Chief Constable, Mr T. Hodgson, Scotland Yard deployed Detective Superintendent William Marchant to head the investigation; they also secured the valuable assistance of Dr Ian Holden, director of the nearby Home Office Forensic Laboratory at Aldermaston.

After visiting the scene of this barbaric double murder, and observing that the gravel pit is obscured from open view and accessible only by a narrow and twisting lane, the investigating officers worked on the assumption that the killer was a local man familiar with the area and with the fact that children used to play around the pit. As a consequence, all 850 villagers, men and women, old and young, were asked to account for their movements after

5.30pm on 17th April. Meanwhile the statements and blood samples taken from all male residents of Beenham between the ages of 19 and 60 which had been taken during the search for Yolande Waddington's killer, were re-examined for possible clues.

In checking the alibis for 17th April, police noticed that a man named David Burgess, a 19-year-old dumper-truck driver working on another of the local gravel pits had left work at 5.30 on the evening in question and had been seen in the area. He had told his brother John – who also worked at the pit – that he was going to look for rabbit snares. On the following morning John Burgess casually asked his brother if he had been to the 'other' gravel pit and was surprised by David's sharp reply of 'it wasn't me!'

With the uncanny perception of the experienced detective, William Marchant directed his attention to David Burgess, instinctively sure that he had already found his murderer. At the beginning of their interview Burgess denied all knowledge of the killings, but then unaccountably broke into a fit of weeping during which he cried 'You catch the one I chased away'. Asked to expand this rather cryptic demand, he replied: 'I was up at the end of the pit where I work. I heard someone scream. When I went across I saw her. A bloke stood there and she was in the water. I shouted at him. I was scared. I picked her up. I saw she was bloody and all that, then I left her.'

While the interview was taking place, Dr Brian Rees, a forensic scientist at Aldermaston, was at work on a pair of shoes worn by Burgess on the day of the crime. As Superintendent Marchant had anticipated, they bore bloodstains belonging to the same group as Jeanette's – the more impressive as evidence because it was one of the rarer groups, shared by only one in seventy people.

In June, David Burgess was committed by the Reading magistrates to appear at Gloucester Assizes to face a charge of double murder.

Just a week before his trial was due to open, Burgess claimed to have a sudden change of mind. He did, after all, know the man he said he saw at the gravel pit – 'Mac'.

Memory did not stretch to a proper name, but he thought it might be MacNab. 'I met him at the Viking Cafe, Caversham Road, Reading and it should be possible to trace him there.' Of his former reticence, Burgess explained that he had subsequently met Mac again in the gents of The Six Bells at Beenham and had been warned to keep his mouth shut if he knew what was good for him. In the event nobody at the Viking knew a MacNab, and such Macs as could be traced had cast-iron alibis.

On 13th July 1967 David Burgess faced Mr Justice Stable; he was defended by Mr Douglas Draycott QC, while Mr Kenneth Jones QC represented the Crown.

Once in the witness box Burgess's character came under critical scrutiny both by the judge and by Mr Jones. Part of that cross-examination follows:

Mr Justice Stable: When did you make up your mind to conceal what you have now told the jury you saw happen in the pit? – *Burgess*: Well, I was already thinking about it, thinking that I would have nothing to do with it.

You have seen this little girl who was brutally murdered, the murderer only two minutes ahead of you. If you had raised a hue and cry, don't you think the police might have caught him? – He would have been miles away by then.

If every police officer in Berkshire had been alerted within a couple of minutes why should that mean trouble for you? – I did not want to be pestered with the law. I did not want the police around me for statements all the time.

Mr Kenneth Jones: Did it ever occur to you that there might even have been one chance in a million that a doctor could have helped that little girl? – No. She looked dead, so I left her.

Why did you not take the direct route back to the quarry where you work? – I did not want to walk up Admoor Lane with blood dripping off my fingers, did I?

Why not? – I did not want to have anything to do with it.

Have you got any normal feelings at all? – There was nothing I could do for that girl.

But there was something you could have done for all the other little girls in Beenham; as long as this monster was free no little girl in Beenham was safe. I ask you again, have you got any normal feelings at all? – For some people.

Not for little girls? – She was dead. There was nothing I could do.

Are you fond of children? – It doesn't make any difference.

Which was clearly not a view shared by the judge. In a summing up that despite its scrupulous fairness gave every sign of Mr Justice Stable's evident disapproval of the prisoner, he presented this crucial question to the jury: 'Did he give any indication at any time that he felt pity or distress or horror? Not about what he had done, but what he found, what he had seen happen to that stricken child?

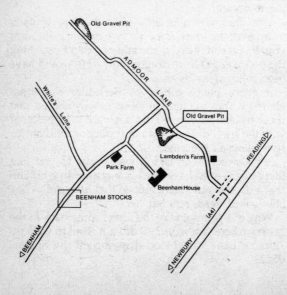

Or did he give the impression that so long as he was not bothered nothing else mattered?'

When they returned to the court after a retirement of three hours and twenty minutes, the jury announced a unanimous verdict of guilty on both counts of murder. Sentencing Burgess to life imprisonment the judge commented: 'I have not the slightest doubt that the verdict is right and you know it is . . . the cloud of fear is lifted from this part of Berkshire.'

With a broad smile on his face, David Burgess was taken down and removed to Durham Gaol.

GUILTY, BUT ASLEEP*

The Killing of Jean Sylvia Constable by Staff-Sergeant Wills Eugene Boshears
On Sunday, 1st January 1961 at his flat in
Great Dunmow, Essex

As a defence it stood unique.

The prisoner in the dock was Wills Eugene Boshears, a 29-year-old husband and father in service as a Sergeant fitter with the American fighter-plane base at Wethersfield.

The date was 4th January 1961; the place, the Essex Assizes at Chelmsford.

The charge against Boshears was one of murder; his defence was that he had killed in his sleep, and therefore no crime had been committed.

When lorry-driver Sidney Ambrose pulled his lorry in to a lay-by just outside the village of Ridgewell on the main Cambridge-Colchester road, murder could not have been further from his mind. Uppermost was that he needed to relieve himself after some time on the road, and with that in view walked the few yards off the road into a field. There, lying under a blackberry bush was the half-naked body of a young woman.

Medical examination revealed that the girl had died of

---

* One of the repercussions of the Boshears case was that Lord Elgin enquired, during a House of Lords discussion, whether the government had any plans to make a change in the law to make possible a verdict of 'Guilty but asleep', which would effectively prevent any similar defendant from walking free from punishment.

asphyxia due to manual strangulation, and the absence of mud on the soles of her feet indicated that she had met her death elsewhere and been dumped.

Command of the police investigation was immediately entrusted to the skill and experience of Detective Chief Inspector Barkway, head of Essex CID, and Detective Inspector Burdon. Within 12 hours they had an identity for the victim and were beginning to piece together the vital last hours of her life. The girl was 20-year-old Jean Sylvia Constable of Abels Road, Halstead, in Essex. On New Year's Day she had left home saying that she was going to a party in London.

Jean Constable had been one of those young women for whom the free-spending American service personnel attached to the local US Army Air Force proved an irresistible attraction, and much of her spare time was spent haunting the pubs in which they drank. The night of her death was no exception, and on this occasion she had been seen, not for the first time, in the company of Staff-Sergeant Wills Eugene Boshears.

But Boshears had started his drinking day somewhat earlier than Miss Constable. He had risen at around 6.15 on that first morning of the New Year in his flat in Great Dunmow. After drawing his pay at the base, Boshears breakfasted at the NCO's club where he started with a couple of vodkas as an aperitif, and concluded with a couple of vodka chasers. After spending the rest of the morning in convivial drinking, he departed the camp clutching a large bottle of 100% proof vodka.

On his way back to the flat, Boshears was diverted by a couple of beers at Great Bardfield, and after dropping in briefly at home for a large vodka and lemonade, the already merry Sergeant weaved his way into Braintree and the open doors of The Bell, The Boar, and back to The Bell again – which had by this time attracted the custom of Jean Constable and 20-year-old David Salt who were already well entrenched when Boshears joined them. After closing time the trio went back to Dunmow where the vodka bottle continued to dispense liquid happiness. Before long, driven no doubt by drink and passion, Salt and Jean Constable disappeared into the bedroom where they got to know each other a lot better. Wills Boshears, meanwhile, dragged a double mattress in front of the lounge fire, and when his companions returned from their love nest he suggested a night-cap before they all fell asleep on the mattress. At around 12.45am David Salt woke up, dressed, woke Boshears to ask where there was a taxi rank, and with this information departed the flat leaving Jean, the worse for drink, and Boshears, in much the same condition, sleeping.

Boshears takes up the narrative in his evidence given before the Essex Assizes:

> 'I went to sleep almost immediately. The next thing I remember is that I felt something pulling at my mouth. I was not awake but this woke me up, and I found I was over Jean and I had my hands round her throat. Jean was dead, and I panicked. I started to cut her hair off. Then I took the body to the spare room and left it. I dressed her in the way in which she was later found. I took the sheets and blankets off the bed and put them in the bath tub to soak [Jean would have soiled them in her fear at being attacked] and went in and went to sleep.'

The following day Boshears disposed of the body in the place where Sidney Ambrose found it.

This extraordinary defence could clearly not go unchallenged, and both Mr Stanley Rees QC, acting for the Crown, and Mr Justice Glyn-Jones, the presiding judge, made quite plain their mistrust of the proposition. And in this they were endorsed by the expert testimony of pathologist Professor Francis Camps. From the witness box, Camps declared that: 'Boshears would probably have felt the girl moving, even if he was half-asleep.'

Judge: He could not possibly have carried this through without waking up? – *Camps*: I should think that it is certainly within the bounds of improbability. My reason, from my findings, is this process would take a certain amount of time, and during that period the person would go through certain phases of movement, and from the description given of finding her suddenly dead like that I don't think it fits in with that type of death.

13   Peter Griffiths
[see 'Through a Mist of Tears', p.256.]

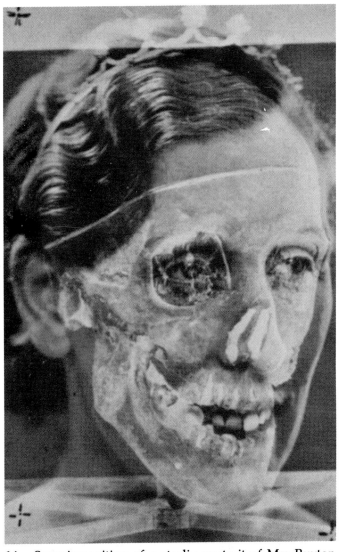

14. Superimposition of a studio portrait of Mrs Ruxton and Skull 2
[see 'Red Stains on the Carpet', p.266.]

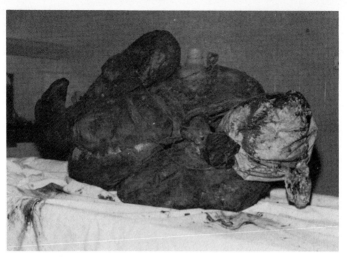

15 The body of James Finlay
[see 'The Rochdale Mummy', p.277.]

16 The military and civilian aspects of Armstrong's life
[see 'The Murdering Major', p.303.]

17   Alfred Potter
[see 'The Devil's Work'. p.334.]

18 Camille Holland's body recovered from the ditch at Moat Farm. [see 'Murder at Moat Farm', p.378.]

19 Sir Bernard Spilsbury at work in his laboratory [see 'No Honour Among Thieves', p.395.]

20 John 'Babbacombe' Lee on his release from prison [see 'The Man They Couldn't Hang', p.437.]

21 Neville Heath (left) under arrest [see 'A Damned Unworthy Son', p.448]

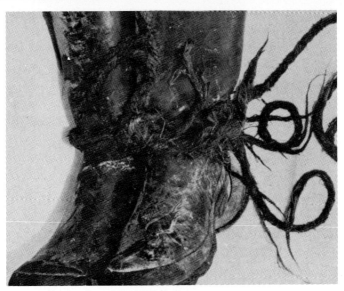

22 Phillips's bound ankles
[see 'The Mystery of Cefn Golau', p.485]

23 The arrest of the Donalds
[see 'With Malice Aforethought?', p.560.]

24 William Burke (left), William Hare [see 'The Resurrection Men', p.566.]

Summing up at the end of the trial, Mr Justice Glyn-Jones asked the jury: 'Have you ever heard of a man strangling a woman while he was sound asleep? We have no medical evidence that there exists any record in all the records of the medical profession that such a thing ever happened . . . You use your common sense and decide whether it happened.' However, on the matter of the law as it applied to the case, he instructed them that if they believed that Boshears had been asleep and committed the act involuntarily, then he was entitled to be acquitted; if they had any doubts about whether he was asleep or not, then Boshears must be given the benefit of that doubt and be acquitted. But if they rejected the defence, only then could they convict. There were, he said, only two possible verdicts in the case – Guilty of murder, or Not Guilty of anything at all.

Returning to the Court after a deliberation lasting 1 hour and 50 minutes, the jury found Sergeant Boshears not guilty; a verdict clearly not shared by many of the observers of the proceedings whose involuntary gasps witnessed their disapprobation. But Boshears was released and declared his complete satisfaction with British justice.

Only a week later another man, in London, stabbed his victim to death while, he claimed, he was asleep. This defence was obviously not destined to become fashionable, for the killer was convicted and sentenced to life imprisonment.

O, RARE TURPIN HERO

The Murder of Mr Thomas Morris by Richard Turpin

On Wednesday, 4th May 1735 in Epping
Forest, between King's Oak and the Loughton
Road

Turpin was for many years the terror of travellers along the Essex road, on account of his daring highway robberies, and the bane of the county's householders by his frequent burglaries. Nevertheless, despite his remarkably successful, if violent, career in robbery he was brought to an ignominious end by the shooting of a chicken – or more properly, a cockerel.

Richard Turpin was born to a farmer and grazier at Thaxted, in Essex, and having received a slight education, was apprenticed to a butcher in Whitechapel, in whose house he was most conspicuous for his gross behaviour and coarse manners. When his apprenticeship had been served, he married into a respectable East Ham family.

Before long Richard adopted the unsocial practice of stealing his neighbours' cattle, which he slaughtered and cut up for sale. Having stolen two oxen belonging to a Mr Giles of Plaistow, he drove them to his own house; but two of Giles's servants, suspecting who the robber was, went to Turpin's yard where they saw two carcases of the size that were missing, but as the hides had been stripped could not tell whether they were the same. Learning that it was Turpin's custom to dispose of his hides at Waltham Abbey, the men went there, where they found the hides of the beasts that had been stolen.

There was now no doubt remaining who was the thief, and a warrant was issued for the apprehension of Richard

Turpin. Learning that peace-officers were in search of him, Turpin made his escape, and informed his wife where he was concealed so that she could despatch some money, whereupon he travelled into Essex and joined a band of smugglers.

Thrown out of this kind of business by the unwelcome attentions of Custom-house officers, Turpin next allied himself with a gang of deerstealers, the greater part of whose depredations was committed in Epping Forest. This business not meeting their expectations, the robbers determined on a career of housebreaking. The plan was to fix their sights on houses that appeared to contain valuable property: and while one of the gang knocked at the door, the others would rush in and seize whatever might be worthy of their notice.

It was Turpin himself who told his associates that there was an old woman living at Loughton who was in possession of £700 or £800. The gang forced their way into the house, tied handkerchiefs over the eyes of the old woman and her maid and fastened a boy, her son, to the bedstead. This done, Turpin demanded money, and since the owner was reluctant to disclose its whereabouts, threatened to push her onto the blazing fire. Still she refused to give them any information, so the villains actually set her on the fire. There she sat until fear and pain loosened her tongue.

Flushed with success, the gang decided to attack the house of Mr Mason, the keeper of Epping Forest, and a time was fixed when the plan was to be carried out. But Turpin having gone to London to spend his share of the previous booty, intoxicated himself to the extent that he totally forgot the appointment. Nevertheless, the rest of the gang, having taken a solemn oath to break every article of furniture in Mason's house (heaven knows why), set out on their expedition. After ransacking the lower part of the house, they went upstairs where they broke everything that fell in their way, and among other things a china punch bowl from which dropped 120 guineas, which they snatched up and then fled.

On 7th February 1735, six of the gang assembled at The White Bear inn, in Drury Lane where they agreed to rob the house of Mr Francis, a farmer, near Marylebone. Unfortunately the farmer arrived home while the burglary was in progress, and was threatened with instant death if he made the least noise or struggle. One of the thieves stood as sentry while the rest of them rifled the house, in which they found a silver tankard, a medal of Charles the First, a gold watch, several gold rings, a considerable sum of money, and a variety of valuable linen, and other effects, which they took to London. A reward of £100 was offered for their apprehension, and in consequence two of them were taken into custody, tried, convicted on the evidence of an accomplice, and hanged.

The whole gang were dispersed by this tragedy and Turpin returned to the trade of the highwayman. On a journey one day in the direction of Cambridge he met a man fashionably dressed and well mounted, and anticipating a fat booty, Turpin presented his pistol to the supposed gentleman and demanded money. However, the man he stopped happened to be one Tom King, a noted highwayman, who knew Turpin. When the latter threatened instant death if he did not deliver his money, King burst into a fit of laughter and said: 'What! dog eat

dog! Come, come, brother Turpin, if you don't know me I know you, and shall be glad of your company.'

The two of them struck a mutually beneficial bargain, and together committed a number of robberies, till at length they were so well known that no public-house would receive them as guests. Thus they fixed on a spot between the King's Oak and the Loughton Road, in Epping Forest, where they found a cave which was large enough to hide both them and their horses. This cave was enclosed in a sort of thicket of bushes and brambles through which they could look, and see passengers on the road, while themselves remaining unseen. From this place they robbed so many people that at length even pedlars travelling the road carried firearms.

It was not long before Turpin became guilty of murder. It happened in the following manner. A reward of £100 had been offered for his arrest, and the servant of a gentleman named Thompson went out with another to see if they could take this notorious offender. Turpin seeing them approach his dwelling, and Mr Thompson's man having a gun, he mistook them for poachers; on which he said there were no hares near that thicket. 'No,' said the servant, 'but I have found Turpin,' and presenting his gun requested him to surrender. Turpin speaking to him in a friendly manner, gradually retreated till seizing his own gun, he shot him dead on the spot.

So serious were the consequences of this new crime that the Secretary of State issued the following proclamation:

'It having been represented to the King that Richard Turpin did on Wednesday the 4th of May last, murder Thomas Morris, servant to Mr Henry Thompson, one of the keepers of Epping Forest; and the same Richard Turpin continually committing notorious felonies and robberies near London, his Majesty is pleased to promise his most gracious pardon to any of his accomplices, and a reward of £200 to any person or persons that shall discover him, so that he may be apprehended and convicted. Turpin was born at Thaxted, in Essex; he is about thirty, by trade a butcher, about five feet nine inches

high, very much marked with small-pox, his cheek-
bones broad, his face thinner towards the bottom,
his visage short; he stands nearly upright, and is
broad about the shoulders.'

Turpin, for his part, fled farther into the country in search
of his old companion Tom King and having found him
and another rogue named Potter the trio set off for London
in the dusk of evening. Passing as they did close by The
Green Man in Epping Forest, they overtook a gentleman
named Major riding a fine horse from which Turpin
compelled the rider to dismount, his own beast being
jaded, and exchange.

The robbers now continued their journey towards
London, and Mr Major, going to The Green Man, gave
an account of the incident, which all agreed was the work
of Richard Turpin. Mr Major, in the meantime, had
printed some handbills asking information on the whereabouts of his stolen horse. Before long, the landlord of The
Green Man was notified that such a horse as Mr Major had
lost had been left at the Red Lion in Whitechapel. Arriving
at the inn, our landlord lay in wait until somebody came to
collect the horse; and sure enough, at about 11.00 at night,
King's brother came to pay for and take it away. He was
immediately seized and taken into the house. Asked what
right he thought he had to the horse, the man said that he
had just bought it. However, when the landlord examined
the whip which he had in his hand, he found a button at
the end of the handle half broken off, with the name
'Major' on the remaining half. With little more ceremony
the horse-thief was taken into the custody of a constable.
As it was clear, however, that he was not the actual robber,
he was told he would be freed if he would give the name
of the man responsible for the horse's removal from
Mr Major's possession. A stout man, he replied, in a
white duffel coat, was waiting for the horse in Red Lion
Street at this very moment. The company returned there
and saw the highwayman Tom King, who drew a pistol
and attempted to fire it, but it flashed in the pan. He then
tried to draw another pistol, but it got entangled in his
pocket. Turpin was watching all this at a small distance,

Dick Turpin shooting Thomas Morris near his cave in Epping Forest

and riding towards the spot, King cried out, 'Shoot him, or we are taken.' At which Turpin fired, accidentally shot his companion-in-arms, and made off at great speed.

For some considerable time Turpin skulked about his old forest lair, but at length decided to retreat to Yorkshire. First he went to Long Sutton in Lincolnshire, where he stole some horses and was immediately taken into custody. He escaped from the constable as he was being conducted before a magistrate, and hastened to Welton, in Yorkshire, where he assumed the name of John Palmer. He frequently crossed into Lincolnshire to steal horses, and brought them back to Welton, either selling or exchanging them.

He was often in the company of neighbouring gentlemen on their parties of hunting, shooting and, it must be said, heavy drinking. It was on the return one evening from just such an expedition that he wantonly shot a cockerel belonging to his landlord. Seeing this, Mr Hall, a neighbour, shouted at Turpin: 'You have done wrong in shooting your landlord's cock,' to which Turpin replied that if he would stay put while he reloaded his gun, he would shoot him too. Irritated by this insult Mr Hall informed the landlord what had passed, and a warrant was granted for the apprehension of 'John Palmer' who was taken into custody and carried before the bench of justices currently assembled at the Beverley Quarter Sessions. For reasons known only to himself, Turpin felt unwilling to give security for his future good behaviour, and was promptly committed to the local Bridewell.

Inquiries revealed that the man calling himself Palmer often journeyed into Lincolnshire, and on his return was always uncharacteristically wealthy and in possession of several new horses. It was only a short stretch of the imagination to guess that he was a horse-stealer and highwayman. The magistrates being far from satisfied with 'Palmer's' own version of things, commissioned the Clerk of the Peace to make inquiries respecting the activities of the supposed John Palmer in Lincolnshire. The letter was carried by a special messenger, who brought an answer from a magistrate in the neighbourhood of Long Sutton stating that John Palmer was well known, though he had never carried on trade there; that he had been accused of sheep-stealing, for which he had been in custody, but had made his escape from the peace officers; and that there were several complaints lodged against him for horse-stealing. It was felt prudent, therefore, to remove the prisoner to York Castle, where he had been lodged about a month when two people from Lincolnshire came and claimed first a mare and foal, then a horse which he had stolen in that county. After he had been in prison about four months, Turpin wrote the following letter to his brother in Essex:

York, Feb. 6, 1739.

Dear Brother – I am sorry to acquaint you that I am now under confinement in York Castle for horse-stealing. If I could procure an evidence from London to give me a character, that would go a great way towards my being acquitted. I had not been long in this county before my being apprehended, so that it would pass off the readier. For Heaven's sake, dear brother, do not neglect me. You will know what I mean when I say,

I am yours affectionately,
John Palmer

This letter was returned unopened to the post-office in Essex, because the brother, inexplicably, had refused to pay the sixpence postage. The letter was there quite by chance seen by a Mr Smith, coincidentally the schoolmaster who had taught Turpin to write. He immediately recognised the handwriting on the envelope, and took the letter to a magistrate who opened it, thereby discovering that the supposed John Palmer was the real Richard Turpin. Smith was consequently despatched to York, where he immediately identified Turpin among all the other prisoners in the Castle.

When the rumour spread that the infamous Richard Turpin was a prisoner in York, people flocked from all over the country to see him, and debate ran high whether he was the real Turpin or not. Among those who visited his cell was a young fellow who pretended to know the famous Turpin; he examined the prisoner for a considerable time before telling the keeper he would bet him half-a-guinea that the man was not Turpin; at which the prisoner whispered to his keeper: 'Lay him the wager, and I'll go halves.'

Being brought to trial, this notorious malefactor was convicted on two indictments upon which he received sentence of death. After conviction he wrote to his father, imploring him to intercede with a gentleman and lady of rank to make interest that his sentence might be remitted, and that he might be transported. The father did what was in his power; but the notoriety of his character was such that no persons would exert themselves in his favour.

This man lived in the gayest and most thoughtless manner after conviction, reckless of all considerations of futurity, and affecting to make a jest of the dreadful fate that awaited him. Not many days before his execution, he purchased a new fustian frock-coat and a pair of pumps in order to wear them at the time of his death; and on the day before, he hired five poor men at ten shillings each to follow the cart as mourners; he likewise gave hatbands and gloves to several other persons, and left a ring and some other articles to a married woman in Lincolnshire with whom he had been acquainted.

On the morning of the 10th April 1739, this hero of highwaymen – for he was held to be the hero of any gang with which he connected himself – was put into a cart and, followed by the mourners he had engaged, drawn to the place of execution; on his way to which he bowed to the spectators with an air of the most astonishing indifference and intrepidity. When he came to the fatal tree, on ascending the ladder, his right leg trembled, and he stamped it down with an air of assumed courage, as if ashamed of discovering any signs of fear. Having conversed with the executioner about half an hour, he threw himself off the ladder and expired in a few minutes. The spectators of the execution were affected at his fate, as he was distinguished by the comeliness of his appearance. He had attained the thirty-third year of his age. At the execution he had a fellow-sufferer in the person of John Stead, who was also found guilty on a similar indictment namely horse-stealing.

Turpin's corpse was taken to the Blue Boar in Castle Gate, York, where it remained till the next morning when it was interred in the churchyard of St George's parish, with an inscription on the coffin, initials of his name, and age. The grave was dug remarkably deep; but notwithstanding the people who acted as mourners took such measures as they thought would secure the body, it was carried off about three o'clock on the following morning: the populace, however, got intimation where it was conveyed, and found it in a garden belonging to one of the surgeons of the city. Gaining possession of it, they laid it on a board and carried it through the streets in a kind of triumphal manner; after which they filled the coffin with unslaked lime and buried it in the grave where it had been deposited.

THE BATH-CHAIR MURDER

The Murder of Archibald Brown by his son Eric
On Thursday, 23rd July 1943 one mile from their home in London Road, Rayleigh, Essex

As the result of a motor-cycle accident some years previously, 47-year-old Archibald Brown had developed a gradual paralysis of the spine resulting, by 1942, in complete immobility of his legs. He did not, however, let this in any way inhibit the extent of his tyranny over the rest of the Brown family – consisting at that time of Mrs Brown and their two sons, Eric aged 19 and Colin aged 16. Eric in particular suffered a constant barrage of bullying, and his mother fared little better.

On the afternoon of Thursday, 23rd July 1943, the family's resident help, Nurse Mitchell, began the familiar routine of preparing Brown senior for an outing in the wheelchair which now substituted for his legs. Going to the air-raid shelter beside the house where the vehicle was stored (remember, it was wartime), the nurse was puzzled to find the door fastened from the inside; eventually it opened and Eric emerged from the shelter. Thinking little of it, Nurse Mitchell settled her patient and began one of their now familiar trips. About a mile from home Brown wanted to stop and smoke a cigarette which Nurse Mitchell obligingly lit for him, at the same time taking the opportunity to straighten his blankets. As she passed round to the back of the wheelchair Miss Mitchell was thrown violently to the ground by a massive explosion; miraculously she escaped unscathed. Not so Archibald Brown, parts of whose body and chair were spread over quite a large area.

Subsequent examination of the debris revealed the cause of the fatal explosion to be a type of anti-tank device listed as a Hawkins No.75 Grenade Mine. Subsequent examination of Eric Brown revealed that although he was a bank clerk in civilian life he was currently serving with the Army. What was more, a store of Hawkins mines were kept at his company's headquarters, and Eric had attended special lectures on their use.

Interviewed by detectives, Eric Brown appeared unrepentant and seemed to find it difficult to understand that he had committed murder: 'My father's now out of his suffering,' he told investigating officers, 'and I earnestly hope that my mother will now live a much happier and normal life.'

On 4th November 1943 young Brown appeared before the Essex Assizes at Guildford charged with parricide. As the result of an attempt to kill himself whilst in custody, Eric had been examined by nerve specialist Dr Rowland Hill who diagnosed schizophrenia. Accordingly he was judged guilty but insane and committed to a mental institution.

MURDER AT MOAT FARM

The Murder of Camille Cecile Holland by Samuel Herbert Dougal
On Friday, 19th May 1899 at Moat Farm, near Saffron Walden

Samuel Herbert Dougal was a man both attracted to and attractive to women; an unashamed womaniser with a string of illigitimate children dotted around the world like markers charting his career with the Royal Engineers.

In 1869 he married for the first time, and despite the inevitable infidelities the marriage lasted until 1885, when Mrs Dougal died in Nova Scotia where her husband was stationed. Within months the second Mrs Dougal had also perished – after a bout of severe vomiting. Dougal married for the third time in Dublin in 1892: in 1896 he was imprisoned for forgery (Samuel Dougal's second weakness was money – other people's money). On his release in 1898 he set about cultivating an attachment to a 55-year-old spinster named Camille Holland. Miss Holland, though well educated, was rather unworldly, and seemed oblivious to the clear fact that Dougal simply wanted to get his hands on her modest fortune. In 1899 they moved to a lonely farmhouse outside Saffron Walden called Moat Farm. Dougal, up to his old tricks, was discovered by Camille trying to seduce the maid and she ordered him to leave the house. Shortly after this episode, on 19th May, Camille Holland and her lover set off on what they announced as a shopping trip; only Samuel returned. It was to be four years before anybody saw Camille Holland again – or what was left of her after spending the time buried in a drainage ditch.

Meanwhile Dougal was making free with her money by the simple expedient of forgery; his wife (explained away to neighbours as his widowed daughter) came to stay at the farm, and the couple settled into a life of comfort and ease underwritten by Camille Holland's bank balance.

But four years is a long time to spend on holiday (Dougal's explanation for Miss Holland's disappearance), and rumour became so strong that the local police were eventually obliged to make serious enquiries. Which was how they found the body in the ditch; it had been shot through the head with a revolver belonging to Samuel Dougal. He fled with what money and valuables he could lay his hands on, but was identified in London and detained.

On 30th April 1903 Dougal was charged with the murder of Camille Holland. On 22nd June the Chelmsford Assizes found him guilty, and after the rejection of his appeal Dougal was hanged at Chelmsford Gaol on 8th July. Before his execution he confessed his crime to the prison chaplain.

However, a much more extensive 'confession' began to appear in serial form in *The Sun* newspaper; this narrative was later published in complete form. Some of which is reproduced here.

The Only Way

'I made up my mind at last that there was only one way out of the difficulty I was in, and that was to put her out of the way. I used to sit and think about it for hours, because, although I had done a lot of things during my life, I couldn't quite make up my mind to go so far as to murder her. I thought once that I would have a bit of an accident, and that I would contrive to get her out of the house in her nightdress so that she might be found drowned in the moat, and that at the inquest I could say she was in the habit of walking in her sleep, and had no doubt fallen into the moat. But when I came to examine the water I found it was only about a foot or so deep, and that the mud had been allowed for years to settle at the bottom. I did not quite see my way clear to do the job this way, because I wanted, if possible, to avoid publicity. If there had been an inquest I thought her relatives would be sure to see it in the newspapers, and that was what I wanted to avoid if possible. I thought of such a lot of plans for getting rid of her, and once I almost decided to let her shoot herself, only she had such a horror of firearms that she would not let me even keep them in the house, I thought I could get her in one of the rooms alone, and while I was fiddling about with the revolver I would contrive to fire it off just as one of the servants came into the room, so that she could give evidence that it was an accident, but again I thought of the inquest.

Got to Hate Her

I tried to get her to make a will, leaving everything to me, while I made one also, leaving everything to her, but she told me she had already made her will, and

The moat at Moat Farm

that she did not intend to alter it. All this caused me a lot of trouble, and I used to sit for hours and hours conjuring up all kinds of schemes to get rid of her. At this time I got positively to hate her, and when we actually moved into the farm I had definitely decided what I should do. I thought that a good place to bury her would be the ditch, and that was why the very first week we were at the farm I gave orders for it to be filled in.

I had made up my mind then that this should be the last drive Miss Holland should ever have, because as we were driving along she started to nag me again, and she was jawing me all the time we were in the Chequers, the public house where we had some whisky. We got up in the trap again, and as it was a beautiful night we let the horse walk slowly home, and I should think it was about a quarter-past eight when we got back to the farm. When I had taken the horse out I thought she would go in the house, but instead of that she made some remark about it being a beautiful moonlight night.

'I Shot Her'

I had pushed the trap into the coach-house by this time, and I could see by the light at the back of the house that the servant girl was still there doing her work. I stepped up on the side of the trap, reached down the revolver, and as Miss Holland stood just near the door looking at the moon I shot her. I wasn't standing very far from her, and, of course, I was a little higher, because I was still on the step of the trap. She dropped like a log, and then I pulled her into the coach-house.

After the Murder

If I lived to be a thousand years old I shall never forget the feeling as I caught hold of both her hands and drew her along until I got her into the coach-house. All kinds of things came into my mind, and my heart seemed almost to stand still as I put my hand inside her dress to feel if her heart was beating.

Of course, I knew that she was dead, and yet I don't know what made me do it, but I knelt down on one knee and pulled up her head, and asked her to speak if she could. Why I did this I cannot tell you, but just at that moment I thought I heard something move outside, so I kicked one of the cushions towards her head, and put my hand underneath her neck, and lifted her head up and put the cushion underneath.

I didn't think this was of much use, and why I did it I can't tell even now, but I thought for a moment that she might come to, because there was no blood about, and I wasn't quite certain where the bullet had struck her.

Terror Stricken

Then all of a sudden I remembered that the noise of the pistol might reach the back kitchen, where I knew the girl would be having her supper, so I stepped outside, put the revolver in my pocket, pushed the doors to, and then went into the house. I lifted up the latch that was fixed to the gate at the entrance of the Moat-bridge, but almost immediately even this noise seemed to frighten me, for I stood still and listened. I could not turn my head towards the coach-house, and great beads of perspiration began to run down my back, for I had a most peculiar sensation as if someone was following me. I thought the doors of the coach-house had opened and she was walking out after me. I could almost feel her touch me, and as true as there is a God in Heaven, I was ready to drop. I must have stood there some seconds, and then I put my hand into my pocket and drew out the revolver, and turned round and looked straight at the coach-house. I could not quite get out of my mind, nor get rid of the feeling, that something or someone besides myself stood between me and the coach-house. I had still an impression that someone would come towards me, so I levelled up the revolver and stood there with it in my hand.

I don't think I could have uttered a word to have

saved my life. My tongue was like a great ball of fire, and I quite hurt myself trying to get some saliva to moisten my mouth and my parched tongue. Then I remembered how silly it was; of course, there was no one, and put the revolver back into my pocket and walked into the house.

We usually kept some brandy in a decanter in the sitting-room, so I pushed the door open and picked up the decanter without waiting for a glass. I think I must have gulped down half of its contents. This seemed to steady me, and I walked along the passage, expecting to see the girl standing there watching me.

'Where is the Mistress?'

She was still going on with her work, and I looked at her to see if I could read in her face whether she knew what had happened outside. Thank God, her first words were, 'Where's the mistress?' and I was just able to jerk out, 'She has gone to London.' I really believe that at that moment if I had even a suspicion that she knew anything about what had occurred I should have shot her, and I knew that would not do, because she had written to her mother to come and fetch her away, and I knew the mother would be sure to be there, so I need hardly tell you how thankful I was when the girl went back into the kitchen, making some remark about she thought it was very unkind of Mrs Dougal to go to London and leave her in the house after what had happened. I don't know quite what I said, but I think I made some remark about it being all right, because the mistress would return and be there before we went to bed. I asked her whether she did not hear me drive in and she said, 'No, I have been working in the kitchen.' I felt quite relieved when she said this, but as I walked away into the front of the house I stopped and listened once or twice, because I fancied she might follow me and watch what I was doing, but she went on with her work just as if nothing unusual had happened, and I could see she really believed what I said – viz., that her mistress had gone to London.

Then I went into the coach-house, but it was dark, and I pushed the door further open, so that some of the light from the moon would come in. She was in exactly the same position as I had left her, so I knelt down and poured some of the brandy over her face, thinking perhaps it might revive her, but really I knew this was impossible because she was dead. I tried to sit her up, but she fell back on the cushion, and I knew all was over then.

Filling in the Ditch

Of course, I had arranged everything, and had started the work of filling in the ditch, and I had mapped out days before where I was going to bury her, but I sat down and began thinking over new schemes, and every few minutes I kept touching her and feeling her pulse and speaking to her. I don't know how it was, but I wanted to get away from her side, and yet I was afraid. Something seemed to keep me there, to make me keep looking at her, wondering whether she would move, and yet I knew that this was impossible. I went outside the coach-house, and walked down towards the lower moat to see if the girl was still in the kitchen, and I could hear her moving about humming to herself.

I stood by the side of the hedge for quite half an hour thinking over all kinds of methods and ways of getting rid of the body, but somehow I had to go back to the coach-house. Why I did this I can't tell you, but it seemed as if something was dragging me there, and I kept fancying that the girl would come out and go into the coach-house and find out what had happened. I daresay she is right when she says that I came back in about half-an-hour, because I wanted to go into the house again and make myself certain that she did not suspect that her mistress was lying in the coach-house dead. I had to make some excuse, so I told her that I was going to the station to meet a train and bring her mistress back. I was in the house, I think, about a quarter of an hour, and I opened another bottle of brandy and filled up the decanter so the girl should not notice that it was all gone.

Still More Brandy

When I left the house this time I had another good drink of brandy, but although it was neat it seemed to have no impression upon me. I could not get rid of the burning sensation in my throat, and I kept on walking backwards and forwards outside the coach-house fancying every minute that someone would come along, or that the doors would open and I should find myself forced to use my revolver again. I went into the coach-house and put the revolver on the shelf, but had to go back for it again, and put it in my pocket, and practically I kept it there all the night. I tried to smoke a cigar, but I had to light it a dozen times because I forgot all about it and it went out. I walked round the farm buildings, I pushed open the doors to see if anyone was inside, and then I went into the house again and told the girl that her mistress had not come, but I thought she might come by the train that got in just after ten o'clock. Once or twice a feeling came over me that the girl was deceiving me, and that she was watching me as I walked about the farm, so the next time I left I stood on the moat bridge in the shadow of the trees and watched the front door to see if she came out. I grew very nervous, and I kept fancying that if I went away very far from the coach-house she would be sure to come out and go in there.

Getting Rid of the Body

Again I began to conjure up all kinds of possible ways of getting rid of the body, and I made up my mind that it would be best not to put her in the ditch, but to take her away and bury her somewhere else. I looked about the farm for a fork, and when I found one I thought I would go up in the fields and dig a hole and put her in. I did go, perhaps a hundred yards along the hedge of the big field, trying to pick out a spot where the ground was soft, and I could dig a grave, but try my hardest I was obliged to go back to the coach-house, and then I had another good dose of brandy, and I determined to carry her up into the fields. I took off her hat and her veil and the jacket she was wearing, and I picked her up in my arms and walked down by the side of the little moat. Her head was leaning over my shoulder, and as I carried her along I wished there was a great big furnace there that I could put her in and watch her burn. I thought of cutting her up into pieces and putting her into the moat, but I thought of the time it would take me, and I was afraid of being interrupted.

She seemed so heavy, and when I got up into the fields I sat her down, and put her head against the bank that runs up by the side of the hedge. I got hold of the fork, and I stuck it in the ground once or twice, but I thought it would be no good, because the hole would sure to be seen by some of the labourers as they crossed the fields to work. I could not make up my mind what to do with her, so I laid her flat on her back and went back to the house again to get some more brandy, for I was shaking from head to foot. I kept burying my nails into my flesh as I walked along, and I had to close my mouth to prevent my teeth chattering. What I said this time I am not quite certain, but I know I said I expected the mistress would come by the twelve o'clock train, and I pretended that the pony and trap was outside waiting for me to drive to the station again.

When I left the house this time I went to the side of the ditch, and I thought that after all it would be the safest way to get rid of her; but somehow I wanted to bury her out of sight and yet I wanted to keep her by the side of me, so I went back to the field and picked her up again and carried her over to one of the haystacks, where I put her down and left her while I went and got some straw and threw it into the ditch.

A Horrible Sight

I went back to the haystack; picked her up and found then that she was getting cold and stiff, for there was a strong breeze blowing, and it was rather a cold night. It was a horrible sight to see her lying on the ground, and before I picked her up the last time I wished that she was alive again, because I thought after all she hadn't done me any harm, so I knelt down and I kissed her once or twice. All the good times we had had seemed to come back to me, and I remembered that once or twice when I had been queer through the drink she had nursed me and tried to get me well, and that after all it was a bit hard to do her in.

But then I began to think what would happen to me if she was found. I should certainly be accused of the crime, and what could I say after I had told the servant that she had gone to London? I thought I would hide her in the haystack for a few days, but finally I made up my mind that I would get rid of her once and for all, so I picked her up again and carried her back into the coach-house and laid her down on the cushions.

I went and got the fork, and I carried some straw and laid it down at the bottom of the ditch. I think the brandy then began to have some effect upon me, and I grew more brutal, and I began to think of the way she had nagged me and the difficulty I had in getting money from her, and the way she had shown me up before the servant, so I caught hold of her hand and pulled the ring off her finger. She was very fond of this ring; it had been given to her by the only man I really believe she ever loved.

Laid Her on the Straw

I picked her up in my arms, and just as you would carry a baby I carried her out of the coach-house and laid her on the straw which I had put in the ditch. Then a change came over me, but the more brandy I drank the more brutal and wicked I seemed to get. One minute I wanted to kiss her, and the next time I wanted to pitch a lot of mould over her, but at last I made up my mind that I would bury her and get her out of sight. I thought of what had happened, but a few days before, when she stood by the side of the ditch, talking to Pilgrim and myself about filling in the ditch.

I thought perhaps unless I covered her over the fowls would scratch away the straw, so I got some brambles and twigs and pieces of wood, and I stretched them over the body, and then put some more straw on top, so that the body would be hidden. Then I made up my mind to go into the house again and tell the servant that I had been to the station, and that there was no possibility of her mistress coming, that evidently she had lost the train, and that she had better go to bed. I then went outside and I picked up the fork and I put a thin layer of earth over the top of the brambles and straw, and I went back into the house and had some more brandy, and then I went to bed. I couldn't sleep, and I got up and walked round the farm and down to the road and back again. I couldn't keep my eyes off the

Springfield Gaol where Dougal was confined awaiting execution

ditch, and I kept thinking that perhaps the fowls would get loose and they would scratch the mould away, so I got down into the ditch and kicked some more earth over her until it was about a foot deep. Once or twice I was tempted to pull the straw away and have another look at her face, but I tore myself away and walked about the farm, and I was glad when daylight came, because I made myself some breakfast, and I called the girl at half-past six.'

(From *Dougal's Life Story: Told by Himself*)

THE BOVINGDON BUG

The Murder of Robert Egle and Frederick Biggs by Graham Young
Between June and November 1971 at John Hadland's Ltd, Bovingdon, Hertfordshire

---

Very few killers, once convicted, get a second chance to commit murder; and those who do seldom take it. Graham Young was one of the few exceptions.

Young was born in 1947; a few months later his mother fell sick and died, and this was certainly a contributing factor in Graham's development into a solitary child and, as an adolescent, a loner among his peers. He was a highly intelligent youth, though in an off-beat and rather sinister way, a great admirer of Adolf Hitler and the Victorian poisoner William Palmer. Graham also took a precocious interest in chemistry, and at an early age was experimenting with explosives.

In 1961, when he was 14, Young expanded his interest to include poisons and their effects on the human body; a piece of academic research that required the administration of small doses of antimony tartrate to members of his immediate family and a school friend named John Williams. His sister Winifred suffered almost continual stomach upsets, vomiting frequently and occasionally publicly. In April 1962 Young's stepmother died. As he continued to lace his father's and sister's food and drink, they became increasingly ill. When Winifred began to suffer from dizzy spells after drinking some 'bitter' tea, she was diagnosed as being the victim of belladonna poisoning; his father, by this time in a very weak condition, was admitted to hospital and diagnosed as suffering from arsenic poisoning. Young's response was a disdainful: 'How ridiculous not being able to tell the difference between arsenic and antimony poisoning!'

However, the family's suspicions had been aroused and they lost no time in confiding them to the police – after all, one of them had already died, who might be next? When Graham Young was picked up he was found to have several packets of antimony tartrate in his pockets and tucked in his shirt, so sealing his guilt. Not that Young made any kind of fight of his case, and readily confessed that, though he had a great affection for his family, they were, nevertheless, expendable victims of his scientific research. Not surprisingly he was found guilty but insane and removed to Broadmoor.

Nine years later, in 1971, Graham Young, now 23, walked free from the Institution presumed 'cured'. Within a short time he had been found employment with John Hadland's Ltd, a photographic instruments firm in Bovingdon, Hertfordshire. In June 1971 – weeks after Young had joined the company – Hadland's head storeman, 60-year-old Bob Egle, was taken ill at work suffering diarrhoea, nausea, extreme backache, and numbness in the tips of his fingers. After eight days of intense pain, Egle died in St Alban's hospital; death was attributed to bronchopneumonia and polyneuritis. Among the mourners at Bob Egle's cremation was Graham Young.

Meanwhile, Ronald Hewitt, another employee of Hadland's, had also been suffering diarrhoea, vomiting and stomach cramps – symptoms which continued until he left the firm two days after Egle's death.

In September 1971 another of the Hadland's workforce fell ill – 60-year-old Fred Biggs. The symptoms were the familiar ones shared by Bob Egle and Ronald Hewitt. Later in the same month the import-export manager, Peter Buck, fell similarly ill.

During the next month David Tilson, a clerk, and Jethro Batt, a storeman, also fell victim to what was now being called 'The Bovingdon Bug'. Both men grew worse. Tilson required hospitalisation and began to lose his hair. Mrs Diana Smart developed stomach and leg cramps, nausea, and other symptoms. On 4th November Fred Biggs was admitted to hospital with severe pains in his chest, the following day he was joined by Jethro Batt. On the 19th Biggs died. Such was the alarm that several members of Hadland's staff handed in their notice.

Eventually the management were worried into holding a full medical enquiry into working conditions at the plant. In an attempt to defuse the mounting panic, and to assure workers that the chemicals they had been handling were safe and in no way responsible for the 'bug', the medical team held a meeting with the entire workforce in the canteen. Dr Arthur Anderson, who had headed the investigation team, made himself available to answer questions, but was quite unprepared for the barrage shot at him by one particular member of Hadland's staff; quite taken aback when Graham Young concluded his outburst with the question: 'Do you not think, doctor, that the symptoms of the mysterious illness are consistent with thallium poisoning?'

It was at this point that Hadland's management decided to check into the background of this young man who had continually evaded talking about his past. Within hours of them learning that he had only the year before been released from Broadmoor whence he had been committed for poisoning his family, Graham Young was under arrest. A search of his bedsit at Hemel Hempstead disclosed various types of poison and a diary, both of which would prove vital in convicting Young of murder – though true to character he finally admitted that he had poisoned six people, two of whom had died. 'I could have killed them all if I wished, as I did Bob Egle and Fred Biggs, but I allowed them to live.'

In July 1972 Graham Young was put on trial at St Alban's for the murder of Egle and Biggs; he pleaded not guilty. Throughout the trial it was evident that he was having the time of his life – an opportunity to show just how clever he was! Incriminating extracts from his diary were read to the court: 'October 30 [1971]. I have administered a fatal dose of the special compound to F[red Biggs], and anticipate a report on his progress on Monday 1st November. I gave him three separate doses.' The court was also told that when arrested and searched, Young was

found to have on his person a lethal dose of thallium –
what he called his 'exit' dose; for as he had written in his
diary: 'I must watch this situation very carefully. If it looks
like I will be detected then I shall have to destroy myself.'

Nevertheless, Young stubbornly and arrogantly continued to protest his innocence; the diary entries, he said
were simply working notes for a novel that he was
writing. And he had no idea how the body of Fred Biggs
and the ashes of Bob Egle came to carry lethal amounts of
thallium.

The jury, however, failed to be persuaded by the cool,
confident manner of the prisoner; they could see through
the shell to the psychopath that lurked beneath, this man
who had callously poisoned his colleagues like guinea-
pigs in a laboratory experiment. Graham Young was
sentenced to life imprisonment.

In August 1990, warders making a routine visit to
Graham Young's cell at Parkhurst prison found him lying
crumpled on the floor. Rushed to the prison hospital,
Young was found to have died from a heart attack; he
was 42 years old.

THALLIUM AS A POISON

Thallium, a heavy metal closely related to mercury and
lead but more toxic than both, was discovered by Sir
William Crookes in 1861. Its usefulness to industry has
been mainly limited to incorporation into pesticides,
although as in the case of arsenic before it, the sale of
thallium-based products is no longer permitted in
many countries.

As an instrument of murder, thallium appears rarely
in homicide records, despite the fact that its properties
suit it well to the purposes of the poisoner. Its salts are
colourless, almost tasteless, and can be easily dissolved in waterbased liquids; furthermore, the symptoms of thallium poisoning can be confused with those
of a number of common virus ailments such as influ-
enza.

Biologically, the human body seems to confuse thallium with potassium – which is essential for the sustenance of cells and nerves – and so interferes with several different systems at the same time. It upsets the metabolism of the B vitamins, inhibits the absorbtion of iron and calcium, and disturbs the nerve cells. Uniquely, thallium causes the hair to fall out, and until the recognition of its dangers, thallium acetate was used by dermatologists to remove body hair in the treatment of fungus diseases.

NO HONOUR AMONG THIEVES

The Murder of Herbert William Ayres (alias 'Pigsticker') by Oliver Newman (alias 'Tiggy') and William Shelly (alias 'Moosh')
On or around 29th May 1931 in a tent-town between the Watford and Barnet by-passes, Hertfordshire

---

That there is not – never was – any such thing as 'honour among thieves' is no surprise to anybody except readers of Harrison Ainsworth and admirers of Gay's Captain Macheath; least of all is it believed by students of true crime.

In the following tale, we visit the denizens of a twilight underworld which, if not entirely criminal, is a community with more than its fair percentage of villains. The landscape of this world is as alien as its inhabitants, a wilderness of unkempt grass and brambles wedged between the Watford and Barnet by-pass roads, dotted with tumble-down shacks and tarpaulin tents. Over everything in this hostile 'country' hangs a pall of acrid smoke from the vast smouldering refuse tip used by the LMS Railway. The population is for the most part unemployed and unemployable, eking out a rudimentary existence by living on their wits. The few that work toil mainly as navvies, or in the underground sewage and drainage systems that ferry Britain's effluent. In this transient, dog-eat-dog world, names are as closely guarded as past histories, not least for the two protagonists of our story: one is called 'Tiggy'; the other 'Moosh'. Their dwelling is a marginally better furbished hut than most of its neighbours, with a board floor and a tarpaulin roof. This reprobate pair are in work; what they earn goes, for the most part, into the brewers' purses.

On 1st June 1931, one of the tent-town inhabitants, named McGlade, was stumbling home past the refuse tip when, protruding from the side of a smouldering mound of rubbish, he observed a human hand.

Usually when a policeman appeared in this overgrown underworld its inhabitants instinctively ran for cover. When a policeman arrived to remove the body from the tip, everybody wanted a front-row seat. Carefully, lest the mound should topple, the body attached to the hand was extricated from the rubbish.

Despite its charred, unrecognisable features, pathologist Sir Bernard Spilsbury set the victim's time of death as around three days previous to its discovery, and the cause of death to a savage blow to the head which had left a rectangular-shaped fracture. Facial identification being out of the question, the police began to work with what little they had; which amounted to a few fragments of clothing and a tattoo on the back of the unburned hand that had been sticking out of the refuse – a red heart pierced by a sword.

As it turned out this latter mark was quickly recognised by a 'neighbour' as having belonged to a man christened Herbert William Ayres, but in this no-man's-land had been known as 'Pigsticker'. 'Pigsticker' had suddenly disappeared from the encampment several days before, but as this was no rare thing among the hut-dwellers, no further attention had been given to it.

The next, and most vital, information was given by an inhabitant whose real name was John Armstrong. Armstrong had recently got a local job as a navvy, and until he could make his own arrangements 'Moosh' and 'Tiggy' had generously allowed him to sleep on the floor of their hut. Awakened one night by a cry from outside the shack, Armstrong had peeped out and seen his two hosts bludgeoning 'Pigsticker' over the head; they had carried the body off in the direction of the rubbish tip and later returned to bed. Fearing for his own life should he open his mouth on the subject, John Armstrong kept his silence and next morning left the hut and the camp.

After mounting an all-night watch on the shack, a police team led by Detective Inspector Bennett moved in to arrest its occupants. For reasons unfathomable to man, the three ferocious dogs which had been set as guards remained where they were, lying beside the hut; perhaps in their own way they knew that the game was up – at any rate they did not even raise a bark. After the arrests a thorough search was made of the dwelling, and a blood-stained axe was pulled from beneath the floor-boards, the back of its blade fitting perfectly the depression in the dead man's skull.

Not that the culprits made any attempt to deny the charge of murder that was brought against them; indeed, they viewed the killing as a perfectly justifiable act of retribution. 'Pigsticker', they claimed with disgust, had been a thief! He had previously been caught in the act of stealing tea and sugar from their hut, and had received a sound thrashing for his ungentlemanly behaviour. Later, some bread and bacon disappeared, and assuming that 'Pigsticker' had been up to his old tricks, 'Moosh' and 'Tiggy' had taxed him with the theft. There had been a fight, and the rest was witnessed by John Armstrong.

At their trial at the Old Bailey, 61-year-old 'Tiggy', and 57-year-old 'Moosh' were indicted in their real names of Oliver Newman and William Shelly. They seemed throughout the two-day trial to be quietly puzzled as to why anybody should want to punish them for ridding society of such a rotten apple as 'Pigsticker'. The only voluble expression of emotion that they gave vent to was when John Armstrong was in the witness box. Asked if there was a clock in the prisoners' hut, Armstrong replied: 'No, but there was one, and here it is', producing an alarm clock from his coat pocket. 'Blimey, look at that!' cried out 'Moosh' with sincere indignation, 'He's pinched our clock!'

Found guilty and sentenced to death by Mr Justice Swift, 'Moosh' remarked enigmatically that the sentence had come twenty years late. Both men were hanged on 5th August 1931; but one doubt remains – if Armstrong had walked off with their clock, perhaps he had also helped himself to their bacon. If he had, then 'Moosh' and 'Tiggy' killed the wrong man.

HANGED IN ERROR

The Murder of Mr Hayes by his Manservant
In 1741 in the city of Oxford and the Execution
in Error of Jonathan Bradford for the Crime

Jonathan Bradford kept an inn at the city of Oxford. A
gentleman named Hayes, attended by a manservant,
put up one evening at Bradford's house, and in the night
the former was found murdered in his bed. The landlord
was later apprehended on suspicion of having committed
this wicked deed upon his guest.

The evidence presented against him was to this effect:
that two gentlemen who had supped with Mr Hayes, and
who retired to bed at the same time to their respective
chambers, being alarmed in the night by a noise in his
room, and soon hearing groans as of a wounded man, one
of these persons got up to discover the cause. He found
their landlord, with a dark lantern and a knife in his hand,
in a state of great astonishment and horror, bending over
his dying guest, who almost instantly expired.

On this evidence the jury convicted Bradford, and he
was executed.

The facts attending this dreadful tragedy were not fully
brought to light until the deathbed confession of the real
murderer, who was the servant.

Mr Hayes was a man of considerable property, and
greatly respected. He had about him when his sad destiny
led him under Bradford's roof, a considerable sum of
money. The landlord, knowing this, determined to murder and rob him. For this horrid purpose he proceeded

Jonathan Bradford on the gibbet

with a dark lantern and a carving knife, intending to cut the throat of his guest, while yet sleeping; but what must have been his astonishment and confusion to find his victim already murdered by a servant!

The wicked and unworthy manservant had just committed the bloody deed, and secured his treasure, a moment before the landlord entered to commit the murder that he also had planned.

THE PEASENHALL MYSTERY

The Murder of Rose Harsent by an Unknown Assassin
In the early morning of Sunday, 1st June 1902
at Providence House, Peasenhall, Suffolk and
the two Trials of William Gardiner for the
crime

The village of Peasenhall lies just north of Ipswich, and not a great distance from Saxmundham. Apart from a quiet, leisurely atmosphere, the village has no claim on our interest but one; the mysterious death of 23-year-old Rose Harsent, and the two trials of William Gardiner – also from the village – accused of her murder.

It was early on the morning of Sunday, 1st June 1902 that Rose Harsent's father approached Providence House where his daughter was in service to Deacon and Mrs Crisp. The Crisps – prominent members of the local Chapel, and pillars of village society – employed just one servant. Rose occupied quarters consisting of a bedroom and a small kitchen that were detached from the house and were reached up a flight of stairs leading from the main kitchen. It was for this humble apartment that William Harsent set his steps; through the main kitchen, and up the stairs. At least, that is the route he would have taken had he not been stopped in his tracks at the foot of those stairs by the lifeless body of his daughter. Rose was in her nightdress, her face towards the wall, and her body supported on the bottom step. She might have been the victim of a tragic accident; stumbling, falling down those steep stairs in the dark, on some nocturnal errand. But that explanation of things takes no account of the terrible gash across her throat, cut from ear to ear, and the jagged stab wound in her breast. No, poor Rose Harsent lay there not the victim of some tragic accident, but of some coldblooded murder. To compound the horror of his unexpected find, William Harsent saw that even in death his daughter had suffered further violation, for it was clear from the smell, the singed nightdress, and the charred flesh, that somebody had tried to burn her body.

In a village notably free from excitement, the news of Harsent's discovery spread like a forest fire. Tongues started to wag, knots of villagers were forming on street corners and at front gates to gossip over the tragedy, each to advance his or her own theory as to what *really* happened, and more important – who the culprit was. But in the end only one name was on *everybody*'s lips – William Gardiner.

William Gardiner, 34 years old was a master carpenter with Messrs J & J Smyth, agricultural implement makers. Gardiner lived with his wife and six children in a house in Peasenhall's main road, only a couple of hundred yards from Providence House; he was an Elder of the Primitive Methodists and also their choirmaster, leading to the not entirely well-meant nickname 'Holy Willie'.

No great feats of memory were required for the villagers to recall the scandal of a year previously. Two young men named Wright and Skinner had followed Rose Harsent and William Gardiner to the small barn-like building known as the Doctor's Chapel. At the door they eavesdropped on the conversation taking place inside. Rose had asked: 'Did you see me reading my Bible last Sunday?' to which Gardiner replied: 'No, what were you reading?' Rose went on to recite several verses from the Book of Genesis, including: 'And Judah said unto Onan, Go unto thy brother's wife, and marry her, and raise up seed to thy brother. And Onan knew that the seed should not be his; and it came to pass, when he went in unto his brother's wife, that he spilled his seed on the ground, lest that he should give that seed to his brother.' (Chapter 38, verses 8–9). All of which made it abundantly clear what had been going on between the couple. The result was a disciplinary inquiry and William Gardiner had been summoned before the Council of Elders.

But to leave the suspect now, and return to the victim and the scene of the crime.

The police have by this time arrived at Providence House, and are making a detailed assessment of the awful sight before them; for the unhappy girl's corpse was surrounded by a number of quite perplexing objects. For example an oil lamp, which had evidently been carried down from the bedroom and placed, in its three component parts, on the floor; the stand was nearest the body, then the reservoir, and farther away the unbroken glass lamp. A candlestick also lay on the ground. Then there was a broken medicine bottle whose label loudly proclaimed it to have contained a preparation prescribed for the Gardiner children. Beneath Rose Harsent's body was a copy of the *East Anglian Daily Times*; this newspaper was later alleged to have been delivered to William Gardiner by the deceased's brother. When the search spread to Rose's bedroom further clues were in evidence, not least among which was an unsigned note of assignation, postmarked 31st May, and delivered by Brewer the local postman on that same fatal evening before the murder.

'Dr R.,

I will try to see you tonight at twelve o'clock at your place. If you put a light in your window at ten o'clock for about ten minutes, then you can take it out again. Don't have a light in your room at twelve, as I will come round the back.'

There were no likely suspects that lived within viewing distance of Rose Harsent's bedroom window except William Gardiner. And what was so important, and so secret, that a midnight rendezvous was called for? Mrs Crisp the Deacon's wife provided the answer to that: having some weeks before noticed a listlessness, a carelessness, about Rose's work, she had confronted the girl with this change in her character. Rose Harsent had confided that she was pregnant! If William Gardiner was the father, then a 12 o'clock assignation was understandable.

William Gardiner's trial opened at Ipswich Assizes on 7th November 1902 before Mr Justice Grantham. Prosecuting were Sir H.F. Dickens KC, and the Hon John de Grey; defending Gardiner were Sir Ernest Wild KC, and Mr Claughton Scott. The evidence collected by the police and detailed above was paraded before the jury, often with such embellishments as had subsequently come to light – such as the fact that the letter of assignation was written on the kind of stationery that would have been available to William Gardiner at Messrs Smyth and Son.

It was then the turn of Mr Wild to present Gardiner's defence, and every eye in court was focussed on him; there was a silence in which a pin could have been heard to drop. How easy it was, he began, in a small village such as theirs, to become the victim of malicious gossip; how characteristic that a pious man should be branded 'Holy Willie' and that the less godly should try to smear his name. As for the incident in Doctor's Chapel, Gardiner was not guilty of any kind of impropriety – indeed he had been cleared by the court of elders and had lost none of his offices of honour within the Chapel.

Providence House

On the night of the murder, as both the prisoner and his wife would testify from the witness box, they were in the company of a neighbour until midnight, and then went to bed together where they remained until 8 o'clock the following morning. His client absolutely denied writing the fatal note, and the pair of shoes with the characteristic sole prints which matched those found outside Providence House, had not been worn by him for many months.

Cross-examination failed to shake any of these rebuttals when Gardiner took the stand, and he stepped down having done much to advance his defence. The judge, however, known to be a truculent man, was clearly against the prisoner from the start, and his summing up to the jury did nothing to dispel this observation.

The jury retired to consider their verdict at 4.15pm; they did not return until 8.40:

Mr Justice Grantham: Are you agreed upon your verdict? – *Foreman*: No, my lord. I don't know whether you can help us in any way.

Judge: Is there any assistance I can give you in answering any questions? (Here a juror stood up and intimated that there were no questions he wanted to ask)

Judge: There is no prospect of you agreeing? – *Foreman*: I am afraid not, my lord. You don't wish to know our position?

Judge: Well, one gentleman says he does not want to ask any questions. I suppose he is the one who does not agree, and has intimated that there is no chance of his agreeing, (to the juror): You have said you don't wish to ask any questions. Do you think time may be of any value to you in considering the question?

Juror: I have not made up my mind not to agree if I was convinced that the prisoner was guilty, but I have heard nothing to convince me he is guilty. (Applause in court)

Judge: I have no doubt that everything has been said, and if it has not convinced you, I do not think it is any good keeping the jury any longer at great inconvenience. I think there is only one thing to do. I am extremely sorry, but that is to discharge you without giving a verdict.

And so William Gardiner, trembling with anxiety, was released into the care of his gaolers.

The second trial took place in January 1903 before Mr Justice Lawrence. The same counsel were retained, the same evidence was given, and, ironically, a different jury came to the same disagreement. Not believing in proverbs, the Crown did not try for a lucky third time; William Gardiner was released to fade into obscurity. It is said that he and his ever-loyal wife moved close to London and opened a small shop.

The death of Rose Harsent has remained a mystery; though there has been no shortage of speculation over the years. Most theories have sought to show that Rose committed suicide – on account of her 'condition'. One of the strongest pieces of evidence for this *felo de se* theory is that the knife wound to Rose's chest was the result of an

Sir H.F. Dickens

upward thrust – such as a suicide might make. But not long after the Peasenhall incident a vicar of Bury St Edmunds named Jones advanced an intriguing – if far-fetched – theory that Rose Harsent was the victim of an accident:

Let us suppose thus:

An unknown man desired to see the girl secretly. He wrote and made an appointment with her at midnight, telling her to put a light in her bedroom window that he might know it was safe for him to come. He gets a pair of indiarubber shoes from somewhere, and creeps up the road to the window of her kitchen. There a horrible spectacle is revealed – the girl lies dead at the foot of a steep flight of stairs, the lamp she carried is shattered; the paraffin has caught fire and is already burning her body. The man is horrified and flies. He is not a murderer, but his intrigue with her had undoubtedly been the cause of her death.

Such was the clergyman's clever supposition.

Rose Harsent, he deduced, had received the letter in the buff envelope. She had determined to see her lover at

Sir Ernest Wild

midnight, and had made all her preparations accordingly. As her mistress forbade her to have a light in the kitchen after ten o'clock, she had filled and trimmed the lamp, prepared a newspaper upon which it should stand in her bedroom and, that she might replenish it, had filled with oil an old medicine bottle given her by Mrs Gardiner some time previously when she had needed some camphorated oil for her chest.

Thus provided, Rose Harsent went up to her bedroom a little before ten o'clock that night; she showed the light in her window as agreed with her lover – then she undressed and sat upon her bed awaiting the momentous interview. Just before twelve o'clock, she put the newspaper under her arm, took the lamp in one hand and the glass bottle in the other and began to descend the steep flight of stairs leading to the kitchen. Half-way down, perhaps, her foot becomes entangled in her long nightdress and she pitched headlong down the stairs into the kitchen. It was at this moment that Mrs Crisp, the deacon's wife, heard the thud and the scream; and but for her husband's persuasion, would have gone to the kitchen to see what was the matter.

Rose Harsent, thus falling, if fall she did, naturally thought first of the lighted lamp she carried and did her best to save it. She stretched out her arm to prevent its breaking; and so we find it upon the floor in three pieces – the unbroken glass farthest away from the body, the reservoir near and then the holder. The paraffin naturally escaping from it, ran back to the rill worn in the stone at the stair's foot, as rills always are worn in the stones of these country cottages. There it caught fire, and for a little while burned briskly. Meanwhile the poor girl herself had forgotten the glass bottle in her other hand, and upon that she had fallen with all her weight. It cut her throat and killed her.

Few people realise what a terrible weapon glass may be and how it will cut more effectively than any knife.

Many years ago, at Eton, a boy was killed by falling with a common glass squirt in his hand. It cut his throat, the doctors said, more deeply than any razor would have done. In motor accidents, terrible injuries are often inflicted by broken glass, and passengers have been almost decapitated by being flung through screens. So it becomes apparent that Rose Harsent could have been killed if she had fallen upon this bottle, and when we examine her wounds, we perceive more clearly the acumen of the clergyman's hypothesis.

The bottle was broken curiously, we remember. One side of it was intact, and that side would have accounted for the great wide wound which severed the jugular vein. The deeper jagged wound below, described by the doctors as an upward stab, might very well have been caused by the broken neck of the bottle – indeed, reflection seems to say that nothing could account for this wound so satisfactorily. Had a knife been used, it seems reasonable to say that there would have been a clean cut – no crude tearing of the flesh or jagged edges. Yet this possibility occurred to nobody at the trial – and we admit unhesitatingly that Sir Ernest Wild could not have raised it without grave danger to his client.

The clergyman's theory of accident is possible – no more. How would any jury of commonsense men have dealt with such an amazing story and what ridicule would prosecuting counsel have cast upon it?

Had the wounds in Rose Harsent's throat been searched for any trace of glass, a different story might have been told. We should then, perhaps, have been able to account for everything, even the footsteps, the light in the window and the letter. But they were not searched, and it remained for a clever clergyman to state this supposition and to advance arguments for it which were convincing. On the other hand there are obvious difficulties. The girl had pitched head foremost into the kitchen, and yet she lay with her head resting on the stairs. Doctors have admitted that people thus wounded mortally have staggered to their feet and even run a few steps. Naturally, faintness would have overcome Rose Harsent almost immediately, but nevertheless, she might have staggered to her feet as our theorist suggests, and then immediately have fallen backward into the position where they found her.

As to the jagged and broken neck of the bottle, it is true that it was found some distance from the body, but it

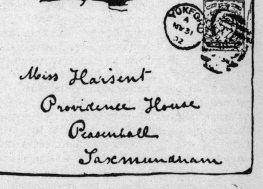

D R

I will try to see you tonight at 1½ oclock at your Place if you Put a light in your window at 10 oclock for about 10 minutes then you can take it out again. dont have a light in your Room at 1½ as I will come round to the back

Miss Harsent
Providence House
Peasenhall
Saxmundham

The mysterious letter of assignation sent to Rose Harsent

might very well have rebounded there after the impact –
or the poor girl might have torn it from her throat and
flung it away from her before passing into unconsciousness. Be that as it may, the Peasenhall murder remains a
profound mystery. It is the addition of one more to that
long list of undiscovered crimes, the stories of which no
man has been able to read truly. It is also another witness
to the deceits of that apparent and seemingly perfect peace
we associate with the remote countryside and its enchant-
ing villages.

THE RED BARN

**The Murder of Maria Marten (or Martin) by
William Corder**
On Wednesday, 18th May 1827 in the Red
Barn, Polstead, Suffolk

Maria Marten, was born in July, 1801, daughter of a
mole-catcher at Polstead, in Suffolk. Blessed as she
was with a pretty face and graceful form, it was no
surprise that as a young woman Maria had her choice
of local manhood; it was to be her regret and the sorrow of
her poor parents that she seemed incapable of choosing
wisely among them. Before many years had passed Maria
Marten had become pregnant and been spurned by two of
these unworthy wretches before, in the year 1826, she
formed her third tragic liaison – with William Corder, the
man who was destined to be her murderer.

Corder, the son of a wealthy farmer of Polstead, had no
sooner become acquainted with the unfortunate Maria
Marten than she once again fell pregnant. It is a measure,
perhaps, of the girl's determination, or that of her parents,
that a promise was elicited from Corder that they would
marry. So it was that on the 18th May 1827, William
Corder persuaded his intended bride to dress in a suit
of men's clothes – the better, he said, to ensure secrecy –
and to meet him at part of his father's farm known as the
Red Barn, where she might change in preparation for the
ceremony.

A few minutes after leaving the Marten house he was
seen by Maria's brother walking in the direction of the Red
Barn carrying a pickaxe over his shoulder. However,
despite the general expectation, Maria was never seen

at home again, and it is surprising perhaps that it was not until two weeks after the supposed marriage that Mrs Marten thought to question Corder, who had returned to his father's farm, on her whereabouts. Having satisfied the good woman that her daughter was alive and well and living on the Isle of Wight, William proceeded to decamp, having first given orders that the Red Barn should be filled with grain.

Several letters were subsequently received by both Mrs Corder and Mrs Marten, indicating that William and Maria were happily enjoying life on the Isle of Wight, the only puzzling feature being that they had all been posted in London.

During the month of March 1828, Mrs Marten was visited by the same horrid dream on three nights in succession – that her daughter had been murdered and buried in the Red Barn. Indeed, so lively were her feelings, so convinced was she of the evil omen, that her husband applied for permission to examine the Barn to lay her fears at rest. Permission having been established, the unhappy father applied himself to the spot where, in old Mrs Marten's dream, his daughter had lain. There, upon digging, the mole-catcher turned up a piece of the shawl which he knew to be Maria's, and when he had dug to a depth of 18 inches, he raked out part of a human body.

The body, as may be supposed, was in an advanced state of decomposition; but the dress, which was perfect, and certain marks on the teeth afforded sufficient proof of identity.

By the time a coroner's inquest had been convened, a full examination of the body had been made, indicating that Maria Marten had come to her death by violent means. There had been blood on the face and on the clothes, and also on a handkerchief around the neck; the handkerchief had been tied extremely tight, and beneath the folds a wound was visible in the throat, such as would have been inflicted with a sharp instrument. There was also a wound in the orbit of the right eye, and it seemed as if something had been thrust in which had fractured the small bones and penetrated the brain.

No sooner had this body been found and named than all

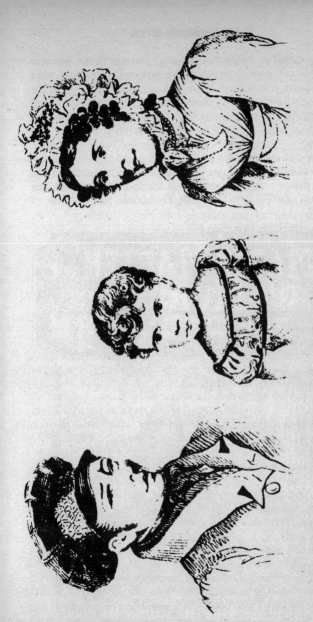

William, Maria and the baby

eyes turned to William Corder as the murderer. He was traced to Grove House, a residence in Ealing Lane, near Brentford, where he lived with a new wife of five months. Though he vigorously denied his identity, articles found in the house were associated with William Corder of Polstead, and he was taken immediately back to that town.

The date set for his trial was 7th August at the Shire Hall in Bury St Edmunds, and though the rain fell in torrents a crowd was waiting from 5.00 in the morning till 9 o'clock to gain admission to the court. Hundreds, too, collected at

REVEALED BY A MOTHER'S DREAM

the jail and along the route to catch a glimpse of the prisoner.

In his own defence, Corder declared that when he and the girl had reached the Red Barn they started to quarrel, and Maria flew into a passion. 'I asked her if she was to go on this way before marriage, what was I to expect after; I told her I would not marry her and turned from the barn.' As he walked away, so he said, Corder heard the report of a pistol and, looking behind him beheld the unhappy girl lying upon the floor: 'I discovered that the dreadful act had been committed by one of my own pistols, and that I was the only person in existence who could tell how the fatal act had taken place.' In short, he panicked, buried the girl's body, and fled.

Even more shortly, he was convicted and sentenced to death. On his return to the jail, the Governor made every effort to induce him to confess. Finally, Corder exclaimed: 'I am a guilty man. I am justly sentenced, and may God forgive me.'

After the execution, spirited bidding took place for the rope that was used by the hangman, and as much as a guinea an inch was obtained for it. Large sums were offered for Corder's pistols, but these became the property of the Sheriff. A piece of the skin of this wretched man was later tanned and exhibited for a long time at the shop of a leather-seller in Oxford Street, and a further piece used to bind a transcript of his own trial.*

* These relics are now on public display in the Moyse's Hall Museum, Cornhill, Bury St Edmunds.

SOUTH-WEST
ENGLAND

Avon

Cornwall

Devon

Dorset

Somerset

Wiltshire

TERMINAL GREED

The Murder of James Pullen by Reginald Ivor Hinks
On Friday, 1st December 1933 at his home
'Wallasey', in Englishcombe Lane, Bath, Avon

On 4th May 1934, after a trial noted for the tenacity of its defence counsel, Reginald Ivor Hinks was hanged at Bristol. Ironically, the only person to mourn the passing of this thoroughly worthless man was his victim's daughter; unfortunately for her, she was also Mrs Hinks.

Hinks had been born in 1900, and after an indifferent education was turned loose on the world to show just what a rotten apple he was. In 1917 he went to lodge with his two brothers in Bath, and managed to secure an apprenticeship as a fitter with a local engineering works. An idle and careless worker, he was also suspected of being responsible for the mysterious disappearances of his workmates' tools. Indeed, had he not left of his own volition in 1921, it is quite likely that the decision would have been made for him. Not so the local branch of the Church Lad's Brigade of which he was a member; they found his behaviour so unacceptable that even this most charitable organisation was obliged to dismiss him.

Hinks's time with the Royal Corps of Signals was equally undistinguished. After joining in 1921, they suffered him only until 7th August 1922, when the Corps opted to do without his further services. His military record reads, in part: 'Character indifferent, slack, lazy and untidy.' On 30th May 1923 he joined the Lancashire Fusiliers under the name Hanks; in December 1925 they discharged him as physically unfit. From this point, Reginald Hinks moved about quite a lot, usually for very good reasons – none of them honest. He became a barman in Lambeth, South London; a job which lasted only a few months. His service as a cloakroom attendant with the Royal Automobile Club in Pall Mall lasted for an even shorter period – he was sacked after four weeks. Hinks then had a spell in domestic service in partnership with a girl-friend with whom he was living – he as butler, she as cook. On 16th January 1929 Hinks appeared before the magistrates at Westminster on two charges of stealing from his employers and their guests. Later that year his girlfriend received a modest legacy of £225 from a benevolent uncle; money which Reginald Hinks speedily converted to his private use. After a quarrel in which Hinks gave her a severe beating, the couple separated. After a further succession of short-lived jobs – short-lived mainly on account of his dishonesty – and occasional appearances in London police courts, Hinks headed back to Bath.

Arriving in that city on Christmas Eve 1932, Reginald Hinks – presumably unaffected by seasonal goodwill – snatched a lady's handbag containing £100. In early 1933 the Bath branch of Messrs. Hoover Ltd became the latest in a long series of employers: Hinks was taken on as a vacuum cleaner salesman. In March of the same year he made the acquaintance of Mrs Constance Anne Jeffries (*née* Pullen), a divorced lady who lived with her 5-year-old

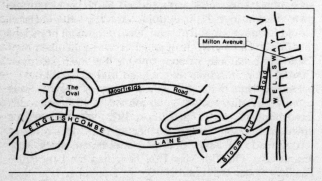

daughter Connie and her ancient father, James Pullen, at 43 Milton Avenue in Bath. Despite his great frailty and the advanced senility that rendered him almost incoherent, Mr Pullen was a great attraction to Reginald Hinks – he had a lot of money. Hinks promptly married Mrs Jeffries and installed himself in her comfortable home. Once settled, Reginald saw no pressing reason to waste his time working while there was so much money around; nonetheless, by way of a small contribution he did economize on poor old Mr Pullen's food – cutting down on both quality and quantity. He also saved the household budget 30/- a week through the simple expedient of dismissing Mr Strange, the male nurse on whom the old man was almost totally reliant. But Hinks's heart was set upon higher things, such as larger amounts of money for himself. Within a short time he had embezzled £900 of Mr Pullen's savings and bought a small mock-Tudor house called 'Wallasey' in Englishcombe Lane, a suburb of Bath. The new family home has been appropriately described by Miss Tennyson Jesse in her own perceptive account of the Hinks case*: 'Wallasey, in short, was a cheap little modern imitation Tudor house and stood in relation to the beautiful houses of Bath much as Hinks must have stood in relation to his honest fellow men.'

But Reginald Ivor Hinks was as impatient as he was greedy. When he learned that an order in lunacy had been made out regarding James Pullen, effectively safeguarding his money from the grasping hands of the likes of himself, and that he was unlikely to have any access to the old man's money until he was dead, Reginald decided to hasten the process. He began, for example, to send the muddled, helpless octogenarian out for walks by himself in the busy city centre in the hope that he might have an accident with the traffic. A local police constable subsequently recalled that on a night in the autumn he had been on patrol and saw James Pullen apparently walking in his sleep; following behind was Reginald Hinks in his car. Hinks breezily explained to the bewildered constable that

* *Comments on Cain*, F. Tennyson Jesse

his father-in-law was on a 10-mile walk, but as they were talking the old man's legs suddenly gave way and he slumped to the ground. Hinks, with some show of concern, bundled him into the back of the car and drove home. On another occasion a different police officer was called to a minor incident aboard a Bath Tramways bus. On his arriving at the scene, the conductor pointed to a customer who had just tendered four match sticks and a pencil for his fare to Dorking; it was Mr Pullen.

But none of this was proving nearly fatal enough for Reginald Hinks. Clearly, stronger methods were called for.

On the evening of 30th November 1933, at about 7.30, Hinks called the Bath Fire Brigade Ambulance; his father-in-law, he explained had been found unconscious in his bath. (It was customary at that time to call the fire brigade in such cases as they had supplies of oxygen in the event of respiratory failure.) One should add that the weekly bath night in the Hinks household was a very bizarre ritual indeed: Once the tub was filled little Connie was bathed, then Mrs Hinks climbed into the same water, succeeded by Reginald Ivor; last of all, old Mr Pullen was immersed in this same poisonous concoction.

Hinks had also summoned the police, and then the doctor, hastening to assure him that he, Hinks, customarily watched over the old man during his ablutions – lest he might do something silly or careless. But on this occasion he had popped downstairs to fetch some clean towels (!), and when he returned he found Mr Pullen with his head under the water: 'He was black in the face.'

By the time the fire brigade, the Chief Constable, and Dr Gibson arrived, old James Pullen seemed to have made a remarkable recovery – he was sitting up in the now empty bath, wrapped in a blanket with a hot-water bottle held to his chest; far from black in the face, he was rather pale. At any rate the doctor could find no cause for alarm, quite the reverse, Mr Pullen was in uncommonly good health for a man of his advanced years. And so the players in Reginald Hinks's elaborately staged scenario gradually left the house. But this had only been the prologue; on the following day the drama proper was to be staged.

Hinks was at home with his father-in-law and step-daughter; Mrs Hinks had gone to the local cinema. On the other side of town the fire brigade was receiving yet another summons to 'Wallasey' via a telephone call from Reginald Hinks. He subsequently called in the police and the doctor. When these players once again found themselves on the stage of Englishcombe Lane they found old Mr Pullen lying in a kitchen smelling strongly of gas; and as a police officer approached the dying man to give assitance, Hinks gratuitously mentioned: 'You might find a bruise at the back of his head; I pulled him out of the gas stove and his head fell with a bump on the floor.' Hinks later gave an account of his discovery of Mr Pullen: 'I found the two gas taps turned on,' he began. 'I don't think he could turn on taps like that,' interrupted the doctor. 'He often turned them on and off,' replied Hinks. The doctor observed that a raincoat had been draped over the stove – presumably in order to enclose the gas in the oven, and protested that, in Mr Pullen's state of mental degeneration, he would have been unlikely to have coped with the complicated series of actions required to commit suicide in this way. Subsequent pathological examination yielded an even more damaging rebuttal to the suicide theory – the injury to the back of James Pullen's head had been sustained before he had inhaled gas. From this lead, a case was built up against Reginald Hinks that would lead to his trial at the Old Bailey on a charge of murdering his father-in-law.

For the prosecution, Mr Croom-Johnson KC dismissed the suicide theory totally and absolutely; summing up his case, he told the jury: 'This old, tottering man was supposed to have gone upstairs to the bedroom, kissed the little girl asleep, gone downstairs, out of the back door to the lavatory, come back into the kitchen, removed coat and waistcoat, placed a piece of blanket into the stove to make himself happy and comfortable, removed three shelves from the stove, arranged the coats around the oven door, turned on the two taps, removed his slippers, and then laid down with his head in the stove to await his Maker – and all this in the space of twenty-five minutes . . .'

For Hinks, Mr O'Connor also emphasized the unbalance of the old man's mind, and suggested that not only was he quite capable of suicide, but had on several occasions been heard to threaten to kill himself. He entreated the jury: 'I ask you to say that Pullen had the intention of committing suicide if he had the opportunity.'

After cautioning them that 'You cannot prove a man has murdered another simply by proof that he would be better off if he did so,' Mr Justice Branson sent the jury into retirement.

Pronounced guilty, Hinks was sentenced to death. His appeal was heard in April, and once again the decision was against him. In dismissing the appeal, Lord Hewart said that there was clear evidence that James Pullen was neither mentally nor physically capable of committing suicide in the manner suggested; the matter had been finally settled.

There was only one sound to break the hush that fell over the court, it was the anguished sobbing of Constance Hinks, a woman who had stood by her husband to the last.

THE BRISTOL TAXI MURDER

The Murder of William Tripp by John Rogers
On Friday, 29th July 1960 at the Powderhall
Farm Cross Roads, outside Chew Magna, Avon

Although the likelihood of a person being murdered in
Britain is statistically very low, there have always
been occupations which, by their nature, carry with them
a proportionately greater risk of lethal assault. As most
killings that are committed by people not known to the
victim are the accompaniment of robbery, those who carry
cash about with them as part of their job are among those
most vulnerable. Tradespeople like milkmen are regularly
the victims of violent attack, and in the days before wide
acceptance of cheques and credit cards, rent-collectors and
tally-men were at the top of the high-risk occupations –
not least because the regular pattern of their calls made
them easily identifiable.

But perhaps the most vulnerable of all have been taxi
drivers. From the days when highwaymen terrorized the
roads, cab drivers have frequently been victims of robbery, physical assault, and even murder. The cabbie,
locked in a confined space for most of his working life
with total strangers needs all his wits and instincts
functioning, as well as a lot of luck, to help him avoid
attack; and with the proliferation of such assaults it is no
surprise that cabmen and women the world over are
arming themselves against such an eventuality.

William Tripp was a taxi driver; and at the age of 41 had
tens of thousands of miles of service behind him. By all
reports he was a gentle, homely man, well-liked and

respected; indeed, as his wife Sybil said after his tragic death: 'It could only have been done by a madman.' Because William Tripp had been brutally murdered in his cab – his only 'fault' was the possession of £20.

Late on the night of Friday, 29th July 1960, Cyril Farrow was cycling towards the Powderhall Farm Cross Roads between Chew Magna and Winford (in those days part of Somerset). As he neared the junction he could hear the sound of a car horn blaring out pointlessly at the night; then, in front of him, he saw the overturned car, its lights staring into the darkness: 'As I approached the overturned cab on my bicycle, a man ran past me. I was wondering what to do when suddenly I heard the footsteps stop. They did not sound again for ten minutes.' Ten minutes during which Farrow crouched in the shadow of the car, expecting any minute to end up as dead as the cab's occupant.

When the police arrived, they found William Tripp slumped over the steering wheel, dead from a gunshot wound; on the back seat lay a tartan duffel-bag, in it the .22 rifle that had so recently blasted its deadly charge into the back of its victim's head. The taxi's meter had stopped, showing a fare of 39s.2d.

Within a few hours, investigating officers led by Detective Superintendent A.C. Brown, head of Somerset CID, had begun to piece together a picture of their suspect and the sequence of events that led up to the murder. Tripp had been observed picking up a fare in Bristol city centre at 10.40pm; the distance to Powderhall Farm Cross Roads was seven miles – a fare of 39s.2d. Combining information from this witness and from Mr Farrow, the police were able to issue a description of the young man they wanted to interview: 5ft 8in tall, slim build, wearing a dark suit, drainpipe trousers and thick rubber-soled shoes. These were characteristics of the clothing worn by the youth cult of the '50s called 'Teddy Boys'. Officers had meanwhile identified the gun as one stolen from a local brewery's rifle club. That it had been stolen with the express purpose of crime could be seen from the sawing down of barrel and stock so that the weapon could be concealed beneath a coat.

Five days later, a suspect was taken into custody; he was 20-year-old John Rogers, clerk in a Bristol brewery and living with his parents in the city. After being cautioned, Rogers remarked: 'It was not the intention of murder, definitely not.'

The trial opened at the Somerset Assizes in Taunton in October 1960. Mr Justice Cassels presided, and Mr N.R. Fox-Andrews QC led for the Crown. What defence Rogers could make was entrusted to Mr Hugh Park QC.

Rogers did not – could not – deny stealing and 'adapting' the rifle for the sole purpose of armed robbery; nor that on the night of 29th July, a taxi-driver was to be the object of that intention. With this in mind John Rogers hired William Tripp to drive him from Bristol to Winford. Rogers' version of the 'accident' was as follows: 'I took the .22 gun from the duffel bag, with intention of robbing the driver. I told him to pull into the side. He turned round, and I jumped up. As I did so I flipped the trigger of the gun, and he flopped over the wheel. I do not know where I shot him, or if I hit him. When he flopped the taxi lurched forward and we went into a hedge and overturned. It took me about three minutes to get out of the thing.'

Having escaped from the car, and from the attentions of Cyril Farrow, Rogers spent the rest of the August Bank

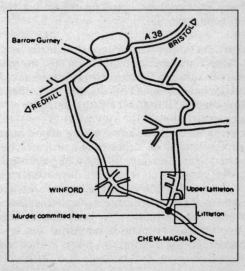

Holiday with friends at the annual Beaulieu Jazz Festival –
no doubt spending freely of the £20 known to have been in
William Tripp's possession up to the night of his death – it
was his weekly takings due to be paid to the taxi company.

When Crown witness Dr Edward Parkes, Director of the
South-Western Forensic Science Laboratory, took the
stand, he described the tests which had been undertaken
by the ballistics experts and the pathologist, the results of
which led to the clear conclusion that: 'The fatal shot was
fired with the gun when the driver was looking forward.
The gun was held virtually horizontally and pointed at the
back of his head.'

Summing up at the end of the trial, Mr Justice Cassels
instructed the jury: 'If a wicked, intentional mind, bent on
killing or seriously injuring, has accompanied an act
which does in fact kill, then in law there is malice aforethought, and that is murder ... If you come to the
conclusion that this may have been an accident you have
to ask yourselves, was it an accident with criminal negli-
gence and was there reckless disregard for the safety of the
taxi driver. If you conclude that there was, he would be
guilty of manslaughter.'

The jury, quite rightly, opted for the former verdict –
guilty of capital murder.

Although John Rogers was sentenced to death, he did not
finally suffer 'the ultimate sanction'. On 6th December, the
day before he was due to hang, Rogers was removed from
Horfield Gaol's condemned cell by order of the then Home
Secretary, Mr R.A. Butler, who had granted an eleventh-
hour reprieve.

Quite why this callous, brutal young man should have
received the benefit of clemency we will never know,
because a Home Secretary is not obliged to give his
reasons for granting or refusing a reprieve. It may be
that the obligatory inquiry into the state of mental health
of a condemned man revealed some factor that indicated a
diminished responsibility. He may have been, in
Mrs Tripp's earlier estimate 'a madman'. But it was of
little comfort to Sybil Tripp; even less to her husband
William.

A KILLER SENT BY GOD

**The Murder of Colyn Bedale-Taylor by
Graham Backhouse**
On Monday, 30th April 1984 at Widden Hill
Farm, Horton, near Chipping Sodbury

Forty-three-year-old farmer Graham Backhouse, appearing at Bristol Crown Court, stood charged with the attempted murder of his wife Margaret in order to collect the sum of £100,000 on her life insurance, and the murder of neighbour Mr Colyn Bedale-Taylor in order to divert police suspicion from himself.

Mr James Black QC for the prosecution described Backhouse as a 'devious, dangerous and determined man, who had carefully planned both crimes and carried them out in cold blood.' Mr Black went on to tell the jury how Backhouse had invented a scenario whereby he and his family were the victims of a supposed village vendetta; he gone as far as to impale a sheep's head on a stake close to the house bearing a note reading 'You Next'. The police had had constant complaints from Mr Backhouse of threatening letters and telephone calls – which later obligingly ceased when a listening device was installed.

On 9th April 1984, Margaret Backhouse climbed into the driver's seat of the family's Volvo estate car and turned on the ignition; the resulting explosion left her with severe injuries to her legs and buttocks. Although the injuries were said by consultant surgeon Colin Davidson to be 'extensive and extremely serious', they were mercifully not fatal, due in large part to the solid design of the vehicle. Believed at the time to be the intended victim, Graham Backhouse was given 24-hour police protection.

On 18th April, at Backhouse's request, the police watch was taken off, and a 'panic button' linked to the local police station fitted at the farmhouse. On 30th April the alarm went off.

When police constable Richard Yeadon arrived at the farm he found 63-year-old Colyn Bedale-Taylor lying dead from shotgun wounds to the chest; in his hand was a Stanley handyman's knife. Pc Yeadon then noticed Mr Backhouse lying in the entrance to the lounge, sobbing; he was covered in blood coming from wounds to the face and chest.

In a statement read to the court by Mr Lionel Read QC, acting for Backhouse, his client claimed that Bedale-Taylor had called at the farmhouse on the evening of the 30th and told him that he had come to repair furniture: 'I told him there was no furniture to repair, and he said that God had sent him.' Bedale-Taylor then went on to accuse Mr Backhouse of being responsible for the death of his son Digby – who had in fact died as the result of a car crash some eighteen months previously. The visitor later went on to confess to having planted the car bomb, and then lunged at Backhouse with the Stanley knife: 'I ran into the hallway and grabbed a gun; Bedale-Taylor was still after me. I shouted I had got a gun but he still kept coming and I shot him. He fell back and I shot him again and that was it.'

This version of the events leading to Bedale-Taylor's death was at variance with the findings of the forensic investigation alleged the Crown prosecutor, and from the witness stand Mr Geoffrey Robinson from the Home Office Forensic Laboratory at Chepstow, Gwent, advanced the proposition that Mr Backhouse's wounds were self-inflicted, and that he placed the knife in his victim's hand after death. Backhouse, he suggested, must have splashed blood in the kitchen after the shooting to simulate an attack on himself. Although there were bloodstains in the kitchen and around the area where the body lay, there was none in the hallway or on the murder weapon (the prisoner and the deceased had different blood groups he emphasised). When Backhouse placed the knife in the dead man's hand, he could not have noticed that the palms were completely covered with blood through clutching at his wounds after being shot. If his story was true, and Bedale-Smith had been holding the knife, then at least part of the palm should have been clear of blood.

Evidence was then offered to the court indicating that even after arrest the prisoner continued in his efforts to incriminate Bedale-Taylor. From his cell at Horfield Prison, Bristol, Backhouse wrote to his wife asking her to smuggle in writing materials: 'The police are fabricating evidence against me and my case is looking black. However, with your help I can improve the case considerably. I want to fabricate a letter to the Press. So please help me. I must get out of this hell hole.'

The jury was told that Backhouse persuaded a fellow-prisoner to smuggle out an unsigned letter, which implicated Mr Bedale-Taylor in the bombing, addressed to the editor of the *Bristol Evening Post*. Forensic examination proved that the handwriting matched the threatening letters supposed to have been received by Graham Backhouse, and that they both matched the handwriting of Backhouse himself.

As evidence of motive, Mr Black for the Crown examined Richard Martin, manager of the Chipping Sodbury branch of the National Westminster Bank. Mr Martin stated that the prisoner had been left to run the farm after his father's death in 1979. As the result of bad harvests and poor management the farm had turned into a liability; within four years, Backhouse had accumulated debts of more than £70,000. The jury was also told that up to 1984 Margaret Backhouse's life had been insured for £50,000; in March of that year a further policy had been taken out for the same amount 'in the event of her death or serious injury.'

On Monday, 19th February, the jury of eight men and five women retired to consider their verdict; after 5½ hours, by a majority of ten to two, they returned a verdict of guilty on both charges. Mr Justice Stuart-Smith, in giving Backhouse two terms of life imprisonment, made no recommendation on the sentences.

On his way from the dock, escorted by prison officers, Graham Backhouse passed within feet of his wife sitting in the public gallery; he did not glance in her direction.

BORN TO LOSE

**The Murder of Charles Henry Giffard and his
wife by their son Miles Giffard**
On Friday, 7th November 1952 at their home,
'Carrickowl', Porthpean, Cornwall

Miles Giffard was born in 1927 at 'Carrickowl', the
extensive family residence overlooking Carlyon Bay,
Porthpean, near St Austell, where Charles Henry Giffard
was Clerk to the Magistrates.

Young Miles was to prove a grave disappointment to
his parents, a disappointment that was first focused in
1940 when his masters at the exclusive Rugby public
school found him uncooperative and virtually impossible
to teach, and were constrained to remove him. In fairness
to Miles, his subsequent examination by Devon psychiatrist Dr Roy Craig revealed him to be suffering from a
form of schizophrenia – a condition for which he was
never treated.

Giffard then failed to make any progress in the study of
law, and enjoyed even less success in a course in estate
management. At the age of 25 he inherited the sum of
£750, gave up hope of mastering the estate agent's profession, and settled comfortably into the day-to-day routine
of a wastrel. Within four months he had squandered his
inheritance and, pausing briefly to spend a couple of
weeks selling ice-cream in Bournemouth, returned in
June 1952 to his parents in Porthpean. Here, he set about
frittering away his father's money as he had his own.

From Porthpean, Giffard began to make frequent sorties
to London, where he became enamoured of 19-year-old
Gabrielle Vallance, who lived with her mother at 40 Tite

Street, Chelsea. By this time an exasperated Charles Giffard was prepared to go to extreme lengths to try to salvage both his son and what was left of his money. He recalled Miles to Porthpean, and after an ugly domestic scene forbade him – on pain of losing his allowance – to return to London. Miles, at the age of 26, totally dependent on his father for financial support, had been forced into a corner. On 3rd November 1952 he wrote in a letter to Gabrielle Vallance: 'I am dreadfully fed up as I was looking forward to seeing you . . . Short of doing him in, I see no future in the world at all. I love you terribly . . .'

At 5.30pm on 7th November he telephoned Gabrielle that he would be travelling up to London later that night, adding that he would phone again in a few hours to confirm it.

At 7.30pm Miles Giffard walked into the garage where his father was at work on his car. Leaving the old man unconscious from a crushing blow to the head with an iron pipe, Miles made his way to the kitchen, where he felled Mrs Giffard with a series of blows from the same blunt instrument.

Miles now made the promised call to Miss Vallance announcing his imminent departure for London, then returned to complete the job of killing his parents. Having tipped the victims of his murderous attack over the cliff some small distance from the house, Giffard took the family car and drove to Chelsea, where he was knocking on Gabrielle Vallance's door at 8 o'clock the following morning. Taking a short time out to pawn some of his mother's jewellery, Giffard and his girl-friend went on the town. That evening, in a public house in Chelsea Mews, Miles confessed the murders to her, observing later: 'it upset her . . .'

While Miles Giffard had been busy raising cash on his unfortunate mother's jewellery that morning, the Cornish police had been busy investigating the discovery of two bodies on the beach below the cliffs at Carlyon Bay; though Giffard, in his ineptitude, had left very little to tax the resources of the investigating officers. A trail of blood led along the cliff path into the kitchen and garage of 'Carrickowl', where only the most rudimentary attempt had been made to clean up the evidence of the previous evening's brutal killings. Miles Giffard had disappeared along with the family car. Within hours, the London police had located Charles Giffard's Triumph outside the house in Tite Street. As Miles and Gabrielle returned that night from drinking they were met by a squad of policemen.

Held overnight on a charge of car stealing, Giffard was interviewed on the Sunday morning by Superintendent Julian, head of the Cornish CID, to whom he admitted killing his parents: 'I wish to tell you everything about it with as little trouble as possible . . . I want to be frank. I did it.'

Driven back to St Austell, Miles Giffard was formally charged with murder in the small courtroom in which his father had been Clerk for twenty-five years. In a statement he had said: 'I can only say that I have had a brainstorm. I cannot account for my actions. I had drunk about half a bottle of whisky on the Friday afternoon, before all this happened.'

Giffard's trial opened at Bodmin Assizes in February 1953; he pleaded not guilty by reason of insanity. Contesting this defence, Mr John Scott Henderson QC pointed out to the jury that this had been a most calculated and cold-blooded murder; that Giffard had killed his father in order to take his car to London, and his mother in order to steal jewellery with which to finance his further extravagance. The fact that he had made little attempt to evade capture was due not to insanity, but to thorough incompetence.

In Giffard's defence, Mr John Maude QC said that there had been no attempt to deny the killings, but that the defence would rely on a proven history of mental instability. In the witness box Dr Roy Craig, who had subsequently retired from practice, recalled his examination of Giffard after his removal from Rugby: 'I do not consider that he has ever been normal mentally. It was found that the origins of his terrors came from some sadistic nurse, who had not only beaten him as a tiny child, but had locked him in a dark cupboard.' Questioned on the probable state of Giffard's mind at the time of the murders, Dr Craig replied: 'I think at the time he did this thing

he was in a schizophrenic episode. He would know what
he was doing, but in schizophrenia there is a split in the
mind – a split between the unconscious or primitive part
of the mind and the more superficial, conventional part.
When the split takes place the primitive mind takes
charge, uncontrolled any longer by the conventional
part. People in this condition know what they are doing
and know the consequences of what they are doing.'

Nevertheless, after a trial lasting four days, Mr Maude
had clearly failed to convince the ten men and two women
who comprised the jury that Miles Giffard was insane at
the time he killed his parents. After a deliberation of only
32 minutes they found the prisoner guilty of murder.
Miles Giffard was hanged at Bristol on 24th February
1953.

THE MAN THEY COULDN'T HANG

The Murder of Miss Emma Keyse by John Lee
On Saturday, 15th November 1884 in her house
at Babbacombe, Devon

Along with stories of people being hanged in error – of which, due mainly to the unsound foundations of the law enforcement system and the huge number of capital offences on the statute in former centuries, there were many – are a host of legends of people who were hanged several times, hanged and then revived, or reprieved just as they had been 'launched into eternity'. In fact, there are a number of reliably recorded cases where, for reasons generally connected with the crudeness of the method of execution, the prisoner simply would not hang.

The most celebrated such case was that of John Lee, the Babbacombe Murderer, who, in 1884, at the age of 19 years, was convicted of the brutal murder of the elderly spinster for whom he served as footman.

John Lee was the son of a yeoman farmer living at 3 Town Cottages, Abbotskerswell, near Newton Abbot, in which village he lived with his mother. Shortly after his 15th birthday, John was taken into service by Miss Emma Keyse of Babbacombe; she had once been a maid to Queen Victoria and around the village was known and loved for her kindness and generosity. Among her servants she was known for her strictness and parsimony.

Though John did well in his employment, it was barely eighteen months before the spirit of adventure rose in him, and the dreams inspired by the passing ships and the tales of the fishermen and seafarers that clustered around the quayside along that stretch of the Devon coast, decided him on a life in the Royal Navy. Sadly, the youthful enthusiasm was not matched by physical strength, and his weak chest failed John Lee in all but the lightest duties. The final disaster struck: after developing pneumonia on board, he was invalided out of the service.

Now whether it was disappointment, depression after his illness, or simply a natural tendency that had not yet manifested itself, back on shore John Lee was a changed young man. A youth who had changed to such a degree that he may already have been marked for the gallows.

From his next employer on dry land, Lee took to stealing; and was rewarded with 6 months' hard labour. And this might have proved the salutary lesson that he needed; but Miss Keyse, hearing of his predicament, and with more generosity than foresight, wrote to the prison Governor offering to take John back into service if he should be released. And so he was. And so John Lee came to return to the house by the sea.

In the early hours of Saturday morning, 15th November 1884, one of the maids woke to the strong smell of smoke. When the household had been roused with cries of 'Fire!', it was discovered that there were no less than five separate fires – all of them started with paraffin, but only one burning human fuel. With utter horror and disbelief, the party which had been despatched to deal with the fire in the dining-room came upon the lifeless body of Miss Keyse, her head terribly injured and her throat slashed through to the vertebra. Around the body, like a ghastly funeral pyre were smouldering newspapers soaked in a mixture of blood and paraffin.

When John Lee's blood-soaked knife and towel were found next to the body of Miss Keyse he was immediately arrested and charged with murder. At his trial, the prisoner owned that it was revenge that had turned him into a killer, resentment that his weekly wage had been reduced by sixpence to two shillings on account of some minor lapse.

On 4th December 1884, Lee was condemned to death. He was to have been executed at Exeter by James Berry, then the official hangman whose competence had never been held in doubt. The prisoner was in position beneath the gallows, a hood over his head and a rope round his

The unsuccessful attempt to hang John Lee

neck. Berry pulled the lever. The trap remained stuck fast, with John Lee standing on it. The hangman pulled again; and again; still the prisoner could not drop. Berry stamped several times on the doors of the trap, so did the warders; still they remained firmly together.

With Lee removed from the 'machine', it was tested and checked, and worked perfectly. Until they tried to hang John Lee for the second time.

A much embarrassed James Berry once again tested his apparatus; once again completed a successful test drop. And was once again unsuccessful in launching Lee, as they say, 'into Eternity'. To the dismay, and by now more that a little disgust, of the observers, the trap refused to open for a third time. The chaplain recorded: 'The lever was pulled again and again. A great noise was heard, which sounded like the falling of the drop. But to my horror, when I turned my eyes to the scaffold, I saw the poor convict standing upon the drop as I had seen him twice before. I refused to stay any longer.'

The only person not surprised by the strange occurrence was Lee himself, for he had dreamed that he would not hang; 'The Lord will never permit me to be executed', he said. And, indeed, He did not. John Lee's sentence was commuted to imprisonment, and he was released in 1907.

Of the subsequent explanations (including many concerning Divine intervention), the most likely seems to be that the flaps of the trap had become swollen as a result of soaking up the recent heavy rain, and when a weight was put directly on them the edges bound.

JAMES BERRY'S ACCOUNT

Executioner's Office,
1, Bilton Place, City Road
Bradford, Yorks.,
4th March, 1885

Re John Lee

Sir,

In accordance with the request contained in your letter

of the 30th inst., I beg to say that on the morning of Friday, the 20th ult., I travelled from Bradford to Bristol, and on the morning of Saturday, the 21st, from Bristol to Exeter, arriving at Exeter at 11.50am, when I walked direct to the County Gaol, signed my name in your Gaol Register Book at 12 o'clock exactly. I was shown to the Governor's office, and arranged with him that I would go and dine and return to the Gaol at 2.00pm. I accordingly left the Gaol, partook of dinner, and returned at 1.50pm, when I was shown to the bedroom allotted to me which was an officer's room in the new Hospital Ward. Shortly afterwards I made an inspection of the place of Execution. The execution was to take place in a Coach-house in which the Prison Van was usually kept. Two Warders accompanied me on the inspection. In the Coach-house I found a Beam about four inches thick, and about a foot in depth, was placed across the top of the Coach-house. Through this beam an iron bolt was fastened with an iron-nut on the upper side, and to this bolt a wrought-iron rod was fixed, about three-quarters of a yard long with a hole at the lower end to which the rope was to be attached. Two Trap-doors were placed in the floor of the Coachhouse, which is flagged with stone, and these doors cover a pit about 2 yards by 112 yards across, and about 11 feet deep. On inspecting these doors I found they were only about an inch thick, but to have been constructed properly should have been three or four inches thick. The ironwork of the doors was of a frail kind, and much too weak for the purpose. There was a lever to these doors, and it was placed near the top of them. I pulled the lever and the doors dropped, the catches acting all right. I had the doors raised, and tried the lever a second time, when the catch again acted all right. The Governor was watching me through the window of his office and saw me try the doors. After the examination I went to him, explained how I found the doors, and suggested to him that for future executions new trap-doors should be made about three times as thick as those then fixed. I also suggested that a spring should be fixed in the Wall to hold the doors back when they fell, so that no rebounding occurred, and that the ironwork of the doors should be stronger. The Governor said he would see to these matters in future. I spent all the Sunday in the room allotted to me, and did not go outside the Gaol. I retired to bed about 9–45 that night. The execution was fixed to take place at eight o'clock on the morning of Monday the 23rd ultimo.

On the Monday morning I arose at 6.30, and was conducted from the Bedroom by a Warder, at 7.30, to the place of execution. Everything appeared to be as I had left it on the Saturday afternoon. I fixed the rope in my ordinary manner, and placed everything in readiness. I did not try the Trap-doors as they appeared to be just as I had left them. It had rained heavily during the nights of Saturday and Sunday. About four minutes to eight o'clock I was conducted by the Governor to the condemned Cell and introduced to John Lee. I proceeded at once to pinion him, which was done in the usual manner, and then gave a signal to the Governor that I was ready. The procession was formed, headed by the Governor, the Chief Warder, and the Chaplain followed by Lee. I walked behind Lee and 6 or 8 warders came after me. On reaching the place of execution I found you were there with the Prison Surgeon. Lee was at once placed upon the trap-doors. I pinioned his legs, pulled down the white cap, adjusted the Rope, stepped on one side, and drew the lever – but the trap-door did not fall. I had previously stood upon the doors and thought they would fall quite easily. I unloosed the strap from his legs, took the rope from his neck, removed the White Cap, and took Lee away into an adjoining room until I made an examination of the doors. I worked the lever after Lee had been taken off, drew it, and the doors fell easily. With the assistance of the warders the doors were pulled up, and the lever drawn a second time, when the doors again fell easily. Lee was then brought from the adjoining room, placed in position, the cap and rope adjusted, but when I again pulled the lever it did not act, and in trying to force it the lever was slightly strained. Lee was then taken off a second time and conducted to the adjoining room.

It was suggested to me that the woodwork fitted too tightly in the centre of the doors, and one of the warders fetched an axe and another a plane. I again tried the lever but it did not act. A piece of wood was then sawn off one of the doors close to where the iron catches were, and by the aid of an iron crowbar the catches were knocked off, and the doors fell down. You then gave orders that the execution should not be proceeded with until you have communicated with the Home Secretary, and Lee was taken back to the Condemned Cell. I am of opinion that the ironwork catches of the trapdoors were not strong enough for the purpose, that the woodwork of the doors should have been about three or four times as heavy, and with ironwork to correspond, so that when a man of Lee's weight was placed upon the doors the iron catches would not have become locked, as I feel sure they did on this occasion, but would respond readily. So far as I am concerned, everything was performed in a careful manner, and had the iron and woodwork been sufficiently strong, the execution would have been satisfactorily accomplished.

I am, Sir,

        Your obedient Servant,

          James Berry

Henry M. James, Esq.,
  Under-Sheriff of Devon.
    The Close, Exeter.

WITH A 'V' OR A 'W'?*

The Murder of Irene Wilkins By Thomas Henry Allaway
On Thursday, 22nd December 1921 at Fifteen-Acre-Meadow, outside Bournemouth

'Lady Cook, 31, requires post in a school. Experienced in a school with forty boarders. Disengaged. Salary £65. Miss Irene Wilkins, 21 Thirlmere Road, Streatham, S.W.16.'

So read the advertisement in December 20th 1921's edition of *The Morning Post*. By midday on Thursday 22nd, Miss Wilkins had already received a reply; the telegram instructed her:

Morning Post. Come immediately 4.30 train Waterloo Bournmouth Central. Car will meet train. Expence no object. Urgent. Wood, Beech House.'

After sending a hasty telegram of confirmation, Irene left her home at 3.00pm carrying a few necessaries in a small attaché case; she arrived in Bournemouth at 7.03. What she did not know was that her telegram had just been returned – address unknown.

At 7.30 on the following morning, Friday December 23rd, labourer Charles Nicklen was well into his regular morning constitutional and had reached a plot of rough ground known locally as the Fifteen-Acre-Meadow, at the

---

* 'Do you spell it with a "V" or a "W"?' inquired the judge. 'That depends upon the taste and fancy of the speller, My Lord,' replied Sam.

(Charles Dickens, *Pickwick Papers*, ch 34.)

point where the Seafield Road meets the Iford to Tuckton lane. With nothing much else to look at, Nicklen's attention wandered to the comparatively interesting sight of two cows worrying at a bundle on the ground; a bundle which on closer inspection turned out to be the body of a young woman.

By 8.00am the police had arrived. At 9.00 Dr Harold Summons, the police surgeon, began his examination of the victim's injuries, concluding that the most severe head injuries had been caused by blows from a heavy instrument such as a hammer, and the more superficial bruising probably by a clenched fist.

Meanwhile the police had determined from signs of a struggle on the path and a trail of blood, that the woman had been attacked before being deposited in the field. In the mud they found footprints belonging to a man and a woman and the tracks of a car fitted with characteristic Dunlop Magnum tyres. Time of death was estimated as being between 7.45 and 8.20 on the previous evening.

Already alarmed by the return of their daughter's telegram, Mr and Mrs Wilkins were no less distressed when they read in their evening paper of the discovery of a young woman's body, wearing a gold watch engraved with the initials 'IMW', and clothes embroidered with the name 'I. Wilkins'. They lost no time in expressing their worst fears to the Streatham police.

In this way the threads were joined together; the unhappy Wilkins family learned the fate of their daughter, the police learned of the advertisement and the telegrams.

Indeed, in the succeeding days they learned of two further similar telegrams, sent from the same area and in response to similar advertisements. It was a matter of great good fortune that neither of the other recipients felt inclined to keep the assignation. The post office clerks in all three cases were vague about their description of the man who sent the messages, though Alice Waters said he might have been a chauffeur, and that he had a 'rough voice'.

It also transpired that Irene Wilkins had been observed

on her fateful journey to Bournemouth by a fellow-passenger. Frank Humphris also recalled seeing the girl get into a chauffeur-driven grey Mercedes at the station. Mr Humphris had no reason to make a note of the vehicle's registration number, but he was to get a second glimpse of the same car driven by the same man on January 4th 1922 – this time with full awareness of its significance – and took the number down and passed it on to the police (it was LK 7405). Had the police not, for some unaccountable reason, ignored this information, Irene Wilkins's killer might have been caught a lot earlier.

As it was, all this talk of a dark Mercedes car and chauffeurs was making one of that latter calling decidedly nervous – especially after a routine visit from the police. Thomas Henry Allaway, driver to Mr Sutton, a resident of nearby Boscombe, fled his lodgings taking with him a book of his employer's cheques. Eight days later, Allaway was traced to Reading, whence he had gone to rendezvous with his wife; when he was arrested, police found a number of betting slips in his pockets, the handwriting on which matched the telegram messages. Further examples of Allaway's handwriting were found at his Boscombe address, and while in custody, Allaway agreed to write out, to the dictation of a police officer, the texts of the three telegrams. Although he made every attempt to disguise his writing, Allaway convicted himself with his bad spelling – reproducing faithfully the 'Bournmouth' and 'expence' of the Wilkins telegram as well as other obvious inaccuracies and illiteracies.

Thomas Allaway was then identified by the postal clerks who had taken his telegram messages, by Mr Humphris, and by a railway signalman who saw him standing at Bournemouth station on the day of the murder.

On July 3rd, 1922, Allaway was put on trial at the Summer Assizes at Winchester, before Mr Justice Avory. In his defence, Allaway attempted to prove an alibi – that he had been at his lodgings on the night of the murder, and had spoken to his landlord. It was an alibi that held only until that landlord was called as a witness; his recollection was that not only had he not spoken to the prisoner, but that it would have been very difficult to have done so, as he had been out of the house since early evening.

Thomas Allaway was found guilty of the murder of Irene Wilkins, and on the morning of August 19th, 1922, he was hanged at Winchester. Shortly before his death, Allaway confessed his guilt to the prison governor.

A DAMNED UNWORTHY SON

The Murder of Margery Gardner and Doreen Marshall by Neville George Clevely Heath
On Thursday, 20th June 1946 and Wednesday, 3rd July 1946 at the Pembridge Court Hotel, London, and Branksome Dene Chine, Dorset, respectively

Margery Aimée Bramwell Gardner, a 22-year-old occasional film extra, first met the young man who had introduced himself as Lieutenant Colonel Heath in May 1946. Somewhat the worse for drink, they booked into the Pembridge Court Hotel, 34 Pembridge Gardens, in London's Notting Hill Gate area. There Mrs Gardner was stripped, tied up, and flogged by Heath. In short, they were doing what they enjoyed most – which was bondage and flagellation. It must have been a very bewildered hotel detective who, attracted by Margery Gardner's screams, rushed through the door to find they were cries of pleasure.

On 15th June, 19-year-old Yvonne Symonds was the focus of attention for the amorous officer. Miss Symonds was staying at the Overseas Club in London, and on the night of the encounter had gone to a WRNS dance in Chelsea. Though he was ten years her senior, Yvonne, like so many girls before her, had succumbed to the gentle manners and easy charm of the man calling himself Lieutenant Colonel Heath. They visited the Panama Club in South Kensington before the gallant officer escorted his companion back to the Overseas Club. After spending the following Sunday in each other's company, and after – perhaps only after – Heath had proposed marriage, did Yvonne Symonds consent to being booked into the Pembridge Court Hotel under the rather premature title 'Mrs N.G.C. Heath'. Sex, if it took place at all, was by Heath's standards disarmingly normal; Miss Symonds was not attracted to flagellation. On the following morning she departed for her parents' home in Worthing leaving Heath to his own devices.

The second time that Margery Gardner shared Heath's room at the Pembridge Court Hotel, on Thursday, 20th June, it was the last. On the following afternoon a chambermaid, irritated by not being able to get in to clean the room, used her pass key. What she found was enough to send her scurrying for the manageress – on the bed nearest the door, covered by bedclothes was the shape of a person, a very still, stiff person. The sight beneath the covers was too much even for Sergeant Fred Averill, sent over from the nearby Notting Hill police station. Margery Gardner's naked body lay on its back, her feet tied together with a handkerchief; her wrists, judging by the marks, had also been bound, though the ligature had been removed. Her face had been severely bruised consistent with having been punched repeatedly. There were no less than seventeen vicious lash marks on various parts of her body – marks with a distinctive diamond criss-cross pattern. In addition the breasts had been bitten, the nipples almost bitten off. Finally, some rough object had been forced into her vagina causing excessive bleeding. The unspeakable savagery of the injuries were compounded by the fact that Margery Gardner had been alive when they were inflicted; death had come later, from suffocation.

On that same morning, Heath's 'fiancée' received a telephone call, the result of which was Heath taking a train to Worthing. After booking himself into the Ocean Hotel, they lunched. On the Saturday morning – for no explicable reason – Heath told Miss Symonds that a terrible murder had occurred in London and that he would tell her about it later. And tell her he did, over dinner at the Blue Peter Club in Angmering. It took place at the Pembridge Court Hotel, he said, in the room that he had booked; what was more, he had actually seen the body: 'a very gruesome sight'. Quite how this was affecting Yvonne Symonds's digestion we can only guess, but in her subsequent statement she recalled that her companion had said he met the victim earlier on the evening of her death, and that he had lent her his room to entertain a gentleman friend, and that on the following day Inspector Barrett had personally invited him to view the body. Heath suggested that a poker had 'been stuck up her'.

It was with understandable dismay that the Symonds family – over breakfast this time – learned not only the details of the murder from the Sunday newspapers, but also that the police were anxious to interview one Neville George Clevely Heath. When Yvonne Symonds relayed their disquiet to her fiancé over the telephone, he sympathised with her parents' upset, and assured her that he was at that moment on his way to London to 'clear things up'.

Of course he did no such thing. Instead he moved along the coast to Bournemouth from where he posted a preposterous letter to Scotland Yard's Inspector Barrett, in which he claimed to have met the late Margery Gardner and lent her his hotel room key in order to accommodate a man friend with whom 'for mainly financial reasons' she was obliged to sleep. He continued: 'Mrs Gardner asked if she could use my hotel room until two o'clock and intimated that if I returned after that, I might spend the remainder of the night with her. I gave her my keys and told her to leave the hotel door open. It must have been nearly 3am when I returned to the hotel and found her in the condition of which you are aware. I realised that I was in an invidious position, and rather than notify the police, I packed my belongings and left. Since then I have been in several minds whether to come forward or not but in view of the circumstances I have been afraid to. I can give you a description of the man. He was aged approximately thirty, dark hair (black), with small moustache. Height about 5ft 9in, slim build. His name was Jack and I gathered he was a friend of Mrs Gardner of some long standing . . . I have the instrument with which Mrs Gardner was beaten and am forwarding this to you today. You will find my fingerprints on it, but you should also find others as well.' The letter was signed 'N.G.C. Heath'. The alleged 'instrument' never arrived.

Heath arrived at the Tollard Royal Hotel on the West Cliff in Bournemouth on Sunday 23rd June, and checked in under the name of Group Captain Rupert Brooke. He occupied room 81. On the morning of the 3rd of July 'Brooke' met 21-year-old Doreen Marshall and entertained her to afternoon tea. In a later statement to the police – when they finally caught up with him – Heath described the events of that Wednesday:

'I met her along the promenade about 2.45 in the afternoon, and after a short stroll we went to the Tollard Royal for tea about 3.45. The conversation was fairly general and covered the fact that she had served with the WRNS. She mentioned the fact that she had been ill and was down in Bournemouth to recuperate. She left the hotel at about 5.45 after accepting my invitation to dinner in the evening. At approximately 7.15 I was standing outside the hotel when I saw Miss Marshall approaching the hotel on foot down West Hill Road. I entered the hotel, went to my room to get some tobacco, and came down again just as she was entering the lounge. We dined at about 8.15pm and sat talking in the lounge after dinner, moving into the writing room at about 10pm. The conversation was again general but she told me she was considering cutting short her holiday and returning home [she lived in Pinner] on Friday instead of Monday. She mentioned an American staying at her hotel and told me that he had taken her for car rides into the country and to Poole. She also mentioned an invitation to go with him to Exeter, but I gathered, although she did not actually say so, that she did not intend to go. Another American was mentioned – I believe his name was Pat – to whom I believe she was unofficially engaged some while ago. Conversation continued general until approximately 11.30pm.

At 11pm (approx) Miss Marshall suggested going away, but I persuaded her to stay a little longer. At about 11.30 the weather was clear and we left the hotel and sat on a seat overlooking the sea.'

When 'Group Captain Brooke' returned to his hotel he decided to 'practice a small deception' on the night porter: 'I guessed he would be waiting for me to come in, and as a ladder had that day been placed up against my window . . . [I] entered my hotel bedroom via the ladder.'

On 5th July the Norfolk Hotel's manager notified the local police that one of his guests – Miss Doreen Marshall – had been missing since the 3rd. At the same time he telephoned his opposite number at the Tollard Royal, a Mr Relf, who on the following morning asked 'Brooke' whether his guest of the previous Wednesday had been the missing Miss Marshall from Pinner. 'Oh, no,' Brooke laughed. 'I've known that lady for a long while, and she certainly doesn't come from Pinner.' Nevertheless, Relf suggested, it might be a good idea to get in touch with the police.

And with amazing bravado, he did just that; presenting himself at Bournemouth police station at 5.30pm. Here, through Detective Constable George Suter, he met Doreen Marshall's father and sister who had travelled down from Pinner to be close to the search for Doreen. Brooke was shown a photograph of the missing girl, and with a great show of surprise and sorrow admitted that it was, after all, the same young woman with whom he had dined on the night of her disappearance. Throughout this exchange, DC Suter had been scrutinizing his guest carefully; he bore an uncanny resemblance to the photograph of the man Heath that Scotland Yard were anxious to interview. Finally, he gave voice to his thoughts: 'Brooke, is your real name Heath?' 'Good Lord no!' he replied, 'But I agree it is like me.'

Nonetheless, with a good detective's instinctive caution, Suter detained his visitor until the Inspector arrived, at which point Brooke's meagre belongings were brought from the Tollard Royal Hotel to the police station. Searched in front of him, Brooke's jacket pockets yielded a left-luggage ticket issued at Bournemouth West station, the return half of a first-class railway ticket issued to Doreen Marshall, and a single artificial pearl from a necklace. When Detective Inspector George Gates redeemed the deposited suitcase from Bournemouth

West, a further damning array of evidence was revealed: clothing and a hat marked with the name 'Heath', and a blue woollen scarf and a neckerchief, both stained with blood and bearing hairs later proved to have come from Doreen Marshall's head. At the bottom of the case was a leather riding switch; a riding switch with a distinctive diamond pattern weave.

Early the following day Detective Inspector Reg Spooner arrived from London, and on Monday, 8th July, Heath was removed to Scotland Yard, where he was charged with the murder of Margery Gardner.

Meanwhile, that same day Kathleen Evans, a young waitress, had been exercising her dog at Branksome Dene Chine on the Dorset/Hampshire border when she noticed a swarm of flies around some rhododendron bushes. When she later read of Doreen Marshall's continued disappearance she was reminded of the flies, and voiced her suspicions to her father. When Kathleen and Mr Evans returned to the Chine later that evening they solved the riddle of Doreen Marshall.

When the police arrived they found the body naked but for a left shoe, and covered by the victim's clothing and some branches of fir-tree. Close to the body, police searchers found Doreen's torn stockings, a powder compact, and a broken string of artificial pearls; on the following morning her handbag was located behind a beach-hut at Durley Chine.

The direct cause of Doreen Marshall's death had been two deep cuts across her throat, though these were but two of a dreadful series of injuries and mutilations committed on the body both before and after death. She had been bludgeoned a number of times on the back of the head, and there were bruises and abrasions to most of the upper body. One rib had been fractured and had pierced the left lung; Doreen's hands, which had been tied at the wrists, bore deep cuts indicating that she had tried to grab the knife from her attacker. But even in death, the tragic girl had suffered further appalling treatment; one nipple had been bitten off, and a ragged knife cut reached from her vagina to her chest where it met a further diagonal slash from each nipple to the middle of her body. In addition, an instrument, probably the branch of a tree, had been forced into her vagina and anus.

The trial of Neville George Clevely Heath opened in the Old Bailey's No. 1 Court on Tuesday, 24th September 1946. Mr Justice Morris presided, and Mr E.A. Hawke and Mr J.D. Casswell led, respectively, the prosecution and defence cases. Heath was charged only with the murder of Margery Gardner to which he pleaded not guilty.

There was never any question of Heath's guilt – he was quite patently a vicious and sadistic killer. The question was, was he insane? Mr Casswell's defence rested heavily on the fact that a man simply had to be mad to have committed such grotesque crimes; that though Heath may well have known what he was doing, he was so morally bankrupt that he had no conception at the time that what he was doing was wrong. For the Crown two prison doctors, while allowing that Heath was both a sexual pervert and a psychopath, refused to agree that he was, within the scope of the M'Naghten Rules – which determined such matters in law – definitely not insane.

As for the prisoner himself, he seemed throughout the three days of the trial to be quite indifferent to the proceedings – even bored. He said not one word in his own defence, nor exhibited the slightest remorse. After a retirement of one hour, the jury were unanimous in their verdict – guilty of murder.

Heath made no appeal and no last minute confession; his sole gesture to decency was to admit, in a letter to his parents, that he had been 'damned unworthy of you both'. On 16th October he stood on the scaffold at Pentonville Prison. Before hangman Albert Pierrepoint carried out his public duty, Neville Heath is said to have asked the prison governor for a whisky, adding: 'You might as well make that a double.'

THE MARTYR KING

**The Assassination of King Edward by a
servant of his step-mother Elfrida**
In March 979 at the gate of Corfe Castle,
Dorset

Edward was born in about the year 963, son of Edgar the
Peaceful, sovereign of all England, and his first wife
Ethelfleda. The queen did not long survive Edward's birth
and Edgar remarried, to Elfrida by whom he had another
son, Ethelred.

On the king's death in 975 Edward, as the eldest son,
succeeded to the throne at the start of a reign that was to
be as unpopular as it was short. Though we know little of
the political life of Edward, his adherence to the strict
guidance of St Dunstan (then Archbishop of Canterbury),
and his own irrepressible ill-temper, made him many
powerful enemies. Opposition was particularly strong
among a group of anti-monastic thanes based in the
influential kingdom of Mercia. In their disaffection for
Edward, they had a dedicated ally in Elfrida who, since
Edgar's death had sought to install her own son Ethelred –
though he was barely ten years of age – on the throne of
England.

It is the historian monk William of Malmesbury who
provides us with the most detailed account of Edward's
eventual assassination. In March 979 Edward had been on
a hunting trip in what is now Dorset. Weary of the chase
and determined to visit his young step-brother, for whom
he entertained a great affection, he approached Elfrida's
castle at Corfe. Apprised of his imminent arrival, Elfrida
rode out with a party of servants to greet the king, and

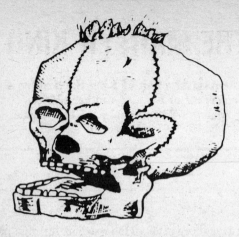

seeing that he was alone embarked on an impromptu plan that was to result in his death. Feigning pleasure at his unexpected arrival, Elfrida called for refreshment for her stepson; while he supped from the cup, one of the servants 'pierced him through' with a dagger. Although Edward spurred his horse to make an escape, he slipped from the saddle, and with one foot caught in the stirrup was dragged along 'his blood leaving a trail' until he died.

William of Malmesbury relates that Elfrida ordered the king's body to be thrown into a bog that it might not be discovered, but a miraculous pillar of light marked the spot, and the corpse was taken up for burial in the church at Wareham. In 980, Dunstan had the relics removed to Shaftesbury Abbey.

In 1001, Ethelred (called 'Unraed' or The Unready,) signed a charter by which his late step-brother was dignified 'Saint and Martyr'; in 1008 he further ordered the observance of an annual feast of St Edward Martyr King.

As for Elfrida, overwhelmed by remorse she expiated her sin by becoming a nun and founding the monasteries of Amesbury and Wherwell, at which latter she died.

THE PRICE OF FRIENDSHIP

The Murder of Jeanne Sutcliffe and her
daughter Heidi by Heather Arnold
On Wednesday, 30th April 1986 at their home
in Westbury, Wiltshire

Teacher Denies Axe Killings
1st April 1987: A jury at Bristol Crown Court was told
yesterday how teacher Paul Sutcliffe arrived home with
two of his children on the evening of 30th April last year to
discover the dead bodies of his wife Jeanne and baby
daughter Heidi lying side by side in the sewing-room of
their house in Westbury, Wiltshire.

In the dock accused of the murders was a colleague of
Mr Sutcliffe, 50-year-old mathematics teacher Heather
Arnold. Divorcee Mrs Arnold, of Orchard Road, West-
bury, has pleaded not guilty to both counts of murder.

Mr David Elfer QC, for the prosecution, told the court:
'The killer probably told Mrs Sutcliffe that she wanted to
buy some dressmaking cotton or thread [Mrs Sutcliffe ran
a small dressmaking business from home], and was
clearly let into the house. As Mrs Sutcliffe bent down to
get whatever it was, the killer hit her on the back of the
head.' She then turned her attention to the baby, and it too
was fatally attacked. The two bodies were then laid side
by side. Mr Elfer said that a household axe, which had at
one time been painted red, was used in the attack, and
forensic evidence had linked the murder weapon with an
axe-head in Mrs Arnold's possession; the accused had
washed the axe and tried to burn it, but fragments of red
paint were found both on Mrs Sutcliffe's body and in
Arnold's car.

Mother's Blood on Baby

2nd April 1987: Continuing the prosecution case today, Mr Bill Kennard, a Home Office pathologist, detailed part of the forensic reconstruction of the murders of 39-year-old Jeanne Sutcliffe and her 8-month-old baby Heidi. He told the court that the cause of Mrs Sutcliffe's death was haemorrhage due to a cut throat; there were thirteen injuries to her head and face, all of them caused by a blunt instrument. Mrs Sutcliffe's skull had been extensively fractured and pushed into the brain, the cut to her throat went through to the spinal cord. The victim had been anorexic and weighed only about 6 stone and stood just over 5ft tall. Stunned before she knew what was happening, Mrs Sutcliffe was able to put up little resistance, though injuries to the backs of her hands were consistent with having tried to protect herself. Blood on the knee of baby Heidi's romper suit was of the same group as Mrs Sutcliffe's, and indicated that the child had crawled into its mother's blood before she too had had her throat cut. The bodies had then been laid side by side, a tea-towel covering the baby's neck wound.

Axe-head Hidden in Skirt

6th April 1987: From the witness stand of Bristol Crown Court, Mrs Caroline Buckley, the solicitor daughter of Mrs Heather Arnold, told how her mother had come to stay at her home over the May Bank holiday (1986), and towards evening broke into tears and told her that she had found a small axe in her garage. She admitted chopping up the handle of the axe and burning the pieces before disposing of them. Mrs Arnold then produced the axe head, wrapped in blue tissue, from the top of her skirt. Mrs Buckley said her mother was obviously very frightened, but told her: 'I didn't do it.'

Detective Constable Bob Richards told the jury that for a week after the murders a team of four detectives had worked under cover with council refuse collectors. Wiltshire CID had played the imaginative hunch that the killer would sooner or later try to dispose of the murder weapon along with household rubbish. DC Richards had seen Mrs Arnold walking out of her front door with a white carrier bag and said to her: 'All right love, I'll take that, it will save your legs.' The carrier bag was later found to contain the three charred pieces of an axe handle.

Court Told of 'Confessions'

7th April 1987: In the case against Mrs Heather Arnold today, the jury was told by Detective Constable Caroline Enright that Mrs Arnold broke down in the back of a police car and confessed to killing Mrs Jeanne Sutcliffe and her baby daughter. The confession was made as Mrs Arnold was being driven to Wiltshire police headquarters after her arrest.

The court then heard that Mrs Arnold had signed the notes taken down of this alleged confession, but on the advice of her solicitor had subsequently denied going to the Sutcliffe house on the day of the murders.

Court Told of Panic

8th April 1987: Mrs Heather Arnold went into the witness box to give evidence in her own defence today. She told the murder trial that when she found a household axe that she did not recognize in her garage she panicked. Mrs Arnold said she felt some 'inexplicable' need to get rid of the axe, and later cut the head from the handle, cut the handle in three pieces, and disposed of it with the household rubbish. She could not remember anything about the axe head until she 'rediscovered' it in her handbag on the evening of her visit to her daughter. Explaining her panic, the prisoner said: 'I just felt I was already under suspicion, why I did not know. This thing [the axe] was going to make the situation even worse and I felt some inexplicable need to get rid of it.'

Murder Jury Retires

14th April 1987: The jury in the Heather Arnold trial will finally be sent out today to make their decision. The judge's summing-up was delayed because one of the jurors injured his back at the weekend and was unable to attend court. With the agreement of defence and Crown counsel, Mr Justice Henry formally discharged the man from further duty and proceeded with an 11-member jury.

Teacher Gets Life for Double Murder

15th April 1987: The jury retired on Tuesday to consider their verdict, but after a 6-hour deliberation were unable to reach a verdict. Mr Justice Henry sent them to a hotel for the night. Today, after a further 90-minute retirement, the jury returned to the court to present their unanimous verdict. Mrs Arnold broke down and wept as the fore-woman gave a verdict of 'guilty' on the first count; she collapsed in the dock when a second 'guilty' verdict was announced and had to be supported by two women prison officers.

Sentencing Mrs Arnold to life imprisonment, Mr Justice Henry told her: 'The jury has rightly convicted you of these two terrible murders, murders which have shocked and horrified the community. That community is now left to mourn the quality of these two innocent lives you took.'

At a press conference after the sentence had been passed, Mr Paul Sutcliffe, the victims' husband and father, spoke about the innocent friendship that had brought tragedy to his family. Mr Sutcliffe and Mrs Arnold had been colleagues at Kingsdown Comprehensive school in Warminster, and when Mrs Arnold was going through a difficult divorce from her husband, both he and his wife had been very supportive. Mr Sutcliffe suggested: 'I think there must have been some form of envy. I have a feeling that Mrs Arnold had a rather empty existence. I had a fairly chaotic family existence which I clearly enjoyed.' Mrs Arnold may have been jealous of Jeanne Sutcliffe's happy marriage, and when new baby Heidi was born felt that the Sutcliffes were about to build a life in which she would have no place.

WALES

Clwyd

Dyfed

Glamorgan

Gwent

Gwynedd

Powys

THE RHYL MUMMY CASE

The Death of Mrs Frances Knight
On a date in April 1940 at 35 Kinmel Street,
Rhyl, Clwyd and the Trial of Sarah Jane
Harvey for her Murder

Number 35 Kinmel Street in the coastal resort town of Rhyl, North Wales, had been home to Leslie Harvey for most of his childhood and youth, his mother, Sarah Jane Harvey, still lived there, and since the death of her husband Alfred in January 1938 she had shared the modest two-storey terrace house with a succession of paying guests. Now at the age of 65, Mrs Harvey was beginning to feel the consequences of a long life, and in April 1960 she was taken into hospital for observation.

Though Leslie was married now, and living in nearby Abergele, the filial affection remained as strong as ever; and it was as a token of this affection that he and his wife stood on the threshold of the family home in Kinmel Street on the afternoon of 5th May 1960. Leslie had decided to take advantage of his mother's confinement in order to decorate the house for her. After making their way to the top of the stairs making mental notes of jobs to be done, clutter to clear, musty corners to air, Leslie and his wife found themselves in front of the large wooden cupboard on the first-floor landing. In Leslie's recollection the cupboard had always been locked, and strictly out-of-bounds. The only explanation ever given to the inquisitive small boy was that it contained some belongings of a long-since departed lodger named Frances Knight.

With a renewed curiosity Leslie Harvey prised open the double doors with a screwdriver, prepared at worst for the task of clearing out some dusty old suitcases. With understandable horror, he stood speechless as the contents of the cupboard were revealed by the invading light. These were not somebody's possessions – it was *somebody*; a body that had obviously been there for a very long time.

By late evening the usually quiet street had become busy with policemen, and inside No.35 Flint's chief constable, Reginald Atkins, and coroner Dr Rhys Llewellyn Jones peered closely at the grim bundle that had so recently occupied the landing cupboard. The body was in a doubled-up position, and clothed in a now-faded and cobweb encrusted nightdress and dressing gown; the skin was shrunken and leathery, what flesh remained was hard as stone. The whole corpse had been mummified – not by art, as was the custom in ancient Egypt, but by the natural process of warm, dry air rising and circulating around the cupboard tomb, slowly desiccating the body tissues. An atmospheric freak which had made it possible to conceal a corpse for many years without the tell-tale stench of putrefaction.

Despite the hideous appearance of the face, Leslie Harvey observed that the mummy bore some resemblance to the former lodger Mrs Knight, whose 'possessions' were supposed to have been deposited behind the locked doors of the cupboard. Mrs Knight, he recalled, had been a divorcee living on a small weekly maintenance payment from her former husband; but she had left in 1940. Could her dead body possibly have lain where it was found for twenty years? And who on earth would have wanted to keep it there? Who had hung a fly-paper over the corpse with with the obvious intention of dealing with the infestation of insects that prey on dead flesh? It was clear that Mrs Sarah Harvey would have a lot of questions to answer.

With the discovery of a body in mysterious circumstances – and there could be few more mysterious circumstances than those surrounding the Rhyl mummy – the well-oiled machinery of a major police investigation is set in motion. Teams of investigating officers and scientists, each with their well-defined areas of expertise combine resources to track down and bring to justice a killer.

First, a minute examination of the human remains
attempts to answer the three seminal questions – who,
how, and when? In this instance it was the job of Dr Gerald
Evans, pathologist to the Home Office, to undertake the
post-mortem; an examination that had to be delayed until
the body had soaked long enough in a tank of glycerine
solution to become pliable enough to examine. It was then
that Dr Evans found the remains of what appeared to be a
knotted ligature, and a groove in the neck consistent with
strangulation by that ligature. While Dr Evans was cautious enough not to be positive about his suspicions, the
police were now treating the case as one of murder; an
opinion endorsed by the extraordinary findings of Detective Inspector Hugh Williams and Detective-Sergeant
William Evans. Williams and Evans had been trying to
confirm a link between Mrs Frances Knight and the
mummified body, and had routinely visited the registrar's office at St Asaph, where there was no record of
a death certificate being issued for the woman in question.
When the two officers transferred their inquiries to the
Rhyl municipal offices, the mystery deepened. Yes, they
knew Mrs Knight, she was an elderly lady who had
resided for many years in Kinmel Street; she lived with
a Mrs Harvey who had been collecting her housebound
lodger's maintenance cheque for the past twenty years!
What came to light next was beyond the belief even of
Hugh Williams. Investigation showed that no less than
seven further deaths had occurred among the occupants of
35 Kinmel Street during the past twenty-five years:

1926, May 30: Thomas Evans, aged 57, died of a
malignant disease.

1928, February 16: Ellen Evans, 60, encephalitis
lethargica and exhaustion.

1928, March 1: Jane Jones (Sarah Harvey's
mother), 64, cerebral edema.

1938, January 28: Alfred James Harvey (Sarah's
husband), 67, cerebral embolism and exhaustion.

1940, December 1: Jonathan Mould, 67, enteritis
and chronic cardiac disease.

1940, December 23: Edith Mould (Jonathan's sister), 69, senile decay, anaemia, and sarcoma of the uterus.

1941, September 4: Herbert Lomas, 74, myocardial degeneration.

Misfortune? They were, after all, elderly people; and with the flow of residents passing through a lodging house there must be a greater percentage of deaths. At any rate the police decided to pursue only one case. The case of Mrs Frances Knight.

On 9th June 1960, at 6 o'clock in the morning, Sarah Jane Harvey was arrested on a charge of murder.

By comparison, the trial was an anticlimax. On 30th June at the Town Hall in Rhyl, the prosecution advanced the proposition that Sarah Harvey had strangled her lodger, on some date during 1940, in order to avail herself of Mrs Knight's weekly £2 maintenance money. In her defence, Mrs Harvey claimed that the victim had died of natural causes and that she had panicked and hidden the body in the cupboard (though one might have thought she was more accustomed than most to having people dying in her house). As to the stocking found knotted around Frances Knight's neck, the somewhat unlikely explanation was offered that an old folk-cure for sore throats was to tie an unwashed stocking or sock around the sufferer's neck – perhaps Mrs Knight had accidentally strangled herself.

In what must be seen as an act of compassion towards an elderly, sick woman accused of a 20-year-old crime that could not even be unquestionably proved, the trial was stopped after three days. Sarah Jane Harvey was found guilty, on her own admission, only of the lesser charge of fraudulently obtaining money, and sentenced to fifteen months imprisonment.

THE 'REGINALD PERRIN' MURDERS

**The Murder of Greeba Healey and her
daughter Marie Walker by Robert Healey**
On Tuesday, 29th July 1986 at their home in
Longmead Avenue, Stockport

Police Plea to 'Perrin' Man
Tuesday, 5th August 1986: Further to the apparent suicide
last Wednesday of Mr Robert Healey, police are now
fearful that his missing wife Greeba, aged 40, and 13-
year-old stepdaughter Marie Walker are dead. Healey, a
37-year-old self-employed driving instructor, has not been
seen since driving away from his home at Longmead
Avenue, Hazel Grove, Stockport, last Tuesday; his metallic silver Vauxhall Chevette (registration TEH 199R) was
left in a multi-storey car park in Park Street, Birmingham,
on Thursday, and police are anxious to talk to anyone who
saw it being parked.

On the previous day a suicide note addressed to
Mr Healey's mother had been found with a pile of men's
clothing on the beach at Prestatyn, in North Wales. The
note stated that Mr Healey felt his marriage was breaking
up, and that life was no longer worth while. A subsequent
police check of the Healey home revealed that Mrs Healey
and Marie were also missing; forensic experts found traces
of blood in the couple's bedroom.

The discovery of video tapes of the television series 'The
Fall and Rise of Reginald Perrin' have aroused grave
doubts about the 'suicide' of Mr Healey. Perrin, the
central character, is seen at the beginning of each episode
undressing and putting his clothes into a pile on the beach
to persuade the police that he has drowned himself, and

then going off to start a new life.

Detective Chief Superintendent Clive Atkinson, who is leading the inquiry, said: 'I am making a personal appeal to Robert Healey to come forward and speak to me, or to any police officer, to relieve the anguish of his parents, his wife's friends and his stepdaughter's father.'

Bloodstains Link with Wife and Daughter

Wednesday, 6th August 1986: Forensic tests on the bloodstains found at the Healey home in Stockport reveal that they match the group of missing Mrs Greeba Healey and her daughter Marie; they were last seen at lunchtime last Monday. Police now believe that Robert Healey's suicide was faked, and Det. Chief Supt. Atkinson said: 'I am now treating this case as a murder hunt, and I am very anxious to trace Mr Healey.'

Quilt Clue to Murder

Saturday, 9th August 1986: Police officers leading the Healey murder investigation revealed yesterday that bloodstains on a quilt found in a ditch off the A5117 near Chester match in group those found at the Healey home earlier this week. These in turn matched the group shared by Mrs Healey and her daughter. Matching stains were also found in the car abandoned by Mr Robert Healey in a Birmingham car park. An RAF helicopter search using heat seeking equipment has failed to trace either bodies or recently disturbed ground.

BODIES FOUND

Man Charged in 'Perrin' Case

Monday, 18th August 1986: Mr Robert Healey who, it is understood, has been living under a false name in the Harrow Road area of west London, was last night charged with the murder of his wife and stepdaughter at their home in Stockport.

Mr Healey, who presented himself at New Scotland Yard on Saturday night, will appear before Stockport magistrates today. Police have issued a statement in which it is stated that Mrs Greeba Healey died of multiple skull fractures, while her daughter had been suffocated. Their naked bodies were found in a shallow grave in a wood at Caerwys, in North Wales, on Friday night.

Tuesday, 19th August 1986: Magistrates at Stockport yesterday remanded Robert Healey in custody until 26th August. During the 3 minute hearing, Mr Healey stood silent as the charges were read to him.

'Reginald Perrin' Trial Opens
Tuesday, 24th March 1987: The trial began at Liverpool Crown Court yesterday of Mr Robert Healey, accused of the murder of his wife and stepdaughter. Mr Healey denied the charges.

Mr Brian Leveson, QC, opening for the prosecution said that after the bodies of Mrs Healey and her daughter Marie were found in a shallow grave in North Wales last August, Healey had given himself up to the police. While in custody he had produced a notebook filled with what appeared to be a rationale for the killings. According to the handwritten entries, after being taunted by his wife over his sexual prowess, Healey had 'as if in a dream' battered her to death with a rolling pin as she lay in bed. His stepdaughter, attracted by the noise, had come into the room, and Healey claims he gripped her by the throat to prevent her struggling.

Mr Leveson then told the jury that a rather different story would emerge from the evidence, that both Mrs Healey and Marie had had sexual intercourse just before their deaths; that Mr Healey, after bludgeoning his wife, had carefully cleaned and replaced the rolling pin in a kitchen drawer, washed down the blood-spattered kitchen walls, and changed the stained bed linen. He then wrote a note cancelling the milk and newspapers, and put the bodies into his wife's car. Shortly afterwards, Healey applied for a passport giving the name of his brother-in-law. On the morning of the following day, a pile of men's clothing was found on the beach at Prestatyn, and in the coat pocket was Mr Healey's wallet containing a note to his mother ending: 'I might as well die now.'

Wednesday, 25th March 1987: The jury at Liverpool Crown Court heard yesterday how 72-year-old William Douglas had been walking in a wood at Caerwys, North Wales, when he kicked aside a pile of leaves and earth to be confronted with a human hand and foot protruding from a shallow grave. Police later removed the bodies of Mrs Greeba Healey and her daughter from beneath twelve inches of soil.

In his evidence to the court, pathologist Dr Donald Wayte said that the injuries to Healey's stepdaughter Marie resembled those that he had seen on victims crushed to death in road accidents. Healey sat in the dock covering his ears as Dr Wayte estimated that it could have taken as long as five agonized minutes for Marie to die.

Thursday, 26th March 1987: In the witness box yesterday, Mr Robert Healey, who pleads not guilty to two charges of murder, spoke of his failing marriage. He had met his wife Greeba through a lonely hearts advertisement in the local newspaper, and after their marriage: 'She started to become obsessive towards me. I must be there constantly, all the time.' He said that often after sex his wife would storm off into the garden and refuse to come in, shouting: 'You don't want me, you don't love me!'

Asked if he had been engaging in sexual intercourse with his stepdaughter Marie, and that he had killed her to prevent her exposing him, Healey replied: 'Nothing of the sort.'

Friday, 27th March 1987: Continuing his evidence, Robert Healey described the killing of his wife and stepdaughter as 'like a film. I was watching myself on television.' He said that on 29th July of last year his wife had once again criticised his love-making, and that: 'I felt like screaming. I felt frustrated'. He walked down to the kitchen: 'I stared at things, objects. There was a rolling pin. I picked it up. I didn't know what I was doing . . . I went upstairs to our bedroom. I walked round the bed. I hit her with the rolling pin on the head. She jumped up; she didn't say anything; she didn't scream, she just moaned. I hit her again; I don't know how many times. Eventually she was down on the floor. Marie came in and I told her to get out. My hand caught her face. She went out and came straight back in again. I didn't want her to see her mother on the floor. I grabbed her by the throat and pushed her up against the wall. The next thing I remember she was down on the floor. I don't know how long it was before I realised they were both dead.'

Healey then staged the fake suicide at Prestatyn before burying the two bodies and returning to London to take up a new identity.

Suggesting that he derived the inspiration for his charade from the Reginald Perrin television series, Mr Leveson for the prosecution asked him: 'Does not the Perrin character walk into the sea, then start a new life with a new name and a beard? You did all these things.' Mr Healey: 'Yes, but I didn't get the ideas from the programme.' He said that he had fully intended to go ahead with the suicide.

In closing, Mr Leveson maintained that Robert Healey had intended to kill his wife and then, after intercourse with her, Marie; the proper verdicts would be guilty of murder.

Judge's Summing-up

Saturday, 28th March 1987: Concluding for the defence yesterday at Liverpool Crown Court, Mr John Hugell, QC, on behalf of the prisoner, invited the jury to consider the following questions: Why should Healey have made such a frenzied attack on the two women? And why should he then, after killing them, fake his own suicide? He continued: 'The case is upsetting for many reasons. One is the sheer ordinariness of everyone concerned . . . it is all so ordinary. You may think you have seen a tortured soul before you. He is a man in considerable distress, and rightly so because, in any view, he has committed a dreadful crime.'

The judge, Mr Justice McNeill, in his summing-up advised the jury of seven women and five men that if they decided that Mr Healey had not committed murder, then it must return a verdict of guilty of manslaughter: 'It is not in dispute here that in the case of each killing it was the defendant who caused death by direct and unlawful violence'. He said that they must consider whether Mrs Healey had given provocation: 'Would a reasonable man take a rolling pin and rain blows down on her head so as to kill her?' There was no suggestion of provocation on the part of Marie Walker.

Guilty Verdict in 'Perrin' Case

Tuesday, 31st March 1987: After a retirement of 3 hours yesterday, the jury returned unanimous verdicts of guilty of murder in the case of Robert Healey. As the verdict was announced, Healey turned away, his hands trembling violently, and burst into tears.

Sentencing the prisoner, Mr Justice McNeill told him: 'You know there is only one sentence. The sentence fixed by law upon conviction for murder is that on each count, to be served concurrently, you will go to prison for life.'

Motive

At no time during the trial was any motive for the murders disclosed. Police, however, are convinced that it was Healey's illegal relationship with his stepdaughter that was the key. Detectives are now able to reveal that Healey was put on 2 years probation four years ago for inciting a young girl to an act of gross indecency. If Marie Walker had threatened to expose him for his current acts of indecency, it was not beyond the bounds of reason that Healey might kill rather than face the inevitable prison sentence consequent upon a second conviction for interfering with a child.

THE MISSING CORPSE

**The Murder of Stanislaw Sykut by Michael
Onufrejczyc
On Monday, 14th December 1953 at Cefn
Hendre farm, Cwmdu, Dyfed**

Michael Onufrejczyc had served as a warrant officer
with the Polish Army during the hostilities of
1939–45, his conspicuous gallantry earning him nine
medals. At the end of the war Onufrejczyc had settled in
Britain, and in 1949, with money borrowed from Polish
Army funds, he realised the dream of a lifetime; at the age
of 58, Michael Onufrejczyc bought a farm. Or rather, he
bought what was left after years of neglect and exposure to
the elements had rendered it virtually derelict. A bleak,
inhospitable patch of land with its ruined farm buildings,
Cefn Hendre was situated about a mile from the village of
Cwmdu, in what was once Carmarthenshire and now lies
in the county of Dyfed. Here Onufrejczyc, himself a withdrawn man, came face to face with the natural reserve of the
Welsh. While not openly hostile, the local community had
an inborn mistrust of this foreigner, and he had a dismis-
sive, almost arrogant approach to his neighbours.

The land at Cefn Hendre soon proved to be as barren as
it was bleak, and after years of stubborn effort, Michael
Onufrejczyc, veteran campaigner in some of Europe's
bloodiest theatres of war, found himself engaged in a
battle he could not hope to win; the farm bordered on
bankruptcy. In a final effort to salvage his future, Onufrejczyc took on a partner in the person of Stanislaw Sykut.
There had been two previous attempts at a partnership,
each of which ended disastrously following Onufrejczyc's

violent outbursts of temper. But this time it might be different. Sykut, like Onufrejczyc, was a Pole, a former military man, and the same age as his prospective partner. In temperament, however, they were at opposite extremes, Sykut being a quiet, meditative man. Thus it was, that only a short time after the partnership commenced in March 1953, Sykut was obliged to report to the local police that Onufrejczyc had physically attacked him. Onufrejczyc bluffed his way out of any serious trouble with the law over the matter, but things had clearly gone too far for Stanislaw Sykut. In the second week of June 1953, he instructed a solicitor to serve a termination order dissolving the partnership as of 14th November and adding that if the £600 that his client had invested in the business was not refunded by that date, then the farm would be auctioned to raise the necessary reimbursement.

Surprisingly, given the general atmosphere of acrimony that had developed over the previous months, Stanislaw Sykut continued in residence at Cefn Hendre. More surprising still, 14th November came and passed with Onufrejczyc still refusing to refund his partner a single penny of his money, and Sykut still remained.

On 14th December, Sykut visited the village blacksmith, whose forge was at the end of the lane leading to Cefn Hendre, and had the work-horse shod. Then the smith watched as he returned along the lane to the farm. It was the last time that Stanislaw Sykut was seen – to this day there has been no trace of him, alive or dead.

That a man is not seen around for a couple of days, particularly a man as reclusive as Sykut, would have attracted no particular attention locally even if the villagers were interested – which they weren't. And when an officer of the Sheriff paid a visit to Cefn Hendre on 16th December, there was no suggestion of a mystery. This man, through a Polish interpreter, spoke briefly to Onufrejczyc who, when asked Sykut's whereabouts, replied that he had taken a trip to Llandilo to visit his doctor. It was only later that this proved to be untrue. Slight suspicion was generated, however, by Onufrejczyc's refusal to conduct this conversation in the shelter of the farmhouse. It was a freezing day with a biting wind blowing down from the hills, and despite his visitors' obvious discomfort, and several suggestions that it might be warmer inside, Onufrejczyc resolutely insisted on conducting the business *al fresco*.

It was on 30th December that official attention was again focussed on the Onufrejczyc farm. This time it was a visit by Sergeant Phillips on a routine check on aliens in the district. In reply to his question, Phillips was told that Stanislaw Sykut had gone to London for a fortnight.

By this time gossip was beginning to spread around the neighbourhood, emanating from that mecca of local tittle-tattle, the village post office. It had been Stanislaw Sykut's daily routine to visit the Cwmdu office in order to set his watch by their clock, and to pick up his mail. He had not been seen since 14th December and his letters were piling up.

By January 1954, rumours and suspicions had reached the ears of the police, and on the 13th of that month a detective from Llandilo, accompanied by a Polish interpreter, once again approached the surly owner of Cefn Hendre on the matter of his partner's whereabouts.

At the end of a particularly frustrating interview, in which Onufrejczyc made extravagant play of his poor command of English and refused even to comprehend questions in his own tongue, the officer was convinced that the farmer was trying to hide something. As a result, Mr T.H. Lewis, Chief Constable of Carmarthenshire and Cardiganshire, requested a magistrate's warrant to search the farmhouse. But despite the most thorough search, police officers were still no nearer finding the missing alien. The farm land, a considerable amount of which was unproductive bog, was combed by police with tracker dogs, men and animals often wading thigh deep in the mud and slime. However, as far as locating Stanislaw Sykut was concerned, the search proved negative.

Detectives, now convinced that Sykut had been murdered, but having no shred of evidence on which to proceed, interviewed their chief 'suspect' again. This time, for no very good reason, Onufrejczyc changed his earlier story. Whereas before he had claimed that his partner had gone to the doctor in Llandilo the previous December, he now maintained that Sykut had gone to London. Onufrejczyc then produced a paper purporting to have been signed by Stanislaw Sykut transferring his interest in the farm to Onufrejczyc for the sum of £600, £450 paid already, the balance in May 1954. Anticipating the obvious question, Onufrejczyc volunteered the information that he had borrowed the money from his niece, a Mrs Pokora.

When Mrs Pokora was traced to London and interviewed by officers of the Metropolitan Police force, she made a full and very intriguing statement. For a start, she had most certainly not lent Onufrejczyc any money. The bizarre truth was that he had asked her to pretend to lend him the money by sending two packets by registered post that looked the size and shape of £450 in one-pound notes. Wisely, she had refused. At the same time, the police learned that it was Mrs Pokora who had written the transfer in Stanislaw Sykut's name returning ownership of the farm to Onufrejczyc. Furthermore, she had written several letters for Onufrejczyc purporting to come from Sykut – written on the assurance that her uncle would get his partner's signature. Examining these documents later, the South Wales and Monmouthshire Forensic Science Laboratory was able to state categorically that the scrawl at the foot of the pages was not Sykut's signature. Predictably, when confronted with this new evidence, Onufrejczyc flew into one of his violent tempers and branded Mrs Pokora a liar, among other things.

Confident of the case they were building up against farmer Onufrejczyc, the police carried out a further search of Cefn Hendre in collaboration with the Forensic Science Laboratory. This time the investigating team identified more than two thousand tiny dark stains on the walls of the kitchen and hallway, and a large dark stain of a familiar shape on the surface of the kitchen dresser. On one of the plaster-board walls a reversed double impression of Stanislaw Sykut's signature was found, as though the wall had been used as a blotter. Partly covering one of these images was a bloodstain; the implication was clear –

the blood had been splashed on the wall *after* Sykut's arrival at the farm.

Onufrejczyc's reluctant explanation was that he had been killing and cleaning rabbits in the kitchen. A story that was quickly changed when the laboratory identified the stains as being blood of human origin; the mark on the dresser, a bloody handprint. The Pole's subsequent version was that Sykut had cut his hand and shaken the blood from his injury so that it splattered the wall. Improbable though the story was, it was unshakeable.

By 19th August, and not without hesitation, the Director of Public Prosecutions decided that a charge of murder could be brought against Michael Onufrejczyc. After a lengthy hearing in the magistrates court, the prisoner was committed for trial at Glamorgan Assizes.

Dispelling a widely held, and quite erroneous belief that still persists – that a charge of murder cannot be brought without a body – the judge, Mr Justice Oliver, told the jury: 'At the trial of a person charged with murder the fact of death is provable by circumstantial evidence, notwithstanding that neither the body nor any trace of the body has been found, and that the accused has made no confession of any participation in the crime. Before he can be convicted, the fact of death should be proved by such circumstances as render the commission of the crime morally certain and leave no ground for reasonable doubt. The circumstantial evidence should be so cogent and compelling as to convince a jury that upon no rational hypothesis other than murder can the facts be discounted'.

The jury clearly felt that the evidence was both 'cogent' and 'compelling', and within three hours had returned a verdict of guilty. At the time of the trial there was only one sentence that a judge could pass on a person found guilty of murder – the ultimate sentence of Death.

Onufrejczyc, though, was still fighting, and when, on 11th January 1955, his appeal was dismissed by the Court of Criminal Appeal, his solicitors immediately applied for leave to appeal to the House of Lords. The application was, in the end, refused; but on 24th January, Onufrejczyc's sentence was commuted to life imprisonment.

In 1965 the Pole was released from prison, still protesting his innocence, and still apparently determined to prove it. His first action was to return to the Cwmdu area to ask if Stanislaw Sykut had reappeared while he had been away! A year later, Onufrejczyc was killed in a traffic accident in Bradford, and with him the true story of Cefn Hendre was buried for ever.

So what could have happened to Stanislaw Sykut's body? That he was killed is certain; that Michael Onufrejczyc was responsible for his death is equally certain. How, then, did he dispose of the corpse? In his own account of 'The Butcher of Cwmdu', ex-Detective Superintendent David Thomas – himself involved in the case – makes this suggestion:

> 'My own opinion, which I put forward at the time of the investigation and which I still hold to, is that the chopped-up pieces of Sykut's body were probably fed to a herd of ravenous pigs which roamed the farm. It would have been a simple matter for Onufrejczyc to have boiled the parts of the dismembered body with the pigs' mash in the days immediately following December 14, and before Sykut was missed . . . Onufrejczyc always seemed confident the body would never be found. What better confidence did he need than to know his pigs had eaten the evidence.'

> (*Seek Out The Guilty*, 1965)

THE CARDIFF
RACE-TRACK GANG

The Murder of Dai Lewis by members of the Rowlands Gang
On Thursday, 29th September 1927 in St Mary Street, Cardiff, Glamorgan

In any pursuit where it is possible to make a few dishonest pennies, there will be gangsters to make them. Men – for the female of the species is rare – who will use muscle rather than brain to keep a few pounds ahead. Sports have always offered good pickings; gambling on sports even better; horse racing one of the best.

The 1920s, particularly, spawned this sub-culture of race-track gangsters, and as in the twilight world of hoodlums everywhere, the race-course was a jealously guarded territory. At Cardiff, the reigning gang was run by the brothers Rowlands – John, and 'Titch' – his real name was Edward, but probably even he had forgotten. Violent men by nature, even without the 'muscle' with whom they surrounded themselves, the Rowlands brothers would suffer no invasion of their territory without retribution.

Now, on the fringe of any society can be found that character popularly fictionalized as 'the lovable rogue' – a sentiment easier to comprehend with the heart than with the head! Dai Lewis was so described by those who knew him well; Dai Lewis: former athlete, and professional boxer in the welter weight class. Like many boxers of his day, Lewis had become attracted to the less glamorous elements of that rather unglamorous sport, and had turned his bulk and pugilistic skills to the 'defence' of others. More accurately, he was a one-man protection racket. Lewis's trade was to hire out to bookmakers on the course small items like stools, chalk, and buckets of water to clean their boards. Those who availed themselves of this service had insured against 'accidents' which might befall them – such as having their stands tipped over, or worse, being attacked and robbed.

Dai's permanent office was Monmouth race-track, and in this uneasy way of business he may have grubbed along at a leisurely pace, on just the right side both of the law and of his clients.

But in September 1927, Lewis made a grave error of business judgement; an error that would cost him not only his livelihood, but his life. On the 28th of that month, Dai Lewis expanded his activities to Cardiff; to the race-course 'owned' by John and Titch Rowlands.

Even before the meeting was over on that Wednesday afternoon, Lewis had received threats against his life; threats that with his customary braggadocio he had scorned and dismissed. Even so, he took the precaution of avoiding his home in Ethel Street, Cardiff, that night, and booked into a hotel in St Mary Street.

On the following morning, 29th September, Dai Lewis was up early and on his way to Monmouth to offer his 'services' on the track. But his want of etiquette on the previous afternoon had not been forgotten, and when Lewis returned to St Mary Street and The Blue Anchor pub, he found himself drinking in the company of a sizeable number of the Rowlands gang – including John and Titch themselves.

Apparently unconcerned, Dai Lewis continued to drink and make merry until closing time, unaware that several of the Rowlands' cronies had detached themselves from the company and moved across to the cafe opposite The Blue Anchor.

Outside on the pavement, Lewis, befuddled by drink, stood looking about him. What he saw was John Rowlands and a man named William Price coming towards him from the gloom of the ill-lit street, followed by less defined human forms. What he did not see were the men creeping up behind his back. In the most unevenly matched fight of his life, Dai Lewis struck out with powerful, desperate blows; but within seconds he was grounded, and from the melée of arms and legs that struck out at him came the momentary flash of the knife blade that was to rob Dai Lewis of his life. He cried out just once as his assailants scuttled off in all directions; then he was still, blood pouring from a deep gash in his throat.

As the ambulance arrived to rush him to the Cardiff Royal Infirmary, Dai Lewis was still breathing, and with a tenacity born of years in the ring, he clung on to his life. And with a stubbornness born of years on the edge of gangsterdom, he refused absolutely to name his assailants. Neither the police, in the person of Detective Chief Inspector Tom Hodges, nor his wife Annie, could budge his determination to prove that there was 'honour among thieves'.

In another part of the Infirmary, a quick-thinking night-nurse on duty in the reception office was taking a telephone call:

'Call you tell me how Dai Lewis is?'

'Who is speaking, please?'

The only reply was the click of a receiver being replaced.

In the early hours of the morning the same nurse answered the same telephone to hear the same rasping voice:

'Can you tell me how Dai Lewis is?'

'Who is that speaking, please?'

Click.

This time the nurse alerted police officers to the reluctant caller, and arrangements were made with the local telephone exchange to trace any further calls. Another hour passed, and while Dai Lewis's grip on life weakened, the duty nurse was startled for a third time by the insistent ring of the telephone on her desk. On this occasion she managed to keep the unknown voice talking for long enough for the call to be traced to the notorious Colonial Club in Custom House Street. At the same time, officers at police headquarters were receiving a mystery call of their own; a hastily spoken claim that the Rowlands gang was responsible for the attack on Dai Lewis. At the Colonial Club, John and Titch Rowlands, Daniel Driscoll, John Hughes, and William Price were arrested on a charge of attempted murder.

When it became clear that Lewis was unlikely to make it through the day, a final desperate attempt was made to cajole him into giving vital information as to the identity of his assailants. A magistrate and his clerk were summoned to the hospital to take the dying man's deposition; the five accused men stood at the foot of Dai Lewis's bed. After informing him that he was near death, the magistrate's clerk told Lewis: 'These men are accused of attacking you . . . take things very slowly, and say what took place.'

The boxer opened his eyes, and in a faint, hesitant voice began to speak: 'I do not know how I have been injured . . . I do not remember how it happened . . . there was no quarrel or fight. Nobody did any harm to me . . . I did not see anyone use a knife.' Inclining his head in Edward Rowlands' direction, he continued: 'You had nothing to do with it . . . we've been the best of friends.' To Driscoll: 'You had nothing to do with it either; we were talking and laughing together. My dear old pal.'

That Lewis was lying was obvious; that he would never alter his story was as pathetically apparent. Later that day he died.

It was several days after Dai Lewis's funeral that John Rowlands, under interrogation, confessed to his involvement in the violence of the night of 29th September. His story was that it had been Lewis who drew the knife and attacked him first; during a fierce struggle he had wrested the weapon from his opponent's grip, but in the process must have accidentally caused the boxer his fatal injury. And improbable though this account sounded, it was gratefully accepted as direct evidence. Brother Edward and Daniel Driscoll still maintained that they were guiltless onlookers who had made off when they saw Lewis fall to the ground wounded. John Hughes was released for want of reliable evidence, and the remaining four were committed for trial.

The trial opened at the Glamorgan Assizes on 29th November before Mr Justice Wright. The case for the Crown was led by Lord Halsbury, who opened with the words: 'This was murder as cruel and beastly as you could possibly imagine, premeditated, and carried out – I might almost say flaunted – in Cardiff's main street'. His case, however, was weak from the start; such witnesses as came forward gave hopelessly conflicting accounts of the sequence of events, and even the policemen who arrived on the scene of the crime were in clear disagreement.

The trial lasted for three days, ending for the jury with as confused a picture as that with which they had begun. Nevertheless, on Friday 2nd December they returned a verdict of guilty against the Rowlands brothers and Daniel Driscoll, and all three were sentenced to hang. William Price was found not guilty and released from custody.

No sooner had the sentences been passed than public dissatisfaction with the verdicts was mobilised into a solid fighting force. Large sums of money were raised by public subscription to fund an appeal; more than 250,000 signatures were collected demanding a Home Office inquiry, and the case was discussed in the Chamber of the House of Commons. Three doctors who had been present at the post-mortem on Dai Lewis's body claimed that the victim had died not from his wounds, but from a heart attack; and in an unprecedented move, eight members of the trial jury petitioned the Home Secretary, Sir Austen Chamberlain, that: 'Sentence of death should be waived as an act of mercy.'

Legal opinion, however, was not to be swayed by sentimentality – or by suggestions of a miscarriage of justice for that matter – and at the Appeal Court hearing on 11th January 1928, Lord Hewart the Lord Chief Justice, Mr Justice Avory, and Mr Justice Branson, declared that there was no further evidence on which to divert the due process of the law.

On 27th January at 8am, Edward Rowlands and Daniel Driscoll stood on the scaffold at Cardiff Gaol. John Rowlands, who had gone berserk in the van on his way to the Appeal Court, and was later certified insane, had already been confined to Broadmoor.

In his autobiography Detective Superintendent David Thomas added this postscript to the case: 'Lewis's killing was to become known, in later years, as the Hoodoo Murder. Within twelve months John Hughes was dead and one of the prostitutes who had given key evidence committed suicide . . . Price, acquitted at the Assizes, was blinded in one eye with a butcher's hook. A police constable who gave evidence died while still young of tuberculosis; another constable who never ceased saying 'We are all doomed, we sent an innocent man to the scaffold', died in his thirties of a mysterious stomach ailment; a detective-sergeant who investigated the case committed suicide; and another sergeant died, while still relatively young, from cancer. Harold Lloyd, the solicitor who represented Price, was sentenced to five years' penal servitude . . . on charges of converting clients' money to his own use.'

THE MYSTERY OF CEFN GOLAU

The Mysterious Death of Tom Phillips
On Wednesday, 4th March 1959 near his home
in Tredegar, Gwent

F arming the inhospitable land of the Welsh mountains is a precarious occupation, and it requires a hardy breed of men to make a living from the harsh, uncompromising landscape in the often uncertain weather of the uplands. Such a family were the Phillipses, headed by 30-year-old David and his 25-year-old brother Tom.

The weather on the night of 4th March 1959 was as wild as any that the Phillips family could remember, the lightning storm and torrential rain had lashed the hillsides for hours, and from the comfort of their home at Half Way House, Tredegar, the two brothers' thoughts returned constantly to the fate of their livestock, the hundreds of sheep and scores of valuable Welsh ponies that would be huddling to what small shelter they could find on the weather-beaten mountain side of Cefn Golau.

As darkness fell, Tom Phillips walked to the window of the farmhouse and took stock of the bleak aspect outside. Characteristically, Tom made his decision with the best interests of the farm foremost in his mind: 'I think I'll go out and bring in some of the ponies. The storm looks like getting worse; they'll be safer nearer the house.' Without another word Tom Phillips wrapped his powerful frame in an old raincoat and set his steps against the darkness.

It was several hours before David Phillips began to get anxious; on a night like this rounding up the half-wild hill ponies was going to be no light work. But there were other considerations playing on David's mind: the perilous outcrops of rock made slippery with the downpour, the deep crevices and cracks that scarred the boulder strewn slopes; Tom must have had an accident. With this awful premonition, David Phillips and another brother were soon facing the gale, soaked before they left the farm gates, calling Tom's name only to have their voices lost in the howling of the wind.

Not far from the house, in the hesitant light of their hurricane lamp, the two brothers saw a group of ponies taking what shelter they could from a clump of sparse trees. It was obvious from their position that the ponies had not been driven there under Tom's command, he would have known that there was safer shelter nearer the house; and if the beasts had wandered down from the mountainside on their own, then where was Tom Phillips? Tormented by the elements, defied by the darkness, the brothers returned to the farmhouse, hardly daring to hope that they would find Tom sitting drying before the fire. And for the rest of the night the family sat, their eyes fastened on the door, waiting, willing the latch to lift.

By morning there was still no sign of Tom, and after reporting the disappearance at the Tredegar police station, David Phillips organized a party to search every foot of the mountain top around Cefn Golau. Eventually the police brought up dogs to try to trace the missing man's scent; but at the end of the day Tom Phillips was still a missing person.

Taking the matter increasingly seriously, Divisional Superintendent Leonard James widened the search across the valley and down to the reservoir, which was systematically dragged – still without solving the enigma of Tom Phillips's disappearance. The discovery near the water's edge of the corduroy hat in which Tom took his last walk, put some impetus back into the search, and the banks of the reservoir were patrolled daily in the expectation that the waters would yield up Tom's body. After four weeks it looked as if the file on this missing person was to remain open.

And then on 19th April, a young man out for a stroll noticed a bulky shape at the edge of the reservoir. Tom

Phillips was missing no longer; he was dead. The body's ankles had been bound with rope, and the wrists with a polka-dot neckerchief. Local gossip was fanned into a new blaze when David Phillips stated categorically that the neckerchief had not belonged to his brother, and the word 'murder' was in every mind if not on every lip.

The police, however, could not afford to jump to so hasty a conclusion; a conclusion that would simply have exchanged an unsolved disappearance for an unsolved homicide. There were other possibilities, and however irrational it may seem in retrospect, the police opted for Tom Phillips committing suicide. True, it was demonstrated by officers at the inquest that it was physically *possible* for a man to tie himself up in such a way as that in which the body had been found and then to hop to the edge of the water and throw himself in. But was it likely? In his evidence to the coroner's court, David Phillips – convinced that murder had been committed – stated that his brother was a very 'jolly' person, poetically describing his frame of mind on the night of his disappearance as 'happy as a bird in springtime'. And would even a suicidal man walk several miles from his home in one of the worst storms of the year, go through the elaborate charade of tying himself up just to jump into the reservoir? There were, after all, plenty of other deep ponds much nearer home. And then, where did the spotted neckerchief come from, and the rope that tied his legs and which the Phillips family had never seen about the farm? Was it credible that Tom's body had been under water for five weeks without having being weighted down? One would normally expect the build-up of gasses generated by putrefaction to re-float the body inside ten days.

Despite these weighty doubts, the coroner, Lieutenant-Colonel K.D. Treasure, decided that the only verdict that was worthy of consideration was one of 'suicide during a period of mental depression'. But there are many people, including some in authority, who feel that the possibility of foul play should not have been dismissed in quite such a cavalier fashion.

NORTH-EAST ENGLAND

Cleveland

Durham

Humberside

Northumberland

North Yorkshire

South Yorkshire

Tyne and Wear

West Yorkshire

THE WEST AUCKLAND POISONING

The Murder of Charles Edward Cotton by his stepmother Mary Ann Cotton
In the month of July 1872 at their home in Johnson Terrace, West Auckland, Durham

Mary Ann Robson first saw the light of day in 1832, in the pit village of East Rainton, a little north of Durham. Her father, a miner, and her mother were both devout Wesleyan Methodists, and it was in this creed that the young Mary was raised. She was not fated to become one of its proudest daughters.

At the age of 20, Mary Robson became Mrs William Mowbray; Mowbray, like Mary's father, was a miner. After a couple of years based in Newcastle-upon-Tyne, the couple moved south to Cornwall, where William Mowbray followed the calling of a navvy, and Mary Ann devoted herself to producing children. Of these, four sons died in infancy, victims, it was recorded, of 'gastric fever' – a not uncommon cause of sickness and death in an unsanitary age. The remaining Mowbrays returned to Durham, where, in a short time, the fifth child, a girl, succumbed to the same 'gastric fever'. Four months later William Mowbray died unexpectedly of diarrhoea – just weeks after taking out a sizeable insurance on his life; Mowbray's hearse was quickly followed by that of another of his children, a victim of 'gastric fever'.

Putting sorrow behind her, Mary started afresh at Seaham with a new husband, George Ward. Was it just bad luck that George should die fourteen months later of 'gastric fever'? Within weeks, Mary Robson (or Mowbray, or

Ward – she made free use of whichever name suited the occasion) answered a newspaper advertisement for a housekeeper to John Robinson, a widowed shipwright, and his five children.

The scope of Mary's duties in the Robinson household was clearly very broad, and an unexpected pregnancy necessitated changing her name yet again – to Mary Ann Robinson.

Tragedy, though, seemed still to dog this unfortunate woman. Already one of the Robinson children had contracted a fatal dose of 'gastric fever' just after Mary Ann's appointment. In 1867 three more children died – on 21st April John Robinson's 6-year-old-son passed over; followed by his daughter Elizabeth, aged 8, on the 26th of the same month. On 2nd May, Mary's daughter by Mowbray, Isabella, 9 years old, joined her father and brothers.

John Robinson, it must be said, was lucky. On previous record, he, too, might have lost his life; as it was, Mary Ann simply helped herself to his savings and fled to Spennymoor. It was in this place that she was sacked from her position as housekeeper to a doctor on grounds of incompetence; the doctor survived this brief encounter.

The next move was to Walbottle, and it was here that Mary met Mr Frederick Cotton and his sister Margaret. When, some months into this new friendship, Mary was once again expecting a child she married Cotton (bigamously, for John Robinson was still alive) at St Andrew's church, Newcastle. She now had the name which, within the decade, was to become notorious – Mary Ann Cotton.

Not surprisingly, the angel of death that seems to have followed Mrs Cotton for most of her adult life, did not relinquish its hold. Margaret Cotton went down with 'gastric fever' and died shortly before her brother's wedding. She had thoughtfully left her savings to Frederick and Mary.

But poor Margaret was not the only one of God's creatures to have their light snuffed out in their prime; a significant number of pigs belonging to Mary Ann's neighbours mysteriously began to die.

Perhaps it was because livestock was valued above human life that those uncharitable neighbours began to point an accusing finger in the direction of the Cotton household; and in Mary's direction in particular. Such was the acrimony over the deceased pigs that the Cottons – Frederick, Mary Ann, two offspring of Cotton's earlier marriage, and Mary's baby – found it expedient to decamp to a house in Johnson Terrace, West Auckland.

Here, the family rapidly decreased in number; Frederick was the first loss, on 9th September 1871. He was followed into the grave by Mary's 10-year-old stepson Frederick on 10th March 1872, and her 14-month-old baby Robert on 27th March. Joseph Nattrass, a lodger who had been imprudent enough to become Mrs Cotton's lover, and unwise enough to make a will in her favour, became the fourth victim of 'gastric fever' on 1st April.

This left only little Charles Edward, a stepson, who had survived the 'illnesses' to attain his 7th birthday. He was never to see his 8th. In the light of the previous four deaths, Mary Ann's observation to her neighbours that Charles Edward would soon be joining his brother in the local cemetery was unwise; not least because he did, on 12th July 1872.

Mary Ann was arrested when a post-mortem on the body of the latest victim of 'gastric fever' revealed abnormal traces of arsenic. Exhumation was ordered for the four previous victims, and examination by Dr Thomas Scattergood, lecturer in forensic medicine and toxicology at Leeds Medical School, proved that they too had met their end through arsenical poisoning.

Nevertheless, it was for Charles Edward's murder only that Mary Ann Cotton was tried at the Durham Assizes. It was on the morning of Wednesday, 5th March 1873, that Sir Charles Russell, QC, (later to be appointed Lord Chief Justice) rose to address the court on behalf of the Crown. Mary Ann's defence, advanced on her behalf by Mr Thomas Campbell Foster, was that her stepson had been accidentally poisoned by some wallpaper in his bedroom, the green pigment of which was derived from arsenic. And it is a defence that stood at least a chance of succeeding had not evidence of the four previous poisonings been deemed admissible in order to refute the proposition of accidental death.

At 5.30pm on the third day of the trial, the jury retired to consider their verdict. It was barely an hour before that decision had been reached and the judge, from beneath the black cap, had intoned the sentence of death.

Mary Ann Cotton died on the scaffold at Durham County Gaol at 8am on Monday 24th March 1873. Already her infamy was assured; already the children in the streets had immortalized her name in rhyme.

> *Mary Ann Cotton*
> *She's dead and she's rotten*
> *She lies in her bed*
> *With her eyes wide oppen.*
> *Sing, sing, oh, what can I sing?*
> *Mary Ann Cotton is tied up wi' string.*
> *Where, where? Up in the air*
> *Sellin' black puddens a penny a pair.*

EVERY TIME LUCKY

The Killing of Mrs Tyler, Mrs Spencer, and Mrs Brookes by William Burkitt In 1915, 1925, and 1939 respectively at various addresses in Hull, Humberside

---

For most of us, life is based upon a comfortable expectancy that luck will be fairly evenly distributed throughout our natural span; sometimes good luck, sometimes bad luck, with an optimistic anticipation that in times of need – times when it really counts – the spirits will smile benignly.

That even murderers share these blessings is amply displayed by the story of William Burkitt. That he did not deserve his good luck is an irrelevance – it was always there when he needed it. Or almost always.

In outline, Burkitt's fortunes ran like this. An unlucky start on account of being born with a gene that inclined him to kill people; on the other hand lucky because on each of the three occasions when he was unlucky enough to get caught, he was tried in a British court in front of a British jury. When he finally made a little bit of legal history it proved, for Burkitt anyway, to be very unlucky.

William Burkitt was a fisherman out of Hull, and whatever his undiscovered misdeeds, he was not singled out by the eagle eye of Justice until 1915, the year in which he appeared before the York Assizes charged with murdering a Mrs Tyler, his mistress. Burkitt had stabbed the unfortunate woman several times in the throat, and was now on trial for his life. If only the guardian angel with the unenviable job of looking after William Burkitt had averted his eyes for an instant, things might have turned out better all round. As it was, Burkitt was as lucky as his victim was short of it; a sympathetic jury reduced the conviction to manslaughter, and Burkitt was given twelve years.

With a few years remission William Burkitt was back on the streets by 1924. Now he set up home with Mrs Ellen Spencer, who had left Mr Spencer for Burkitt, presumably to effect some kind of change in her fortunes. Although she didn't know it, her luck was running out very fast; within a year, Mrs Spencer had joined Mrs Tyler, and William Burkitt was back in the dock at York.

Helped by the unfailing fairness of the British legal system in not allowing a prisoner's previous record to be made known to the jury, Burkitt enjoyed every consideration of the law, and once again had his murder charge reduced to manslaughter; and the hangman's rope exchanged for a 10-year stretch.

Burkitt was released from prison in August 1935, and during the next three and a half years enjoyed the comforts of Mrs Emma Brookes. In the early hours of Wednesday, 1st March 1939, Burkitt succeeded in terrifying his sister by presenting himself on her doorstep, foaming at the mouth, and claiming to have swallowed 600 aspirins. Either he had miscounted, or his personal genie was working overtime, because Burkitt was still active enough by the afternoon to hurl himself into the waters of the River Humber, from whence he was dragged, protesting, to Hull Infirmary.

Such behaviour cannot long escape the notice of the police, and by the time Burkitt had been tucked into a hospital bed, officers had broken into his home and discovered Mrs Brookes – she had been stabbed to death!

In May 1939, William Burkitt stood before the bench of Leeds Assizes facing his third charge of murder. Unbelievably, the jury reduced the charge to manslaughter.

It was quite apparent that the judge, Mr Justice Cassels, who in his days at the Bar had come across more than a few notorious murderers and who knew a rogue when he saw one, was not prepared to exercise such clemency. Besides, he was privy to the information from which the jury had been so carefully shielded. Passing sentence on

Burkitt, Mr Justice Cassels gave muted voice to his misgivings over the verdict when he told the prisoner: 'They did not know what you know and what I knew, and what they were not allowed to know – that this was the third time you have stood in the dock on a charge of murder. Each time it has been the murder of a woman with whom you had been living. Each time the jury have taken a merciful view . . . I can see in your case not one redeeming feature. You will be kept in penal servitude for the rest of your natural life.'

By the time William Burkitt had served some 9 years of his sentence, the new Criminal Justice Bill had wound its weary way through Commons and Lords, and had been made an Act of Parliament by Royal Assent on 30th July 1948.

Among the numerous reforms to existing criminal law, the Act provided for the abolition of 'penal servitude'*, a development which was not lost on the captive William Burkitt. Clearly believing in the continuance of his own good luck, Burkitt made application to appear before the Court of Criminal Appeal. And so it came about that a three-times killer appealed against his current sentence on the unique grounds that he was suffering a punishment (penal servitude) which had become 'illegal'.

In fact, the Act had simply put onto the statute what was the prevailing prison practice – to make no practical distinction between the offenders sentenced to penal servitude and those sentenced to ordinary imprisonment.

In dismissing Burkitt's somewhat frivolous appeal, Lord Goddard, the Lord Chief Justice, commented: 'There was nothing at all in Burkitt's contention that he had been sentenced to a term that was illegal.'

Burkitt, meanwhile, remained where he rightly belonged – behind bars. Fate, perhaps, had decided that William Burkitt had already enjoyed more than his fair share of good luck.

---

* The Act also, incidentally, suspended the death penalty for five years, though public outcry eventually forced the clause to be deleted and capital punishment to be restored.

THE ROOT OF ALL EVIL

**The Murder of Oliver Leonard and Ernest
Wilson by Mary Elizabeth Wilson
During 1957 at Felling-on-Tyne, Tyne and Wear**

There was hardly a good thing anybody could say about
Mrs Wilson; perhaps it was because she inflicted the
excruciatingly painful death of phosphorus poisoning
upon her husband, and was discovered to have disposed
of a lover and two earlier husbands as well.

At the time of her trial, Mary Wilson was 66 years old,
arrogant and grasping.

Mary's first husband had been John Knowles, a
labourer. Displaying an early greed for just about everything, Mrs Knowles took John George Russell, a chimney
sweep who lodged with them at Windy Nook, as a lover.
By 1957 both were dead, both certified as the victims of
'natural causes'; both leaving their worldly goods to Mary
– a total of £46!

During the summer of 1957, Mary met Oliver James
Leonard; she was 64 at the time, and he was 75, a retired
estate agent. As with her previous 'attachments', it was
money to which Mrs Wilson was attracted, a fact she made
no secret of when enquiring of Leonard's landlady: 'Has
the old bugger any money?' Apparently he had. In a trice
she was Mrs Leonard, the marriage being solemnized in
September 1957 at Jarrow Register Office. Thirteen days
after the wedding Mrs Russell, a neighbour, was called in
during the night and found Leonard in such a poor state
that she felt constrained to observe that she feared he

might be dying. 'I think so too,' Mrs Wilson replied, 'I've called you because you will be handy if he does.' By the following morning Oliver Leonard was, indeed, dead; and after a cursory examination the doctor accounted for his sudden demise as due to myocardial degeneration and chronic nephritis. His wife had bettered her lot by £50.

The next death to occur by Mrs Wilson's hand was that of her namesake, Ernest Wilson. Like Oliver Leonard, Wilson had also reached his 75th year; like Leonard, he was not fated to reach his 76th. Mrs Wilson saw the immediate advantage of marriage when Ernest confided that in addition to being provident enough to have a fully paid up insurance policy on his life, he also had £100 invested with the Co-op. No sooner had Mary moved into the rather squalid bungalow which Wilson rented from the council, than the old man suddenly died – of what the doctors described as 'cardiac muscular failure'.

It was only now that Mrs Wilson's 'jokes' – in poor taste even at the time – began to show in a decidedly sinister light. She had, for example, joshed with the undertaker that she had put so much business his way that she should be entitled to 'trade rates'. At the modest reception after her marriage to Wilson, Mary had told the caterer: 'Save the leftover cakes – they will come in handy for the funeral,' adding later: 'Better not save them, I might give him a bit longer to live.'

Little surprise, then, that Mary Wilson came to the attention of the police; no surprise that the bodies of Messrs Leonard and Wilson were exhumed for post-mortem examination.

The conclusion reached by pathologists Dr William Stewart and Dr David Price was that both men had died of phosphorus poisoning.

Mary Wilson was defended at her trial by Miss Rose Heilbron QC, who pointed out to the court that at the time phosphorus poisoning was relatively little known to forensic toxicology – and the fact that the rate of oxidization of phosphorus was then unknown, there was no reliable method of assessing how much of the poison had been ingested. It was advanced that both victims had been taking sex-stimulant pills, one of whose ingredients was phosphorus. Miss Heilbron had also been wise enough to secure for the defence an expert medical witness, Dr Francis Camps, later to become one of Britain's foremost forensic pathologists. While Camps had not personally examined the two bodies in question, he was familiar with several instances of phosphorus poisoning, and stated that, in his opinion, this was not necessarily the direct cause of death in the cases of Leonard and Wilson.

Mary Wilson did not give evidence on her own behalf, which prompted Mr Justice Hinchcliffe to remark, rightly or wrongly: 'Has she helped us all she could?' Found guilty as charged, Mrs Wilson was sentenced to death, though in the event her advanced years earned her the clemency she had no right to expect. She served 4½ years of a life sentence, then died in Holloway Prison, aged 70.

It only remains to add that when the bodies of John Knowles and John George Russell were exhumed for pathological examination, they were found to contain appreciable traces of phosphorus.

THE NEWCASTLE TRAIN MURDER

The Murder of John Innes Nisbet by John Alexander Dickman
On Friday, 18th March 1910 aboard a train between Stannington and Morpeth, Northumberland

---

The train leaving platform 5 at Newcastle on Friday, 18th March, 1910, was the 10.27am stopping train to Alnmouth, a journey of a little less than 35 miles, and was due to arrive at its destination at 12.08pm.

Among the passengers on that train was John Innes Nisbet, a clerk for twenty-eight years with the Stobswood Colliery Company, and whose job it was, on alternate Fridays, to deliver wages to the mine near Widdington. He carried the money – £370 9s 6d in gold, silver and copper – in small canvas bags which in turn were locked into a small black leather bag. Nisbet, contrary to his regular routine sat in the front of the train's three carriages, next to the engine.

The next carriage was occupied by two young men named Spink and Hall – cashiers as it happened, and on the same errand as Nisbet, delivering wages to their respective collieries. Just before the train set off on its journey, Hall looked out of the window and saw Nisbet, whom he knew by sight, get into the front carriage in the company of a man with whom he seemed acquainted.

Heaton was the second station along the Newcastle-Alnmouth route, and it was also where John Nisbet and his wife lived – at 180 Heaton Road. It was an affectionate habit on these fortnightly trips for Annie Nisbet to walk to the station and greet her husband as his train passed through. This she did on 18th March, later recalling that in the shadows cast by the tunnel under which the train had come to a stop, she had seen a man in a light overcoat sitting on the opposite side of the compartment to her husband.

At Stannington station, Messrs Spink and Hall left the train, and in passing, gave a friendly nod to Nisbet. They, too, were vaguely aware of another person sharing his compartment.

Beyond Stannington is Morpeth; about two-and-a-half miles beyond. Here a man in a light overcoat left the train and handed the ticket collector an outward half of a return ticket from Newcastle to Stannington, plus tuppence-halfpenny, the excess fare. A passenger boarding the train at Morpeth noticed that the first compartment – that occupied by Nisbet and another – was empty.

It was when William Charlton, foreman porter at Aln-mouth station, made a brief inspection of the train before it left on the return journey, that the 10.27 from Newcastle became more than just another routine suburban run.

Opening the doors of the first carriage behind the engine, Charlton was confronted with three streams of blood oozing from beneath the seat where, pushed under as far as it would go, was a body. A soft felt hat on the floor of the compartment identified the unfortunate man as Mr John Nisbet.

The post-mortem examination of Nisbet's body showed that he had been shot no less than five times in the head; forensic investigation of the bullets posed a puzzle; of the two projectiles that were recovered from Nisbet's head, one was a common lead bullet, the other was nickel capped. Furthermore, each was of a different calibre – .320 and .250, respectively.*

As soon as they were informed of the tragedy, Nisbet's

---

* The truth of the matter was more curious still. The killer had in fact used only one gun, and had attempted to make the smaller bullet fit the barrel by wrapping a strip of paper around it; one of these pieces of paper had been found in the carriage, though at the time its purpose was not realized. It must be added that no gun was ever found in John Dickman's possession, and indeed the murder weapon has never been found.

employers felt inclined to offer a substantial cash reward for information leading to the arrest of his killer. A description was given, and the hunt was on for the man in the light overcoat.

£100 REWARD MURDER

Whereas on the 18th of March, 1910, John Innes Nisbet, a clerk or cashier, late of 180 Heaton Road, Newcastle, was murdered in a third-class carriage on the North-Eastern Railway between Newcastle and Alnmouth, and a black leather bag containing £370 9s 6d in money (mostly gold and silver), which was in charge of the deceased man, was stolen.

A man of the following description was seen in the same carriage as the deceased at Newcastle and Stannington railway stations, and appeared to be on friendly terms with the deceased:- About 35 to 40 years of age, about 5 ft 6 in. high, about 11 stones in weight, medium build; heavy, dark moustache, pale or sallow complexion; wore a light overcoat, down to his knees; black, hard, felt hat; well dressed and appeared to be fairly well to do.

The above reward will be paid by the owners of the Stobswood Colliery, near Widdington, to any person (other than a person belonging to the police force in the United Kingdom), not being the actual murderer, who shall be the first to give such information and shall give such evidence as shall lead to the discovery and the conviction of the murderer or muderers.

The result of this notice and other pieces of official investigation was an interview with one John Alexander Dickman, who had been identified by several persons acquainted with both men as Nisbet's companion on his last earthly journey.

Dickman had until comparatively recently been employed in the position of secretary to a mining syndicate, but since that syndicate had disbanded he derived the greater part of his slender income from gambling on horses and acting 'on commission' to various bookmakers

– a less mobile version of what used to be known as 'bookies' runners'. On the day in question, however, Dickman claimed he had been on his way to see a man named William Hogg, manager of the Dovecot Colliery, on mining business.

With a coolness that he maintained throughout the investigation and his subsequent trial, John Dickman freely admitted that he and Nisbet had a passing acquaintance, and that he had travelled on the same train as the deceased after having exchanged pleasantries at the booking office. However, he was emphatic that he had not travelled in the same compartment of the train – on the contrary, Dickman claimed, he had travelled in the rear carriage.

Dickman then made a voluntary statement to Superintendent Weddell covering his actions subsequent to boarding the train. His journey had been to Stannington, where he should have alighted to visit the man Hogg at Dovecot Colliery. Unfortunately he had been preoccupied with the racing pages of his newspaper, and passed through his destination without noticing. When he got off at Morpeth he had handed in his ticket and paid the excess fare of tuppence-halfpenny. The day being fine, if chilly, Dickman had it in his mind to walk the couple of miles back to Stannington, but after being taken ill on the way, and having to rest a while in a field, he returned to Morpeth intending to catch the 1.12pm express back to Newcastle. As it happened, he missed the train by a few minutes and was obliged to wait around town for the 1.40pm. The truth of this was later confirmed by a man with whom Dickman had a conversation in Morpeth.

Far from entirely happy with the story, detectives made a search of the Dickman house at 1 Lily Avenue, Jesmond, and removed a number of items that were to have some influential bearing on John Dickman's trial – among them a number of financial documents and a pair of trousers and a pair of suede gloves bearing stains which were later shown to be mammal blood – though Dr Boland, who gave expert medical evidence at the trial, declined to conclude that it was human.

On 9th June, a seminal discovery was made by Mr Peter

Spooner, a manager at the Hepcott Colliery. On a routine inspection of an air-shaft at Isabella pit (see map), Spooner had found the leather bag in which John Nisbet had been transporting money on the day of his murder. The bag had been cut open, and the contents removed (but for a few copper coins) before being pushed through the iron grille that covered the air-shaft. The suspicion that robbery had been the motive for the killing now became a certainty.

Meanwhile, police officers were piecing together the sorry story of John Dickman's finances up to the events of 18th March. Bank books found at his home revealed that Dickman had two accounts – one with Lloyd's, which had been closed, and another with the National Provident Bank. Further investigation uncovered the fact that in October 1909 Dickman had borrowed £20 from the Cash Accommodation and Investment Company, and although he had been assiduous in paying the interest on the loan, he was still unable to repay the principal at the beginning of March 1910. On 14th February 1910, Dickman pawned some modest items of jewellery to Cush and Company, of Newcastle, receiving £5. A further indication of the dire straits in which the Dickmans found themselves during the first quarter of 1910 is revealed in a letter from Mrs Dickman to her husband while he was away on 'business':

'Dear Jack,

I received your card, and am sorry that you have no money to send. I am needing it very badly. The weather here is past description. I had to get in a load of coals, which consumed the greater part of a sovereign. The final notice for rates has come in – in fact, came in last week – which means they must be paid next Thursday. Also Harry's school account. With my dividend due this week and what is in the Post Office I dare say I can pay the most pressing things, but it is going to make the question of living a poser, unless you can give me some advice as to what to do . . . Trusting to hear from you soon regarding what you think I had best do.

I am, yours faithfully,
Annie Dickman'

In evidence at his trial, Dickman made strong protestation that he was not short of money, but in the face of clear contrary evidence, it probably harmed his case far more than admitting the truth. It is interesting, however, to note that when John Dickman was arrested on 21st March, he had only £17 9s 11d. The proceeds of the robbery, the £370 which cost John Nisbet his life, were never found, and certainly never associated with Dickman.

The trial of John Alexander Dickman opened before Mr Justice Coleridge at the Newcastle Summer Assizes during the first week of July 1910. On his way to the court on the first day, Monday the 4th, Dickman was mobbed by hostile crowds – indicative of the atmosphere of hysterical hatred (largely generated, it must be said, by the Press) in which he was supposed to receive an 'impartial hearing'.

With alarming predictability, the circumstantial evidence led the jury to a verdict of guilty. Mr Justice Coleridge, in sentencing Dickman, was brief: 'Prisoner at the bar, the patient, careful trial is now ended, the irrevocable decision has now been given. The jury have found you guilty of murder. In your hungry lust for gold you had no pity upon the victim whom you slew, and it is only just that the nemesis of the law should overtake the author of the crime. The scales of justice are now balanced by the verdict which your fellows have pronounced. The punishment is death.'

If the outcome of the trial had been predictable, the reaction of the general public to that verdict was little less than astounding. With that innate sense of fair-play that is characteristic of the British personality, the crowds that only four weeks previously had been baying for Dickman's blood, were now demonstrating in the streets for his reprieve. Placards proclaimed: 'Dickman is the Victim of Circumstantial Evidence', 'Stop the Hanging!' Thousands of signatures were put to a petition to the Home Secretary to commute the sentence; individual letters and telegrams made the same demand. On the day before John Dickman's execution, 'reprieve fever' had hit the capital as well; London was flooded with leaflets, left in bars,

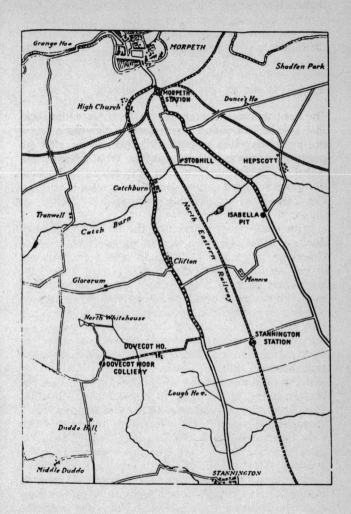

Locations in the Newcastle train murder

restaurants, shops, and handed out in the streets by demonstrators:

> 'Must Dickman be Hanged Tomorrow?
> NO! NO! NO!
> Wire Home Secretary at once
> and Wash Your Hands of
> Complicity in the
> LEGAL CRIME'

The campaign was without success. John Alexander Dickman was hanged within the precincts of Newcastle Prison on Wednesday 10th August 1910. But was he, after all, guilty? The answer is, quite probably. What is less certain is that the Crown proved its case – beyond any reasonable doubt.

THE MYSTERY OF THE BURNED-OUT CAR

The Murder of Evelyn Foster by an Unknown Assailant
On Tuesday, 6th January 1931 at Wolf's Neck, near Otterburn, Northumberland

---

It was at about 9.30 on the night of 6th January 1931, that Mr Johnson pulled his bus sharply in to the side of the road, his attention attracted by what looked like a car on fire about seventy yards on to the moor that abutted the Otterburn/Newcastle thoroughfare. Johnson and his conductor went to investigate, and found to their astonishment that the vehicle was a hire-car belonging to the same transport company that they themselves worked for, and for whom they were now driving the last bus back from Newcastle; the fire had all but subsided, leaving only the back wheel burning. At first the men thought that the car was abandoned, but got the shock of their lives when they saw a girl lying face downwards on the ground some yards from the vehicle, and seemingly licking the frost which covered the rough grass. Their horror was the greater to discover on closer examination that the girl was Evelyn Foster, the 27-year-old daughter of their employer. Wrapping Evelyn's terribly burned body in his overcoat, Johnson drove her home to Otterburn at speed. On the way she kept repeating over and over, as in a delirium: 'Oh that awful man. He has gone in a motorcar. Oh that awful man . . .'

Once home, and between intermittent lapses of consciousness, Evelyn Foster told the story which was to puzzle generations. She was an accomplished driver, and frequently handled the hire-car side of the business at her father's garage. On the previous day she had carried three passengers to Rochester, and on the return journey, at Elishaw, a man approached her and said he had missed a bus and wanted to go to Ponteland to meet a connection to Newcastle. Evelyn arranged to pick up her fare at The Percy Arms Hotel, but when she got there he was nowhere to be found. A few minutes later, at about 7.30pm, Evelyn caught sight of the man, stopped, and then at his request started to drive him to Newcastle. They had got as far as Belsay when Evelyn's passenger ordered her to stop, turn round, and drive back. Not surprisingly she asked why, and was answered with a vicious punch in the eye. After a short distance the man began to wrestle Evelyn for control of the steering wheel, eventually succeeding and driving them back along the road to Otterburn, to an isolated spot called 'Wolf's Neck', where he drove the car off the road, down a steep bank, and across the moor for a distance of about 200 feet. The man then got out of the car and seemed to pull something from his pocket which he set light to; there followed a burst of flame and a small explosion. Evelyn Foster, still in the car, and choking with the fumes, struggled to get out of the car which was obviously on fire. After what seemed an age, she managed to open the door and crawl out. As she did so she was aware of her attacker walking back towards the road, saw a car come along the road, and the man get into it. She remembered feeling terribly thirsty and licking at the icy puddles in the grass; then everything was a blur until Mr Johnson arrived.

Having told her story, Evelyn cried out: 'I have been murdered!' and shortly afterwards she died.

As soon as the police were alerted to the incident they put out a warning that there was a dangerous lunatic at large; it was assumed that they were dealing with a madman because Miss Foster's handbag was intact – still containing 30 shillings in cash – and there was no evidence of sexual interference, thus depriving the attack of any rational motive.

Resulting from information pieced together from Evelyn Foster's story, a description was circulated of the man who had tried to kill her: Aged about twenty-five, 5ft 6in tall, clean-shaven, and wearing a dark tweed suit, bowler hat, and overcoat. The man seemed quite well educated, and spoke with a Tyneside accent.

He was never found.

The coroner's inquest into the death of Evelyn Foster opened on Thursday 8th January at the Ottershaw Memorial Hall, where the jury heard evidence from Evelyn's mother, her father, and from the police. After an adjournment of several weeks, the inquest re-opened on 5th February.

Professor Stuart McDonald, pathologist, at Durham University gave evidence of the post-mortem carried out on Evelyn's body:

> 'The features were obscured by burns, but there appeared to be discoloration about the root of the nose. Extensive burns were distributed about various parts of the body. No external marks suggesting injury apart from the burns were found on any other part of the body. An internal examination showed no injuries except severe burning. From these appearances we [the post-mortem was carried out with the assistance of Dr McEachran] are of the opinion that the cause of death was shock, the result of severe external burning. The distribution of the burns and their severity suggest that certain portions of the clothing had contained some inflammable substance. The distribution of the burned areas suggests that Miss Foster was sitting during some period of the burning. The situation of other burns indicates that there had been splashes of an inflammable liquid.'

Professor McDonald then stated that, contrary to Evelyn Foster's claim that she had been punched, there was no evidence of bruising to the face.

At this point the coroner, Mr P.M. Dodds, put a question to the witness that was to raise a most controversial doubt:

> 'Assuming the car was where you saw it, and she threw some petrol into the back of the car and set fire

> to it, with her left leg probably on the running board and her right on the edge of the step, could the flames have come back and blinded her?'

'I think it quite possible,' replied the Professor.

Here, then, was a clear suggestion that Evelyn Foster might not have been telling the truth about her 'attack'; indeed, that for reasons best known to herself, she had set fire to the car.

In summing up the evidence to the jury, the coroner pointed out that there were two fundamental points to consider:

> 'Was the girl murdered or did she set fire to the car and in doing so obtain the burns accidentally? If it was a case of murder, then the man must have been a homicidal maniac.
>
> If the girl has done it herself you must consider what her object might have been. Was her object to obtain money through the insurance on the car?
>
> There were two policies, one for £450, covering the car in a garage only, and another one covering cars up to 30 horse-power in the sum of £700.
>
> On the other hand, there are cases of persons obsessed with the idea of notoriety. That might be a factor in this case.'

When the jury returned after considering the case in retirement, the verdict that they delivered was that Evelyn had been murdered 'by some person or persons unknown' – that Miss Foster had been deliberately set alight by an assailant.

The verdict seems to have come as something of a relief to all concerned; only Mr Foster, Evelyn's father, was dissatisfied, and in a strongly-worded complaint to the Home Secretary, made it clear that he resented even the suggestion that his daughter might have set fire to the car herself.

And there the mystery remains, as unlikely to be solved now as it was sixty years ago.

THE HAND OF GLORY

A Sinister Murder Associated with the Gruesome Artefact late of Danby, Yorkshire

---

Safely encased in glass in a room of the Whitby Museum is a dried up mass of a thing which resembles nothing so much as a shrivelled human hand. And that is exactly what it is – a dead hand.

The Danby Hand of Glory, so named because it was once in the possession of an antiquarian of Danby-in-Cleveland, is a relic of an unknown death in that dark realm where murder and Black Magic meet.

This object – the Hand of Glory – has its ancestry far back in the sorcery of the Middle Ages, when the hand of a gibbeted corpse, cut off, pickled and dried, was credited with miraculous powers. The Jesuit demonologist Martin Antoine Del Rio related how thieves would light the fingers of the hand of glory to put to sleep the inhabitants of the dwelling they planned to rob and murder (*Disquisitionum Magicarum*, Louvain, 1599). It was this attribute, above all others, that survived into the comparatively recent past (having first been recorded by Petrus Mamoris in the 15th century). The Danby Hand itself was last used in this manner, so it is said, in 1820.

In an earlier local variant of the tale, a traveller wearing women's clothing came seeking lodgings for the night at the Old Spital Inn at Stainmore one night in 1790. Having forewarned her hosts of an early start next morning, the traveller retired to a corner bench next to the fire. The landlady obligingly stationed a servant girl in the kitchen

to be on hand and make sure their guest woke in time and was well breakfasted before taking to the road. While she attended to the guest's bedding the perceptive servant noticed that she was wearing men's boots beneath her skirts, and when she went to her own bed, lay watchful whilst pretending to sleep. When all the lights were out, and the inn was silent, the bogus female crept from his bed and drew from his pocket a hand of glory, and lit a candle that was clenched between the dead fingers, chanting:

> *'Let those who rest more deeply sleep,*
> *Let those awake their vigils keep [ie the burglars],*
> *Oh Hand of Glory, cast thy light,*
> *And guide us to our spoils tonight.'*

The Hand of Glory, from an ancient French textbook on magic

THE HAND OF GLORY
A Recipe

The following extract is translated from the 16th-century Latin work *Libellus de Mirabilibus Naturae Arcanis* by Alberto Parvi Lucii, and is the most complete early record of the use of the Hand of Glory:

The Hand of Glory is used to stupefy all those to whom it is shown – rendering them incapable of movement, as though they were dead.

It is prepared thus –

Cut the hand from a felon who has been hanged from a gibbet and wrap it in a scrap of funeral pall. Squeeze the hand; then put it into an earthenware pot with powdered zimat, nitre, long peppers, and salt. It should be left in this state for two weeks and then taken out into the sunlight of the dog-days [July 3rd-August 11th, when the Dog-star Sirius rises and sets with the sun] until it is quite dried out. If the sun does not shine either hotly or often enough, the drying can be completed in an oven kindled with ferns and vervain herb. Next make a candle with the fat of the gibbeted criminal, some virgin beeswax, sesame, and peony. This should be fitted into the Hand of Glory after the manner of a candle-holder.

When you wish to work your spell of binding with this loathsome relic, simply carry it into the presence of your victim.

He then went quietly to the inn door to admit his companions-in-crime. As the burglar opened the door, the courageous maid leapt from her bed and pushed with all her strength till the rogue was out, and the door securely bolted from within. While the frightened servant tried in vain to wake her master, sleeping now as though dead, the candle continued to cast its eerie glow around the kitchen; the cutthroats, intent on victory, were breaking down the inn door.

In a desperate flash of inspiration, the servant girl

remembered an old story told by her grandmother – that only milk will douse the flame of the hand of glory. Throwing a pan of milk over the ghastly hand, putting out the light, the whole family and servants were now easily roused, and in force laid hold of the would-be robbers.

A romance, no doubt, but it is a tale that with few changes to the narrative is recorded all over Europe. One version, with an added element of bloody murder, occurs in the Ingoldsby Legends, the burlesque masterpiece of the Rev. Richard Harris Barham.

A VERY ANGRY MAN

The Murder of Frederick Ellison Morton by Ernest Brown
On the evening of Tuesday, 3rd September 1933 at Saxton Grange, Towton, North Yorkshire

In 1933 a case came before Mr Justice Humphreys at the Leeds Autumn Assizes that exemplified the kinds of advances that were being made by the forensic sciences, the better to detect and to convict the nation's rogues.

The case really began some years before, developing from one of those spontaneous 'amours' that some women find irresistible, into a frightening and sordid finale.

Ernest Brown, the man whose role it was to be the villain of the piece, had for some time been engaged as groom to a wealthy Yorkshire cattleman named Morton. In the early days of his employment, Brown had also been of service to Mrs Dorothy Louise Morton, the lady of the house. This was decidedly *hors contract*, and consisted in servicing Mrs Morton's more romantic needs. The tragedy, in hindsight, is that while the lady's passion cooled after the first piquancy of clandestine love, Ernest Brown's did not, and he continued to make a nuisance of himself long after even simple affection had died.

At the beginning of 1933, the Mortons took up the residence of Saxton Grange, an isolated farm near Towton, itself no great distance from Leeds. In June of the same year Ernest Brown, who had accompanied his master in order to attend to the hunters, was instructed to mow the lawn. For reasons best known to his psychiatrist, this imagined indignity angered Brown to such a degree that, in a fit of unconcealed rage, he withdrew his services. Whatever Morton's feelings at losing a good horseman, Dorothy Louise doubtless found the removal of her erstwhile lover's tiresome attentions most timely.

However, like many before him and a great many since, Ernest Brown came to regret the consequences of an uncontrollable temper, which had lost him not only his livelihood but his mistress as well. Thus it was that a contrite groom sought, through the offices of Mrs Morton (which he had secured by the simple expedient of threats of violence), to get back into his former master's favour.

If being asked to mow the lawn had wounded Brown's pride, then his reinstatement in Morton's employ as a lowly odd-job man sparked off an all-consuming hatred. Frequently over the succeeding weeks the brooding violence that had always characterized Brown when he had been crossed, began to erupt in bouts of cursing and threatening that might – if he had ever witnessed them – have worried even Frederick Morton.

On the morning of Tuesday 5th September, Morton announced his intention of 'driving out' for the day, and left in one of the family's two cars. Later, seizing the opportunity to pester Mrs Morton, Brown confronted her with the fact that she had been sunbathing that afternoon with a gentleman friend. The row that followed ended, unsurprisingly, in Ernest Brown knocking his former lover to the ground.

That evening, at around 9.30, a somewhat shaken Dorothy Morton was in the kitchen with her young companion/help Ann Houseman, when they heard the noise of a shotgun being discharged somewhere close to the house, followed by the rattle of pellets against the window-pane. Shortly afterwards, Brown burst into the house and announced that he had just shot a rat out near the barn. Ten minutes later the shrill ring of the telephone broke an uneasy silence, and the caller – a business acquaintance wanting to speak to Mr Morton – was invited to call back later. He did try again, but by this time the telephone wires outside the house had been cut.

The women, unnerved now to a point of anxiety, sat and waited for the return of Frederick Morton: by midnight he had still not arrived, and though they were too nervous to sleep, the two women locked themselves in upstairs rooms. Ann Houseman from her bedroom window saw Brown cross the yard and enter the back door of the house. Both Ann and Mrs Morton, reunited now for mutual support listened silently to the sounds coming from below. At 2am all was silent. Ninety minutes later, there was a huge explosion outside, and the watching women could see through the window that the garage was an inferno. Finding the telephone dead, they collected Mrs Morton's baby and fled to the village to raise the alarm.

Meanwhile Brown, after an unsuccessful attempt to round up the terrified horses and cattle that were stampeding about the grounds, drove the horse-box into Towton to rouse the farm bailiff, and together they returned to Saxton Grange. By now the fire had spread from the garage to the main outbuildings, and it was not for some hours that the conflagration was sufficiently under control to allow investigation of the debris.

In the burned-out garage police found the charred remains of Morton's motor-car; and in the driver's seat, the charred remains of Frederick Morton. A subsequent post-mortem examination revealed that the unfortunate man had been dead before the fire, and that the hole in his lower trunk was consistent with a gunshot wound.

Ernest Brown's account of the events was that his master had arrived home at about 11.30 the previous night, and that somewhat the worse for drink must accidentally have set fire to himself whilst smoking a cigarette. Brown, so he said, had been dismissed for the night and was in bed at the time the garage caught fire.

To a great extent, the trial of Ernest Brown was something of an anti-climax to the bizarre events that had led to his arrest. The prosecution contended that Frederick Morton had in fact got home at 9.30 on the night of his death, and that as he sat in his car in the garage, his groom had shot him. Fearing the occupants of the house had heard the gunfire, Brown fired a second shot outside the garage in order to give credence to the claim that he was killing rats.

He had then cut the telephone wires with the intention of delaying the arrival of help, and set fire to the garage, which had exploded due to the presence of quantities of petrol.

The Crown case was helped to a great extent by scientific evidence offered in the matter of the cut telephone wires. Both Mrs Morton and Ann Houseman had testified that the apparatus had gone dead just after Brown had been in the kitchen (to explain the shooting) and taken out with him a knife from the cutlery drawer. Mrs Morton explained that the drawer contained two sharp knives – a white-handled game-knife, and a general purpose knife with a black handle. Brown, she said, had taken the game-knife.

In his evidence to the court, Professor Tryhorn, then Professor of Chemistry at Hull University College, outlined the tests which had been carried out on the knives and the wires:

> 'He had taken photographs, magnified more than one hundred times, of the marks and scratches made by the severing instrument upon the leaden casing of the wires, as well as photographs of the edges of both knives and of many similar knives, all magnified to the same extent. The edge of a knife so magnified looks, of course, very much like a saw. He had similarly photographed the result of cuts made by himself with a part of the white-handled knife, upon other portions of the same telephone wire cut off with pliers for the purpose. On comparing the photos, which were produced to the jury, the witness was able to express a definite opinion that the wires had been severed by one particular portion of the edge of the white-handled knife and definitely not by any of the other knives which he had examined, including the black-handled one. He could not say with certainty that no other knife existed which could have made those marks, but the evidence, as it stood, afforded strong corroboration of Mrs Morton's evidence as to which knife was taken by Brown, and at least some evidence that the

person who had taken the white-handled knife from the drawer had used it to cut the telephone wire.'

The jury returned a verdict of guilty, and Ernest Brown was subsequently hanged at Armley Road Gaol, Leeds.

MURDER BY INSULIN

The Murder of Mrs Elizabeth Barlow by her husband Kenneth
On Friday, 3rd May 1957 at their home in
Thornbury Crescent, Bradford, West Yorkshire

A t around 11.30 on the night of 3rd May 1957, a 35-year-old male nurse named Kenneth Barlow summoned a doctor to his home at Thornbury Crescent with the dramatic news that he had found his wife Elizabeth dead in her bath.

Barlow subsequently elaborated on his grisly discovery; Elizabeth had been feeling unwell for most of the evening, and they had retired early. After vomiting in bed, Elizabeth had gone to take a hot bath, leaving her husband to clear up and change the bed linen. Barlow then returned to bed and dozed off. When he awoke some time later and went in search of his wife, he found her in the bath, submerged in the water, and apparently dead. He claimed he then pulled out the plug to drain the water and tried to pull Elizabeth from the bath. Being too weak to lift her, he then tried unsuccessfully to resuscitate his wife by artificial respiration. At this point he went next door to Mr and Mrs Skinner, his neighbours, and telephoned the doctor.

The doctor's initial examination could find no obvious reason why Mrs Barlow should have slipped beneath the bath water and drowned. In accordance with the legal requirements in any case of unexplained death, the police were called, and a post-mortem examination carried out on the body of the late Elizabeth Barlow.

There were no marks of physical violence, and though

her eyes were widely dilated it was clear that if Elizabeth had taken or been given drugs that substance had not been administered orally. On 8th May, West Riding pathologist Dr David Price made a minute examination of the surface of the body and found four small puncture marks on the buttocks, consistent with the use of a hypodermic syringe; one of these marks appeared to have been made as recently as a few hours before death.

Police investigation had meanwhile turned up two hypodermic syringes in the house at Thornbury Crescent. Barlow at first denied using the syringes on his wife, claiming that he had been given them in order to treat himself with penicillin for a carbuncle on the neck. In a subsequent statement to Detective Superintendent Cheshire, Barlow admitted to having injected his wife with ergometrine in order to terminate her current pregnancy. The syringes were routinely sent to the West Riding Forensic Laboratory at Harrogate for examination; they did contain traces of penicillin, but not of ergometrine.

With no more than a few injection marks to guide them, Dr Alan Currie, senior scientific officer at Harrogate, and his team of specialists began an exhaustive examination into the possible causes of Elizabeth Barlow's death. There was no evidence of disease, and the possibility of any common drug or poison being in the body had been eliminated.

The question remained – what substance could have accounted for the symptoms that had led to Mrs Barlow's untimely death? Her husband had spoken of vomiting, her discarded nightwear had been wet with perspiration, and she had clearly been too weak to prevent herself slipping down in the bath and drowning. In addition, her eyes had been so widely dilated that the coloured parts could not be seen. There was one condition which satisfied all these symptoms – hypoglycaemia, a deficiency of blood sugar; a condition which might be caused by injecting insulin – used to correct the blood sugar level in a diabetic patient – into the body of a non-diabetic.

A series of tests was carried out on mice, in which a control batch were injected with insulin, resulting in coma and death. Other mice were injected with an extract distilled from tissue from the dead woman's body; the reaction was identical – coma followed by death.

The analysts now began working on the theory that Mrs Barlow had been put into the bath and drowned while in a coma induced by a large injection of insulin. In all, 127 tests were carried out, leading to the conclusion that on the basis of finding 240 units of insulin-type substance in the body tissues after death, and given the rapid rate at which it is absorbed into the bloodstream, Elizabeth Barlow's body would have contained a massive dose at the time she drowned.

In December 1957, Kenneth Barlow was put on trial at the Leeds Assizes charged with the murder of his wife by insulin poisoning – the first time that such a charge had ever been brought.

Sir Harry Hylton-Foster, the Solicitor-General opened the case for the Crown, and in the course of his evidence introduced a number of witnesses who claimed that during the previous two years, Barlow had spoken on several occasions to hospital colleagues about the suitability of insulin to committing the perfect murder. To Nurse Joan Waterhouse he had said: 'You could kill someone with insulin as it can't be found very easily.'

Giving evidence about the circumstances leading to Mrs Barlow's death on 3rd May, Detective-Sergeant Naylor told the court that on entering the bathroom, he was immediately struck by the absence of condensation on the walls, despite Barlow's talk of a 'hot bath' and of having dozed off for some time while his wife was in it. As for Barlow's attempts at resuscitation, DS Naylor remarked that he found the prisoner's pyjamas to be completely dry.

Representing the accused, Mr Bernard Gillis QC sought to prove that Elizabeth Barlow's death had been, as her husband claimed, accidental. Evidence was presented of the happy state of matrimony enjoyed by the Barlows, and the total lack of motive for murder. In refuting the medical evidence, Mr Gillis called on Dr Hobson of St Luke's Hospital, Muswell Hill, London. Dr Hobson explained that insulin is a protein occurring naturally in the human body; that in a state of emotional excitement – such as fear

– the body will secrete greater than normal amounts of insulin. If Mrs Barlow had slipped down into the bath and panicked that she might not be able to get out, this could have resulted in the symptoms found at the post-mortem examination. In short, Mr Gillis submitted to the court, the scientific evidence against his client fell short of the proof required to convict him of murder.

Cross-examining, the Solicitor-General asked Dr Hobson if he was aware that 80 units of insulin were found in just 170 grammes of tissue taken from the deceased's body. Answered in the affirmative, Sir Harry continued: 'The body of the woman weighed 32,000 grammes, and if it came from the natural pancreas, it would mean that Mrs Barlow had 15,000 units of insulin in her body, which was quite impossible.' He also took the opportunity to remind the jury that nine times as much insulin had been found in one buttock – that bearing the puncture marks – as in the other.

In his summing-up, Mr Justice Diplock advised the jury: 'This is murder or nothing. It is not suggested that Barlow did not know that an injection of insulin could kill. If you are satisfied that he injected insulin into his wife and knowingly injected it, you will probably find no difficulty in reaching the conclusion that he did so with intent to kill . . . If you are satisfied that that story of giving her artificial respiration cannot be true you will ask why he lied, and no doubt why he did not give her artificial respiration. Was it because he intended her to die?'

The jury were in retirement for 1½ hours before returning a unanimous verdict of Guilty. Sentenced to life imprisonment, Kenneth Barlow persisted in protesting his innocence: 'I am not guilty. I did not murder my wife. I had no reason to murder my wife. Somewhere, someone must know something more than has come out and I beg leave to appeal.'

So ended the first trial in which insulin was alleged to have been used as a 'weapon', and detected as such only because of the exhaustive and totally new lines of investigation followed by the Home Office analysts and biologists. Mr Justice Diplock concluded: 'Information has been obtained which will be of value in other cases – if other cases of this kind should arise.'

As a postscript, Elizabeth was Barlow's second wife. The first Mrs Barlow died in 1956 at the early age of 33. At the inquest, doctors were unable to find the cause of death, and a verdict of 'natural causes' was returned.

'JUST CLEANING UP STREETS'*

The Murder of Thirteen Women by Peter Sutcliffe (called 'The Yorkshire Ripper') On various dates between October 1975 and November 1980 at locations in Yorkshire, Lancashire, and Greater Manchester

In November 1980, shortly after the brutal killing of Leeds student Jacqueline Hill, one national newspaper published its story under the headline 'Did one man really do all this?' It seemed incredible at the time, and no less worrying in retrospect, that one man – Peter Sutcliffe – *was* able, over a period of five years, to bludgeon, stab, and mutilate an admitted total of 20 women, 13 of whom died from their savage treatment.

These tragic victims, aged between 16 and 46, with occupations between student and prostitute, had only one thing in common – they were alone on the street after dark.

The full story of the investigation into the atrocities committed by the man who came to be known as 'The Yorkshire Ripper' through its painful five years, is too complex and too lengthy for a book such as this. There is, however, a plethora of books on the Yorkshire Ripper; they range from the downright sordid to the excellent *Somebody's Husband, Somebody's Son*, by Gordon Burn (1984). It is a story of determination and frustration – of a police force desperate to put a stop to one of the worst serial murderers in Britain's history, but seemingly powerless to end the carnage. Above all, it is the story of a county in the grip of terror, its women fearful of being out of

* 'I were just cleaning up streets, our kid. Just cleaning up streets' (Peter Sutcliffe to his younger brother Carl).

doors at night. Thirteen of them paid with their lives for that freedom; this text stands as a modest memorial.

Diary of a Murderer

Saturday, 5th July 1975, 1.30am: Keighley. Thirty-seven-year-old Anna Rogulskyj attacked and stabbed twice. This was the first 'Ripper' attack, and the victim survived.

Friday, 15th August 1975, 11.45pm: Halifax. Olive Smelt, 46, bludgeoned about the head and stabbed. Ms Smelt recovered and was able to give a partial description of the man who had attacked her: '5 feet 6 inches tall with darkish wavy hair'.

Thursday, 30th October 1975, 1.30am: Leeds. Wilma McCann had left her home on the Old Scott Estate earlier in the evening for a night's drinking in town. After a late meal at the Room at the Top Club, Mrs McCann hitch-hiked home. The driver dumped her body, with fifteen stab wounds, a bare 150 yards from her house. Two of the McCann children went out into the street in the early hours to look for their mother; mercifully, it was a local milk roundsman who discovered the body. Twenty-eight-year-old Wilma McCann was the first of the victims to lose her life over the next five years.

Thursday, 20th November 1975, 10.20pm: Preston. Joan Harrison, aged 26 killed by a single blow to the back of the head.

Tuesday, 20th January 1976, 7.00pm: Leeds. Emily and Sydney Jackson and their three children lived in the town of Morley, and by day Mr and Mrs Jackson ran their own successful roofing business. At night, it was customary for Emily to drive into Leeds, meet her husband for a drink, spend several hours pursuing her second job as a prostitute, then pick Sydney up from the pub and drive home. On the night of 20th January this pattern changed; Sydney Jackson waited for his wife until closing time, and when she failed to turn up, took a taxi home. Shortly afterwards Mrs Jackson's mutilated body was found; she had been severely beaten, and in a frenzied attack, had been stabbed fifty times. On the victim's thigh, police found a significant clue in their search for the killer – the print of a size 7 Dunlop boot.

Sunday, 9th May 1976: Leeds. Marcella Claxton survives a 'Ripper-type' attack late at night.

Saturday, 5th February 1977, 11.30pm: Leeds. Irene Richardson, 28, was a most unlikely woman to be wandering the streets alone late at night. As a result of being evicted by her boyfriend some months previously, and after living in a series of squalid lodging-houses, Irene was now penniless, homeless, and luckless. At 11.30pm she met Peter Sutcliffe. The following day her stabbed and mutilated body was found in Soldiers' Field, a local park. Close by, tyre tracks were found which would be of significance to the investigation.

Saturday, 23rd April 1977, 11.15pm: Bradford. The only victim of the Ripper attacked indoors was 33-year-old prostitute Patricia Atkinson. Ms Atkinson was bludgeoned, stabbed, and mutilated in what was becoming an identifiable 'style'. A print was found made by the same boot as that left at the scene of the Emily Jackson murder.

Sunday, 26th June 1977, 1.45am: Leeds. Up to this point there had been a general complacency on the part of the public towards the Ripper attacks – the victims had so far been prostitutes plying their trade; this attitude was about to change dramatically. Sixteen-year-old Jayne MacDonald had been to a disco in Leeds city centre with her boyfriend – she kept to her customary soft drinks, but her escort drank rather more beer than was good for him, and Jayne ended up seeing the boy home. The short cut back to her parents' house was through the red-light district of Chapeltown where, presumably mistaken for a prostitute, Jayne MacDonald died of multiple stab wounds.

June 1977: George Oldfield, Assistant Chief Constable of the West Yorkshire force, is given charge of the Ripper investigation.

Sunday, 10th July 1977, 2.15am: Bradford. Forty-two-year-old Maureen Long beaten and stabbed several times, but survives the ordeal.

Saturday, 1st October 1977, 9.30pm: Manchester. The series of murders becomes more repellent with the killing of 21-year-old mother of two, Jean Jordan. Sutcliffe, after leaving Jean's battered body on a Manchester allotment, returned after eight days to further mutilate the already decomposing corpse. Eventually, it was only by her fingerprints that Jean Jordan could be identified.

October 1977: Police find a new £5 note in the handbag of the latest victim, identified as part of a batch issued by a Yorkshire bank two days before the attack. Police begin interviewing 5,500 people who may have had the note in their wage-packet.

2nd November 1977: Peter Sutcliffe interviewed by police about the £5 note.

8th November 1977: Sutcliffe seen by police for the second time about £5 note.

Wednesday, 14th December 1977, 8.00pm: Leeds. Marilyn Moore, 25, attacked and severely bludgeoned; however, she was not stabbed, and survived. Scene-of-crime officers identify car tracks as identical to those left at the scene of the Irene Richardson killing.

Saturday, 21st January 1978, 9.30pm: Bradford. Yvonne Pearson, 22, was bludgeoned to such a severe degree that her face was unrecognizable, then dumped on a derelict site and hidden by rubble. Her body was not found until 26th March, eight weeks later. She had not been stabbed. The irony was that Yvonne was known to have taken such precautions as were possible given the usual hazards of her job as a prostitute – she had begun to seek a 'better class' of clientele, and she never took men back to her flat. In common with many women living in fear of the Ripper, she carried a weapon for protection in the form of a long pair of scissors.

Tuesday, 31st January 1978, 9.10pm: Huddersfield. Helen Rytka and her sister Rita had devised their own makeshift method of protection. The teenage prostitutes always patrolled their Huddersfield beat together – one either side of the road. When one was picked up, the other would wait at the spot for her return. On the night of the 31st, Helen was seen by her sister getting into a dark-coloured car and driving off with a 'thinly built' client of about 30 to 40. Rita never saw her sister alive again.

8th March 1978: Assistant Chief Constable Oldfield received the 'Ripper letter'.

For the past four years a vicious killer has been at large in the North of England. There have been to date 12 horrific murders and four brutal attacks. The evidence suggests that the same man may be responsible for all of them. If so, he has struck 13 times in West Yorkshire, twice in Manchester and once in Lancashire. Large teams of police officers, including Regional Crime Squads, are working full time in West Yorkshire, Sunderland, Manchester and Lancashire to catch him. His original targets were prostitutes but innocent girls have also died. You can help to end this terror . . .

HELP US
CATCH THE
RIPPER

● HAVE YOU SEEN THE HANDWRITING?

IF YOU HAVEN'T IT'S ON THE BACK PAGE

● HAVE YOU HEARD THE TAPE?

IF YOU HAVEN'T, RING THE NEAREST OF THE FOLLOWING TELEPHONE NUMBERS:

LEEDS (0532) 464111   MANCHESTER (061) 246 8060
BRADFORD (0274) 36511   NEWCASTLE (0632) 8075

DO ANY OF THESE QUESTIONS DESCRIBE SOMEONE YOU KNOW?

- Has a Wearside (Geordie) accent?
- Is physically fit and reasonably strong?
- Travels between, or has connections in, the Yorkshire, Lancashire and Sunderland areas?
- Perhaps shows disgust of low moral standards?
- Is a manual worker or has access to tools?
- Possibly lives alone or with aged parents?
- Is prone to sudden outbursts of emotion?
- Owns a car of his own or has access to one?
- Sometimes stays out late at night?

- BUT DON'T DISCOUNT ANY SUSPICIONS BECAUSE OF THE QUESTIONS. IF YOU HAVE ANY DOUBTS AT ALL, CONTACT THE POLICE AND HELP CATCH THE RIPPER.

IF YOU ARE AN EMPLOYER

- Does your firm possibly have business connections throughout the North of England, especially in the Yorkshire, Lancashire and Sunderland areas
- Have you an employee who was available in Sunderland to post an envelope on the following dates:
  March 7/8, 1978.
  March 12/13, 1978.
  March 21/22, 1979.
  Shortly before June 18, 1979.

Through his duties or being absent from work he was available to attack the 'Ripper' victims (see centre pages) on:

July 5, 1975.	February 6, 1977.	December 14, 1977.
August 15, 1975.	April 24, 1977.	January 21, 1978.
October 30, 1975.	June 26, 1977.	January 31, 1978.
November 20, 1975.	July 10, 1977.	May 17, 1978.
January 20, 1976.	October 1, 1977.	April 5, 1979.
		September 2, 1979.

FIRST RIPPER LETTER

Dear Sir, – I am sorry I cannot give may [spelling is as it was written] name for obvisous reasons I am the ripper. Ive been dubbed a maniac by the press but not by you, You can call me clever and I am. You and your mates havent a clue That photo in the paper gave me fits and that lot about killing myself no chancee Ive got things to do. My purpose to rid the streets of them sluts. my one regret his that young lassie Mcdonald did not know cause change routine that nite, Up to number 8 now you say 7 but remember Preston 75, Get about you know, you were right I travel a bit You probably look for me in Sunderland dont bother I am not daft just posted letter there on one of my trips. Not a bad place compared with Chapeltown and Manningham and other places.

Warn whores to keep off the streets cause I feel it coming on again, sorry about young lassie.

Yours respectfully
Jack the Ripper

13th March 1978: A second letter, signed 'Jack the Ripper' sent to the *Daily Mirror* offices in Manchester.

SECOND RIPPER LETTER

Dear Sir, – I have already written Chief constable, Oldfield a 'man I respect' concerning the recent Ripper murders. I told him and I am telling you to warn them whores I'll strike and soon when the heat cools off. About the Mcdonald lassie I didn't know that she was decent and I am sorry I changed my routine that night, Up to number 8 now You say seven but remember Preston 75. Easy picking them up dont even have to try, you think they're learn but they dont Mare young lassies, next time try older one I hope. Police havent a clue yet and I dont leave any I am very clever and dont think of looking for any fingerprints cause there arent any and dont look for me up there in Sunderland cause I not stupid just passed through the place not a bad place compared with Chapeltown and Manningham cant walk the street for them whore, Dont forget warn them I feel it coming on again if I get the chance, Sorry about lassie I didn't know

Yours respectfully
Jack the Ripper

Tuesday, 16th May 1978, 10.00pm: Manchester. Widowed, with five children and in the poorest of health, 41-year-old Vera Millward is believed to have been meeting a man friend on the night she was murdered. When her friend failed to turn up, Vera Millward picked up another 'client'. Her battered and stabbed body was found in the grounds of the Manchester Royal Infirmary. Tyre tracks near the body matched those found in the Richardson and Moore cases.

13th August 1978: Because his car had been identified driving through the Leeds and Bradford red-light districts, Peter Sutcliffe was interviewed by police for a third time. He told them, truthfully, that this was his route for work.

23rd November 1978: Routine examination of the tyres on Peter Sutcliffe's car to see whether they matched those left at the scenes of three murders. Sutcliffe had already replaced the tyres.

Wednesday, 4th April 1979, 11.30pm: Halifax. Nineteen-year-old building society clerk Josephine Whitaker had been visiting her grandmother and decided to walk home by a short cut. Her terribly injured body was found just 150 yards from her house. For the third time in this investigation, the print from a size 7 Dunlop boot was found close to the victim.

June 1979: Police receive a tape recording purporting to be made by the Ripper. Investigating officers decide to make the tape public in an attempt to identify the voice.

29th July 1979: Peter Sutcliffe interviewed by police for the fifth time.

Sunday, 2nd September 1979, 1.00am: Bradford. University student Barbara Leach was walking to meet friends after a social evening at a local pub. Three hundred yards from Bradford's central police station she became the Ripper's eleventh victim. Ms Leach was hit over the head and stabbed eight times with a knife identical to that used to kill Josephine Whitaker.

23rd October 1979: Peter Sutcliffe again interviewed after his car had been repeatedly reported in local red-light areas.

January 1980: Assistant Chief Constable George Oldfield taken off the Ripper investigation.

13th January 1980: Sutcliffe interviewed again about £5 note.

30th January 1980: Sutcliffe interviewed to confirm previous statements.

2nd February 1980: Sutcliffe interviewed for the fourth time about the £5 note.

Monday, 18th August 1980: Leeds. Forty-seven-year-old Marguerite Walls, a civil servant, was murdered as she walked home after working late. The fact that Ms Walls had been strangled put her killing outside the *modus operandi* of the Ripper, and the case was dismissed from the main investigation. Peter Sutcliffe subsequently confessed to the killing.

Wednesday, 24th September 1980: Leeds. Upadhya Andavathy Bandara attacked in the street.

Wednesday, 5th November 1980: Huddersfield. Teresa Sykes attacked in the street.

Monday, 17th November 1980, 9.23pm: Leeds. Although it was not known at the time, Jacqueline Hill was to be the last victim of the Yorkshire Ripper. The 20-year-old student was walking the hundred yards to her flat on Leeds University campus when she was attacked. Although Jacqueline's bloodstained handbag was found and handed in to the police, it was treated as lost property, and her body was not found until the next morning.

28th November 1980: Trevor Birdsall, a friend of Peter Sutcliffe, sent an anonymous letter to the police Incident Room accusing Sutcliffe of being the Ripper.

29th November 1980: Birdsall interviewed by Bradford police who set aside his claim that Sutcliffe is the Ripper.

2nd January 1981: Peter Sutcliffe arrested in Sheffield.

5th January 1981: Sutcliffe remanded for trial by Dewsbury magistrates.

22nd May 1981: Sutcliffe sentenced to life imprisonment at the Old Bailey. The judge recommended that he serve at least 30 years.

CHICAGO, YORKSHIRE

**The Murder of Abraham Levine by Walter
Sharpe and Gordon Lannen**
On Wednesday, 16th November 1949 at his
shop in Leeds, West Yorkshire

At around 10 o'clock on a bleak November morning on a
bustling city street, two young men, their raincoats
belted against an icy wind, hover outside the window
before entering a little jewellery store. The elderly Jewish
proprietor looks up as a tinny bell above the door jangles.
His eyes register danger; paying customers these are not,
but the pistols in their hands tell him that these men mean
serious business of some kind. Their only words confirm
his worst suspicions: 'Give us the money!'

'Give you my money?' he thinks, 'Give you my money!'
The guns give him a moment's pause; but then he is round
the counter, and without his uttering a word the two men
know his thoughts: 'Old Levine, give you his money? Abe
don't work all week just to keep you punks!' With more
courage than good sense he grabs hold of one of the
robbers; as he does so, his companion rains down blow
after blow with the butt of his gun on the old man's head.
Still he keeps fighting. Twice a gun bursts into life; twice
the old jeweller's body recoils with the impact of its deadly
missiles. In an instant the two men are across the shop,
leaving behind them one more statistic on the city's crime
list. In another instant they are out into the crowd of
shoppers, shooting wildly to scatter the terrified pedes-
trians, each scrambling for cover, women screaming.
Some public-spirited citizens give chase; more shots,
and in the panic and confusion two fugitives are born.

In the uncanny silence that follows, the old jeweller, bleeding from his head and his body, stumbles out of his shop and collapses onto the pavement.

Chicago 1929?
LEEDS 1949!

After being lifted from the pavement outside his Albion Watch Depot on that morning of 16th November, Abraham Levine was rushed to the Leeds General Infirmary.

Within hours, the West Riding Chief Constable, Mr J.W. Barnett, had 1,000 officers combing Leeds for information on the jeweller's attackers; the police forces of surrounding districts were alerted to be on the lookout for two dangerous gunmen. Back in Leeds Infirmary Abraham Levine was losing his grip on life; the next night he died.

Forensic experts had soon confirmed that a bullet taken from Mr Levine's body was part of an ammunition haul stolen from a local gunsmith, and with their fingers firmly on the pulse of the Leeds underworld, detectives were beginning to piece together information that would identify the two fugitives.

Only two days after the shooting, and one day after the death of its victim, the killers were tracked down to Southport, across the border. Walter Sharpe, 20, and Gordon Lannen, just 17, were arraigned before Mr Justice Streatfield at the Leeds Assizes. On that March morning both youths stood, condemned not only by the evidence, but also by their own ill-graced personalities.

Rarely could a defence counsel have had such a thankless task as that facing Mr G.R. Hinchcliffe. In mitigation he proposed that it was their diet of violent movies that had encouraged Sharpe and Lannen into a life of crime – 'these wretched gangster films', as the judge described them. More specifically, Sharpe, who had fired the gun that robbed Mr Levine of his life, claimed that it was an accidental killing, that he was not even aware of the gun going off he was so confused.

The verdict was a foregone conclusion; the jury obviously felt that there was little, if anything, to discuss, and delivered their verdict within twenty minutes: Guilty of murder.

In passing sentence, the judge first addressed Gordon Lannen: 'The jury have very properly convicted you on this evidence of a most shocking and disgraceful murder. You come under the protection of the Children and Young Persons Act, and, because you are under the age of eighteen, you cannot suffer the supreme penalty of the law. The Act protects even young gangsters.'

In an atmosphere of gravity such as no other occasion can produce*, the black cap was placed on Mr Justice Streatfield's head and he sentenced Sharpe: 'For your part in this most shocking crime it is my duty to pass upon you, young though you are, the sentence which is prescribed by law for this offence.'

Walter Sharpe was hanged at Armley Gaol on 30th March 1950.

The murder of Abraham Levine is not a great classic, not a classic of any degree, simply a pointless crime of greed and stupidity. But it is useful to recall it even if it reminds us simply of this: wherever guns are available, there will be gangsters ready to use them. Chicago 1929, Leeds 1949 . . .

* The atmosphere in court at the moment of passing of the death sentence is perfectly described by Mr Rowan-Hamilton in his introduction to the trial of John Alexander Dickman for the Notable British Trials series: 'There is a silence which creeps round a Court of justice while the sentence of death is being pronounced. Just for a few seconds it seems as if the noise of the world is hushed, and time stands still. Each hears his own heart beat; the crowded gallery strain and crane to get a look at the man that is holding on to the rail, with a warder on each side. His friends sob audibly; tears stream from the eyes of women who have cared for him with all his faults; sometimes a wife or lover faints. Hardly a soul that does not feel an instant's terror when the Spirit of Death stalks in to claim his prize.'

THE MAN WHO CAME BACK

The Murder of Zoe Wade by James Pollard
On Wednesday, 13th June 1984 at Fairbourne
House, The Crescent, Buttershaw, Bradford,
West Yorkshire

Quiet, timid, 42-year-old Zoe Wade had lived with a silent fear locked in her head for four-and-a-half years – ever since the night a vicious double rape left her life in ruins, and both her body and her spirit indelibly scarred. Imagine, then, the abject panic she must have endured when she learned that the man responsible for her agony, former neighbour James Pollard, had been paroled early from prison, and had been seen, like a nightmare from the past, walking free near her home.

Within weeks she was dead, brutally murdered, and raped again in her home, in the same room and, unbelievably, by the same man. In an attempt to cover his tracks, Pollard had set fire to the bed where he left Miss Wade's body – and then sat drinking in a public house opposite, watching the fire brigade and police.

James Pollard was born on 29th July 1958, in Halifax. As a child at Lightcliffe Infants' School, he had been noticeably backward, though not classed as educationally subnormal. Between the ages of 9 and 12 he attended Quarry House, a special school. He subsequently rejoined the conventional education system until he was 16. School reports informed his parents that he progressed 'slowly'.

Up until 1982, Pollard had a satisfactory employment record in a number of jobs, including apprentice painter and decorator, metal presser, and textile worker. He was

inclined to be a solitary youth, and had particular difficulty in communicating with girls of his peer group.

In 1980 he was convicted of theft and put on probation,
a condition of which was that he lived in the Cardigan
House hostel at Leeds; the probation officer assigned to
him was Mr Richard Hayes.

Like many young criminals before him, and since, this
first taste of institutionalization only served to harden
Pollard's anti-social outlook; he began to get involved in
heavy drinking sessions with the hostel's other residents.
Shortly afterwards, he moved into a council maisonette at
Fairbourne House, The Crescent, Buttershaw, where Zoe
Wade had lived since 1976. At thirty minutes after midnight on Saturday 30th January 1982, Pollard broke into
Miss Wade's home in order to steal her television set;
wakened by the noise, she got up to confront the intru-
der, though she had little time to do or say anything before
Pollard savagely beat her about the head with a frying pan,
causing seven deep wounds requiring twenty stitches.

Pollard, who had consumed fourteen pints of beer
during the day, ordered Miss Wade to clean herself up
and take her clothes off; when she returned from the
bathroom he raped her twice before leaving with the
television set, hissing the chilling warning: 'Don't phone
the police or I will kill you.' This threat was never made
known by the police to either Pollard's probation officer or
the Parole Board; it is just one of a series of blunders that
characterised the inability of any of the forces of authority
involved in the Zoe Ward case to prevent a very unne-
cessary tragedy.

At Crown Court, Mr Justice Glidewell jailed Pollard for
4½ years after he had admitted rape, wounding, and two
charges of burglary; he spent time in several prisons,
ending up in Durham. His sentence was due to run until
31st June 1985, but on 18th August 1983, Pollard was
paroled.

Before his release from Durham, James Pollard asked
his probation officer, Mr Hayes, for Miss Wade's address
so that he could write to her and apologize. His request
was naturally refused, but the police were not informed of
Pollard's interest in his victim's address.

Leaving prison, Pollard did not take up regular employment, though part of his parole condition was that he attend four days a week at the Crow Trees hostel at Idle, Bradford, where he had been given the task of painting the outside of the building. At the time he was living with his parents at Hillcrest Drive, Queensbury. The probation officer had made only a verbal parole condition that Pollard was to stay away from the Buttershaw Estate.

Frightened after neighbours spotted Pollard on the estate, Miss Wade applied to Bradford Council's housing department for an urgent transfer. With an unbelievable lack of concern, they advised her simply that no other house was available. The housing director of Bradford, Mr Jack Feather, subsequently claimed: 'I have now investigated this matter. Miss Wade did apply for a transfer, and we had discussions with her. However, a social worker became involved and had talks with Miss Wade. After this we received a telephone call from the social worker saying Miss Wade had decided to withdraw her application. I don't know why.'

On the morning of Wednesday, 13th June 1984, Pollard did not have to attend the hostel, but reported to the probation service at 10.30. He then went on a drinking spree in Wyke with a friend who was also on parole, returning to the city centre in order to get a bus out to the Buttershaw Estate. Pollard hid himself in the entrance hallway of the flats, and lay in wait for his victim to return from her job with Allied Industrial Services in Lidget Green.

When she arrived home, Zoe Wade came face to face with her nightmare; face to face with the man whom she had last seen viciously attacking her. Pollard forced her into the flat, raped and murdered her. He left and went to visit a friend nearby to establish an alibi, and then calmly went into The Beacon public house opposite Miss Wade's flat and began drinking.

However, the police were already on Pollard's trail, neighbours had reported seeing him, and he was arrested in the public house.

James Pollard came to trial for this senseless murder during three days in early February 1985, at the Leeds Crown Court. Despite a defence half-way between accident and provocation, the jury brought in a verdict after just one hour – guilty, not of manslaughter, but as charged, of murder. Sentencing Pollard to life imprisonment, Mr Justice Simon Brown stipulated: 'You are not to serve a sentence of less than twenty years.'

A NOTORIOUS BURGLAR

The Murder of Arthur Dyson by Charles Frederick Peace
On Wednesday, 29th November 1876 in
Ecclesall Road, Sheffield, South Yorkshire

Charles Peace was one of those villains who, bad as he was, squalid and murderous as he was, succeeded in entering British folklore as almost a hero; transformed, like Dick Turpin, into that figment of romance, the 'loveable rogue'.

Peace was born in 1832 in Angel Court, Sheffield. In 1859 he married Hannah Ward and became stepfather to her small son. It is from about this date that Peace's nocturnal occupations around the Manchester area were beginning to attract the frequent attentions of the police, and the 'notorious burglar' spent several short terms as a guest of Her Majesty's prison service.

When Manchester became too hot for him, Charlie Peace decamped, en famille, for Sheffield, where he took up residence at 40 Victoria Place, Britannia Road. Next door but one lived the Dysons – Arthur, a civil engineer, his wife, and their young son. Mrs Dyson soon became the object of Peace's flirtatious attentions and, despite the suitor's rather shambling appearance and the gap of some twenty years in their ages, the lady, for a time at least, responded. Quite understandably, Arthur Dyson did not give the liaison his blessing, and made his feelings known to the amorous Peace. Charlie responded perfectly in character by attacking Dyson in the street and threatening to shoot dead both him and his wife.

Both families now moved house, the Dysons to a

residence in Banner Cross Terrace, Ecclesall Road, on the other side of Sheffield, the Peaces to Hull. Not that this in any way impeded Peace in pestering Mrs Dyson; indeed, on the very day that they moved into their new home, the Dysons found Charlie skulking on the doorstep greeting them with: 'You see, I am here to annoy you, wherever you go!' Which he continued to do for some time.

A little after 8 o'clock on the evening of 29th November 1876, Mrs Dyson lit a lantern and walked across her back yard to use the communal privy; there outside, lurking in the shadows, was Charlie Peace, revolver in his hand and a curious request on his lips: 'Speak, or I'll shoot!' Mrs Dyson did more than that, she screamed at the top

Charles Peace, as he appeared sitting in the dock, when I defended him for murder in 1879. FL

Caricature of Peace drawn by Frank Lockwood, his defence counsel

of her voice and locked herself in the lavatory. Peering through a crack in the door, the terrified woman was in time to see Peace shoot her husband, who had rushed out in response to her alarm, and make off across the back gardens.

Wisely, Charlie Peace transferred his 'business' to London, operating for some time from 5 Evelina Road, Peckham, under the alias 'Mr Thompson'.

In the early morning of 10th October 1878, a Police Constable named Edward Robinson apprehended 'Thompson' after a struggle outside a house in St John's Park, Blackheath, which he was in the act of burgling. His alias soon stripped away, Charles Peace was put aboard a train for Leeds where he was to be tried for the murder of Charles Dyson. On the journey, Peace made an attempt at escape when he threw himself, handcuffed, out of the carriage window; he succeeded only in cracking his head severely.

Charlie Peace was found guilty of Dyson's murder, and paid the supreme penalty at Armley Gaol on 25th February 1879. Before he was hanged, Peace made an unexpected death-cell confession – to the murder of PC Nicholas Cock at Whalley Range in August 1876. What is more, he admitted being in the court when William Habron was found guilty and sentenced to death for the murder. It was only on account of his youth that Habron's sentence was commuted to life imprisonment – and had it not been for Peace's last-minute confession, that is where the unfortunate boy would have remained.

THE EXECUTIONER'S STORY

[Shortly after the execution of Charles Peace the following interview took place between a journalist and William Marwood, the public hangman 1874–83.]

'. . . a kind hearted enough man, despite his profession, the executioner had promised me a private interview, and as soon as we were alone he referred to the great skill he had attained in the science of hanging, and told me how Peace had met his death.

'A firmer step never walked to the scaffold,' he said, 'I admired his bravery; he met his fate like a man; he acknowledged his guilt, and his faith in God with regard to his future was very good.'

'But,' I asked, 'don't you think he feared death?'

'No' replied Marwood; 'During the seven years I have officiated as executioner I never met a man who faced death with greater calmness.'

'You mean to say, then, that he met his fate without a tremor?'

'Yes,' responded the executioner. 'It's true he shivered a bit; but not through fear. It was a bitter winter's morning, and he complained of the cold.'

'It is not surprising,' said I, 'that a man like Peace, who has been face to face with danger so often should endeavour to die without betraying any weakness or timidity'.

'The bravery was an outcome of his nature,' replied Marwood, 'He was ignorant alike of weakness and timidity. I will prove it to you. He had been suffering with a bad cough for some days. The night before his execution he said to one of his warders, "I wonder whether Mr Marwood can cure this bad cough of mine?" The warder replied "I have no doubt he could." And I can tell you that a man who jokes about getting hanged to cure a cough is no coward.'

'Do you think he suffered much?'

'Not in the least; he was dead instantly. But perhaps I had better tell you what occurred just before the execution: it is a most curious thing. He had got hold of the idea that I should terribly punish him at the scaffold and he repeatedly asked the chief warder to be sure to tell me that he wished for an interview about a quarter of an hour before he was led out to die. Accordingly, ten minutes to eight o'clock I went to the condemned cell, which stands about in the centre of the gaol, some hundred yards from the place where the scaffold was erected. Peace was seated – he was in his convict dress, and there were several officials attending upon him. The

bandage had been removed from his head [Peace
had been injured in trying to leap to freedom from
the train taking him to trial in Sheffield]; and he did
not wear spectacles. He was neither weak nor
prostrate, but sat upright in his chair, as if he had
never known a moment's illness. When I appeared
in the doorway, he seemed pleased, and holding out
his hand said "I am glad to see you Mr Marwood. I
wish to have a word with you. I do hope you will not
punish me. I hope you will do your work quickly."
"You will not suffer pain from my hand" I replied;
and then Peace, grasping my arm, said, "God bless
you. I hope to meet you all in Heaven. I am thankful
to say my sins are all forgiven." It was now time to
pinion him. He stood up at my request, but did not
really need the support of the two warders by his
side. He was not at all nervous, and quietly submitted to my operations. Pinioning is a very ingenious process. I run a main strap round the body,
and connected to it are two other straps, which take
the small of the arm, so that the elbows are fastened
close to the body and the hands are free. Peace
complained, saying: "The straps fit very tight." I
replied, "It is better so; it will prevent you from
suffering". He made no further objection, and taking
hold of the main strap, so as to keep my hand on
him, we started for the scaffold. The Governor and
the Under-Sheriff went first, then came the Chaplain; and I followed with the condemned man, two
warders attending him, one on each side. They
grasped him by the arms, but did not support
him. He was bareheaded. His face was pale, but
pinched with cold rather than fear. As he arrived
near the scaffold he gave a very wistful look at my
arrangements. They were all right, and seemed to
satisfy him, for he made no remark. He went up the
steps leading to the drop with a firm tread, whilst
the Chaplain read the burial service. I brought him
to a proper stand under the cross-bar, and then
strapped his legs. When that was done he wished
to say something to the reporters, and made a

beautiful speech. Such a speech has never come from a condemned man I have executed. It was a really good speech. When he had finished it he asked for a drink; but you know that was unreasonable, and it could not be admitted, for the time fixed for execution had fully expired. So I placed the cap over his face, and adjusted the rope, when he said: "I say, the rope fits very tight!" I replied: "Never mind; its all for the best; hold up your chin", and he did so immediately, so that I could properly fix the rope.

The Bannercross Murder – Peace threatening Mrs Dyson

"Good-bye all; God bless you," he kept repeating as I went towards the lever. At this time he did not require anyone to support him, but I told one of the warders to take hold of the back strap. Whilst he stood in this manner on the drop, with the noose round his neck, I pushed the lever forward; it withdrew the bolt from the swinging doors, and Peace's body fell through the aperture beneath the platform. The drop was exactly nine feet four inches. Peace was dead in a moment; he never moved a finger or a muscle after he fell; so I carried out my promise to do it well and quickly.'

GUN LAW

**The Murder of Danielle Lloyd (née Ledez)
and her daughter Stephanie by Ian Wood**
On Sunday, 21st September 1986 at Ughill Hall,
Stannington, South Yorkshire

The following account derives from contemporary press releases, and newspaper and court reports. It adopts the format of a hypothetical collection of press cuttings in order to illustrate the piecemeal progression of a murder case from the discovery of a body in suspicious circumstances to the conviction of a killer.

Solicitor Hunted
Tuesday, 23rd September 1986: Police last night began the search for 37-year-old solicitor Ian Wood, who disappeared from his home after shooting his lover and her two children.

The bodies of Mrs Danielle Lloyd, 38, her daughter Stephanie, 3, and son Christopher, 5, were found shot at Wood's country mansion, Ughill Hall in the village of Stannington, Yorkshire. Mrs Lloyd was found dead in the bathroom, Stephanie in her playroom, and Christopher, who is presently in hospital undergoing emergency treatment for serious injuries, was found in his bedroom. The three had moved into Wood's home after his wife Margaret left him in January taking their children with her.

Detective Chief Superintendent Robin Herold, in charge of the case, said Wood disappeared in a hired Ford Granada Scorpio, registration number C832 AMS; he is thought to be armed.

Wood Phones from hiding

Wednesday, 24th September 1986: Events took a dramatic turn yesterday in the hunt for runaway solicitor Ian Wood. In a telephone call to reporter Brenda Tunney of the *Sheffield Gazette*, Wood confessed to the killing of his mistress and her daughter, and of attempting to kill her son; he claimed that he and Danielle, who was in the process of a difficult divorce from her husband Colin Lloyd, had made a suicide pact. Wood, who also admitted having serious financial problems, continued: 'It was a most appalling thing, but I must keep my side of the bargain'. He added that if certain 'conditions' were not met, he would kill Colin Lloyd. The conditions were that Danielle be buried in her home town of Amiens, in France, and that Lloyd should not attend the funeral.

New Phone Clue

Sunday, 28th September 1986: Sheffield reporter Brenda Tunney received another call yesterday from fugitive Ian Wood – the 14th since his disappearance. Wood, a former secretary of the Sheffield law society, was inquiring about the arrangements made for the funeral of his mistress Mrs Danielle Lloyd and her daughter Stephanie. Informed that the funerals could not take place until police had completed their investigation, Wood rang off. Detectives have still been unable to trace the calls, though they believe Wood is still in the Yorkshire area.

Wood in France

Friday, 29th October 1986: The hunt ended last night for Sheffield solicitor Ian Wood. Wood surrendered to French police after spending the afternoon perched precariously on one of the towers of Amiens' famous cathedral. He had been on a guided tour of the building, and after passing a note to the guide, leapt over the 200 ft high parapet onto one of the gargoyles. His note read: 'I am psychologically depressed. Please call a priest.'

After six hours, during which police commissaire Robert Camonges, mayor René Lamps, and a priest tried to reason with him, Wood was seized by three gendarmes in an unguarded moment. An angry crowd had gathered below the cathedral to jeer at Wood, whose victim, the former Danielle Ledez, was born in Amiens.

The Director of Public Prosecutions, on behalf of the South Yorkshire Constabulary, is expected to start extradition proceedings immediately. Meanwhile, Christopher Lloyd, who miraculously survived the shooting by Wood, was described as 'much improved'.

Wood Agrees to Extradition
Friday, 29th October 1986: A French court has ruled that Ian Wood will be extradited to Britain to face charges in connection with the deaths of his mistress and her daughter. Wood waived his right to oppose the order, stating: 'I will explain to the British courts that it was not the real me.'

Back in England, a police guard was mounted at the bedside of Christopher Lloyd in the Royal Hallamshire Hospital, Sheffield, and on four relatives of Ian Wood; this was in response to threatening telephone calls from a man claiming to be Wood.

Solicitor Charged
Wednesday, 4th February 1987: Ian Wood, accused of murdering his mistress Danielle Lloyd and her daughter Stephanie, was yesterday committed in custody for trial at Sheffield Crown Court. He is also charged with the attempted murder of Danielle's son Christopher, and of appropriating £84,800 of his clients' money.

Trial of Ian Wood Opens
Wednesday, 22nd June 1987: The trial opened at Sheffield Crown Court yesterday of Mr Ian Wood. Wood pleaded guilty to murdering 3-year-old Stephanie Lloyd, and to the manslaughter of her mother Danielle Lloyd (née Ledez). Rejecting the latter plea, the Crown will pursue a conviction on the greater charge of murder. The prisoner is also charged with the attempted murder of Christopher Lloyd, and with stealing two large sums of money from his clients.

Opening the case for the prosecution, Mr Geoffrey Rivlin QC told the court that Wood was separated from

his wife Margaret, and had been living with Danielle
Lloyd and her two children at his home, Ughill Hall,
near Sheffield. Mrs Lloyd, who had left her husband
Colin, was pregnant by Wood at the time of her death.

Mr Rivlin continued: 'At about midday on that Sunday
in the playroom, the defendant shot and killed Danielle
and in a child's bedroom he shot and killed Stephanie and
in the bathroom he shot and very nearly killed Christopher. When he realised Christopher was still alive he beat
his head with a wooden stick and left him for dead.
Miraculously, Christopher is still alive . . . [Although he
does not deny shooting Mrs Lloyd] Wood claims that he
shot her but that he should not be convicted of her murder
because when he shot her he did so as a result of an
agreement between him and Danielle that he should first
shoot her and the children and then kill himself. He says
that he and Danielle entered into a suicide pact together
and that is why he shot her.'

The Crown contended that there were no grounds for
accepting the genuineness of the 'suicide pact': 'In the
circumstances of this case it would, in our submission,
mean the defendant showing two things – that there was
at the time a genuine common agreement between him
and Danielle that they should commit suicide and that at
the time Danielle died the defendant did have a second
intention of dying himself in pursuance of that suicide
pact. Little children cannot, in law, agree to die and these
little children did not agree to die. In relation to them there
is no such defence available to the defendant, and he has
pleaded guilty to killing Stephanie and attempting to kill
Christopher . . . The prosecution does not accept that
Danielle agreed she should die, let alone, as he claims,
that the children should die with her, or that the defendant
intended to take his own life.'

Wood had already given his account of the killings to
the police, which Mr Rivlin recounted for the jury. After
agreeing to the suicide pact, Wood had claimed: 'We told
each other we loved each other. She put her hands up to
the side of her head to cover her ears. I went to get the
revolver. I picked it up, and I walked back to just behind
Danielle. I don't think she heard me or even knew I was

there. I shot her through a cushion. I wanted to make it so I couldn't see the bullet hit her. She made a noise and it was horrible. The cry stopped almost as soon as it had started.'

He had then shot Mrs Lloyd's daughter and son Christopher: 'I shot her [Stephanie] twice. I got up off the bed and I think my weight coming off the bed caused her to roll onto the floor. Her eyes were open and I thought she was dead. I had to be sure. I pointed the gun at her and shot again. I told Christopher I had a surprise and took him to the bathroom and said that he should close his eyes and, so he did not cheat, he should lie on the floor. I put a towel over his head. I shot him twice and thought he was dead.'

Friday, 24th July 1987: The jury at Sheffield Crown Court yesterday heard a tape recording made by accused Ian Wood while he was in flight from the police. It had been Wood's hope that the message would explain to 5-year-old Christopher Lloyd why his mother and sister had been killed: 'She [Danielle Lloyd] was my wife, my lover, my friend, my all. She gave herself so completely, she was and always will be my love. We agreed what to do and I did it. It was the most appalling thing and has haunted me ever since. The fact I am now in a position where I can die is the greatest thing for me. My fear now is that God will not let me be with the woman I love. My tryst dictates I must now try and die with her. There is an ultimate irony . . . the beautiful and lovely are dead.'

Saturday, 25th July 1987: Giving evidence in his own defence, Ian Wood told the court that he and his mistress had spent ten minutes discussing their suicide, and had discounted sleeping tablets as impracticable – not least because 3-year-old Stephanie would have had to be held down and force-fed the pills. Instead Wood offered to shoot them all.

On the fifth day of her son's trial, Mrs Barbara Wood told the court that, as a consequence of the difficulties with her husband, Mrs Danielle Lloyd had made as many as ten suicide threats – two of them including her children in the plan; Danielle had told her: 'There is no joy in living in the constant fear of Colin.' Two days after her son had shot

Mrs Lloyd and her two children, Mrs Wood received a telephone call: 'He rang me to say goodbye, to say he loved me, and how sorry he was. He was saying there had been a suicide pact.'

Continuing her evidence, Mrs Wood said: 'He [Ian] had financial problems, emotional problems, problems about the children, and he used to worry about me. He was a very conscientious and nice son, but he did worry.'

Closing Speeches
Thursday, 30th July 1987: Closing the prosecution case, Mr Geoffrey Rivlin told the jury that the prisoner, Ian Wood, was 'an utterly ruthless and cold-blooded killer', and claimed that the alleged suicide pact was 'a pack of lies'. 'If it was not so desperately serious it would be laughable. Wood is a man with an unusually fertile imagination, and he uses that imagination when it seems convenient, and it serves him well in different circumstances. In our submission, this man has the capacity to dream up an extraordinary tissue of lies when it suits his purpose. Call it lies or romancing, it all comes very easy to him.'

Mr Gilbert Gray QC, representing Wood, restated his client's defence of a suicide pact in the matter of Mrs Lloyd's death. Asking the jury to question what possible benefit Wood could derive from lying after pleading guilty to the murder of Stephanie Lloyd, Mr Gray said: 'Greed? No. Sadistic pleasure? No. This was a suicide pact, and into this pact two normal, rational people pooled their tension, their stresses and extraordinary personalities, and came out with the most calamitous of all schemes.'

In his summing-up, Mr Justice Taylor urged the jury not to be swayed by feelings of revulsion: 'What you have heard in this case must create horror and perhaps indignation in the minds of ordinary, reasonable people.' Wood, he continued, must prove 'that it is more probable than not that he and Danielle agreed that both of them should die, and it is more probable than not that when he killed Danielle he had a settled and firm intention of dying himself in pursuance of the agreement.'

Wood Found Guilty

Friday, 31st July 1987: The jury at Sheffield Crown Court yesterday returned a majority verdict of guilty of the murder of Danielle Lloyd and her daughter Stephanie against solicitor Ian Wood. Sentencing Wood, Mr Justice Taylor told him: 'The jury have rejected your story of a suicide pact, although I think, no doubt, you were under great pressure at the time . . . These were cold-blooded shootings of your mistress and her daughter and son, and you were prepared to kill all three of them. And, having shot them, you packed methodically, dressed smartly, had a drink in your favourite bar, and set off for France in a hire car for which the police would not be looking . . . You then tried to put a better complexion on it by sending a stream of messages saying Danielle had agreed to do it. You stuck to that tale through this long and anguished trial.'

Wood was given two life sentences for the murder of Mrs Lloyd and her daughter, and 12 years' imprisonment, to run concurrently, for the attempted murder of Christopher Lloyd. Wood also received a further 3 years concurrent sentence on charges of stealing money from his clients.

Postscript

August 1987: Police are at the centre of a new row over gun laws. After the trial of Ian Wood on two counts of murder and one of attempted murder, a senior officer of Yorkshire CID admitted that 'mistakes had been made' over police interpretation of the 1968 Firearms Act.

It was revealed that Wood shot his mistress, Danielle Lloyd and her two children with a gun and bullets given to him by Sussex police without the knowledge of the South Yorkshire force who were responsible for supervising Wood's firearms certificate. The gun, an ex-service Enfield revolver, had been used by Wood's father to commit suicide, and had been passed on to Wood at his request after the Coroner's inquest. This despite the fact that he did not have the correct firearms certificate, and without notifying the Yorkshire police.

In November 1985, when Wood's marriage began to

disintegrate, officers from Sheffield had seized several guns from his home when it was feared that the balance of his mind was upset; the weapons were returned after seven weeks. Later, in April 1986, Wood had a violent argument with the owner of a local gunshop who had, in error, sold him the wrong size ammunition. Mr Andrew Sumner reported the incident to the police next day, adding that he felt Wood's violent temper made him an unfit person to possess a firearm. Nevertheless, Ian Wood's firearms certificate was renewed. The Home Office is to look into the matter in collaboration with South Yorkshire police.

Meanwhile, Mr Bill Michie, Labour MP for Sheffield Heeley, is demanding an independent medical assessment of all firearms certificate applicants.

SCOTLAND

Borders

Central

Dumfries and Galloway

Fife

Grampian

Highlands

Lothian

Strathclyde

WITH MALICE AFORETHOUGHT?

**The Murder of Helen Wilson Robertson
Priestly by Jeannie Donald**
On Friday, 20th April 1934 at 61 Urquart Road,
Aberdeen, Grampian

The law draws a very clear distinction between the crimes of murder and manslaughter, which, though of less practical use now that capital punishment has been abolished as the automatic sentence for the former, it can still reflect in the severity of custodial punishment. The standard definition of Murder was laid down by Sir Edward (Chief Justice) Coke: 'Murder is when a man of sound memory, and of the age of discretion, unlawfully killeth within any county of the realm any reasonable creature in rerum natura under the King's peace, with malice aforethought, either expressed by the party or implied by law, so as the party wounded, or hurt, etc. die of the wound or hurt, etc. within a year and a day after the same.' Its rather archaic wording may benefit from some explanation: *a man of sound memory* is anybody not, in a legal sense, either 'insane' or, since the Homicide Act of 1959, of 'diminished responsibility'; *the age of discretion* is over 10 years (though under 14 it is considered 'mischievous discretion'). *Within any county of the realm* is rather misleading as by the Offences Against the Person Act (1861) and the British Nationality Act (1948) both murder and manslaughter committed by a British Subject anywhere abroad can be tried in the United Kingdom as if the crime had been committed 'within the realm'. *Any reasonable creature in rerum natura* includes any human being, the only contention being the point at which a foetus becomes a 'human being'. *Under the King's peace* covers everybody, except an enemy killed during war operations. *Malice aforethought* – and this is the phrase upon which the definition of Murder rests – can be seen as one of the following:

1. An intention to kill another person.
2. An intention to commit an act knowing it is highly probable that it will kill another person.
3. An intention to cause grievous bodily harm to another person.
4. An intention to commit an act knowing that it is highly probable that it will cause grievous bodily harm to another person.

Within a year and a day means that if, for example, A pushes B off a cliff at sometime on 1st January 1990, and B dies of the injuries he has sustained before midnight on 1st January 1991, A is guilty of unlawful homicide. It is not particularly useful here to go into the origins of this arbitrary length of time.

Thus we can say that unlawful homicide *with* malice aforethought constitutes Murder, and unlawful homicide *without* malice aforethought constitutes Manslaughter.

The case of Jeannie Donald highlights the difficulty of attributing to some crimes the correct definition. Found guilty of 'murder', she was sentenced to death; but was she, perhaps, guilty only of the lesser charge of man-slaughter (or, in the law of Scotland where Mrs Donald was put on trial, 'culpable homicide').

Jeannie Donald was the 38-year-old wife of an Aberdeen hairdresser. Her victim, 8-year-old Helen Priestly, lived with her parents in a flat on the first floor of a tenement at 61 Urquart Road, Aberdeen. Below them on the ground floor lived the Donalds, although they were neighbours only in a strict locational sense; Mrs Donald and Mrs Priestly had not spoken to each other for five years, the result of some long-forgotten real or imagined grievance.

At a quarter-past midday on 20th April 1934, young Helen arrived home from school for the lunchtime meal.

With the speed achieved only by small children in a hurry to be out to play, Helen finished her food and rushed round to visit a friend, Mrs Robertson. She returned home at about 10 minutes past 1 o'clock, and was immediately sent out again to the local Co-op store to buy her mother a loaf of bread. Helen was seen by several people walking back from the shop with her purchase – it was around 1.30. Helen Priestly was never seen alive again.

When her daughter failed to return home, Mrs Priestly alerted the neighbours to her fears, and the well-oiled machinery of working-class community spirit burst into action. During the whole of the rest of that day and through the night, the police searchers were assisted by parties of local people anxious to offer their support in the Priestlys' hour of crisis. At 5 o'clock in the morning, one volunteer who had been home for a few hours sleep, entered 61 Urquart Road to tell Mr Priestly he was ready to resume the hunt for missing Helen. Here, in the half-light of the communal lobby, his search ended; in a recess under the stairs was a brown sack, and as his eyes became accustomed to the gloom, he saw the hand and foot of a child protruding from it. Within minutes people had collected, it seemed, from far and wide in the neighbourhood. Helen Priestly had been found – dead.

At first sight it appeared to police officers that little Helen had been strangled and sexually assaulted, and considerable time was wasted hunting for a mysterious man who, it was claimed, had been seen by one of Helen's school chums.

Only when a thorough post-mortem had been conducted was it established that, despite some instrument having been intruded into her body, there were no signs consistent with rape or attempted rape; the most logical conclusion being that Helen had been slain by a woman who faked the abuse in order to deflect suspicion. The post-mortem revealed that the victim's death had taken place around 2 o'clock on the afternoon of her disappearance, and the cause of death was asphyxia, possibly from manual strangulation, although vomited particles were found in the windpipe and smaller air tubes.

By the middle of the week following Helen Priestly's

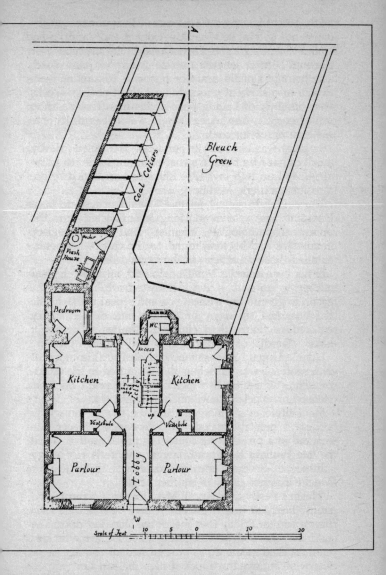

Plan of the house in Urquart Road

death, gossip had reached the ears of the police about the longstanding feud between Mrs Donald and the Priestlys (Helen had often taunted Mrs Donald with the nickname 'Coconut'). After lengthy questioning at Urquart Road, both Jeannie Donald and her husband Alexander were taken into custody at midnight on 25th April. Two weeks later, his alibi of having been at his hairdresser's shop proved correct, Alexander Donald was released; Jeannie was committed for trial.

So great was local public outrage at the Helen Priestly murder, that Mrs Donald's trial was transferred to Edinburgh, and on 16th July 1934, she stood arraigned before Lord Justice Clerk Aitchison.

The evidence against Jeannie Donald proved to be a damaging jigsaw of interlocking facts collated from the reports of pathologists, chemists, and bacteriologists. Bloodstains and bacteria found on the child's garments, matched those on articles in the Donald flat.

In her own defence, Mrs Donald said only that she had nothing to do with Helen Priestly's death, and saw no reason to go into the witness box and repeat the fact. The trial occupied six days, but at the end of it the jury required no more than eighteen minutes to return a majority verdict of thirteen 'guilty' and two 'not proven'.

Jeannie Donald was sentenced to death, although that grim sentence was subsequently commuted to life imprisonment – which for Mrs Donald was 10 years. She was released on special licence on 26th June 1944.

No motive ever emerged from the trial – though in fairness it must be stated that it was not – never is – required of a prosecuting counsel to prove motive. But if the late William Roughead, lawyer and author of many volumes of Scottish criminal trials was right, Jeannie Donald was not guilty of murder at all:

'Helen Priestly used to call Mrs Donald 'Coconut', and plainly held her in low esteem. It may be that by a fatal chance on that Friday they met at the Donalds' door. The child may have done something to rouse the woman's wrath: kicked at the door, put out her tongue at her, or otherwise annoyed or mocked her. She lost her temper, seized the child by the throat, and shook her. Such a shock, owing to the child's physical defect [she had an enlarged thymus gland], would result in a sudden collapse, passing into coma. [If she vomited during this period of uncon-sciousness she could easily have choked on her own vomit, which would have been consistent with the post-mortem finding of asphyxia.]

The woman, horrified, thought she had killed her. She carried the child into the kitchen and frantically strove to revive her, but without avail. What was she to do? There was always bad blood between them; doubtless she would be accused of deliberate murder. Then to her, panic-stricken and distraught, the very Devil suggested as the sole means of safety the vile expedient of simulated rape . . .'

THE RESURRECTION MEN

**The Murders of Mary Patterson, James
Wilson, Margaret Docherty and others by
William Burke and William Hare**
On various dates between December 1827 and
October 1828 in Edinburgh

L ike those of Jack the Ripper, the dark deeds of the
notorious body-snatchers Burke and Hare are almost
too familiar to need repeating. Instead, here is a brief
synopsis of the sinful lives and ignoble ends of the
'Monsters of Edinburgh'.

Burke and Hare were Irish immigrant labourers who
arrived in Scotland around 1818, and had been working

William Burke

William Hare

as navvies on the Union Canal being built between Glasgow and Edinburgh. In 1826 Burke and Hare became acquainted whilst fellow-residents at Logue's lodging-house, a squalid heap of a building in Tanner's Close in Edinburgh's West Port.

Sharing these same lodgings was an army pensioner known as Old Donald, and in the November of 1827 the old man succumbed to a combination of ill-health, old-age and poverty, which was a source of great distress to William Hare, because the old man had died owing him £4. Between them, Burke and Hare opened Old Donald's coffin and substituted a sack of bark for his body, and sold the latter for £7.10s. to Dr Knox at the Anatomy School. Over the next ten months Knox was to become a valued customer.

Dr Knox was a brilliant anatomist and head of the successful academy at 10 Surgeon's Square; quite how much he really knew of his suppliers' methods is a matter for conjecture, but with classes of upwards of 500 students, getting hold of bodies for dissection was not always easy in those pre-Anatomy Act days*, and a committed teacher was not wise to ask too many questions.

In fact, most of the trade was done in newly-dead bodies 'resurrected' from their graves; Burke and Hare broadened the scope of their craft, and created their own fresh supplies. Their *modus operandi* was that a promising 'subject' was lured to Burke or Hare's lodgings either by Maggie Laird – Hare's 'wife' – or Helen McDougal – Burke's. Here the victim would be rendered senseless with drink, and then lifeless by means of a blanket over the face (suffocated for preference, to avoid 'spoiling the merchandise').

The shutters were pulled down on Burke and Hare's enterprise at the beginning of November 1828. On the last day of October an elderly beggar named Margaret Docherty fell victim to the demands of medicine, and was lying

---

* The Anatomy (or Warburton's) Act of 1830, repealed the existing law that required every corpse to receive a 'Christian burial', and effectively put a stop to the private trade in dead bodies.

around awaiting delivery when her body was found under a pile of straw by fellow-lodgers, who summoned the police.

Burke and Helen McDougal, and Hare and Maggie Laird were arrested, the latter pair escaping prosecution by turning King's evidence.

At their trial on 24th and 25th December (at the time the festival of Christmas was not observed in Scotland) at the High Court of Justiciary in Edinburgh, Burke and McDougal were charged jointly with the murders of Mary Patterson, a prostitute, James Wilson (called 'Daft Jamie'), and Margaret Docherty. After a short deliberation, the jury found the case against Helen McDougal 'Not Proven', and against Burke 'Proven'.

In passing sentence, Lord Justice-Clerk Boyle told Burke: 'Rest assured you have no chance of a pardon. The only doubt I have in my mind in order to satisfy the violated laws of your country and the voice of public indignation is whether your body should not be exhibited in chains to bleach in the winds, to deter others from the commission of such offences, but taking into consideration the public eye would be offended by such a dismal

Burke and Hare carrying off the body of Old Donald

spectacle, I am willing to accede to a more lenient execution of your sentence, that your body should be publicly dissected.'

While in Calton Gaol awaiting execution, William Burke is said to have complained bitterly to his warder that Dr Knox still owed him £5.00. He was hanged on the gallows at Liberton's Wynd on 27th January 1829.

Helen McDougal and Maggie Laird were both mobbed by a bloodthirsty rabble and escaped lynching only through the intervention of the police. William Hare fled to London, where he was recorded as eking out an existence by begging in Oxford Street.

Dr Robert Knox was also hounded out of Edinburgh

Burking!

and is said to have ended his days as an obscure general practitioner in Hackney, London.

It will never be known what the full tally of Burke and Hare's murderous career was, but between December 1827 and October 1828, no fewer than sixteen people ended up on a slab at No.10 Surgeon's Square.

MY FIRST EXECUTION

The Murder of John Fortune and John McDiarmid by Robert Vickers and William Innes
In the year 1884 at Gorebridge, near Edinburgh, Lothian

It is sometimes the case that a murder, historically and socially insignificant, will have an interest through circumstances quite peripheral to the crime itself. Such is the case of Robert Vickers and William Innes, two poachers who during their nocturnal activities shot and killed John Fortune, a gamekeeper, and John McDiarmid, a rabbit trapper. Tried and convicted in Edinburgh, the pair were sentenced to be executed at Calton Gaol on 31st March 1884.

The public servant whose duty it was to hang them was James Berry, official executioner from 1884 until 1892, when he left the profession having arrived at the conclusion that capital punishment was a barbarous and ineffectual means of dealing with criminals.

Berry was a flamboyant character, proud of his craft, and noted for his meticulous recording of its finer technical details. Vickers and Innes were Berry's first 'commission', and in that elevated capacity became the subject of a lengthy entry in his notebook, subsequently published in his memoirs.

James Berry had been selected by the Sheriffs of London and Middlesex in September 1883 from a list of some 1,400 applicants.

Despite the disapprobation of his friends and the active opposition of his relatives, who went so far as to petition the Home Secretary to dismiss the application on the grounds that it would disgrace the family name, Berry made overtures by letter to the magistrates of Edinburgh who were looking for a man to dispatch Vickers and Innes:

> 52, Thorpe Street, Shearbridge,
> Bradford, Yorkshire
> March 13th 1884

To the Magistrates
of the City of Edinburgh.

Dear Sirs.

I beg most respectfully to apply to you, to ask you if you will permit me to conduct the execution of the two Convicts now lying under sentence of death at Edinburgh. I was very intimate with the late Mr Marwood [Public executioner 1874–83], and he made me thoroughly acquainted with his system of carrying out his work, and also the information which he learnt from the Doctors of different Prisons which he had to visit to carry out the last sentence of the law. I have now one rope of his which I bought from him at Horncastle, and have had two made from it. I also have two Pinioning straps made from his, also two leg straps. I have seen Mr Calcraft [Public executioner 1829–74] execute three convicts at Manchester 13 years ago, and should you think fit to give me the appointment I would endeavour to merit your patronage. I have served 8 years in Bradford and West Riding Police Force, and re-signed without a stain on my character, and could satisfy you as to my abilities and fitness for the appointment. You can apply to Mr Jas. Withers, Chief Constable, Bradford, also to the High Sheriff of the City of London, Mr Clarence Smith, Mansion House Buildings, 4, Queen Victoria Street, London E.C., who will testify as to my character and fitness to carry out the Law. Should you require me I could be at your command at 24 hours' notice. Hoping these few lines will meet with your approval.

> I remain, Sirs
> Your most obedient servant
> James Berry

To the Chief Magistrates,
  Borough of Edinburgh,
    Scotland.
P.S. An answer would greatly oblige as I should take
it as a favour.

On March the 21st, the Clerk of Magistrates sent the
following reply:

City Chambers, Edinburgh,
March 21st 1884

Sir,
  With reference to your letters of the 13th and 15th
instant, I am now directed by the Magistrates to
inform you that they accept the offer you have made
of your services to act as Executioner here on Monday, the 31st March current, on condition (1) that
you bring your Assistant with you, and (2) that you
and your Assistant arrive in Edinburgh on the
morning of Friday the 28th instant, and reside
within the prison (at the Magistrates' expense) till
after the Executions are over.

  The Magistrates agree to your terms of ten guineas
for each person executed and 20s. for each person
executed to your Assistant, with second-class railway fares for both of you, you finding all the
necessary requisites for the Execution.

I am, Sir,
Your obedient servant
Deputy City Clerk

P.S. Please acknowledge receipt of this letter immediately – A.C.'

The narrative is taken up by executioner Berry himself:

'On Thursday, March 27th, 1884, I departed from
my home, Bradford and made my way to the Midland Station, and booked 3rd class for Edinburgh, to
carry out the execution of the Gorebridge murderers.
I arrived at Waverley Station 4.20pm, and I hired a
cab to drive me to the gaol. On arrival at the prison I
was met at the doors by a good-looking warder,

dressed in ordinary prison garb, and very courteous; and on entering the large portal gate, was asked my name, and after entering it down in the prison book, time, etc., he pulled a string, which rang the Governor's bell, and in a few moments I was confronted with the Governor, a very nice gentleman, of military appearance, and very good looking. After passing the usual conversation of the day, and the weather, and what kind of journey I had up from Bradford, he said after such a long journey I should require a good, substantial tea; and as soon as I had washed, and combed my hair, the tea was there, everything that could be desired. I sat down, and quite enjoyed my first Scotch meal in Bonnie Scotland . . . I returned to my room, and stayed in during the daytime. I spent Thursday night smoking and reading. At 10.0 o'clock p.m. I was escorted to my bedroom, a round house at the back part of the gaol, about 40 yards from the back entrance, a snug little place, and was informed that the last man who slept inside that room was Wm. Marwood, five years previous to my visit. He was then there for the same purpose as myself, but the culprit in his case was a poisoner. The chief warder, whom I spoke to, seemed to touch upon the subject with great reluctance, and said that he felt quite upset concerning the two culprits, and that he hoped they would get a reprieve. I could see in his countenance a deep expression of grief, which was making him look no better for his occupation . . . I sat me down on my bed after he had gone, locked my door, and could hear the trains depart from the station under the prison walls I looked out of my window at the mail taking its departure for the South . . . I then knelt down and asked the Almighty to help me in my most painful task, which I had undertaken to carry out . . . [The night was much disturbed by the persistent smoking of the chimney.] . . . At 8.0 a.m. on the morning of the 28th, Friday, my breakfast was brought into my room, consisting of toast, ham and eggs, and coffee . . . At 10.0 a.m. on Friday morning, 28th March, 1884, I was introduced to the Magistrates and those responsible to see the execution carried out. I exposed my ropes and straps for their inspection, and, after a long and careful investigation of all points, they retired, quite satisfied with their visit. After that we paid another visit to the scaffold; the builders, not having finished the contract, were making a final touch to the new-erected shed to keep the execution private, and so that nobody outside could see. After testing it with bags of cement, same weight as the prisoners, and calculating the length of drop and its consequences, and other details, the committee departed. After, I filled my time walking about the prison grounds, and thinking of the poor men who were nearing their end, full of life, and knowing the fatal hour, which made me quite ill to think about. My meals did not seem to do me good, my appetite began to fall off, nothing felt good to me, everything that I put into my mouth felt like sand, and I felt as I wished I had never undertaken such an awful calling. I regretted for a while, and then I thought the public would only think I had not the pluck, and I would not allow my feelings to overthrow me, so I never gave way to such thoughts again.

At 1.0 p.m. my dinner had arrived. I went up to my room, and sat down to pudding, beef, and vegetables, Scotch broth, and Cochrane and Cantrell's ginger ale. At that time I was a total abstainer; and I think it is the safest side, since what I have seen brought on by its sad consequences of taking too much alcoholic liquor . . . After tea, I had a chat with the warders coming off duty for the day. As they passed through the wicket gate, one remarked, 'He looks a nice fellow for a job like that;' another says, 'But he has a wicked eye,' and he would be sure I could do it . . . I was left smoking in the lodge with the gatekeeper and one (warder) who stayed behind to see what he could hear me say; but I looked him over, and could see by the look of his face that I was not to

SCALE SHOWING THE STRIKING FORCE OF FALLING BODIES AT DIFFERENT DISTANCES.

Falling Distance in Feet	8 Stone	9 Stone	10 Stone	11 Stone	12 Stone	13 Stone	14 Stone	15 Stone	16 Stone	17 Stone	18 Stone	19 Stone
	Cw. Qr. lb.	Cw. Qr. lb.	Cw. Qr. lb.	Cw. Qr. lb.	Cw. Qr. lb.	Cw. Qr. lb.	Cw. Qr. lb.	Cw. Qr. lb.	Cw. Qr. lb.	Cw. Qr. lb.	Cw. Qr. lb.	Cw. Qr. lb.
Zero	8 0 0	9 0 0	10 0 0	11 0 0	12 0 0	13 0 0	14 0 0	15 0 0	16 0 0	17 0 0	18 0 0	19 0 0
1 Ft.	11 1 15	12 2 23	14 0 14	15 2 4	16 3 22	18 1 12	19 3 0	21 0 21	22 2 11	24 0 1	25 1 19	26 3 9
2 ,,	13 3 16	15 2 15	17 1 14	19 0 12	20 3 11	22 2 9	24 1 8	26 0 7	27 3 5	29 2 4	31 1 2	33 0 1
3 ,,	16 0 0	18 0 0	20 0 0	22 0 0	24 0 0	26 0 0	28 0 0	30 0 0	32 0 0	34 0 0	36 0 0	40 0 0
4 ,,	17 2 11	19 3 5	22 0 0	24 0 22	26 1 16	28 2 11	30 3 5	33 0 0	35 0 22	37 0 16	39 2 11	41 3 15
5 ,,	19 2 11	22 0 5	24 2 0	26 3 22	29 1 16	31 3 11	34 1 5	36 3 0	39 0 22	41 2 16	44 0 11	46 2 5
6 ,,	21 0 22	23 3 11	26 2 0	29 0 16	31 3 5	34 1 22	37 0 11	39 3 0	42 1 16	45 0 5	47 2 22	50 1 11
7 ,,	22 2 22	25 2 4	28 2 14	31 0 23	34 0 5	36 3 15	39 2 25	42 2 7	45 1 16	48 0 26	51 0 8	53 3 19
8 ,,	24 0 11	27 0 12	30 0 14	33 0 23	36 0 16	39 0 18	42 0 19	45 0 21	48 0 22	51 0 23	54 0 25	57 0 26
9 ,,	25 1 5	28 1 23	31 2 14	34 3 4	37 3 22	41 0 12	44 1 2	47 1 21	50 2 11	53 3 1	56 3 19	60 0 9

Scale used by Berry to calculate the 'drop'

say much in his presence, as he was built that way. I was left alone with the gatekeeper, and he looked like a straight, honest man, and he was like myself. He said, 'I am glad you never began to say anything in the presence of that man, as he would stop until morning.' ... Saturday morning, 29th ... After breakfast, had another interview with the Magistrates, and made the final arrangements. I tested the scaffold in their presence, with the ropes I was going to use on the Monday morning, with bags of cement, each bag being placed in the same places as was marked for the criminals; Vickers, weighing 10 stones and over, 8 feet (drop); and Innes, 9 stones, 10 feet. One bag represented one, and the other bag the other. I tested the ropes by letting off the traps, and down went the bags, and I got my calculations from that point, after seeing the ropes tested with the weight of cement. They all looked quite satisfied with the results. The rope was of Italian silk hemp, made specially for the work, 1/8 inch in thickness, and very pliable, running through a brass thimble, which causes dislocation and a painless death if rightly adjusted ... After dining, I had the honour of having a drive in an open carriage (provided by the Governor) for a couple of hours ... which I enjoyed, after being inside the prison gates since my arrival on Thursday ... I gave my friend another night's visit at the lodge gate. We chatted on different topics of the day, and spent a nice, jovial evening together, smoking our weed; when a voice came to the door from a visitor from the offices of the town, that a reprieve was refused, and the law was to take its course, and I had a paper sent, with the words in full, 'Gore-bridge Murderers – No Reprieve', which made me feel as bad as the condemned men for a time. But, what with the jolly gate-keeper, and another of the warders, I drove it out of my mind for a while ... I retired to bed as usual at 10.0 p.m., after reciting my prayers, and thinking only another night and I shall be back with my wife and children. Saturday night

I was very restless, and I did not feel so much refreshed for my night's sleep, as I was thinking of the poor creatures who slumbering their hours away, in the prison cell, just beyond where I was laid, thinking of the dreadful fate that awaited them in such a short space of time. Two men, in full bloom, and had to come to such an untimely end, leaving wives and large families. One poor woman, I was informed, her mind was so affected that she was removed to the asylum, she took so to heart . . . I retired to my day-room at the front entrance, where I only partook very sparingly of the nice and tempting ham and poached eggs put before me. I spent most of the forenoon looking round inside the prison, while the prisoners was at chapel, until dinner time. My dinner did not arrive until 4.0 o'clock, which is called late dinner, consisting of rice pudding, black currants, chicken, vegetables, potatoes, bread, and the usual teetotal beverages. I tried to make the best of it, but all that I could do was to look at it, as my appetite was gone; but I managed to eat a little before going to roost for the last night . . . I retired at 10.0 on Sunday, but only had cat naps all night, one eye shut and the other open, thinking and fancying things that never will be, and which is impossible. I was dressed and up at 5.0 a.m.; and felt more dead than alive as I had such a responsible part to play in the programme for the day. I fancied the ropes breaking; I fancied I was trembling, and could not do it; I fancied I fell sick just at the last push. I was nearly frantic in my mind, but I never let them know. 6.0 a.m. arrived. I heard the sound of the keys, clattering of doors, sliding of bolts. Breakfast had to be served earlier than usual. No prisoner allowed out of his cell until all was over. The public had begun to assemble on Calton Hill in groups. 7.0 a.m. arrived. I made my way to the scaffold, made my arrangements secure, and cleared the scaffold shed, the principal warder locking the door, not to be opened again until the procession enters for the great event of the day . . .

At 7.45 the living group wended their way to the prison, and into the doctor's room, ready for the last scene of the drama. The prisoners were brought face to face for the first time since their conviction. They kissed each other; and the scene was a very painful one, to see mates going to meet their end on the gallows. They were conducted to the room adjoining the doctor's room, and were in prayer with the two ministers in attendance after 8.5. I was called to do my duty. I was handed the warrant, which was made out by the judge who condemned them to die. I then proceeded to pinion the prisoners, previously shaking hands, bidding goodbye to this world. Both men seemed to feel the position very much. The procession was formed, headed by the High Bailiff, the Chaplain reading the litany for the dead. Both the prisoners walked without assistance to place of execution; they was at once placed under the beam on the drop, where everything was done as quick as lightning, and both culprits paid the highest penalty of the law . . . The magistrates, and doctors, and even the pressmen, admitted that

The condemned cell

the execution of the two men had been carried out in an humane manner as possibly could be, and that the poor fellows had not suffered the slightest pain in going through the execution; doctors giving me a testimonial as to the skilful way I had carried out the execution. 9.0 a.m., my breakfast arrived; and I was so much affected by the sad sight I had witnessed, that I had not appetite, but just merely drank a cup of coffee; but eating was out of the question.'

That Berry carried out his duties with distinction is attested to by a collection of references – solicited by Berry himself – from the official representatives of the the prison authorities:

H.M. Prison, Edinburgh

31st March, 1884.

We hereby certify that we have this day witnessed the Execution of Vickers and Innes, and examined their bodies. We are of the opinion that the Execution of these men was admirably managed; and that the Executioner Berry and his Assistant conducted

Executioner William Marwood

themselves in a cool, business-like manner, to our entire satisfaction; death being instantaneous.

James A. Sidey, M.D.
(Surgeon to H.M. Prison, Edinburgh)
Henry D. Littlejohn, M.D.
(Surgeon of Police)

POST SCRIPT
On the Gallows

The first two men whom I executed, though strong chums and partners in crime, were totally different from each other in their conduct. They both showed deep emotion, although they belonged to a low type of humanity, and they both attentively listened to the chaplain as often as he was willing to visit them, and to such outside ministers as took any interest in their fate, but I believe they did this with the view of making the best of a bad job – if any 'best' were possible – rather than from any deep conviction of the sinfulness of their offence. Beyond this, their demeanour was totally different. Vickers was buoyed up with hope throughout, and continually asked if 'the reprieve' had come. Even when I was introduced to him on the morning of the execution he had not despaired, and his hope rendered him almost cheerful. Even when we were on the scaffold he was convinced that he was not to die, and seemed to listen as people on the scaffold did in olden times for the horseman wildly dashing across the courtyard and crying, 'Reprieve! Reprieve!' at the very last moment. It was not until the noose touched his neck that he realised that his execution was to be an actual solemn fact, and when the dread reality burst upon him, he fainted.

His companion in crime and death stood unmoved upon the scaffold, resigned and calm, without either hope or fear. The white cap was over his face when Vickers fainted, and no sound from the bystanders gave him any hint that Vickers was overcome. The fainting man was supported for a moment, then a touch on the lever, and it was necessary to support him no longer. The Gorebridge murder, for which these men were executed, caused a great sensation at the time.

James Berry

'HE WHOM THOU CURSEST'*

The Mysterious Death of Norah Emily Farnario
On Tuesday, 19th November 1929 on the Isle of Iona, Strathclyde

I have not been to the Isle of Iona for many years now – too many years; for what the Holy Island lacks in size (it is barely five square miles) it compensates for in beauty and mystery. Even the seemingly endless tread of visitors' feet cannot spoil the majesty of the graves of the Scottish kings, nor the clicking of their cameras disturb the serenity of the Abbey, founded 1,500 years ago by the Irish monk Columba, who brought Christianity to the Pagan Picts of the North.

But there is a more recent mystery commemorated there in the quiet Reilig Odhrain burial ground. I am told the stone still remains, its simple message cut into the white marble: 'N.E.F. died 19 November 1929. Aged 33 years.'

Sixty years ago. Before MacBrayne's ferries ran their Three-Island pleasure tours from Oban, round Mull, to Staffa and Iona; before electricity; before telephones and running water. In those days few but the hardy islanders would journey along the thirty-odd miles of rough track, through Glen More, along the shoreline above Loch Scridain, and across the weather-beaten Ross of Mull to the Fionnphort ferry, there to cross the mile-and-a-half of water that is the Sound of Iona.

* He whom thou blessest is blessed, and he whom thou cursest is cursed' (*Numbers* xxii, 6)

Norah Emily Farnario was what in London would have
been called a 'bohemian', a 'free-spirit' – much given to
wearing colourful folk-weaves and exotic jewellery. Like
most of her type, Norah was passionately interested in
folklore and 'earth-mysteries'; which would have been
very cosy had it not led to a somewhat more dangerous
fascination with the study of occult forces. Miss Farnario
spent what some may think an unhealthy amount of her
time trying to contact the spirits of the dead; in this pursuit
she was greatly encouraged by Mrs Moina Mathers, a
gifted spirit-medium and clairvoyant, and wife of the
magician Samuel Liddell Mathers. The Mathers also encouraged Norah Farnario to experiment with telepathy
and faith-healing, and she had become a member of the
Order of Alpha and Omega, one of the many occult
groups inspired by Mathers' Hermetic Order of the Gold-
en Dawn.

For Norah, the hardships of the journey to Iona were
seen through the eyes of one enlightened, and when she
arrived in the autumn of 1929 it was as though she had
come to a spiritual home. She took lodgings at an island
croft, and if the local people found her habits a little alien,
a little 'weird', they were gracious enough to leave her
alone to pursue her poetry and her lonely treks across the
barren, windswept moors; nocturnal journeys on which
she spoke of having communion with the spirits of the
island.

Whose these spirits were we can only guess – the long-
dead islanders of those pagan times before St Columba
replaced their ancient rituals; or the shades of the monks
whose lives were savagely taken by the Norse pirates?

In the course of time, the state of Norah Farnario's mind
appears to have unbalanced, and she became restless and
anxious, sometimes rambling incoherently about contact
with 'the world beyond'. Then quite suddenly she seemed
to be gripped by a great panic, accompanied by an urge to
immediately leave the island. Whether things would have
turned out differently if it had not been a Sunday, or if the
Fionnphort ferry had operated on the Sabbath, it is
difficult to say; probably by this time it was already too
late. Norah, her bags packed and waiting, was marooned

on the island for at least another night – and at this point she almost certainly knew she would never again cross the Sound of Iona.

The following morning, Norah's landlady found her room empty, her bed unslept in, and her clothes neatly folded beside it. When she had not returned by early afternoon, a search party was raised among the crofters to search for Norah; a search which failed to find any trace of the strange woman who roamed the moors at night.

Next day, the searchers were successful – two islanders found Norah Farnario's body. Not, as was earlier expected, at the foot of the craggy shoreline, but spreadeagled on the bleak heather moor, naked but for the magical robe of her Order and a tarnished silver chain round her neck. Her face was frozen in a grimace of stark horror, and the soles of her feet cut to ribbons in her desperate flight from who knows what? One hand still gripped tightly a long-bladed knife – her ritual athamé, a weapon of magical power; and when her body was moved it was seen that she had used it as a last bid for protection, for with the sacred instrument of Art she had cut a crude cross in the rough turf on which she lay. Her last act of invocation had been in vain.

And there, officially, the case of Norah Farnario ended. The local doctor, as bewildered as everybody else by the mystery, simply wrote 'heart failure' on her death certificate; and Norah hopefully found peace in her small plot in God's little acre.

But there were many in the occult world who were not as easily satisfied as the island police. They knew how Norah Farnario had met her death: she had been the victim of a vicious psychic murder. Some – among them the celebrated occultist Dion Fortune – were prepared to go as far as to name a suspect, a person with a history of involvement in psychic attacks: Mrs Moina Mathers.

Had Norah offended her one-time mentor? Had she broken some vow connected with the Alpha and Omega? Was she engaged in some rivalry with an Adept more powerful than herself? One thing is sure; whatever attacked Norah Farnario on that freezing November night, it seemed poor Norah had looked straight into the mouth of Hell.

'A Blasphemous Sect . . .'

It is difficult to understand the implications of Norah Farnario's mysterious death without some appreciation of the risky nature of the occult studies in which she was clearly immersed, and the people with whom she was involved in London.

Norah had for many years been a friend and associate of Mrs Moina Mathers, a gifted clairvoyant and occultist. Mrs Mathers' husband, Samuel Liddell Mathers, was to a very great extent responsible for the introduction to Britain of the occult practices current in 19th century mainland Europe – particularly France and Germany. This revival of interest in Magic – generally known as the 'Western Esoteric Tradition' and based broadly on the Cabbala – had been generated by the French mage Eliphas Levi (Alphonse Louis Constant), and popularised by such contemporary novelists as Honoré de Balzac and Bulwer-Lytton.

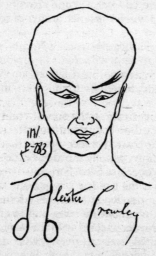

Aleister Crowley, a self-portrait

In 1884, a clergyman by the name of Dr William Woodman purchased an esoteric manuscript from a bookstall in London's Farringdon Road and showed it to the then London Coroner, William Wynne Westcott, an authority on the Cabbala and member of the group known as the Rosicrucians (which had been formed in Paris by Levi's chief disciple, the Marquis Stanislas de Guaita). Westcott in turn recruited the aid of Liddell Mathers (also a Rosicrucian) and, with his wife's help, Mathers translated the manuscript which dealt, in the main, with a Cabbalistic interpretation of the Tarot. This became the basic working document of a whole new 'tradition' of occult study, and the foundation of the Hermetic Order of the Golden Dawn. According to Moina Mathers writing in the introduction to her husband's *Kabbalah Unveiled*, the Order 'studied the intellectual forces behind Nature, the constitution of man, and his relation to God'; in reality it became the theatre of war for a psychic battle between the immense egocentricities of its leading members. Within a short time Mathers who, convinced that he was descended from the clan McGregor, had taken to calling himself 'McGregor Mathers' and 'Comte McGregor de Glenstrae', had forced out the founders and taken over total control of the Golden Dawn and its lodges in Edinburgh, Paris, London, Bradford, and Weston-super-Mare.

In 1898, a young man named Aleister Crowley joined the Order, and attempted to unseat Mathers from its leadership. Space does not allow a discussion of the remarkable personality and magical career of the man they called 'The Beast', but suffice it to say that when Crowley sought power it was a fight without rules. In *The Great Beast*, his biography of Crowley, John Symonds describes the psychic war that resulted from Crowley's attempt to wrest the Golden Dawn from Mathers.

Mathers, his pride wounded by such temerity, conjured up a vampire to smite down his enemy; Crowley combated the she-devil and finally overcame it 'with her own current of evil'. The struggle was described later by J.F.C. Fuller:

'At once recognising the power of her sorcery, and knowing that if he even so much as contemplated her Gorgon head, all the power of his Magick [sic] would be petrified, and that he would become but a puppet in her hands, but a toy to be played with and when broken cast aside, he quietly rose as if nothing unusual had occurred; and placing the bust on the mantelpiece turned towards her and commenced with her a magical conversation; that is to say a conversation which outwardly had but the appearance of the politest small talk, but which inwardly lacerated her evil heart, and burnt into her black bowels as if each word had been a drop of some corrosive acid.

She writhed back from him, and then again approached him even more beautiful than she had been before. She was battling for her life now, and no longer for the blood of another victim. If she lost, hell yawned before her, the hell that every once-beautiful woman who is approaching middle-age, sees before her; the hell of lost beauty, of decrepitude, of wrinkles and fat. The odour of man seemed to fill her whole subtle form with a feline agility, with a beauty irresistible. One step nearer and then she sprang at Frater P. [Crowley] and with an obscene word sought to press her scarlet lips to his.

As she did so Frater P. caught her, and holding her at arm's length smote the sorceress with her own current of evil, just as a would-be murderer is sometimes killed with the very weapon with which he has attacked his victim.

A bluish-green light seemed to play around the head of the vampire, and then the flaxen hair turned the colour of muddy snow, and the fair skin wrinkled, and those eyes that had turned so many happy lives to stone, dulled and became as pewter dappled with the dregs of wine. The girl of twenty had gone; before him stood a hag of sixty, bent, decrepit, debauched. With dribbling curses she hobbled from the room.

As Frater P. left the house, for some time he turned

over in his mind these strange happenings and was not long in coming to the opinion that Mrs M[athers] was not working alone, and that behind her probably were far greater forces than she.'

Crowley then responded by setting a pack of psychic bloodhounds on the Mathers. After mortal combat, Mathers created a spell which struck dead the whole baying pack with one blow; and for good measure he put a curse on the Crowley servant who went mad and tried to kill Mrs Crowley. Incensed, Crowley summoned up from Hell the demon Beelzebub and forty-nine of his cohort of devils and despatched them to Paris to torment the Mathers.

Expelled from the Golden Dawn, Aleister Crowley later founded the society called AA (*Argentinum Astrum* – Silver Star)*. Ironically, perhaps, it was in the year of Norah Farnario's death, 1929, that Crowley published his masterpiece *Magick in Theory and Practice*, arguably the best single volume written on the subject.

---

* Described by *The Looking Glass* as 'a blasphemous sect whose proceedings conceivably lend themselves to immorality of the most revolting character . . .'

MY DEAR EMILE . . .

**The Death by poisoning of Pierre Emile
L'Angelier**
On 23rd March 1857, at Franklin Place,
Glasgow and the Trial and Acquittal of
Madeleine Smith for the crime

Madeleine Smith was born in Glasgow, eldest daughter
of James Smith, architect of that city, and a man of
considerable wealth and influence. Like many of his social
eminence, Smith kept a town house at India Street,
Glasgow, and a country home called Rowaleyn, at
Row, to which the family retreated during the summer
months. At the time at which it is convenient to begin this
narrative, the year 1855, the Smith family comprised
James and his wife, daughters Madeleine, aged 19, Bessie, aged 17, two sons, 16 and 14, and little Janet, aged 12.
The Smiths kept two servants, Charlotte McLean, cook,
and Christina Haggart.

In keeping with the convention for children of her class,
Madeleine had been sent to boarding school in London (in
Clapton – at the time considerably more genteel than it
now is), and returned home in 1853 a 'finished' young
lady – well-bred, well-read, and with an above average
aptitude for music.

Madeleine was also a singularly vivacious and attractive young woman and, on the streets of her native city,
what was quaintly termed a 'head-turner'. Certainly, she
turned the head of Pierre L'Angelier.

But there, young L'Angelier had a head for turning, as
they might have said. He had been born in Jersey in 1827
of French extraction, and at the time Madeleine crossed his
path he was a humble clerk with the firm of Huggins and

Company (and for what interest it may be, his wage was 10s per week). Despite his modest circumstances, Pierre affected the manner of the dandy, and with his flowing whiskers and coiffed hair was, in his 'continental' way, considered attractive by the opposite sex. A histrionic youth, L'Angelier had already chalked up one 'tragic' love affair (with a lady in Fife) and several threats of suicide. In fact this auto-destructive tendency had seemed to grow more acute over the years, and lately Pierre would scan the daily press for reports of suicides, commenting to a friend on one occasion: 'There is a person who has had the courage to do what I should have done. I wish I had the courage to do the same' (this, presumably, referred to his ill-fated romance in Fife). When he was not preoccupied with death and tragedy, Pierre was preoccupied with women – or at least with talking about being preoccupied with women, especially 'beautiful girls with a considerable sum of money'. Indeed, it was his passionate hope one day to marry into social and financial security.

By the slightly devious intervention of Robert Baird, a mutual friend of his and Madeleine's, L'Angelier contrived to meet the young lady in question by 'chance' in the street. In fashionable Sauchiehall Street, Robert and Pierre, Madeleine and sister Bessie, were mutually introduced.

And it would seem that this introduction was not all that was mutual, for Madeleine was as attracted to Pierre L'Angelier as he was to her. These, 'casual' meetings in the street continued until gossip reached the ears of Mrs Smith who, rightly or wrongly, wanted better for her daughter than a poorly-paid warehouse clerk. So the blossoming romance went underground, and Madeleine and Pierre continued their courting by the surreptitious exchange of letters. From Madeleine, vacationing at Row in April 1855:

'My dear Emile
I do not feel as if I were writing to you for the first time. Though our intercourse has been very short, yet we have become as familiar friends. May we long continue so. And ere long may you be a friend of Papa's is my most earnest desire. We feel it rather

dull here after the excitement of a Town's life. But
then we have much more time to devote to study
and improvement. I often wish you were near us, we
could take such charming walks. One enjoys walking with a pleasant companion, and where could we
find one to equal yourself . . .

   . . . We shall be in Town next week. We are going
to the Ball on the 20th of this month, so we will be
several times in Glasgow before that. Papa and
Mama are not going to Town next Sunday. So of
course you do not come to Row. We shall not expect
you. Bessie desires me to remember her to you.
Write on Wednesday or Thursday. I must now
say adieu. With kind love, believe me, yours very
sincerely,

Madeleine'

It was in this same month that Mr Smith himself inter-
vened and, on the face of it, made Madeleine 'see sense'.
At any rate, a letter dated 18th April leads us to believe as
much:

'My dear Emile
I think you will agree with me in what I intend
proposing, viz. that for the present the correspondence had better stop. I know your good feeling will
not take this unkind; it is meant quite the reverse. By
continuing to correspond harm may arise; in dis-
continuing it nothing can be said . . .

Madeleine'

At about the same time Madeleine wrote a letter to Miss
Mary Perry, a sort of confidante of L'Angelier's:

'Dearest Miss Perry
Many kind thanks for all your kindness to me. Emile
will tell you I have bid him adieu. Papa would not
give his consent so I am duty bound to obey him.
Comfort dear Emile; it is a heavy blow to us both. I
had hoped some day to be happy with him, but alas!
it was not intended; we were doomed to be dis-
appointed. You have been a kind friend to him: oh,
continue so. I hope and trust he will prosper in the

step he is about to take and am glad he is now leaving the country, for it would have caused me great pain to have met him . . .

Mimi [a pet name used by L'Angelier]'

It is, in hindsight, a pity that Miss Perry chose not to intervene to calm the situation down, for L'Angelier himself clearly had not the slightest intention of giving up graciously – or at all. His response is typically self-pitying and recriminatory by turns:

'Show my letters to anyone, Madeleine, I don't care who, and if any find that I mislead you I will free you from all blame. I warned you repeatedly not to be rash in your engagement and vows to me but you persisted in that false and deceitful flirtation, playing with affections which you knew to be pure and undivided and knowing at the same time that at a word from your father you would break all your engagement.'

Then, no doubt to boost his sense of self-importance, unlucky Pierre repeated the threat to exile himself to Peru. He subsequently abandons this gesture in order to wheedle his way back into Madeleine's active affections by means of undisguised threats:

'. . . my intentions of going to Lima are now at an end. I would have gone for your sake. Yes, I would have sacrificed all to have you with me, and to leave Glasgow and your friends you detested so very much. Think what your father would say if I sent him your letters for a perusal. Do you think he could sanction your breaking your promises? No, Madeleine, I leave your conscience to speak for itself.'

And very effective it was; in no time the secret affair was resumed. Furthermore, Madeleine was now so entrenched in the romance that her father's anger at discovering the continuance of the amour merely served to harden Madeleine's resolve. Pierre L'Angelier, on the other hand, was not so unbusiness-like as to content himself with the girl and the devil take the money – he wanted both.

Madeleine had not been unaided in conducting her postal love affair; the servant, Christina Haggart, had been acting as courier – collecting Pierre's letters to her young mistress from the post office, and taking hers to L'Angelier's lodgings in Franklin Place. On more daring occasions, it was Miss Haggart who let Pierre into the Smiths' house to keep his secret assignations with Madeleine in the laundry.

If L'Angelier had been completely overwhelmed by his own drama, then he had been as successful in carrying Madeleine with him; by 3rd December she was addressing her letters to 'My Own Darling Husband', and signing them 'Mimi L'Angelier'. She was also actively encouraging Pierre to elope with her. This, quite understandably, did not at all fit in with his plans – he still had his eye firmly set on the family fortune. In a quite heartless letter, L'Angelier begins to get menacing:

'My Dearest and Beloved Wife Mimi
I got home quite safe after leaving you [he had journeyed to the house at Row], but I think it did my cold no good. I was fearfully excited the whole

The house occupied by the Smiths in Blythswood Square

night. I was truly happy with you, my pet; too much
so, for now I am too sad . . . Mimi, unless Huggins
helps me I cannot see how I shall be able to marry
you for years. What misery to have such a future in
one's mind. Do speak to your father, open your
heart to him and try to win his friendship. Mimi,
dearest, you must take a bold step to be my wife. I
entreat you, pet, by the love you have for me, Mimi,
do speak to your mother – tell her it is the last time
you ever shall speak of me to her. You are right,
Mimi, you cannot be the wife of anyone else than
me. I never, never can be happy until you are my
own, my dear, fond wife. Oh, Mimi, be bold for
once, do not fear them – tell them you are my wife
before God. Do not let them leave you without being
married, for I cannot answer what would happen.
My conscience reproaches me of a sin that marriage
can only efface.'

There followed some anxious months during which poor,
terrified Madeleine found it impossible to approach her
father. L'Angelier added further to her misery by vowing
to depart first for Africa, then for Australia.

In the meantime, James Smith had moved his family to
Blythswood Square, and in their next-door neighbour – a
certain Mr Minnoch – thought he had found the ideal
suitor for Madeleine.

It is known that L'Angelier met Madeleine inside the
new house at least once, and that they used her semibase-
ment bedroom window as a place not only to leave their
letters, but to hold secret conversations. For Madeleine,
the despair at her situation became acute and her letters to
L'Angelier became cloying and pathetic: 'I do vex and
annoy you, but, oh, sweet love, I do fondly, truly love you
with my soul, to be your wife, your own sweet wife.'

Things were looking increasingly desperate to Pierre as
well, and out of frustration he went so far as to return
unopened some of Madeleine's letters – the consequence of
which must have been very different from his expectations:

'I felt truly astonished to have my last letter returned
to me; but it will be the last you shall have an

opportunity of returning to me. When you are not pleased with the letters I send you, then our correspondence shall be at an end; and as there is coolness on both sides our engagement had better be broken. This may astonish you; but you have more than once returned me my letters . . . I trust to your honour as a gentleman that you will not reveal anything that may have passed between us. I shall feel obliged by your bringing me my letters and the likeness on Thursday evening at seven.

> I am, etc. M.'

As might have been expected, Pierre L'Angelier behaved in neither an honourable nor a gentlemanly fashion. Not only did he flatly refuse to surrender Madeleine's letters, but held out the threat that he might well be inclined to show them to her father.

Madeleine made another appeal, and the depth of her despair is apparent in every line:

> 'Monday night,

Emile

I have just had your note. Emile, for the love you once had for me, do nothing till I see you. For God's sake do not bring your once-loved Mimi to an open shame. Emile, I have deceived you. I have deceived my mother. God knows she did not boast of anything I had said of you, for the poor woman thought I had broken off with you last winter. I deceived you by telling you she still knew of our engagement. She did not. This I now confess, and as for wishing an engagement with another, I do not fancy she ever thought of it.

Emile, write to no one – to Papa or any other. Oh! do not till I see you on Wednesday night. Be at the Hamiltons' at twelve, and I shall open my shutter, and then you come to the area gate, and I shall see you. It would break my mother's heart. Oh, Emile, be not harsh to me. I am the most guilty miserable wretch on the face of the earth . . .

On my bended knees I write you and ask you, as I

hope for mercy at the Judgement Day, do not inform
on me – do not make me a public shame. Emile, my
love has been one of bitter disappointment. You, and
only you, can make the rest of my life peaceful. My
own conscience will be a punishment that I shall
carry to my grave. I have deceived the best of men . . .

I shall be ruined. Who would trust me? Shame
will be my lot. Despise me, hate me, but make me
not the public scandal. Forget me for ever. Blot out
all remembrance of me.

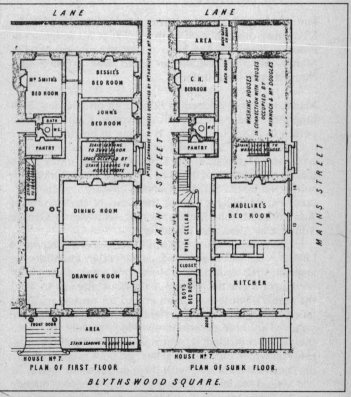

*First floor and sub-basement plans of the house in Blythswood
Square*

I could stand anything but my father's hot displeasure. Emile, you will not cause my death. If he is to get your letters I cannot see him any more; and my poor mother, I will never more kiss her. It would be a shame to them all. Emile, will you not spare me this? Hate me, despise me, but do not expose me. I cannot write more. I am too ill tonight.

P.S. I cannot get to the back stair. I will take you within the door. The area-gate will be open. I shall see you from my window at twelve o'clock. I will wait till one o'clock.'

Pierre L'Angelier never returned Madeleine's love-letters. L'Angelier died on 23rd March 1857, at his lodgings in Franklin Place; he had been poisoned with arsenic. On March the 31st, Madeleine Smith was arrested and charged with his murder.

Madeleine's trial opened in Edinburgh on Tuesday, 30th June 1857, where she faced three charges of administering poison to Pierre L'Angelier, resulting in his death.

On the bench sat Lord Justice-Clerk Hope and Lords Ivory and Handyside. The Crown case was in the more than capable hands of the Lord Advocate James Moncrieff, supported by the Solicitor-General Edward Francis Maitland. For Madeleine Smith, the Dean of the Faculty of Advocates, Mr John Inglis appeared, with Messrs. George Young and Alexander Moncrieff.

Evidence established that Miss Smith, on the pretence of killing rats, had purchased considerable quantities of arsenic first from Mr Murdoch's and then from Mr Currie's chemist shops; a previous attempt to send the family's house-boy on an errand for prussic acid had failed when the chemist, rightly, refused to serve the youth. The three occasions on which arsenic had been purchased coincided, the court was told, with three occasions on which Pierre L'Angelier had been taken violently ill. They also coincided with three occasions on which he had visited Madeleine at their private rendezvous outside her bedroom window at Blythswood Square and was given a warming cup of cocoa. The last date had been

The house in Franklin Place where L'Angelier died. His room was on the first floor, immediately over the doorway.

22nd March, after which assignation, L'Angelier had returned to his lodgings so painfully ill that the landlady, Mrs Jenkins, summoned a doctor. Mrs Jenkins gave this touching account of her lodger's last hours on this earth:

> 'I drew the curtains; he looked very ill and I asked if there was anyone he would like to see? He then asked to see a Miss Perry, in Renfrew Street. I sent for her. He said that if he could get five minutes' sleep he thought he would be better. These were the last words I heard him use. I came back into the room in about five minutes; he was then quite quiet and I thought he was asleep. The doctor then returned and I told him he was asleep. The doctor then went in and felt the pulse and lifted L'Angelier's head, which fell back, and said he was dead.'

However, this evidence was in no way assisted by the post-mortem results. The arsenic bought by Madeleine Smith had been mixed with other substances – in these cases with soot and indigo. It was a simple precaution to avoid the naturally-white powdered arsenic being mistaken for a more innocuous substance. When L'Angelier's stomach was opened up for examination, no trace of either soot or indigo were found – just arsenic. Furthermore, Mr Inglis emphasised the evidence of Madeleine's younger sister Janet and the Smiths' household staff that Madeleine had never even left her room on the night she was charged with administering the fatal dose. In all, the Dean drew a sufficiently convincing picture of Madeleine's innocence for the jury, after a deliberation just short of half an hour, to find the case against her Not Proven.

It is a matter for conjecture whether, deprived of that convenient Scottish alternative, the jury would have found her Guilty or Not Guilty. As it was, Madeleine Smith left the court a free woman.

EVERY WORD BE ESTABLISHED*

The Death by Strangulation of Chrissie Gall
On Saturday, 21st November 1931 at
539 Dumbarton Road, Glasgow and the Trial
and Conviction of Peter Queen for her Murder

It is a frightening thought that a person's guilt or innocence may be established by a single word: a single word that can be, literally, a matter of life or death. This is the case of a man for whom that thought became a frightening reality, and but for the intervention of Mercy would have cost him his life.

At around 3 o'clock on the morning of Saturday, 21st November 1931, Peter Queen rushed into a Glasgow police station and in a state of great agitation told the duty officer: 'Go to 539 Dumbarton Road, I think you will find my wife dead'; he added. 'Don't think I have killed her.' At least, that is what Queen claims he said. A lot different from 'I think I have killed her,' which is what the police claimed he said. One word; a single syllable. Peter Queen's life will depend on it.

Queen was a clerk in his father's bookmaker's office. When he was only 18 he made an unfortunate marriage to a girl who was an alcoholic; two years later she was confined to a home. Four years after this tragic upset, Peter's father engaged a nursemaid, a young woman of modest background who, after leaving school at 14, had been in domestic service with a number of families. When

---

* 'In the mouth of two or three witnesses shall every word be established.' (II *Corinthians* viii, 1)

she went to work for Mr Queen, Chrissie Gall was 21 years old, Peter Queen was 24. Not surprisingly, the two young people became close friends, and when Chrissie left the Queen household after a year, she and Peter continued to see each other.

Chrissie Gall found herself homeless when her father, with whom she had been living, took up residence with another of his daughters, and Peter made arrangements with his friends James and Fay Burns for her to lodge with them. In December 1930, Peter Queen moved in. Events might have gone more smoothly for Mr and 'Mrs' Queen had Chrissie been able to control her intake of alcohol; but like a nightmare returned to haunt him, Peter was soon forced to recognize that she too was an alcoholic. With immense patience and understanding, Peter and James and Fay Burns tried to help Chrissie overcome her dependence on the drug that was beginning to ruin all their lives. As alcoholics will, poor Chrissie alternated between penitence and defiance, and a gradual descent into depression. At the same time she began to make threats on her own life, on one occasion telling Mrs Burns that she would 'make a hole in the Clyde', and on a second occasion promising 'some day some of you will come in and find me strung up.'

In fact, the main cause of Chrissie's problem was a deep sense of Christian shame at living as she saw it 'in sin' with Peter Queen. Remember, this was 1931; it was to be another thirty-odd years before unmarried couples even sharing the same address was viewed as socially acceptable behaviour, and Chrissie Gall was so terrified that her family would get to hear of it that she had woven a fabric of lies about being in domestic service, even to the point of visiting her sister regularly on a Wednesday, claiming it was her 'half-day off'.

After several half-hearted attempts to gas herself – once, but for Fay's vigilance, she would have taken the whole household with her – Peter Queen rented a house in Dumbarton Road, and took Chrissie to live with him as 'Mrs Queen'. Here she continued to drink excessively and to threaten suicide by a variety of means, but usually by hanging. On 12th November 1931, Fay and James Burns came to Dumbarton Road for tea, and when he went to hang his coat on the peg behind the kitchen door, James found it had been broken off. He made a joke in passing about breaking up the happy home, and Peter explained: 'That must have happened during the night. Chrissie tried to do herself in.' Queen had apparently been woken up by a noise in the kitchen and found her slumped on the floor with the line from the clothes-pulley twisted round her neck.

Two days later Chrissie Gall was visited by Leonard Johnson, Fay Burns' brother-in-law. His wife Helen had already made several unsuccessful attempts to persuade Chrissie to stop drinking, and now it was his turn. In answer to Leonard's pleas, she simply said she was sick of living a lie, concluding, 'some day Peter will find me behind the door.' An indication of the fear of exposure under which Chrissie laboured can be judged from the one occasion on which, much the worse for drink, she invited her brother Bert back to Dumbarton Road. Regretting her action afterwards, Chrissie persuaded Peter to go through the charade of pretending that it was his aunt's house that they were meeting at, and later walking down the road with Bert as though he, Peter, was also going 'home'.

On the following day, Friday the 20th, Chrissie was so drunk that Peter tried to call a doctor. As one was not immediately available, he arranged for a house-call the following morning, and put her to bed with the help of the Johnsons, who were visiting. Four hours later, Peter Queen was in the police station announcing that his wife was dead.

Chrissie Gall's body was found lying on her bed, a thin cord tightly tied in a half-knot around her neck just below the Adam's apple. She was dressed in her night-clothes which were undisturbed, and there was not the slightest evidence in the room of any struggle. The post-mortem revealed that the internal organs showed signs of asphyxia, and that death was due to strangulation. But was that death the result of a homicidal attack, or had Chrissie Gall eventually carried out her threat and strangled herself?

The case of HM Advocate v. Peter Queen opened in

Glasgow on 5th January 1932, before Lord Justice-Clerk Alness. The Crown evidence was best described by the judge in his summing-up: 'Scanty and unconvincing in so far as it supports the theory of homicide by the accused.' The main evidence brought against Queen was his statement to the police, the words of which they recalled as being: 'I think I have killed her.' Under cross-examination, the police witnesses seemed ill at ease and evasive, and it was only on the intervention of Lord Alness that they were obliged to admit that, in fact, no record had been made of what Peter Queen said at all.

There followed a stream of friends and relations, all of whom spoke in such unqualified terms of Queen's love, patience, and understanding towards his wife that it was difficult not to think that they had been summoned by counsel for the defence.

Peter Queen exercised his right to speak in his own defence, and for the benefit of the court relived the hours leading up to his wife's tragic death. After he and the Johnsons had got Chrissie into bed on the evening of 20th November, the three of them sat downstairs talking until about 10.45, when Helen and Leonard Johnson left. Later, Peter went in to his wife and they briefly discussed her proposed holiday in Aberdeen. Chrissie then became anxious about whether her brother Bert had really believed the house belonged to Queen's aunt, and feared that her unsanctified 'married' life might already have reached the ears of her family. Peter reassured her, and reminded her that the doctor would be calling in the morning. Chrissie then appeared to sleep, and Peter sat smoking a cigarette before preparing for bed himself. When he pulled down the sheets he saw that Chrissie had a cord tied around her neck and her face was swollen: 'I called out "Chris! Chris!" and shook her. I was shocked and completely knocked out. I don't know what I did for some time. When I came to my senses the first thing I thought of was to go to the police.' Queen then reaffirmed that his words to them were: 'Don't think I have killed her.'

To present the expert medical evidence the defence retained the services of two of Britain's most eminent pathologists, Sir Bernard Spilsbury and Sir Sydney Smith. Spilsbury was adamant that Chrissie Gall's death was self-inflicted, though Sir Sydney had strong reservations and could admit only the possibility of suicide.

Broadly, Sir Bernard Spilsbury's evidence supporting his stand was this:

1. The undisturbed state of the room and the deceased's clothing – her 'boudoir cap' was still in place on her head, as were her dentures in her mouth.

2. The absence of bruising to the deeper parts of the neck and thyroid, indicating that relatively little force had been used to pull the cord tight – which is at variance with what might be expected of a murderer anxious to ensure success.

3. The position of the cord – low down on the neck with the knot to the right of centre – was inconsistent with homicidal strangulation in which the noose would be expected to be higher up on the neck with the knot more to one side as the killer would have to bend over the bed in order to tie it.

But verdicts are not given by pathologists, not given by counsel, or even judges; they are given by juries. And this jury decided, by a majority, that Peter Queen was guilty of murder as charged, adding a strong recommendation to mercy. Another jury, perhaps, might have taken advantage of the Scottish alternative verdict of 'Not Proven'. As it was, Lord Alness could do nothing but pass upon Queen the only sentence available to him in the case of murder – that of death.

Nevertheless, Peter Queen did receive the mercy to which he was so strongly recommended, and three days later the Secretary of State for Scotland commuted his sentence to life imprisonment.

In retrospect, it seems unlikely that Peter Queen should have broken his pattern of loving care for Chrissie Gall to the extent of murdering her, and it was Sir Sydney Smith who summed this feeling up in his wry comment that: 'In the only case where Spilsbury and I were in pretty complete agreement, the jury believed neither of us.'

I HEREBY CONFESS . . .

The Murder of Anne Knielands, Marion Watt, Mrs George Brown, Vivienne Brown, Isabelle Cooke, Peter and Doris Smart, and their son by Peter Manuel
On various dates between 1st January 1956 and 1st January 1958 in Glasgow

---

Peter Manuel's Statement to the Police
'I hereby confess that on January 1st, 1956, I was the person responsible for killing Anne Knielands. On September 17th, 1956, I was responsible for killing Mrs Marion Watt and her sister Mrs George Brown, also her daughter Vivienne. On December 28th, 1957, I was responsible for killing Isabelle Cooke. On January 1st, 1958, I was responsible for killing Mr Peter Smart, his wife Doris and their son. I freely admit and acknowledge my guilt in the above-mentioned crimes and wish to write a statement concerning them.

On January 1st, 1956, I was in East Kilbride at about 7pm. About 7.30, I was walking towards the Cross, when I met a girl. She spoke to me and addressed me as Tommy. I told her my name was not Tommy, but she said she thought she knew me. We got talking and she told me she had to meet someone, but she did not think they were turning up.

After a while I asked her if she would like some tea or coffee. We went into a cafe. When we came out she said she was going home and I offered to take her home.

She said she lived miles away and I would probably get lost if I saw her home. But I insisted, so she said: 'All right.' We walked up to Maxwelltown Road. There we went along a curving road which I can't remember the name of. About halfway along this road I pulled her into a field, but she struggled and ran away. I chased her across the field and over a ditch. When I caught up with her I dragged her into a wood. She started screaming, I hit her over the head with a piece of iron I picked up.

After I killed her I ran down a country road which brought me out at the General's Bridge, on the East Kilbride road. I don't know where I flung the piece of iron. I ran down to High Blantyre and along a road. I went along the road and over a railway, up to where I lived. I got home about 10.15pm.

On September 16th, 1956, I left Woodend Hotel, Mossend, at 10pm. I took two women into Glasgow – one called Jessie I dropped from the taxi in the High Street, Glasgow. The other one, who I only knew as Babs, I took to Merchiston Street, in North Carntyne. After leaving her, I took the taxi to Parkhead Cross where I got a bus home to Birkenshaw.

When I arrived home I met a man I knew and he took me in a car to High Burnside. He had got another man and a woman in the car. They broke into number 18 Fennsbank Avenue. We were there for some time – and someone went to bed. I did not know much about the house. The car was left in the lane.

After a while I went scouting about and looking at the other houses. I found a house that looked empty. Then I went back to see the others at number 18.

Someone had got the car around. I told them to drive me to the other house. I got out, but the others did not like the look of it and went back.

I broke into the house by breaking a glass panel in the front door. I then went in and opened a bedroom door. There were two people in the bed. I went into the other room. There was a girl there.

She woke up and sat up. I hit her on the chin and knocked her out.

I tied her hands, then went back to the other room. I shot the two people there. Then I heard someone making a noise in the other room. The girl had got loose. We struggled, then I threw her on the bed and shot her.

I then went back to number 18 Fennsbank Avenue and found them all asleep. I took the car after waking them –

and they dropped me at home at about 5am. I did not steal anything from number 5.

That same day I went into Glasgow and dropped the gun into the Clyde at the suspension bridge. I got it in a public house at Glasgow Cross. I don't remember the date I got it. I got it as one of a pair of guns. The man who fixed it for me told me the way he had got it.

On December 28th, 1957, I went to Mount Vernon about 7pm, going by bus from Birkenshaw to Mount Vernon. I walked up the road leading to the railway bridge that runs from Bothwell to Shettleston.

Just over the bridge, I met a girl walking. I grabbed her and dragged her into a field on the same side as Rylands riding school. I took her along with me, following a line going in the Bothwell direction. I took her handbag and filled it with stones from the railway. Before going any farther, I flung it in a pond in the middle of a field.

I then made her go with me along towards the dog track and she started to scream. I tore off her clothes, tied something around her neck and choked her.

I then carried her up the line into a field and dug a hole with a shovel. While I was doing this a man passed along the line on a bike. So I carried her again over the path opposite the brickworks and into another field.

I dug a hole in the part of the field that was ploughed, and put her in. I covered her up and went back the way I had come. I went back to the road and got her shoes, which had come off at the outset. I took these and her clothes and scattered them about. The clothes I flung in the river Calder at Bromhouse, the shoes I hid on the railway bank at the dog track. I went up the same path and came out at Baillieston. I walked along the Edinburgh road and up Aitkenhead Road to Birkenshaw, and got there about 12.30am. The first hole I dug, I left it as it was.

On the morning of January 1st, 1958, I left my home about 5.30am, and went down the path to the foot of the brae crossing the road and into Sheepburn Road and broke into the bungalow. I went through the house and took a quantity of banknotes from a wallet I found in a jacket in the front bedroom. There was about £20 to £25 in the wallet. I then shot the man in the bed and next the woman. I then went into the next room and shot the boy.

I did not take anything from the house except money. I got the gun from a man in Glasgow at a club. I took the car from the garage and drove it to the car park at Ranco. Later that day I took the gun into Glasgow and threw it into the Clyde at Glasgow Green.

The next day – Thursday, January 2nd – I saw the car was still in the car park. So I drove it into Glasgow at 8am and left it in Florence Street. Then I got the bus back home and got into the house through the window. I left by the back door.

(Signed) Peter Manuel'

A STUDY OF HAIRS

**The Murder of Catherine McIntyre by
Stanislaw Myszka
On Friday, 26th September 1947 at Kenmore,
overlooking Loch Tay, Tayside**

On 26th September 1947, 47-year-old Catherine McIntyre had been alone in the isolated Tower Cottage which she shared with her family on the slopes of Bolfracks Hill, commanding an unbroken view over Loch Tay below. Her son Archie had left at 8 o'clock to go about his business on one of the nearby estates, and daughters Annie and Mary were taking their summer holidays together. Her husband, head shepherd on the Tombuie Estate had also left early for work.

First to leave that morning, young Archie McIntyre was also the first home, and finding the cottage locked, sat down on the doorstep to read a newspaper while he waited for his mother to get back from afternoon tea, which she had planned to take with Mrs McKerracher on her nearby farm. It was not until he saw Duncan McKerracher striding up the hill that any misgiving troubled Archie's thoughts. It had been a neighbourly custom that had grown up over the years, this exchange of gossip and home-made cakes between the women, but on this occasion not only had Mrs McIntyre not kept her appointment, she had sent no message either, which was most uncharacteristic. Archie McIntyre listened with some concern to McKerracher's story, and immediately climbed into the house through the back kitchen window. The cottage seemed empty, but it was an eerie kind of emptiness, an emptiness almost of desertion. Unusually, the breakfast dishes still stood in the sink waiting to be washed up; on the table was a half-written letter that Mrs McIntyre had left in mid-sentence. With growing apprehension young McIntyre went up to the bedrooms – empty, save for his own, which, inexplicably, was locked, and the key missing.

On the other side of that door, when he had smashed his way through with an axe, was a scene of horror that Archie McIntyre would carry around in his head for the rest of his waking and sleeping life. In the middle of the upturned bedroom, sprawled across his bed, was the twisted body of his mother, bound and gagged and with frightful wounds to her head and face; everything, it seemed, was impregnated by her blood.

The motive for this appalling assassination became clear as soon as the police arrived with Mr McIntyre; the £90 cash with which he was to pay his shepherds' wages was missing, more tragically, the thin gold band had been brutally wrenched from Catherine McIntyre's wedding-ring finger.

Within hours the police, supplemented by volunteers from all the local estates, were combing the moor around the cottage, and were rewarded by finding a recently-occupied hideout deep in the bracken. Inside were the clues to the killer that would cost him his life; amid the detritus of the makeshift shelter were a sawn-off shotgun with fresh blood still on the butt, a bloody handkerchief, the return half of a Perth-Aberfeldy railway ticket of a distinctive type issued only to servicemen, and a used razor blade.

It was the railway ticket that pointed in the direction of Mrs McIntyre's murderer, and the discarded razor blade that helped to prove, beyond all reasonable doubt, his guilt.

On the banks of Loch Tay stood the venerable Taymouth Castle, once seat of the Duke of Breadalbane, now, in the unsettled state in which the whole of post-war Europe found itself, a camp for the Polish Army in Exile, allies who had chosen to start their lives over in a free Scotland rather than return to life under the communist dictatorship that gripped their homeland.

As the result of a police appeal, the shotgun retrieved from the moorland hideout was quickly identified by a farmer of Old Meldrum in Aberdeenshire, who had borrowed it from a neighbour and later found it missing. It happened that at the time a Polish soldier named Myszka had been casually employed on the farm and had been suspected of the gun's theft.

Next a taxi driver came forward with information about one of his recent fares, a foreigner who looked as though he had been sleeping rough, but paid with money peeled from a thick wad of banknotes. A similar story was told by a young woman from nearby Ardallie who had married one of the Polish soldiers based at Loch Tay. A friend and compatriot of her husband's, something of a joke between them because he was always so hard-up, had suddenly taken them on a spending-spree in town. His name was Stanislaw Myszka.

The 23-year-old Polish deserter was finally run to ground and arrested on 2nd October, at a disused RAF airfield at Longside, near Peterhead, and confined to Perth Gaol. Hidden in his shoe, officers found Catherine McIntyre's wedding ring.

The case for Stanislaw Myszka's guilt was never in any question, but at his trial it was the celebrated Scottish pathologist Professor John Glaister who provided the corroborative scientific evidence that was to put the hangman's noose around Myszka's neck. On the used razor blade found in the bracken hideout – and with which Myszka disclaimed any association – several beard shavings were found adhering. Glaister had made a special study of hairs and their importance as forensic evidence, and his exhaustive work *A Study of Hairs* (1931) was for a long time the scientific authority on the subject. With hairs taken from the razor used by Myszka in prison, it was possible for Professor Glaister to conclude that the two samples of hair matched in colour and detailed structural characteristics, and although hair is not unique to a person – as fingerprints are – it was possible to state that they were 'consistent with a common source'.

Although Stanislaw Myszka had pleaded not guilty to the charge and entered a special defence of insanity, the jury were clearly unconvinced. After a retirement of only 20 minutes they returned the verdict that empowered Lord Sorn to adopt the black cap and pass upon the prisoner the dread sentence of death. He was hanged at Perth on Friday, 6th February 1948.

THE ANALYSIS OF HAIR

Although inferior in accuracy to either fingerprint or blood identification, hair can prove of great assistance to forensic scientists. Besides certain evidence as to age, sex and race, microscopic examination of hair can often lead to placing a suspect at the scene of a crime, or as having been in contact with a victim.

Categorized according to the place of origin on the body, human hairs can be divided into six types – head, eyebrows and eye-lashes, beard, body, pubic, and axillary (underarm) – each with distinctive characteristics.

Head hair for example, is generally circular in cross-section, and the ends are frequently split. Eyebrow hairs are also circular, but the ends tend to taper. Hair from the beard is generally triangular in section, and body and pubic hairs are oval or triangular and tend in most cases to curl. Identification of pubic hair is often instrumental in identifying attackers in cases of rape – particularly as the hairs, with their shorter roots are more easily deposited.

Under a powerful microscope, hair can be seen to consist of three layers – the cuticle, or outer sheath of overlapping scales, the cortex, which is formed of keratin and contains the pigment that determines the hair's natural colour, and the central core, or medulla. It is the cuticle that mainly determines the animal origin of the hair, and can be classified so as to attribute it to human or animal, and between different species of animal. This can be useful in, for example, placing a suspect or victim, by a comparison of animal hairs found on the clothing with those found at the location of crime.